Recipes from the WORLD of Beta Sigma Phi

FAVORITE RECIPES® OF

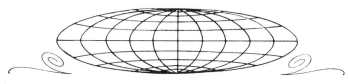

BETA SIGMA PHI INTERNATIONAL

©Favorite Recipes® Press/Nashville EMS MCMLXXVIII
Post Office Box 77, Nashville, Tennessee 37202
Library of Congress Cataloging in Publication Data
Main entry under title:
Favorite Recipes of Beta Sigma Phi International.
   Includes index.
1. Cookery, International. I. Beta Sigma Phi
TX725.AIF297   641.5'9   78-15779
ISBN 0-87197-121-6

Recipe on page 166.

Recipes on pages 67, 94, 142 and 170.

Beta Sigma Phi

JOIE DE VIVRE . . .

. . . is the world of Beta Sigma Phi. It is made up of busy women who handle the various demands of social, home and community service activities with great style and grace. We hope the international sharing and exchange of recipes will add "a touch of flavor" to our sorority social life.

Throughout the world, sisters are being brought together in a favorite pastime shared among good cooks — exchanging beautiful and exciting recipes.

Beta Sigma Phi cookbooks span over a decade of cooking, with the most compliment-drawing recipes contributed by Beta Sigma Phis for your enjoyment. We now pay homage to these generous, good cooks throughout the world. We wish to thank each Beta Sigma Phi for her prized recipe and for helping to make this international cookbook complete.

To bring you, the homemaker, the finest recipes available (and with them, the delight of fine dining!) is the Beta Sigma Phi goal. The basic principle of our lives includes the insistence on a "joie de vivre" that will bring a bit of perfection to us and to others throughout the world.

I sincerely hope you enjoy this cookbook from "the world of Beta Sigma Phi."

Sincerely,

Marge Thomas

Marge Thomas
International Cookbook Chairman
Beta Sigma Phi

CONTENTS

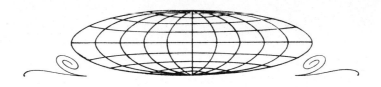

What is Beta Sigma Phi?

A pledge hears it right away, and the experienced member knows it from her heart: Beta Sigma Phi is an Invitation To Life. Almost 50 years ago, Beta Sigma Phi founder Walter W. Ross recognized that women needed a way to express themselves and grow as individuals, whether married or single, following a career, or raising children. So, choosing the words "Life, Learning, Friendship" as a motto, he created Beta Sigma Phi, a social, cultural and service sorority for women from every walk of life and every age, educational and financial group. He wanted the organization to expand a woman's horizons and to give her ways to enrich her mind, and to cultivate her talents, tastes and feelings. That is exactly what Beta Sigma Phi is today: a warm and open sisterhood of members who each day enjoy life in a new way, who learn something new everyday, and who contribute wholeheartedly to the world around them.

When a woman joins Beta Sigma Phi, new opportunities begin to unfold for her almost immediately. The International Office provides each member with a guide to cultural study, which also serves as the program for many of the sorority meetings throughout the year. This study encompasses poetry, art and literary projects, field trips and expeditions, dicsussion groups on current events, and campaigns for social causes. Members learn about politics, mental health, drug abuse, history, science, languages, and international customs. As members progress, this structured form of learning advances to a completely open process of cultural and social investigation of everything of possible interest to today's women.

Also, every chapter strives to provide its members with ways to serve their fellow man, through gifts of time and energy for community projects, national and international organizations, and for the needs of their own chapter members. Beta Sigma Phi fund-raising power brings in money for everything from local historical preservation to world illiteracy and hunger. They make quilts to sell, have raffles, sponsor house and garden tours, telethons, bloodmobiles, and cookbook sales to build playgrounds and hospital wings, among other important community projects.

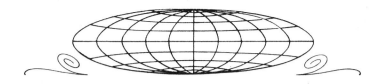

The first chapter of Beta Sigma Phi was chartered in Abilene, Kansas in 1931. Today, 12,000 chapters stretch from Abilene to Australia, from South Dakota to Saudi Arabia, and from Finland to Florida. Two hundred and fifty thousand Beta Sigma Phi sisters now enjoy ever-widening social lives, deep and lasting friendships, expanding cultural lives, and many rewarding deeds of service to their fellow man. Beta Sigma Phi will continue to thrive because, as each chapter progresses, every member progresses — and there is always room for more members. Once a Beta Sigma Phi, a woman need never again be alone, bored, or dissatisfied with her life's goals. Beta Sigma Phi's Invitation To Life is never withdrawn, and its spirit endures because the sorority is ever guided by the words of its motto, "Life, Learning, Friendship."

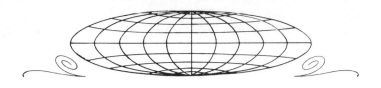

New Horizons for the Kitchen

The art of cooking holds such an important place in society that cookbooks were among the very first books printed after Gutenberg began printing his first Bible in the mid-1400's. This opened many new horizons for cooks everywhere. Before that, cookery information was handed down from mother to daughter by spoken word and instruction. This was an excellent way for cooking to develop, but because only the very wealthy could afford hand written cookbooks, knowledge of the cooking of far away lands was very limited. Today, of course, cookbooks featuring the foods of many lands are far more common and now kitchen horizons for creative cooks are virtually unlimited. Interestingly, though, many cooks today still prefer a cookbook that has grandma's, mom's or Aunt Lucy's notes and hints written in the margins. This is great, because it is the collective imagination of experienced cooks like these that makes cooking an art.

Cooking was considered a fine art, however, long before printed cookbooks became available. Today, we know that it is an important expression of the personality of the inhabitants of a nation, past and current. The Greeks, centuries before Christ, and the Romans, after that, enjoyed many now famous gourmet feasts that required exacting chefs and a wide array of high-quality ingredients. Ancient Chinese writings also show us that cooking was considered an art thousands of years ago, just as it is today. An expert chef was never expected to serve the same meal twice in one year, because he was supposed to know as many as 1000 different dishes.

It may be that the culinary accomplishments of some countries are more famous than others, but there is no question that the world's many varied and superb cuisines prove what fine things can be done with what nature and agriculture provide. It is interesting to note that cooks all over the world create a fantastic array of meals and menus from the same basic group of foods — meats, fish, fruits, grains, vegetables, and seasonings. Yet, the unique ways in which cooks in each country combine the foods and use the seasonings make all the difference. And, for all of us who love food, this assures all the variety, fun, and excitement one could hope for in dining.

More than anything else, it is probably the desire for variety that has shaped the individuality of the world's myriad cuisines. Imagination is the key. Think, for example, how many Oriental and Eastern cooks depend on rice as the staple food in their menu. Yet, Japanese, Chinese, and Indian cuisines are among the most varied and respected in the world. Pasta, in one form or another, appears over and over again in Italian cooking. Yet, Italian cooks have developed a mouth-watering array of sauces, stuffings, and other accompaniments for pasta. It seems that cooks learned long ago that nutritious food is useless if it is boring.

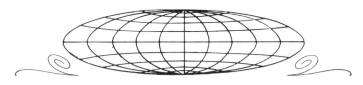

British cooking, long and falsely accused of being lifeless, is actually so wholesome, direct and hearty that it almost makes the foods of other countries seem extravagant. Certainly there is nothing dull about Irish Stew, Yorkshire Pudding, an English Trifle, Scones, Heather Honey, or Welsh Rarebit. Teatime in Britain proves how truly superb British cooks can be. Cold meats, fresh plums and strawberries, mouth-watering tarts, puddings and cakes, served with cups of perfectly brewed tea are the attractions, and all are set out on the finest linen with the most impeccable china and silver available. Even a simple tea — of only a muffin and a mug — is an occasion unmatched in any other land.

Scandinavian cookery abounds in fish and seafood and is earmarked by the *smorrebrod* (Danish), or *smorgasbord* (Sweden). These words loosely translate as "buttered bread," and the meal includes plenty of that, plus a table-bending array of fish cooked in every way, as well as smoked reindeer, cold meats, salads, pate, meatballs, sausages, omelets, fresh fruits, Danish pastry, and cheeses. In the Land of the Midnight Sun, the sun never sets on fantastic eating!

The flavors of European cooking range from the distinctively robust character of German cooking and elegantly rich Austrian pastries to the lively cooking of Italy and the cool cuisine of Spain. France, of course, is famous for its marvelous food and has set the pace for dining in the Western world for hundreds of years.

Mid-Eastern cooking reflects the glory of the great civilizations that have flourished in this part of the world — Greece, Turkey, Saudi Arabia. Mid-Eastern specialties include *shish kabob*, rice and grain *pilaus*, as well as the use of spices, raisins, yogurt, lamb and eggplant. Cooks from this area also make deliciously sweet desserts with almonds, pistachios and walnuts. Greek cooking combines all these features with the best from the Mediterranean area, especially the use of vegetables, olive oil, garlic, citrus fruits and honey.

The Japanese and Chinese cuisines are the pacesetters for the cooks of the Far East and Pacific Islands. Chinese and Japanese chefs prepare, cook, and serve every morsel of food with the utmost care and attention. Vegetables are quickly stir-fried to retain their color, shape and texture. Meats marinated in soy sauce are deep fried in a delicate tempura batter, one serving at the time. Bamboo shoots, snow peas, water chestnuts, carrots, shrimp, pork and chicken, as well as pineapple and other Pacific fruits complete the list of foods typical to this extraordinary style of cooking.

There is nothing more exciting for Beta Sigma Phis than to know their sisterhood extends to the horizons of the world. As they have learned about The World of Beta Sigma Phi, they have found that delicious food is one thing all people have in common — even though they do not share language, dress, or climate. Most of all, Beta Sigma Phis want to share **Recipes from the World Of Beta Sigma Phi** with everyone who loves good food. So, enjoy! Before you know it, your kitchen horizons will begin widening and you will be trying an exciting, new recipe from a different country every night!

International Diners Guide

ITALIAN

Aceto: vinegar
Aglio: garlic
Al Dente: cooked, as pasta, for a slight resistance "to the tooth"
Antipasto: appetizers
Cacciatora: cooked "in hunter style"
Caffe: coffee
Cipolla: onion
Con Carne: with meat
Dolce: sweet
Formaggio: cheese
Funghi: mushrooms
Gnocchi: dumplings
Melenzana: eggplant
Minestra: soup
Olio: oil
Pane: bread
Patate: potato
Pasta: wheat paste in many sizes and shapes
Pesce: fish
Pollo: chicken
Pomodoro: tomato
Prosciutto: smoky Italian ham
Riso: rice
Scalloppini: thinly sliced meat
Spargi: asparagus
Tartufata: truffle
Umido: stew
Uova: eggs
Vitella: veal
Zuppa: soup

GREEK AND MID-EASTERN

Amygathala: almonds
Anginara: artichoke
Arni: lamb
Avga: egg
Avgolemono: Greek lemon and egg soup
Baklava: phyllo pastry layers filled with nuts, honey and spices
Bulgur: whole wheat grains
Couscous: rice-like pasta pellets steamed with sauce
Dolma: stuffed cabbage leaves, also Dolmathes
Domates: tomatoes
Feta: Greek cheese from goat or sheep milk
Halvah: farina-based sweet, flavored with fruit and nuts
Kafes: coffee
Kibbi: ground lamb and bulgur
Marzipan: a sweet almond paste confection
Melitzanes: eggplant

Mezethakia: appetizers (Greek); also Mezes or Mazza
Moussaka: eggplant and lamb casserole
Ouzo: a nise-flavored spirit or aperitif
Phyllo: tissue-thin sheets of rich pastry
Psari: fish
Psomi: bread
Retsina: resin-flavored Greek white wine
Rizi: rice
Skordo: garlic
Spanaki: spinach
Yiaourti: yogurt

GERMAN

Bier: beer
Blumenkohl: cauliflower
Braten: roast
Brot: bread
Eier: eggs
Eis: ice cream
Fisch: fish, seafood
Fleisch: meat
Frucht: fruit
Geflugel: poultry
Gemuse: vegetables
Gurken: cucumber
Huhn: chicken
Kaffee: coffee
Kalbsfleisch: veal
Kartoffel: potato
Kase: cheese
Kraut: cabbage
Kuchen: baked goods
Mittagassen: lunch
Rindfleisch: beef
Salate: salad
Sauer: sour
Schinken: ham
Schnitzel: cutlet
Schokolade: chocolate
Schweinfleisch: pork
Spargel: asparagus
Speck: bacon
Suss: sweet
Vorspeisen: appetizers
Zucker: sugar
Zweibeln: onion

JAPANESE

Aji-no-moto: monosodium gluatamate (MSG)
Awabi: abalone
Daikon: large white radish
Dashi: soup stock
Goma: sesame seed

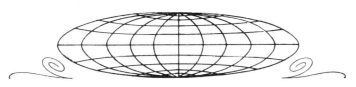

Jagu-imo: potato
Mikan: mandarin oranges
Miso: soybean paste
Sake: rice wine
Sashimi: raw poultry or seafood
Shoga: ginger
Shoyu: soy sauce
Takenoko: bamboo shoots

SPANISH AND MEXICAN

Aceite: oil
Agua: water
Ajo: garlic
Arroz: rice
Aves: poultry
Bebidas: drinks
Burrito: a soft filled tortilla

Carne: meat
Comida: main meal
Desayuno: light breakfast
Ensalada: salad
Frijoles: beans
Huevos: eggs
Mole: sauce
Naranjos: oranges
Pescados: fish
Pollo: chicken
Queso: cheese
Sopa: soup
Taco: tortilla sandwich
Tortilla: unleavened cornmeal flat cake
Venduras: vegetables

FRENCH COOKING TERMS

Aperitif: Before dinner drink.

Bombe: Ice cream or softened ices arranged in layers, then refrozen.

Bouqet Garni: Combination of parsley, thyme and bay leaf tied in cheesecloth bag, used for flavoring stews and sauces; remove before serving dish.

Brioche: Individual sweet roll prepared from light yeast dough, hollowed out, and filled with a sweet or savory sauce.

Coquille: A shell or scallop, or a dish shaped like either.

Court Bouillon: Stock made from water, root vegetables, wine or vinegar, seasonings and herbs, used primarily for poaching veal or fish, and in sauces.

Creme Brulee: Baked, rich custard with caramelized or caramel sauce.

Crepe: Thin, delicate pancakes spread with jam or jelly, or stuffed with savory meat or vegetable, then rolled up, and served as hors d'oeuvres or main dish.

Etouffer: Food that is cooked in its own juices.

Fines Herbes: Chopped parsley, or mixture of herbs, including parsley, chervil, tarragon and chives.

Flambe: Pouring warmed spirits, brandy or sherry over food, igniting as the food continues to cook, adding flavor to the food and helps burn off excess surface fat.

Frappe: Sherbet or flavored ice that is frozen to a mushy texture.

Glace: Thin sugar icing for cakes, biscuits and crystallized fruits.

Gratine: To brown the top of a sauced dish under a broiler. Bread crumbs, grated cheese and dots of butter help form a light brown covering over the sauce.

Huitre: Oyster.

Liqueur: Distilled spirit such as brandy, flavored with herbs, bark, fruit, nuts, seeds, leaves, flowers or honey, then sweetened and redistilled. Served with coffee to end a meal and is thought to aid digestion.

Macedoine: A salad of a medley of vegetables or fruits.

Mirepoix: A mixture of diced vegetables cooked gently in butter, used as a basis for sauces or for foods to be braised.

Mousse: Molded dessert of whipped cream or beaten egg whites mixed with a sweet, flavorful custard; or meat dish chilled in savory stock until congealed.

Noisette: A small, round slice of meat cut from fillet or eye of chop; or butter or other food cooked to a nut-brown color.

Roux: A mixture of shortening and flour used as a thickening for sauces.

Souffle: A sweet or savory baked dish that puffs dramatically high while cooking, made from an egg yolk sauce to which stiffly beaten egg whites are added before baking.

Appetizers and Accompaniments

Appetizers have been a part of the world cuisine for many hundreds of years. Early Chinese and Japanese writings mention appetizer foods, as do ancient Greek and Roman writings. But, it seems that appetizers as we know them today began with the Scandinavian custom of serving an attractive assortment of piquant dishes with before dinner drinks. Their *aquavit table,* as it was called, migrated from there to Russia where *zakuski* (little bits) were served with vodka. France then renamed them *hors d'oeuvres,* meaning "outside the chef's main work." Other countries developed their own appetizer theme: Italian *antipasti,* German *vorspeisen,* Middle Eastern *mese,* Spanish *topas,* South American *entremeses,* Japanese *zatsuki.*

These foods are typically expensive luxury ingredients served in bite-sized amounts — yet the flavors always reflect the personality of the cuisine. These foods are served "in miniature," prepared and flavored to heighten the appetite, then arranged and served to appeal to the eye. Raw vegetables, dried meats, olives, hard-cooked eggs, fish and seafood, various fruits, cheese, caviar and mushrooms are all popular appetizers because they are either light with lots of flavor and color, or they are easy to marinate, pickle or otherwise season with herbs and spices without becoming ponderous and filling. Light, crisp bite-sized pastries are common appetizers in cuisines all over the world, too, because they can be filled with savory mixtures of cheese, chopped meat or seafood, or vegetables — for a tantalizing bit of flavor.

Beta Sigma Phi hostesses know the value of beautiful, taste-tempting appetizers when entertainment is in the air. There is no more hospitable way to introduce the meal than with an array of delicious foods "in miniature," and certainly no better way for guests to relax and enjoy conversation. Whether you concentrate on foods from one country, or those from many lands, remember that appetizer foods can do whatever the occasion calls for, providing foods to whet the appetite, or to appease the appetite during a relaxed evening of music, fun, and enjoyable conversation.

BAKED BANANAS IN ORANGE AND LEMON JUICE

8 bananas, cut lengthwise
1 c. orange sections, free from
    membrane
1/3 c. sugar
2 tbsp. orange juice
2 tbsp. lemon juice
1/4 c. butter, melted

Place bananas in lightly greased baking dish. Arrange orange sections over bananas. Sprinkle with sugar. Combine remaining ingredients. Pour over fruit. Bake in 450-degree oven for 15 minutes. Serve hot or cold. Delicious with chicken or as a dessert. Yield: 8 servings.

Marguerite R. Hamon
Laureate Alpha No. 265
Boise, Idaho

SCALLOPED PINEAPPLE

5 slices white bread, cubed
3 tbsp. milk
2 c. sugar
3/4 c. butter or margarine, softened
3 eggs, beaten
2 15 1/4-oz. cans crushed pineapple

Soak bread cubes in milk. Beat sugar and butter until fluffy. Add eggs; mix well. Fold in pineapple. Add bread cubes. Place in 9 x 13-inch pan. Bake at 350 degrees for 1 hour.

Debbie Skahan, Sec.
Gamma Zeta No. 3248
Pittsburg, Kansas

JOHN CLAMMER

2 med. onions, chopped
2 bell peppers, chopped
3 lg. firm tomatoes, chopped
3 cucumbers, chopped
1 jalapeno pepper, chopped (opt.)
Salt to taste
1/4 c. pepper
White vinegar

Combine all ingredients except vinegar. Cover with vinegar. Let stand in refrigerator for at least 2 hours. May be kept for several days. This is great for a relish with red or navy beans.

Jeanie Echols, Pres.
Xi Pi Lambda X4413
Albany, Texas

EGGPLANT DRESSING

2 med. eggplant, peeled
1 lb. ground beef
2 tbsp. cooking oil
1/2 c. chopped onion
1/2 c. chopped celery
1/2 c. chopped green pepper
Salt and pepper to taste
1/3 c. catsup
2 c. cooked rice

Cut eggplant into bite-sized pieces. Brown beef in oil. Add next 4 ingredients. Simmer for 5 minutes. Stir in eggplant and 3/4 cup water. Cover and simmer over low heat, stirring occasionally, for about 45 minutes or until eggplant breaks up. Add catsup; simmer for 15 minutes longer. Remove from heat; stir in rice. Serve as a main dish or as stuffing for green peppers. Yield: 6 servings.

Loretta H. Cline
Xi Beta Epsilon X3136
Pineville, West Virginia

GERMAN DRESSING

1 lg. cabbage, cut in sm. chunks
5 or 6 med. onions, diced
Vegetable oil
1 egg, beaten
8 to 10 slices bread, toasted and
    cubed
1 tsp. cinnamon
1 tsp. poultry seasoning
Salt and pepper to taste
Butter

Combine cabbage and onions in large frypan with small amount of cooking oil. Simmer for about 30 minutes or until quantity has reduced and vegetables are slightly browned, using additional oil, if necessary. Place mixture in casserole. Add egg, toast, cinnamon and seasonings to frypan; mix well. Pour over onion mixture; dot with butter. Bake in 300-degree oven for about 3 to 3 hours, stirring occasionally and turning browned crust in as formed. This dressing is a side dish to be used with fowl or roast beef or pork.

Marion Deem
Preceptor Epsilon Chap.
Stratford, Ontario, Canada

POTATO BALL DRESSING

8 c. soft bread cubes
1/2 c. chopped onion
1 c. chopped celery
2 tbsp. chopped parsley
1/2 lb. butter, melted
1 1/4 c. milk
2 eggs, beaten
1 1/2 c. mashed potatoes
Salt and pepper to taste

Combine all ingredients; mix well. Form into balls, using an ice cream scoop. Place side by side in buttered baking dish. Pour small amount of additional

melted butter over potato balls. Bake, uncovered, in 375-degree oven for 20 minutes.

Lois McCarty, Scrapbook Chm.
Laureate Beta PL117
Trenton, Missouri

EASY YORKSHIRE PUDDING (ENGLAND)

1/2 c. all-purpose flour
1/4 tsp. salt
1/2 c. milk
1 egg

Mix all ingredients together in bowl. Beat with wire whisk or rotary beater just until smooth. Pour batter into greased 6-section muffin tin. Bake at 350 degrees for 20 to 25 minutes. Serve at once with gravy from roast beef.

Tommye G. Duncan, Pres.
Iota Rho No. 9859
Tulsa, Oklahoma

LIGHT YORKSHIRE PUDDING (ENGLAND)

1 c. flour
1/2 tsp. baking powder
1/2 tsp. salt
1 c. milk
2 eggs, separated

Sift flour, baking powder and salt together. Add milk and beaten egg yolks; mix well. Fold in stiffly beaten egg whites. Turn into earthenware baking dish. Bake in 400-degree oven for about 20 minutes. Baste with drippings from roast. Cut in squares; serve on platter with roast.

Joan Stines, Pres.
Gamma Phi No. 1391
Champaign, Illinois

HIGHLANDER MAYONNAISE (NEW ZEALAND)

1 c. minus 1 tbsp. sweetened
  condensed milk
1/2 c. salad oil
1/2 c. vinegar or lemon juice
2 egg yolks
1/2 tsp. salt
1 tsp. dry mustard
Dash of cayenne pepper

Place all ingredients in bowl or blender container; beat until mixture thickens. This makes a delicious salad dressing for green salad or vegetable salad. Keeps for several weeks in refrigerator. This is usually served with wedges of lettuce and sliced tomatoes. New Zealanders have this on the menu for at least one meal each day.

Nancy M. Darnell
Xi Eta X1357
Newcastle, Wyoming

HOMESTYLE MAYONNAISE

1 egg
1/4 tsp. salt
2 tbsp. sugar
1 tbsp. flour
2 tbsp. prepared mustard
1 tbsp. butter
1/2 c. milk
1/4 c. vinegar

Beat egg and salt together in saucepan. Combine sugar and flour; stir into egg mixture. Add mustard, butter and milk. Cook over medium heat, stirring constantly, until thickened. Remove from heat. Stir in vinegar. Cool, then refrigerate. Will keep well. May be diluted to desired consistency with additional milk.

Mrs. Alice P. Dougall
Xi Alpha Chi X1661
North Miami Beach, Florida

FINADENE SAUCE

1 c. soy sauce
Juice of 3 or 4 lemons
5 green onions, finely chopped
3 sm. red peppers, crushed

Mix all ingredients together. Store in refrigerator. Use over cooked meats or as a marinade.

Lordes Beam, 2nd V.P.
Xi Alpha X2868
Dededo, Guam

GUAMANIAN SAUCE FOR RICE

3 oz. soy sauce
3 oz. lemon juice
Finely chopped jalapeno peppers
  to taste
Finely chopped fresh green onions
  to taste

Combine all ingredients; mix well. Serve over cooked rice.

Joan Hummer, Sec.
Xi Mu Gamma X3553
Portland, Texas

ORANGE SAUCE

1/2 c. butter
2 c. confectioners' sugar
2 c. orange juice
1 tbsp. grated orange rind

Combine all ingredients in top of double boiler over hot water. Heat and mix thoroughly. Serve very hot over French pancakes or French toast.

Elsie L. Birkett
Preceptor Eta XP241
Gulfport, Florida

Cook for 5 minutes. Add anchovies; cook for 2 minutes longer. Place in sterilized jars; seal. Process in waterbath for 10 minutes.

Pat Stanley
Omicron No. 2245
Victoria, British Columbia, Canada

CHEESE WAFERS

1 1/2 c. sifted all-purpose flour
1 c. butter, softened
2 c. shredded sharp cheese
2 c. chopped pecans
Worcestershire sauce to taste
Tabasco sauce to taste
Red pepper to taste
1/2 tsp. salt

Blend all ingredients together until well mixed. Roll a small amount of dough into a ball. Dip fork in flour; flatten each ball with fork tines. Place on ungreased cookie sheet. Bake at 350 degrees for 10 minutes. Let stand overnight. Keeps indefinitely in airtight container.

Nell Hiatt, Soc. Chm.
Xi Mu X1629
Walterboro, South Carolina

AVOCADO HALF SHELLS WITH CAVIAR

3 fully ripe avocados
Lemon juice
6 tbsp. black caviar

Cut avocados lengthwise, twisting gently to separate halves. Insert a sharp knife directly into seeds; twist gently to lift out. Brush cut surfaces with lemon juice. Spoon caviar into cavities. Arrange half shells on ice. Garnish with chopped egg and onion or sour cream. Yield: 6 servings.

Photograph for this recipe above.

ANTIPASTO

2 lb. onions, chopped
2 lb. sweet red peppers, chopped
2 lb. sweet green peppers, chopped
2 lb. cauliflower, chopped
1 1/2 c. oil
1 1/2 c. vinegar
9 1/2 c. catsup
1   2-lb. jar dill pickles, chopped
2   1-lb. cans green beans
2 cans mushrooms, sliced
2 jars green olives, sliced
2 cans black olives, sliced
Salt to taste
4 cans tuna
1   2-oz. can anchovies

Place onions, peppers and cauliflower in saucepan with water to cover. Bring to a boil. Boil for 3 minutes. Drain. Add oil, vinegar and catsup; cook for 3 minutes longer. Add remaining ingredients except anchovies.

SCHNITZELBANK CHEESE POT

2 Camembert cheese
1 Liederkranz cheese
1/4 lb. Roquefort cheese
1 c. butter
1/4 lb. cottage cheese
2 tbsp. flour
2 c. cream
1 1/2 c. chopped pimento-stuffed green olives
Cayenne pepper to taste

Remove outer skin from Camembert cheese and Liederkranz cheese. Place in pan with Roquefort cheese, butter, cottage cheese, flour and cream. Cook until melted, stirring constantly. Mix olives with melted cheese. Season with cayenne. Pour into 1 1/2-quart cheese pot. Chill. Serve with crackers. Will keep for months.

Twyla Magnesa
Xi Gamma Delta X266
Johnson County, Kansas

CORNED BEEF MOLD (IRELAND)

1 pkg. unflavored gelatin
1 c. mayonnaise

1 15 1/2-oz. can corned beef,
    broken up
1 med. onion, grated
3 tbsp. horseradish
Salt and pepper to taste
Worcestershire sauce to taste
Dash of garlic salt

Soften gelatin in 1/2 cup cold water. Add 1 cup hot water and mayonnaise; stir well. Add corned beef; mix well. Add remaining ingredients. Pour into a mold. Chill until set; garnish with parsley. Serve with party rye.

Claudia Pratt, Pres.
Laureate Beta PL341
Richmond, Virginia

BAGNA CAUDA (ITALY)

1/4 c. butter
2 lg. cloves of garlic, finely
    chopped
1/2 c. olive oil
14 flat anchovy fillets
2 tbsp. red wine vinegar
Freshly ground pepper to taste
Salt to taste

Simmer butter in hot crepe pan over direct heat until butter begins to brown. Add garlic; brown lightly. Add olive oil and anchovies; heat through. Add vinegar. Season with pepper and salt. Bagna Cauda may be used as a dressing over shredded cabbage or simmered in a fondue pot for dipping fresh vegetables, breadsticks or cubed Italian bread. Yield: 6-8 servings.

Paulette Brunskill, V.P.
Iota Theta No. 8543
Pittsburg, Kansas

BEAU MONDE DIP

1 1/3 c. sour cream
1 1/3 c. mayonnaise
2 tsp. Beau Monde seasoning
2 tsp. minced onion flakes
2 tsp. parsley flakes
1 whole round loaf rye bread

Combine all ingredients except rye bread. Cut off top of bread. Remove center of loaf; tear into bite-sized pieces. Place dip in cavity of loaf. Use bite-sized pieces of rye bread for dipping.

Peg Dubbelde
Xi Delta Mu No. 1967
East Alton, Illinois

CHEESE AND SAUSAGE DIP

1/2 c. chopped onions
2 lb. hot sausage

1 can cream of celery soup
1 can Cheddar cheese soup
1 roll jalapeno cheese
1 roll garlic cheese
1 roll smokelde cheese

Saute onions until soft. Add sausage; cook for 15 to 20 minutes. Drain. Heat soups in double boiler; add cheeses, stirring until melted. Stir sausage into cheese mixture. Keep warm; serve with chips.

Frances McGee, City Coun.
Xi Rho Alpha X4614
Athens, Texas

BEEFY CHILI CON QUESO (MEXICO)

1 lb. ground beef
1/4 c. chopped green onion
1 8-oz. can tomato sauce
1 4-oz. can chili peppers, drained,
    seeded and chopped
1 tsp. Worcestershire sauce
1 lb. Velveeta cheese, cut in
    sm. cubes
Dash of garlic powder

Brown beef. Add green onion; cook just until tender. Add tomato sauce, chili peppers, Worcestershire sauce and cheese; cook until cheese is melted. Stir in garlic powder. Serve hot in chafing dish or fondue pot with corn chips for dipping.

Deloris Carter, Rec. Sec.
Xi Theta Xi X4087
Wooster, Ohio

HOT CHILI CON QUESO (MEXICO)

1 1/2 lb. Velveeta cheese, cubed
1 can Ro-Tel tomatoes and chilies
1 4-oz. can Old El Paso taco
    sauce
4 tbsp. Masa Trigo
1/2 tsp. salt
1/2 tsp. garlic powder
3 tbsp. hot catsup

Melt cheese in double boiler over hot water. Process remaining ingredients in blender. Pour over cheese; stir until well mixed. Cook for 10 minutes. Serve in chafing dish with tortilla chips or corn chips.
Masa Trigo is a flour mixture for flour tortillas. All-purpose flour may be substituted but flavor will be slightly different.

Sandra McMillen, Pres.
Epsilon Gamma No. 9707
Daleville, Alabama

CROCK·POT CHEESE DIP

1 lb. ground beef
1 lb. process American cheese, cubed
1 10-oz. can chopped tomatoes and green chilies
2 tsp. Worcestershire sauce
1/2 tsp. chili powder

Brown beef; drain well. Place beef and remaining ingredients in Crock·Pot; stir well. Cover; cook on High for 1 hour, stirring occasionally. Turn Crock·Pot on Low for serving up to 6 hours later. Place in fondue pot or chafing dish over low heat to serve.

Barbara J. Middlesworth, Pres.
Alpha Psi No. 9803
Sidney, Montana

FONDUE ITALIANO

1/2 lb. ground beef
1/2 env. spaghetti sauce mix
1 15-oz. can tomato sauce
3 c. shredded Cheddar cheese
1 c. shredded mozzarella cheese
1 tbsp. cornstarch
1/2 c. Chianti
Italian bread, cut into bite-sized pieces

Brown ground beef in a saucepan. Drain off excess fat. Stir in spaghetti sauce mix and tomato sauce. Add cheeses gradually; stir over low heat until cheeses have melted. Blend cornstarch and Chianti together; add to cheese mixture. Cook and stir until thick and bubbly. Transfer to fondue pot; place over burner. Spear bread with fondue forks; dip into fondue, swirling to coat. Add a small amount of warmed Chianti if fondue becomes thick.

Barbara Henry
Xi Tau X1104
Lawton, Oklahoma

SIMPLE CHEESE FONDUE (SWITZERLAND)

2 1/2 c. light cream
5 tbsp. flour
2 tsp. steak sauce
1 med. onion, finely chopped
6 tbsp. butter or margarine
2 tsp. instant chicken bouillon
1 1/2 c. grated Swiss cheese
1 c. grated Parmesan cheese

Combine cream, flour and steak sauce; set aside. Saute onion in butter. Add bouillon; stir to dissolve. Reduce heat to medium. Add cream mixture; cook, stirring constantly, until thickened. Add cheeses gradually; stir

until melted. Fondue may be prepared in advance and reheated in fondue pot.

Gerri Catalano
Theta Delta Chap.
Lorain, Ohio

HOT CHEESE-CHILI DIP

1 2-lb. box Velveeta cheese
1 15-oz. can chili without beans
6 or 7 green onions, chopped
4 green chilies, chopped

Melt cheese in a Crock·Pot. Add remaining ingredients; mix thoroughly. Keep warm; serve with corn chips, fresh vegetables or crackers.

Sue Samuel, Treas.
Alpha Sigma Chap.
Effingham, Illinois

HOT HAMBURGER DIP

1 lb. hamburger, crumbled and browned
1 can Frito-Lay Bean Dip
2 or 3 green onions, chopped
1 lb. Velveeta cheese, cubed
1/2 green pepper, chopped
1 8-oz. can tomato sauce

Place all ingredients in a Crock·Pot. Cook on Low for 10 to 12 hours or on High for 5 hours. Watch for scorching at higher setting. Set on Low to keep warm. Serve with cheese chips. May be used as topping on hot dogs or hamburgers.

Mrs. Judy Flannery, Treas.
Alpha Rho XP1721
Perry, Iowa

DIP A LA DILL

2/3 c. mayonnaise
1 c. sour cream
1 tbsp. minced onion flakes
1 tbsp. parsley flakes
1 tsp. dillweed
1 tsp. Beau Monde seasoning

Mix all ingredients together. Let stand in refrigerator for at least 1 hour before serving. Serve with fresh vegetables.

Donna Wagner, Rec. Sec.
Delta Gamma Psi No. 7756
Sunnyvale, California

GUACAMOLE DIP (MEXICO)

2 med.-sized ripe avocados
2 med. tomatoes

Appetizers

1 bunch green onions, minced
1/2 tsp. Tabasco sauce
2 tsp. salt
2 tbsp. lemon juice

Peel avocados; reserve 1 seed. Mash pulp into small pieces but not smooth. Place tomatoes in boiling water for 1 minute. Rinse in cold water; peel and chop fine. Fold all ingredients together until well blended. Place in serving bowl. Place avocado seed in center to prevent discoloration. Cover and chill until serving time. Remove seed and stir before serving. Yield: 3 cups.

Lynne J. Lotvedt, V.P.
Xi Alpha Pi X4041
Burley, Idaho

HOT PECAN DIP

1 8-oz. package cream cheese, softened
2 tbsp. milk
1/2 c. sour cream
1/4 c. chopped green pepper
1 tbsp. minced onion
1/2 tsp. garlic salt
1 2 1/2-oz. jar dried beef, chopped
2 tbsp. butter
1/2 c. coarsely chopped pecans
1/2 tsp. salt

Combine cream cheese, milk and sour cream. Add green pepper, minced onion, garlic salt and dried beef. Place mixture in 8-inch pie plate. Melt butter; add pecans and salt. Spread pecan mixture over cheese mixture. Bake at 350 degrees for 30 minutes or until light brown. Serve warm with crackers.

Loween Clayberg, Treas.
Iota Mu No. 9513
Gilbert, Iowa

CHICK PEAS WITH SESAME OIL SAUCE (SAUDI ARABIA) HUMMUS

2 cans chick peas
1 c. sesame oil
1 1/2 c. lemon juice
5 cloves of garlic
1 1/2 tbsp. salt
2 tbsp. chopped parsley
Olive oil

Cook chick peas until soft; drain and mash. Add sesame oil and lemon juice slowly and alternately. Crush garlic with salt; add to peas. Add just enough water for dipping consistency. Pour sauce into serving bowl. Garnish with parsley and several whole cooked peas. Pour a small amount of olive oil over top. Chill. Serve with toasted Arab bread strips or crackers.

Louise M. Warner, V.P.
Zeta Upsilon No. 9480
Perry, Georgia

MOCK REMOULADE

6 hard-cooked egg yolks, sieved
4 cloves of garlic, minced
3 tbsp. creole or dark mustard
2 tbsp. prepared mustard
4 c. mayonnaise
2 tbsp. paprika
3 tbsp. (about) horseradish
Dash of Tabasco sauce
1/4 c. vinegar
1/4 c. finely chopped parsley
Salt and pepper to taste

Combine all ingredients. Refrigerate until serving time. Great relish tray dip.

Teresa Wagner
Theta Lambda No. 2916
McAllen, Texas

CREAMY SHRIMP DIP

1 8-oz. package cream cheese
1 sm. carton sour cream
1/4 c. finely chopped onion
2 tbsp. A-1 sauce
2 tbsp. lemon juice
2 tbsp. catsup
1 tsp. salt
Dash of Worcestershire sauce
Dash of hot sauce
2 lb. cleaned boiled shrimp, chopped

Soften cream cheese to room temperature. Beat cream cheese until smooth. Add remaining ingredients except shrimp; blend well. Stir in shrimp. Refrigerate before using.

Paula Stephens, Rec. Sec.
Theta Kappa No. 2914
Denton, Texas

MOLDED SHRIMP DIP

2 pkg. unflavored gelatin
1 can tomato soup
3/4 c. chopped celery
3/4 c. chopped green onion
1 c. mayonnaise
1 tbsp. Worcestershire sauce
3 tbsp. lemon juice
1/2 tsp. salt
2 sm. cans cocktail shrimp

Soften gelatin in 1/4 cup cold water. Heat soup to boiling point. Add gelatin mixture and let cool. Add remaining ingredients; blend well. Pour into mold. Chill until firm. Make several days ahead of use. Serve with celery sticks or crackers.

Evelyn Miller
Exemplar Preceptor Gamma XP124
Lawrence, Kansas

SWEDISH RYE WITH DILLWEED DIP

2 round loaves Swedish rye bread
2 c. mayonnaise
2 c. sour cream
3 tbsp. minced onion flakes
3 tbsp. parsley flakes
3 tsp. dillweed
3 tsp. Beau Monde seasoning

Hollow out insides of loaves. Break bread from center into bite-sized pieces; place on serving tray. Mix remaining ingredients together well. Fill centers of rye loaves with mixture. Use bite-sized pieces of bread for dipping.

Brenda Hart
Epsilon Xi No. 8293
Manassas, Virginia

HOT MEXICAN APPETIZERS

1 can refried beans
1 pkg. tostados
1 can green chilies
Shredded sharp cheese

Place generous portion of refried beans on each tostado. Slice green chilies; remove seeds. Place a slice of chili on beans; top with cheese. Place under broiler. Broil until cheese is melted. Keep hot to serve.

Hope Fricks, Pres.
Preceptor Tau XP516
Rockledge, Florida

HOT OLIVE SURPRISES

1/4 c. soft butter or margarine
1 c. grated sharp Cheddar cheese
1/4 c. sifted flour
36 med.-sized stuffed olives

Combine butter and cheese; stir in flour. Chill dough. Shape a small portion of dough around each olive. Place on baking sheet. Bake at 400 degrees for 15 minutes.

Edwina L. Cage, Parliamentarian
Xi Lambda Phi X3388
Amarillo, Texas

ITALIAN EGG BALLS

4 eggs, beaten
3/4 c. white bread crumbs
3/4 c. grated Parmesan cheese
1 tsp. parsley flakes
1 tsp. salt
1/5 tsp. pepper
Vegetable oil for frying

Combine all ingredients except oil; mix until smooth. Heat oil in frypan until hot. Drop mixture by table-spoonfuls into oil; brown on both sides. Drain on paper towels. Yield: About 18 balls.

Joann Semancik, Treas.
Beta Psi No. 5796
New Providence, New Jersey

KIBBE (LEBANON)

2 c. cracked wheat
2 med. onions, minced
1 1/2 lb. lamb, ground twice
1 1/2 tsp. salt
1 tsp. freshly ground pepper
Dash of Tabasco sauce

Soak cracked wheat in water for 30 minutes to 1 hour. Drain thoroughly. Combine all ingredients; shape into balls. Serve raw or insert a sliver of ice into center and broil for 8 to 10 minutes.

Cynthia A. Dewberry
Zi Alpha Theta Chap.
Milwaukee, Wisconsin

PARTY PIZZA

1 lb. hot pork sausage
3/4 lb. ground beef round
1 tbsp. Worcestershire sauce
1 tsp. oregano
1/2 tsp. garlic powder
2 loaves party rye bread

Brown sausage and beef; drain. Mix next 3 ingredients with browned beef mixture; spread on rye bread. May be frozen for 1 hour, then stored in plastic bags. Place on cookie sheet. Bake at 350 degrees for 10 minutes. Yield: 70 servings.

Ora Lee Nelson, V.P.
Gamma Lambda No. 5529
Hobbs, New Mixico

MARINATED DOLMADES (GREECE)

1/3 c. chopped onion
1/2 lb. ground beef
Olive oil
3 tbsp. lemon juice
1 c. cooked rice
1/2 c. chopped roasted almonds
1 tbsp. dried mint
2 tbsp. beef gravy
1 tbsp. honey
1/2 tsp. salt
1/4 tsp. cinnamon
1/4 tsp. pepper
30 Athena Vine leaves

Brown onion and ground beef in 1 tablespoon olive oil in 8-inch skillet over medium heat until onion is tender. Stir in 1 tablespoon lemon juice and next 8 ingredients. Stir and cook over low heat for 5 minutes. Remove from heat. Cool. Rinse grape leaves in warm water. Place leaves flat on a board with the shiny side down. Place 1 tablespoon beef mixture on each leaf.

Fold and roll leaves to cover beef completely. Ends of leaves may be secured with toothpicks, if necessary. Place in shallow dish. Pour mixture of 1/4 cup olive oil and 2 tablespoons lemon juice over stuffed leaves. Marinate in refrigerator for 2 to 3 hours or overnight. Serve cold on toothpicks. Yield: 30 servings.

Photograph for this recipe on page 12.

BEEF TURNOVERS (RUSSIA)
PIROSHKI

1/4 c. minced onion
Margarine
1/2 lb. ground beef or chopped cooked
    fish
1/2 tsp. crushed dillseed
2 tbsp. minced parsley
2 c. flour
1 tsp. salt

Saute onion in 2 tablespoons margarine. Add next 3 ingredients. Cook until lightly browned. Sift flour and salt in a bowl. Cut in 2/3 cup margarine until mixture is crumbly. Add 1/3 cup water gradually, stirring with fork until mixture holds together. Roll pastry thin on floured board. Cut into 3-inch rounds. Place filling on one side of round; fold over and press edges together. Place on baking sheet; brush lightly with additional melted margarine. Bake in preheated 400-degree oven for 10 minutes or until brown.

Mrs. Nina A. Keitel
Epsilon Chi No. 5612
Muskogee, Oklahoma

FRIED EMPANADITAS
(PHILIPPINE ISLANDS)

2 cloves of garlic, crushed
1 tbsp. oil
2 lb. ground beef
Salt
Pepper to taste
Diced celery to taste
Diced carrots to taste
Diced potatoes to taste
2 c. flour
4 tsp. baking powder
1 tbsp. sugar
1/4 c. butter
2 eggs, slightly beaten

Saute garlic in oil. Add ground beef; cook over medium heat until done, stirring occasionally. Add salt and pepper to taste. Add diced vegetables; continue cooking until vegetables are tender. Drain off excess fat. Cool. Sift flour with baking powder and 1/2 teaspoon salt. Add sugar and resift. Mix butter and eggs together. Pour egg mixture in center of flour. Stir to mix, adding about 3/4 cup water or enough to make a soft dough. Roll out dough on slightly floured board. Cut into squares. Place about 1 spoonful beef mixture into center of each square. Press edges together with

tines of fork. Fry in deep hot fat until golden brown. Serve hot as an hors d'oeuvre with taco sauce or hot sauce.

Betty J. Buckles, V.P.
Preceptor Omega XP1751
Phoenix, Arizona

CHEESE TRIANGLES (GREEK)
TIROPETES

1 lb. feta cheese
4 eggs
1 1-lb. package cream cheese, softened
1 lb. phyllo
1 c. butter, melted

Mash feta cheese with fork until well crumbled; set aside. Beat eggs with electric beater for about 15 minutes or until very fluffy. Beat in cream cheese, small amount at a time, until well blended. Fold in feta cheese. Cut phyllo into 6 x 12-inch pieces. Brush half the phyllo with melted butter. Place about 1 teaspoon mixture at one end of strip. Fold end over mixture, then fold lengthwise in thirds, then fold diagonally until triangle is formed. Brush with butter. Place on ungreased cookie sheet. Bake in 350-degree oven for 30 minutes or until golden. Serve warm. Place unbaked triangles in plastic container, separating layers of triangles with waxed paper. Place in freezer. Will keep for 2 months. Yield: 40 triangles.

Sharon McCabe, Rec. Sec.
Xi Tau X3299
Charleston, South Carolina

BAKED EMPANADAS (SPAIN)

1 8-oz. package cream cheese, softened
1 c. butter, softened
1 tsp. salt
2 to 3 c. flour
1 lb. ground beef
1 med. onion, chopped
2 garlic cloves, crushed
1 med. can tomato sauce
1/4 c. chopped olives
2 dashes of Tabasco sauce
1 tbsp. Worcestershire sauce

Blend cream cheese and butter together with electric mixer. Add salt and flour gradually, beating until thick and blending in last flour by hand. Refrigerate for at least 1 hour or overnight. Fry ground beef, onion and garlic, stirring to separate beef. Add remaining ingredients. Simmer until most of the liquid is absorbed. Roll cut dough as thin as possible on floured board. Cut circles with cutter. Spoon beef mixture into circles. Fold over; crimp edges together. Prick with fork. Place on baking sheet. Bake at 350 degrees for 12 to 15 minutes. Serve as appetizer. Yield: 50 empanadas.

Mrs. George Schrader, W. and M. Chm.
Xi Zeta Sigma X3667
Hollywood, Florida

BRAUNSCHWEIGER PATE (GERMANY)

1 lb. braunschweiger
2 pkg. green onion dip mix
1 tsp. sugar
1 tbsp. garlic spread
2 3-oz. packages cream cheese, softened
1 tbsp. milk
1/8 tsp. hot pepper sauce

Mash braunschweiger. Combine dip mix, sugar and 2 teaspoons water. Add to braunschweiger; blend thoroughly. Shape mixture into a mound; place on serving plate. Chill. Melt garlic spread. Whip cream cheese with milk and hot pepper sauce. Blend in melted spread. Spread cream cheese mixture over braunschweiger; chill. Garnish with parsley and radish slices.

L. Main, Pres.
Xi Gamma Kappa X3534
Agincourt, Ontario, Canada

DANISH LIVER PATE

1/4 c. margarine
1 lg. onion, chopped
1 lb. ground beef
1 lb. liver, cut in sm. pieces
1 tsp. garlic salt
1/2 tsp. salt
1/4 tsp. pepper

Place margarine and onion in heavy skillet. Cook until tender. Add ground beef and liver; cook until tender. Do not overcook liver. Place 1 cup water and seasonings in blender container. Add cooked meat and drippings. Process until well blended. Chill.

Marian Taylor, V.P.
Preceptor Nu XP841
Atlantic, Iowa

ANGOSTURA LIVER PATE (FRANCE)

2 lb. beef liver
2 env. unflavored gelatin
3 vegetable bouillon cubes
1 sm. onion, grated
3 tbsp. lemon juice
1 tbsp. salt
1 tbsp. Angostura aromatic bitters

Cover beef liver with water. Bring to a boil. Reduce heat; simmer for 10 minutes or until liver is tender. Drain; put through food chopper. Sprinkle unflavored gelatin into 1 cup cold water. Let stand for 5 minutes. Add bouillon cubes and stir over low heat until gelatin and cubes are dissolved. Stir in 2 cups water, onion, lemon juice and salt. Chill until mixture is syrupy. Fold in ground liver and Angostura bitters. Beat with rotary egg beater until well blended. Pour mixture into a lightly oiled 9 x 5 x 3-inch loaf pan. Chill until firm.

Unmold. Cut into slices to serve as first course on lettuce leaves. Cube and serve on crackers or on top of bread squares for hors d'oeuvres.

Photograph for this recipe above.

FRIED BACON-WRAPPED OYSTERS

2 eggs, beaten
1/4 c. milk
24 select oysters, drained
1 c. cracker meal
12 bacon strips, halved
Salad oil for frying

Combine eggs and milk in a shallow dish. Dip oysters in egg mixture, then in cracker meal. Repeat process. Wrap each oyster with bacon; secure with a toothpick. Fry in shallow hot oil until golden. Drain on paper towels. Yield: 2 dozen.

Mary Lee Carter
Theta Rho No. 6047
Kennett, Missouri

CRAB MEAT BALLS WITH AVOCADO (PHILIPPINE ISLANDS)

2 tbsp. butter or margarine
2 tbsp. flour
1 1/2 c. evaporated milk
Dash of salt and pepper
2 c. finely diced avocado
2 c. crab meat
Graham cracker crumbs
3 eggs, beaten
Oil for frying

Melt butter. Add flour and milk, mixing well. Season with salt and pepper. Simmer, stirring constantly, until

thick. Stir in avocado and crab meat; mix well. Remove from heat. Cool. Shape into balls; roll in cracker crumbs. Dip into eggs. Fry in deep fat until golden brown.

Erlinda P. West, Prog. Com. Chm.
Alpha Beta No. 2901
Westminster, Maryland

CRAB MOLD

1 can cream of mushroom soup
1 env. unflavored gelatin
2 3-oz. packages cream cheese, softened
1 c. salad dressing
1/2 c. chopped celery
1/2 c. chopped green onion
1/2 lb. crab meat

Heat soup and gelatin until gelatin is dissolved. Stir in remaining ingredients. Place in greased mold. Refrigerate for 24 hours. Serve with crackers.

Terry Lo Conte
Omicron Epsilon No. 4430
San Jose, California

CRAB MEAT SPREAD

1/2 c. softened butter
2 to 4 tbsp. chopped onion
1 6 1/2-oz. can king crab meat
1/4 c. mayonnaise
3 hard-boiled eggs, chopped

Combine all ingredients; mix well. Chill thoroughly. Remove from refrigerator about 1 hour before serving. Serve with crackers.

Mrs. Robert K. Mathis
Xi Mu Chap.
Saint Augustine, Florida

SHRIMP-CHEESE BALL

11 oz. cream cheese, softened
3 tsp. mustard
2 tsp. grated onion (opt.)
2 tsp. lemon juice
Dash of salt and pepper
2 4 1/2-oz. cans shrimp, cut very fine
Crushed salted nuts

Combine all ingredients except nuts, mixing well. Shape into ball. Roll in crushed salted nuts. Chill.

Linda Davis
Lambda Tau No. 10495
Pendleton, Indiana

SHRIMP COCKTAIL (GERMANY)

2 egg yolks
1/8 tsp. salt
1 tsp. hot mustard
1 tsp. Worcestershire sauce
1 tsp. paprika
1 c. oil
Few drops of lemon juice
1 tsp. catsup
1 c. shrimp
1/2 c. mandarin orange slices
1 tbsp. Cognac

Beat egg yolks with a wire whisk. Add salt, mustard, Worcestershire sauce and paprika. Add enough oil in a slow stream to make mixture thick, beating constantly. Add lemon juice, to thin mixture. Add remaining oil, beating constantly. Stir in catsup, shrimp, orange slices and Cognac. Serve as an appetizer with toast.

Carol Lang, City Coun. Rep.
Alpha Pi No. 8865
Hastings, Nebraska

SWEDISH MEATBALLS

1 lb. ground beef
1/3 c. minced onion
1 egg, beaten
1 tsp. salt
1/2 tsp. Worcestershire sauce
1 tbsp. snipped parsley
1/8 tsp. pepper
1/2 c. dry bread crumbs
1/4 c. milk
1/4 c. shortening
1 12-oz. bottle chili sauce
1 10-oz. jar grape jelly

Mix first 9 ingredients together; shape into 1-inch balls. Melt shortening in large skillet; brown meatballs. Remove meatballs from skillet; pour off fat. Heat chili sauce and jelly in skillet, stirring occasionally, until jelly is melted. Add meatballs; stir until thoroughly coated. Simmer, uncovered, for 30 minutes. Serve in chafing dish. Yield: About 3 1/2 dozen.

Blanche N. Goldsmith, V.P.
Laureate Gamma PL182
Las Cruces, New Mexico

WATER CHESTNUT HORS D'OEUVRES

1 can water chestnuts
Bacon
1 c. catsup
1/2 c. sugar

Cut water chestnuts in half. Wrap each section with one half strip bacon; secure with toothpick. Place in baking dish; cover. Bake in 350-degree oven for 30 minutes. Mix catsup and sugar. Pour over wrapped chestnuts. Bake for 30 to 40 minutes longer.

Marcheta Ellsworth, Recipe Chm.
Epsilon Alpha Chap.
Canton, Illinois

Soups and Stews

The word *soupe* is French, but it is probably the most basic dish to the cookery of most countries. Though it was first considered peasant food because it was developed in the countryside, all cooks now recognize that soup is one of the most flavorful, nutritious and economical ways to use food. The French *pot-au-feu,* or stock pot, is an excellent example of the peasant wife's wise use of every bit of food. She always kept a cauldron bubbling at the back of the fire, and here she put bone and meat scraps, providing a rich and tasty broth. Every day or so, this broth was enriched with whatever meat, vegetables or grain was available. Needless to say, the French housewife was not alone in her frugal practices, so a wide variety of flavorful soups have developed all over the world.

Famous versions of these stock pot soups might include Russian *borsch,* Italian *minestrone,* German beer soups, as well as Scottish *Cock-a-Leekie,* and the three-course Spanish *cocido.* All of these are prepared and served today, just as they have been for generations, by cooks in the cities, the suburbs and on the farms. Soups from the Orient are known to be as much a work of art as they are masterpieces in flavor and texture. Most have a clear meat or fish stock as a base, to which artfully cut vegetables are added and cooked only until tender-crisp. Both created hundreds of years ago and considered a delicacy, bird's nest and shark fin soups are still enjoyed by discriminating gourmet diners. These two may seem a little extravagant, but it is light, clear, deeply flavored soups such as these that introduce many meals today, such as French onion soup and madrilene.

Because soups and stews are such an important part of meal planning, Beta Sigma Phis believe that "the more the better" applies to the number of soup and stew recipes used by any homemaker. Served with bread, and maybe a salad or fresh fruit, soups make an economical and convenient meal that no cook can overlook! Moreover, these soup and stew recipes from all over The World of Beta Sigma Phi are the best of all!

BUTTERBALLS FOR SOUP

24 day-old hamburger buns
1 c. eggs, beaten
1 c. melted butter
1/2 tsp. salt
1 tbsp. allspice

Crumble buns finely; add eggs. Mix well. Add butter, salt and allspice; mix well, kneading thoroughly. A small amount of cream may be added if mixture seems too dry. Shape into walnut-sized balls. May be used immediately or may be frozen. May be cooked in chicken broth, adding noodles or rice as preferred.

Grace Wilkerson, Sponsor
Lambda Epsilon No. 10011
Russell, Kansas

ARTICHOKE SOUP

2 cans artichokes
1 onion, chopped
3 tbsp. olive oil
1/4 c. margarine
3 cloves of garlic, minced
1 tsp. lemon juice
Pinch of thyme
Dash of Tabasco sauce
2 tsp. basil
3 tbsp. dried parsley
9 chicken bouillon cubes
1 tbsp. flour
1 c. vermicelli

Cut artichokes in half; drain. Saute onion in olive oil and margarine until soft. Add artichokes; saute for 10 minutes. Add 8 cups water, garlic, lemon juice, thyme, Tabasco sauce, basil, parsley and bouillon cubes. Cook on medium heat for 1 hour and 30 minutes. Make a paste of flour and small amount of water; stir into soup. Add vermicelli; cook until vermicelli is soft.

Avis Lewis
Xi Alpha Chi X3827
Slidell, Louisiana

AVGOLEMONO SOUPA (GREECE)

1 4-lb. hen, disjointed
1 onion, sliced
1 stalk celery, chopped
Salt and pepper to taste
3/4 c. rice
Avgolemono Sauce

Cover hen with water; add onion, celery, salt and pepper. Cook until hen is tender. Remove hen; strain broth. Return broth to kettle; bring to a boil. Stir in rice; cook slowly until rice is soft. Remove bones from hen; cut into bite-sized pieces. Add to soup. Add Avgolemono Sauce to broth; serve immediately. Chicken may be served separately, if desired.

Avgolemono Sauce

1 egg, separated
Juice of 1 lemon
1 c. broth or stock

Beat egg white well; add beaten yolk and lemon juice. Add hot broth gradually to eggs, beating constantly.

Chrysanthy Cawood
Eta Mu No. 2691
Bay City, Texas

GERMAN BORSCH

1 4-lb. chuck roast
1 16-oz. can tomatoes
1 med. peeled onion, quartered
1 stalk celery, cut up
3 sprigs of parsley
10 peppercorns
2 bay leaves
3 c. coarsely shredded cabbage
1 1/2 c. coarsely grated carrots
2 tbsp. chopped fresh dill
1 c. chopped onion
1/3 c. cider vinegar
2 tbsp. sugar
1 16-oz. can julienne beets

Cover roast with 2 quarts water in 8-quart kettle; bring to a boil. Simmer for 1 hour. Add next 6 ingredients; simmer for 2 hours. Remove from heat; lift out beef. Discard bone; cut up beef. Strain broth through colander. Return broth and beef to kettle; add remaining ingredients except beets. Bring to boil; reduce heat. Simmer for 30 minutes. Refrigerate overnight. Remove fat from soup; add beets. Heat thoroughly. Serve hot with dollop of sour cream.

Ava Kiefer, Pres.
Gamma No. 190
Fort Wayne, Indiana

RUSSIAN BORSCH

1/2 c. finely chopped carrots
1 c. finely chopped onions
1 c. finely chopped beets
1 c. finely chopped celery
1 c. finely chopped parsnips
1 tbsp. butter
2 c. beef stock
1 c. finely chopped cabbage
1 c. tomato pulp
Sour cream
Chopped fresh dill

Combine carrots, onions, beets, celery and parsnips; add just enough water to cover. Simmer, covered, for 20 minutes. Add butter, beef stock, cabbage and tomato pulp. Cook, covered, for 15 minutes; season with salt and pepper. Pour into bowls; garnish with 1 teaspoon sour cream and sprinkling of dill.

Norma Vold, Rec. Sec.
Preceptor Alpha Phi XP1391
Montrose, Colorado

UKRAINIAN BORSCH

1/4 c. butter
1 c. finely chopped onion
2 cloves of garlic, minced

2 c. chopped beets
1 c. chopped celery
4 tomatoes, peeled and diced
1/2 tsp. sugar
2 tsp. salt
1/4 c. vinegar
8 c. beef stock
1 lb. potatoes, cut in 1 1/2-in. cubes
1 sm. cabbage, shredded
1 lb. boiled ham, cubed
3 tbsp. minced parsley
Sour cream (opt.)

Melt butter in saucepan; add onion and garlic. Cook until tender but not brown. Stir in beets, celery, tomatoes, sugar, salt, vinegar and 1 1/2 cups beef stock. Simmer for 40 minutes. Combine remaining 6 1/2 cups beef stock, potatoes and cabbage in a large soup pot; cook for 20 minutes. Add beet mixture and ham. Simmer for 15 minutes. Check for seasoning. Sprinkle with parsley. Serve with sour cream. May substitute 1-inch pieces of cooked sausage for ham, if desired.

Sandra Freeman, Pres.
Xi Gamma X399
Manchester, Connecticut

CALIFORNIA BOUILLABAISSE

2 lb. halibut steak
1 carrot, sliced
1 bay leaf
2 tsp. salt
1/4 tsp. pepper
2 med. onions, sliced
3 tbsp. olive oil
1/4 c. flour
1 lb. shrimp, peeled and deveined
1 c. oysters and liquor
1 1-lb. can tomatoes, cut up
1 tbsp. lemon juice
1 2/3 c. pitted California ripe olives
2 tbsp. chopped parsley

Cut halibut in large pieces, removing skin and bones. Combine carrot, 4 cups water, bay leaf, salt and pepper in saucepan. Bring to a boil. Add halibut; reduce heat to low. Cook slowly for 10 minutes. Remove fish, carrot and bay leaf. Cook onions in oil until tender but not browned. Stir in flour until smooth. Strain stock. Stir into onion mixture gradually. Cook until thickened, stirring occasionally. Add shrimp. Cook slowly for 5 minutes. Add oysters, tomatoes, lemon juice, olives and halibut. Heat together for 5 minutes. Add parsley just before serving. Yield: 3 quarts.

Photograph for this recipe on page 24.

CABBAGE AND RICE SOUP
(SWITZERLAND) KABISSUPPE

1 sm. cabbage, shredded
1 lg. onion, thinly sliced
2 tbsp. butter
6 c. beef or chicken bouillon
1/2 c. rice
Grated Parmesan cheese

Wash cabbage and shake dry. Combine cabbage, onion and butter in a 3 to 4-quart kettle. Cook, covered, over low heat until cabbage is golden and tender crisp. Add bouillon; season with salt and pepper. Simmer, covered, for 10 minutes. Add rice; simmer until rice is tender. Serve with cheese.

Martha W. Jackson, Soc. Co-Chm.
Xi Gamma Mu No. 4350
Forest, Virginia

HEARTY CABBAGE SOUP
(GERMANY) ROTKOHLSUPPE

1/2 lb. knackwurst
1/4 c. finely chopped onion
1/2 c. diced celery
1 c. diced potato
1 13 3/4-oz. can chicken broth
3 c. milk
2 c. finely chopped cabbage
2 tsp. salt
1/4 tsp. pepper
2 tsp. brown sugar
1 tsp. caraway seed in cheesecloth bag
1 c. light cream

Cut knackwurst into 1/4-inch slices; place in 4-quart kettle. Add onion, celery, potato and chicken broth. Bring to a boil. Reduce heat; simmer, covered, for 15 minutes. Add milk, cabbage, salt, pepper, brown sugar and caraway seed; return to a boil. Reduce heat; simmer, covered, for 25 minutes longer. Discard caraway seed. Stir in cream. Serve hot. Yield: 6-8 servings.

Patty Goodger, Rec. Sec.
Beta Theta No. 7510
Laurel, Maryland

CAULIFLOWER SOUP (GERMANY)
BLUMENKOHL SUPPE

1 lg. head cauliflower
1/4 c. butter
2 tbsp. minced onion
3 ribs celery, minced
1 tsp. salt
1 tsp. white pepper
1/4 c. flour
4 c. chicken stock
2 c. milk or cream, scalded
1 tbsp. chopped fresh parsley

Cook cauliflower in small amount of water until just tender; drain. Reserve 1 cup flowerets. Puree remaining cauliflower in blender or food mill. Melt butter in saucepan; add onion and celery. Saute until celery is tender. Stir in salt, pepper and flour. Add stock slowly, stirring constantly. Bring to a boil. Add pureed cauliflower and milk. Remove from heat; add reserved flowerets. Sprinkle with parsley. Garnish bowls of soup with grated cheese, if desired. Yield: 6 servings.

Joann E. Kelly, V.P.
Beta Chi No. 5996
Tucson, Arizona

Soups

CHICKEN SOUP AND DUMPLINGS (FINLAND)

1 chicken, disjointed
1 1/2 tsp. salt
1 tsp. pickling spices
1 med. onion, diced
3 med. potatoes, diced
4 carrots, sliced
1/4 c. rice
1 bay leaf
2 c. flour
2 tsp. (heaping) baking powder
1 c. milk
1 egg, lightly beaten

Place chicken pieces in large kettle; cover with water. Add 1 teaspoon salt, pickling spices and onion; cook until chicken is tender. Remove chicken. Add potatoes, carrots, rice and bay leaf; cook for 2 hours and 30 minutes. Combine flour, baking powder and remaining 1/2 teaspoon salt; stir in milk and egg. Drop on top of boiling soup; cover. Cook for 20 minutes. Serve with chicken.

Sandy Davis
Xi Eta Psi X3740
Uniontown, Ohio

CONCH CHOWDER

4 carrots
2 med. onions
5 med. potatoes
3 stalks celery and leaves
1 green pepper
1/4 lb. salt pork, diced
2 cloves of garlic
2 to 4 lb. ground conch
1 20-oz. can tomatoes
1 sm. can tomato paste
6 bay leaves
3 tbsp. barbecue sauce
1 tsp. poultry seasoning
1 tbsp. oregano
1 tsp. pepper
1 tbsp. salt

Scrub and cut vegetables into large pieces. Chop vegetables in blender with small amount water; do not puree. Place in large kettle. Add remaining ingredients. Fill kettle with water; stir and cover. Place on low heat; cook overnight. Turn off heat. Let rest for several hours. Remove cover. Cook for 8 hours longer. Add water or tomato juice if too thick. Taste for salt, adding more if needed. Yield: 8 quarts.

Jeanne Balcerzak
Beta Omega No. 3215
Key West, Florida

SEAFOOD CHOWDER

1 lb. frozen cod
1/2 lb. shrimp
1/2 pt. oysters

2 chicken bouillon cubes
1 med. potato, diced
1/2 c. chopped leeks or green onions
1/2 tsp. salt
1/8 tsp. pepper
1/2 lb. scallops
1/4 c. flour
1/3 c. melted butter
1/2 c. cream

Thaw cod; rinse with cold water. Cut into small pieces. Cut any large shrimp in half. Drain oysters; reserve liquid. Combine 1 1/2 cups boiling water, reserved oyster liquid and bouillon cubes in soup pot. Add potato, leeks, salt and pepper; cover. Bring to a boil. Simmer until potato is tender. Add shrimp, scallops and cod; simmer for 3 minutes. Combine flour and butter; stir into hot soup. Add oysters and cream. Cook for 5 minutes or until oysters are plump and edges ruffled.

Carolyn Gierrish
Omega Chap.
Sussex, New Brunswick, Canada

ZARZUELA (SPAIN)

1/4 c. olive or salad oil
1 med. onion, chopped
1/2 c. whole blanched almonds, toasted
1/2 c. dry white wine
3 cloves of garlic
3 parsley sprigs
1 1/3 c. Spanish-stuffed green olives
1 16-oz. can whole tomatoes, undrained
8 hard-shell clams or 1 can whole baby clams
1 lb. fresh or frozen king crab legs, cut into chunks
1/2 lb. fresh or frozen shelled and deveined shrimp
1/2 lb. fresh or frozen scallops
1 lb. fresh or frozen cod fillets, cut in chunks
1/2 tsp. salt
1/4 tsp. pepper

Heat olive oil in 5-quart Dutch oven. Add onion; saute for about 3 to 5 minutes or until tender. Blend almonds, wine, garlic, parsley and 1/3 cup whole pimento-stuffed olives until well combined in blender container. Add pureed olive mixture and undrained tomatoes to onion; heat to boiling. Cook for 1 minute, stirring constantly. Add clams and crab; return mixture to a boil. Reduce heat; cover. Cook for 5 minutes, stirring occasionally. Add shrimp, scallops, cod fillets, remaining 1 cup olives, salt and pepper; cover. Continue cooking for 5 minutes longer or until cod flakes easily when tested with a fork, stirring occasionally. Serve immediately in soup bowls.

Photograph for this recipe on page 36.

CLEAR SOUP WITH MARROW BALLS (GERMANY) FLEISCHBRUHE MIT MARKKLOSSCHEN

1 soupbone
1 lb. boiling beef
1 carrot, diced
2 onions, diced
4 green onions, sliced
4 cherry tomatoes, chopped
1 tbsp. minced chives
Maggi seasoning to taste
Salt and pepper to taste
2 oz. round or alphabet noodles
1 lg. marrowbone
1 egg
Bread crumbs
Chopped fresh parsley to taste
Nutmeg to taste

Place soupbone, beef and next 5 ingredients in 2 quarts cold water; boil for 2 to 3 hours. Strain; season with maggi seasoning, salt and pepper. Cook noodles in salted water for 15 minutes; add to soup. Scrape marrow from bone; melt over low heat in pan. Cool. Add egg and enough bread crumbs to hold mixture together. Add parsley and nutmeg. Season with salt and pepper. Shape into small firm balls. Refrigerate. Add to soup and simmer for 3 minutes.

Ursula Carlberg, V.P.
Xi Alpha Omicron X3371
Bossier City, Louisiana

CORN SOUP WITH CRAB (CHINA)

1 1/2 c. chicken broth
2 c. canned creamed corn
1 can crab or tuna, flaked
2 eggs
2 green onions with tops, minced

Bring broth to a boil in saucepan over moderate heat; add corn. Cook, stirring, for 3 minutes. Add crab slowly, stirring constantly. Beat eggs with a small amount of water; add slowly, stirring vigorously. Season with salt. May thicken soup with 1 tablespoon cornstarch mixed with 1/2 cup water if soup is too thin. Serve in bowls; sprinkle onions on top. Serve with soya sauce.

Peggy Cavin, Publ Chm.
Preceptor Xi XP491
Farmington, New Mexico

CREAM OF BROCCOLI SOUP (GERMANY) SPARGELKOHLSUPPE

1 bunch broccoli
1/4 c. butter or margarine
1/3 c. flour
4 c. chicken bouillon
2 egg yolks, beaten

1 c. heavy cream or evaporated milk
Salt and pepper to taste

Wash and trim broccoli, discarding most of thick stalks. Cook in 3 cups boiling salted water for about 10 minutes or until just tender. Drain, reserving cooking water. Set aside several small flowerets for garnish. Melt butter in a saucepan; blend in flour, stirring constantly, until well blended and foaming. Do not brown. Add bouillon and 2 cups reserved cooking water gradually; cook, stirring constantly, until smooth and thickened. Add chopped broccoli; simmer for 30 minutes. Puree until smooth in blender or press through fine sieve. Combine egg yolks and cream; stir into hot soup. Season with salt and pepper. This may be served hot or cold. Garnish each serving with reserved flowerets.

Pam Wright
Lambda Beta Chap.
Carbondale, Illinois

CUCUMBER SOUP (FINLAND) KURKKUKEITTO

1/2 c. butter
1 sm. onion, chopped
4 cucumbers, peeled and sliced
3 tbsp. flour
6 c. chicken stock
1/4 tsp. pepper
2 egg yolks, beaten
1 c. light cream
1 tbsp. Sherry
3 tbsp. chopped parsley

Melt butter in saucepan; add onion and cucumbers. Cook over low heat for 10 minutes, stirring frequently. Do not brown. Sprinkle with flour; mix well. Add stock gradually, stirring constantly until boiling point is reached. Add pepper; cook over low heat for 10 minutes, stirring occasionally. Force mixture through sieve or puree in blender. Return to saucepan. Combine egg yolks and cream; stir into soup. Add Sherry. Heat thoroughly, stirring constantly. Sprinkle with parsley before serving.

Nancy Louis, Rec. Sec.
Xi Alpha Eta No. 3444
Waukesha, Wisconsin

EGG DROP SOUP (TAIWAN)

12 thin scallions
3 tbsp. oil
1/2 tsp. salt
1/2 tsp. MSG
3 eggs
Salt and pepper to taste

Chop scallions into 1-inch pieces; saute in oil in soup pot. Add 1 quart water; bring to a boil. Add salt and MSG. Beat eggs; add salt and pepper. Feather egg mixture into boiling soup with a fork. Serve immediately. Yield: 4 servings.

Rosemary Bouffard
Xi Alpha Alpha X3822
Danbury, Connecticut

CUBAN BLACK BEAN SOUP

2 lb. black beans
1 hambone
1 bay leaf
1 8-oz. can tomato sauce
5 cloves of garlic
2 green peppers
2 lg. onions
1 sm. can pimentos with liquid
1/2 c. olive oil
1 tsp. oregano
1 tsp. salt
1 tsp. sugar
1 tsp. cumin
1/4 c. white vinegar

Soak beans overnight in 1 gallon water. Add hambone, bay leaf and tomato sauce. Cook for 3 to 4 hours or until beans are tender. Chop garlic, green peppers, onions and pimentos with liquid in blender. Saute in olive oil. Add to soup with oregano, salt, sugar, cumin and vinegar. Simmer for 1 hour longer. Serve each bowl soup with 1 tablespoon rice, marinated in vinegar and olive oil and 2 finely chopped onions added.

Marilyn MacDonald
Delta Chi No. 2063
El Paso, Texas

CURRIED CARROT VICHYSSOISE
(FRANCE)

1 10 1/4-oz. can frozen cream of
    potato soup, thawed
1 10-oz. package frozen whole baby
    carrots
1 tsp. curry powder
2 c. light cream
Chopped fresh mint

Press potato soup through a sieve or whirl in a blender. Cook carrots until tender; drain. Press through a sieve or whirl in a blender. Combine pureed potato soup, pureed carrots and curry powder. Stir in cream gradually. Chill in refrigerator for at least 4 hours. Serve in chilled bowls. Garnish with chopped mint. Yield: 6 servings.

Photograph for this recipe on this page.

MIXED FRUIT SOUP (NORWAY)

1 11-oz. package mixed dried fruits
1/2 c. seedless raisins
1 3 to 4-in. stick cinnamon
1 orange with peeling, cut into 1/4-in.
    slices
1 No. 2 can unsweetened pineapple juice
1/2 c. sugar
2 tbsp. quick-cooking tapioca
1/4 tsp. salt

Combine dried fruits, raisins, cinnamon and 4 cups water; bring to a boil. Simmer for about 30 minutes or until fruits are tender. Add remaining ingredients; bring to a boil again. Cover; cook for 15 minutes over low heat, stirring constantly. Serve hot or cold.

Katherine McGiffin
Exemplar Preceptor Eta Gamma XP1546
Auburn, California

SCHNITZ SOUP

1 pkg. mixed dried fruit
1 c. raisins
1 tsbp. flour
2 tbsp. sugar
2 tbsp. dark Karo syrup
Cream

Cook fruit and raisins in 1/2 cup water until fruit is tender, adding water as needed. Combine flour, sugar and syrup with enough cream to make a smooth paste; stir slowly into fruit. Bring to a boil, stirring constantly. Simmer for 10 minutes.

Connie Walters, Soc. Com
Xi Alpha Pi X404.
Paul, Idaho

COLD VEGETABLE SOUP
(SPAIN) GAZPACHO

2 med. cucumbers, peeled and chopped
5 med. tomatoes, peeled and chopped
1 lg. onion, chopped
1 med. green pepper, chopped
2 tsp. chopped garlic
4 c. crumbled French bread
1/4 c. red wine vinegar

4 tsp. salt
1/4 c. olive oil
1 tbsp. tomato paste
Chili powder to taste

Combine all vegetables with garlic and bread in large bowl. Stir in 4 cups cold water, vinegar and salt. Puree about 2 cups at a time in blender; pour all puree into bowl. Beat in oil, tomato paste and chili powder with wire whisk. Cover; refrigerate for several hours. Stir with whisk before serving. Serve in chilled soup bowls. Garnish with onions, green pepper and tomatoes.

Nivia M. Wilson
Preceptor Epsilon XP217
Galveston, Texas

EASY GAZPACHO

2 med. tomatoes
1 med. cucumber, pared and chopped
1 sm. onion, chopped
1 sm. green pepper, chopped
1 1/2 c. tomato juice
1/3 c. olive oil
1/3 c. red wine vinegar
1/4 tsp. Tabasco sauce
1 1/2 tsp. salt
1/8 tsp. pepper
1/2 c. chopped chives
Seasoned croutons

Peel and slice tomatoes; add cucumber, onion and green pepper. Add 1/2 cup tomato juice; toss to combine. Place half the mixture in blender at a time; puree, covered, at high speed for 1 minute. Repeat with remaining mixture. Combine pureed vegetables and remaining 1 cup tomato juice in large bowl; add olive oil, vinegar, Tabasco sauce, salt and pepper. Refrigerate until well chilled. Sprinkle with chives and seasoned croutons to serve. Yield: 6 servings.

Shirley Joan Wells, Pres.
Xi Beta Beta X4020
Lincoln, Nebraska

EASY JAMBALAYA

1 1/2 c. diced cooked ham
1 c. chopped onion
3/4 c. sliced celery
1 med. green pepper, cut in thin strips
1 clove of garlic, minced
2 tbsp. vegetable oil
1 10 3/4-oz. can chicken broth
1 15-oz. can tomato sauce
1 c. chopped cooked chicken
3/4 c. rice
2 tbsp. minced parsley
1 bay leaf
1/4 tsp. leaf thyme
1/4 tsp. Worcestershire sauce
1/8 tsp. cayenne papper

Cook ham, onion, celery, green pepper and garlic in oil in large skillet until onion is soft. Add 3/4 cup water and remaining ingredients. Bring to a boil. Cover; simmer for 40 minutes, stirring once or twice. Yield: 4-6 servings.

LaVonne Barthels
Iota Omicron No. 3206
Gonzales, Texas

GUMBO FILE

1 cooked chicken, chopped
1 c. cooked shrimp
1 c. chopped cooked ham
1 c. chopped cooked hot sausage
2 cans golden mushroom soup
1 pkg. dry onion soup mix
1/2 c. chopped celery
1/2 c. chopped bell pepper
1/4 c. chopped onion
1 tbsp. salt
Pepper to taste
1/2 tsp. file

Bring 6 cups water to a boil in large soup pot; add all ingredients except file. Cook over low heat for 4 hours. Stir in file. Serve over rice in soup bowls.

Lorraine Herron, Pres.
Xi Eta Beta X1932
Santa Maria, California

MARYLAND CRAB SOUP

1 can cream of celery soup
1 can pepper pot soup
1 pt. half and half
8 oz. crab meat

Combine all ingredients; mix well. Heat to serving temperature.

Jeanne Fradiska
Xi Beta X551
LaVale, Maryland

MEXICAN VERMICELLI SOUP

3 tbsp. oil
1/2 pkg. coiled vermicelli
1 8-oz. can tomato sauce
2 tbsp. minced onion
1 clove of garlic, minced
2 qt. chicken stock
Salt and pepper to taste
1 tbsp. chopped fresh parsley

Heat oil; add broken vermicelli. Stir until golden brown. Drain off oil. Add tomato sauce, onion and garlic; return to heat. Cook, stirring, until sauce is well mixed. Add stock, salt, pepper and parsley. Cook until vermicelli is tender. Yield: 8-10 servings.

Betty Price
Preceptor Beta XP313
Guthrie, Oklahoma

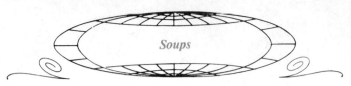

LIVER DUMPLING SOUP
(GERMANY) LEBERKNODELSUPPE

1 lb. beef shank or soupbone
1 tbsp. salt
2 stalks celery, quartered
1 lg. onion, chopped and fried
2 carrots, halved
1 sprig of parsley
1 bay leaf
1 leek
6 to 8 peppercorns
1 whole clove

Combine beef, 2 quarts water and salt in large kettle; bring quickly to a boil. Reduce heat; simmer for 1 hour. Add remaining ingredients. Cook for 1 hour longer. Strain through fine sieve; season with additional salt or 1 or 2 cubes beef bouillon, if desired. This is a clear soup and makes a good basis for a number of other soups with varying garnishes.

Liver Dumplings
Leberklosschen

1 lb. beef or goose liver
1 onion
1 clove of garlic
1 egg
1 tsp. salt
3/4 c. bread crumbs
1 tsp. dried or minced fresh parsley

Process liver, onion and garlic through food processor or meat grinder until finely minced. Add remaining ingredients; shape with a teaspoon into dumplings. Drop in boiling soup or salted water. Simmer for about 10 minutes or until dumplings rise to the top.

Mary L. Partoll
Preceptor Alpha Kappa XP939
Freeport, Illinois

EASY ITALIAN MINESTRONE

2 lg. onions, chopped
3 stalks celery with tops, chopped
1 tbsp. salad oil
4 carrots, chopped
2 10 1/2-oz. cans beef broth
1 soup can water
1 16-oz. can tomatoes, blended
1 can chick peas
1 can pork and beans
Salt and pepper to taste
Minced parsley to taste
4 oz. spaghetti or macaroni

Saute onions and celery in oil until tender; add carrots, broth, water and tomatoes. Cook for 30 minutes. Add peas, pork and beans, salt, pepper and parsley; simmer for 10 to 15 minutes, stirring occasionally. Break spaghetti into soup mixture; simmer for 7 to 8 minutes or until spaghetti is done.

Marie De Feo
Xi Alpha Upsilon No. 1667
Somerset, New Jersey

ITALIAN MINESTRONE WITH HAM

2 ham hocks
1 sm. onion, chopped
3 celery stalks and leaves, chopped
1 c. white beans
1 lg. onion, diced
1 c. diced celery
1 carrot, sliced
1 clove of garlic, minced
Vegetable oil
2 c. Italian tomatoes
1 tsp. basil
Salt and pepper to taste
1/2 tsp. Italian seasoning (opt.)
1 c. coarsely shredded cabbage
1/2 c. macaroni

Cover ham hocks with about 4 quarts water; add chopped onion and celery stalks. Simmer until very tender. Remove ham hocks; add beans to ham stock. Cook until just tender. Saute next 4 ingredients in small amount of oil until lightly browned. Remove meat from ham hocks; add to bean mixture. Add tomatoes and seasonings. Simmer for about 30 minutes. Add remaining ingredients; cook until macaroni is tender. Serve with grated Parmesan cheese. Add more tomatoes or broth if soup is too thick.

Alma Leeming, Corr. Sec.
Preceptor Laureate No. 260
Monterey Park, California

NORWEGIAN SPINACH SOUP

1 can cream of chicken soup
1 c. milk
2 chicken bouillon cubes
1 10-oz. package frozen chopped spinach, thawed
1 tsp. salt
1/4 tsp. pepper
2 tbsp. chopped parsley
2 hard-boiled eggs, quartered

Combine soup and milk in a large saucepan. Dissolve bouillon cubes in 2 cups boiling water; add to milk mixture. Add spinach. Place spinach mixture in blender container, process for several seconds on medium speed until spinach is very finely chopped. Do not puree. Return to saucepan; simmer for 10 minutes. Add salt and pepper. Garnish with parsley and egg quarters.

Myrna L. Liepins, Pres
Xi Epsilon Zeta X489
Birmingham, Michigan

VEGETABLE SOUP (ITALY)
MINESTRA ALLA GENOVESE
CON PESTO

1/2 lb. fresh green beans or 1/2 pkg. frozen
French-style green beans
3 potatoes, peeled and sliced
3 tomatoes, peeled and sliced

1/2 lb. vermicelli
1 tbsp. salt
1/2 tsp. pepper
1 clove of garlic, minced
1/8 tsp. thyme
1/8 tsp. basil
2 tbsp. tomato paste
3 tbsp. olive oil
1/2 c. grated Parmesan cheese

Combine beans, potatoes, tomatoes and 2 1/2 quarts water in a saucepan. Cook over medium heat for 15 minutes. Add vermicelli, salt and pepper. Cook for 12 minutes longer. Mix garlic, thyme, basil and tomato paste in a bowl. Add oil, a drop at a time, mixing constantly until smooth. Add to soup very gradually, stirring constantly. Serve hot; sprinkle with cheese.

Jane Smith, Rec. Sec
Preceptor Eta XP916
Menomonie, Wisconsin

FRENCH ONION SOUP

8 bouillon cubes
3 tbsp. instant minced onion
1 tsp. minced garlic
3 tbsp. butter or margarine
1/2 c. grated Parmesan cheese
1/8 c. grated Romano cheese
1 4-oz. package grated mozzarella cheese
1 4-oz. package grated Swiss cheese

Dissolve bouillon cubes in 6 cups water in 12-inch skillet; bring just to a boil. Add onion and garlic; cook for about 15 minutes. Add butter; let melt completely before adding cheeses. Add Parmesan and Romano cheeses; boil for 5 minutes, stirring constantly. Add mozzarella and Swiss cheeses to simmering mixture about 10 minutes before serving. Heat until cheeses melt. Turn off heat. Pour into soup bowls. Yield: 6 servings.

Bonnie F. Carr
Epsilon Rho No. 8379
Staunton, Virginia

EASY ONION SOUP

2 lg. onions, sliced
1/4 c. butter or margarine
1 1/2 c. beef bouillon
2 tbsp. Worcestershire sauce
Salt and pepper to taste
Mozzarella cheese slices

Saute onions in butter; add bouillon and Worcestershire sauce. Season with salt and pepper. Simmer for 3 to 4 minutes. Pour into individual bowls; place slice of mozzarella cheese in each bowl. Melt slightly under broiler. Serve immediately.

Jeanie Felts, Treas.
Epsilon Sigma Phi No. 9956
Siloam Springs, Arkansas

ORSINI'S CREAM OF ONION SOUP

1 tsp. oil
2 c. (scant) butter
2 1/2 lb. onions, chopped
2 tbsp. flour
1 qt. beef broth or bouillon
1 c. grated Parmesan cheese
Salt to taste

Heat oil and 1 cup butter in large pan. Add onions; saute until golden. Stir in flour. Add beef broth; cook for 2 hours. Puree, using blender or food mill. Add remaining butter and Parmesan cheese. Season with salt. Serve hot.

Connie Ditommaso, 2nd V.P.
Italy Alpha No. 10224
Aviano, Italy

OVEN-BAKED ONION SOUP (GERMANY)

1 onion
Butter or oil
1 1/2 c. beef broth or hot water
Salt to taste
1 slice bread, cut into thin strips
Grated Parmesan cheese

Slice onion into thin rings; saute in small amount butter until light brown. Pour in beef broth; boil for 15 minutes. Season with salt. Remove from heat. Place bread strips on soup; cover thickly with grated cheese. Bake in preheated 400-degree oven until cheese is light brown. Yield: 1 serving.

Joanne Carr
Xi Gamma Tau Chap.
Grants Pass, Oregon

PEANUT SOUP (WEST AFRICA)

1/2 lb. dry-roasted peanuts
1/2 c. finely chopped onion
1 qt. chicken broth
1 tbsp. cornstarch
1 c. half and half
2 tsp. paprika
1/8 tsp. cayenne pepper

Rinse peanuts quickly under running water to remove excess salt. Place in large pan with onion and broth; cook over low heat for 1 hour. Puree peanuts and onion in blender. Return to pan; add cornstarch dissolved in half and half. Season with paprika and cayenne pepper. Simmer over low heat for 10 minutes or until hot. Season with salt, if needed.

Judy Kroon, Treas.
Xi Beta Kappa X2368
Rochester, New York

PORK-CUCUMBER SOUP (THAILAND)

1 lb. pork, cut in thin strips
1 med. onion, finely chopped
1 tbsp. fish sauce
1/2 tsp. pepper
2 cucumbers, peeled and sliced
2 c. cooked rice

Simmer pork and onion in 4 cups water for 2 to 3 hours. Add fish sauce and pepper. Add sliced cucumbers just before serving; let stand, covered, for 10 minutes. Add rice and serve.

Marian M. Davis, 1st V.P.
Xi Alpha Kappa No. 1975
Albuquerque, New Mexico

PORTUGUESE SOUP

2 lb. beef brisket, cut in 1-in. cubes
1 lg. onion, chopped
3 cloves of garlic, crushed
2   15-oz. cans tomato sauce
1/4 c. chopped parsley
2 tsp. salt
1/2 tsp. crushed coriander
1/4 tsp. pepper
1 bay leaf
2 lg. peeled potatoes cut in 1-in. cubes
1 c. Port or dry red wine
1 bunch Swiss chard or spinach, chopped
French bread

Combine first 9 ingredients with 1 quart water in kettle or Dutch oven. Simmer, covered, for 3 hours. Stir in potatoes and Port; simmer, covered, until potatoes are tender. Add Swiss chard; cook, uncovered, for 10 minutes or until crisp tender. Remove bay leaf. Ladle soup over French bread in bowl. Yield: 6-8 servings.

Virginia E. Bryant, Serv. Chm.
Preceptor Beta XP346
Anchorage, Alaska

AUSTRIAN POTATO SOUP

2 lb. boiling potatoes
6 tbsp. butter
1 c. chopped celery
1/4 c. diced parsnips
1 c. finely chopped onions
1 c. diced carrots
2 tbsp. flour
1 qt. chicken stock
1/4 tsp. marjoram
1/2 tsp. salt
Freshly ground pepper to taste
1/2 c. chopped fresh mushrooms

Cook unpeeled potatoes for 6 to 8 minutes in boiling water to cover. Peel and dice into 1/2-inch chunks. Melt butter in heavy 4-quart saucepan. Add potatoes, celery, parsnips, onions and carrots; cook for 10 minutes, stirring occasionally. Sprinkle flour evenly over vegetables; stir until well coated. Add stock, marjo-

ram, salt, pepper and mushrooms. Bring to a boil, stirring almost constantly. Reduce to very low heat; partially cover pan. Simmer for 25 to 30 minutes or until vegetables are tender.

Kristin Lewis
Xi Zeta Alpha X4152
Sikeston, Missouri

BAVARIAN POTATO SOUP KARTOFFELSUPPE

1/2 c. butter
1 carrot, diced
1 leek, diced
4 med. onions, diced
1/2 c. celery, diced
2 cloves of garlic, diced
2 bay leaves
2 to 3 qt. chicken broth
4 c. diced potatoes
° Salt and white pepper to taste
Dash of nutmeg
1 bouquet garni
1 c. light cream or evaporated milk

Melt butter in heavy soup kettle; add carrot, leek, onions, celery and garlic. Saute for about 5 minutes; do not brown. Add bay leaves and chicken broth; simmer, partially covered, for 10 to 15 minutes. Add potatoes, salt, pepper, nutmeg and bouquet garni. Cover; simmer until potatoes are tender. Remove bouquet garni. Stir in cream just before serving. Yield: 8-10 servings.

Rosemary C. Dodd, V.P.
Gamma Upsilon No. 5969
Fredericksburg, Virginia

SCOTCH BROTH (GREAT BRITAIN)

1 lb. lamb stew meat
1/2 c. split peas
1/2 c. barley
1 lg. onion, chopped
2 carrots, diced
2 med. turnips, diced
1 sm. cabbage, coarsely chopped
1/2 c. chopped parsley
1/8 tsp. pepper
1 tbsp. salt

Combine lamb and 8 cups water in stock pot; bring to a boil. Reduce heat; simmer for 1 hour. Add remaining ingredients; simmer for 1 hour longer or until barley and peas are tender.

Ruth Prengle, Pres.
Preceptor Beta XP 13
Houston, Texa

Recipe on page 8

SUPREME TOMATO SOUP

1 med. onion, chopped
2 tbsp. butter
1 3-oz. package cream cheese, cubed
2 cans tomato soup
3 c. milk
1/8 tsp. garlic powder
1/2 tsp. paprika
2 hard-cooked egg yolks, sieved

Saute onion in butter until lightly browned. Combine all ingredients except egg yolks in blender. Blend until smooth. Pour into saucepan; heat thoroughly but do not boil. Garnish with egg yolks.

Kathleen Johnson
Preceptor Beta Alpha Chap.
London, Ontario, Canada

WHITE WINE SOUP (GERMANY)
WEINSUPPE

Cinnamon to taste
Lemon peel to taste
4 tsp. cornstarch
2 c. white wine
5 tbsp. sugar
1 egg yolk, beaten

Combine 2 cups water, cinnamon and lemon peel; bring to a boil. Mix cornstarch with a small amount of cold water; stir into boiling mixture. Boil for 1 minute. Add wine and sugar; heat through but do not boil. Add a small amount of hot mixture to egg yolk; stir back into remaining hot mixture. May be served hot or cold.

Gerda M. Cote, Rec. Sec.
Preceptor Alpha XP133
Manchester, New Hampshire

ALBERTA RED-EYE STEW

1 1/2 lb. stewing beef
1/4 c. all-purpose flour
2 tsp. salt
Pepper to taste
1/4 c. salad oil
2 lb. onions, peeled
1 clove of garlic, minced
12 oz. flat beer
1 tbsp. soy sauce
1 tbsp. Worcestershire sauce
1 tbsp. steak sauce
1/2 tsp. thyme
2 bay leaves
2 to 3 c. tomato juice
3 potatoes, peeled and cubed
3 carrots, peeled and cubed
1 c. frozen peas

Dredge beef with mixture of flour, salt and pepper. Brown in hot oil. Add onions and garlic; cook until

Recipe on page 28.

onions are transparent. Add beer, soy sauce, Worcestershire sauce, steak sauce, thyme and bay leaves. Bring to a boil; cover. Reduce heat; simmer for 1 hour. Add tomato juice; simmer for 30 minutes. Add potatoes and carrots; simmer for 20 minutes. Add peas; simmer for 10 minutes longer or until vegetables are tender. Remove bay leaves. Yield: 6 servings.

Jean Berger, Pres.
Alpha Eta No. 8851
Nanton, Alberta, Canada

AMERICAN-STYLE ITALIAN STEW

1 lb. ground beef
1 lg. green pepper, diced
2 16-oz. cans zucchini
1 14-oz. can pear-shaped tomatoes
1 6-oz. can tomato sauce
1 sm. can whole mushrooms
1/2 jar sm. whole onions
Dash of hot crushed red peppers
1/2 tsp. chili powder
1 tsp. Italian seasoning
3 med.-sized hot sausages, sliced

Brown ground beef; pour off excess fat. Add green pepper; saute until limp. Add remaining ingredients except hot sausages. Fry sausages lightly; add to beef mixture. Simmer for 1 hour. Yield: 8 servings.

Jean Stouffer, W. and M. Chm.
Sigma No. 2148
Hagerstown, Maryland

EASY OVEN BEEF BURGUNDY
(FRANCE) BOEUF BOURGUIGNONNE

2 lb. chuck or beef round steak
1 tbsp. Kitchen Bouquet
1/4 c. cream of rice
4 carrots
2 c. thinly sliced onions
1 c. thinly sliced celery
1 clove of garlic, minced
2 tsp. salt
1/8 tsp. pepper
1/8 tsp. marjoram, crushed
1/8 tsp. thyme, crushed
1 c. Burgundy or dry red wine
1 6-oz. can mushroom crowns or slices

Trim beef; cut into 1 1/2-inch cubes. Place in a 2 1/2-quart casserole; toss gently with Kitchen Bouquet, coating on all sides. Mix in cream of rice. Cut carrots in quarters lengthwise, then in half crosswise. Add carrots and remaining ingredients. Mix gently. Cover. Bake in preheated 325-degree oven for about 2 hours and 30 minutes or until beef and vegetables are tender, stirring every 30 minutes. Serve with potatoes, rice or noodles. Yield: 4-6 servings.

Barbara Bashaw, V.P.
Xi Nu X1805
Phoenix, Arizona

bles are tender. Remove bay leaf. Sprinkle top with parsley.

Photograph for this recipe on this page.

FAMILY BEEF BURGUNDY (FRANCE)

3 strips bacon
1 onion, sliced
1 1/2 to 2 lb. stew meat
1 1/2 tbsp. flour
1 can beef broth
2 c. dry red wine
Salt and pepper to taste
1/4 tsp. marjoram
1/4 tsp. thyme
1 clove of garlic, minced
1/2 lb. mushrooms
1 jar boiled onions

Fry bacon until crisp; remove from pan. Drain and crumble. Add sliced onion; fry until limp. Remove from pan; set aside. Brown stew meat on all sides; stir in flour. Add broth, wine, spices and garlic. Cook for 2 hours and 30 minutes to 3 hours or until meat is tender. Add mushrooms and fried and boiled onions; cook for 30 minutes longer. Add crumbled bacon. Serve with French bread for dipping and dunking.

Diana Sundermeier
Xi Gamma Kappa X1441
Bowling Green, Ohio

FLEMISH BEEF STEW
CARBONNADES FLAMANDE

3 tbsp. flour
2 tsp. salt
1/4 tsp. pepper
2 lb. lean beef stew meat, cut in
        1 1/2-in. cubes
2 tbsp. cooking oil
1/2 c. frozen chopped onion
1 tbsp. dark brown sugar
1 12-oz. can beer
1 10-oz. can beef broth
1 bay leaf
1/4 tsp. dried thyme, crumbled
2 tbsp. red wine vinegar
1 1 1/4-lb. bag frozen stew
        vegetables
1 c. frozen peas
Frozen whole mushrooms
2 tbsp. finely chopped parsley

Blend flour, salt and pepper together; roll meat pieces in flour mixture. Heat oil in a 4-quart Dutch oven. Brown meat, several pieces at a time, until all meat is browned. Add onion; cook until transparent. Sprinkle with brown sugar; mix well. Return meat to casserole. Add beer, broth, bay leaf, thyme and vinegar. Bring to a boil. Reduce heat; cover. Simmer slowly for 1 hour. Add frozen vegetables and mushrooms. Continue to cook for 20 to 30 minutes or until meat and vegeta-

FRENCH CANADIAN STEW

1/2 c. flour
2 tsp. salt
3/4 tsp. pepper
1/2 tsp. paprika
2 lb. stew beef, cut into 1-in. cubes
2 tbsp. oil
1 1/2 c. coarsely chopped onions
2 cloves of garlic, minced
8 prunes, pitted and chopped
2/3 c. pearl barley
1 2-lb. can tomatoes
1/2 tsp. basil
1/4 tsp. thyme
2 bay leaves
1 c. diced potatoes
1 c. sliced carrots
1 1/2 c. chopped celery
1/2 c. frozen peas

Combine flour, 1 teaspoon salt, 1/2 teaspoon pepper and paprika; coat beef with seasoned flour. Heat oil in heavy Dutch oven over high heat. Brown beef in oil. Remove from heat; add 2 cups boiling water, remaining salt and pepper and remaining ingredients except potatoes, carrots, celery and peas. Bake, covered, at 325 degrees for 1 hours and 30 minutes, stirring occasionally. Add vegetables and 1 or 2 cups boiling water

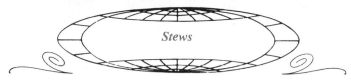
if too thick. Return to oven; bake for 30 minutes longer or until vegetables are tender.

Marie Melnichuk
Eta Xi No. 8940
Orangeville, Ontario, Canada

SPANISH STEW

1 1/2 lb. stew meat, cut in 1-in. cubes
1 med. onion, chopped
4 to 6 tbsp. margarine
2 sm. cans tomato paste
2 tbsp. sugar
4 med. peeled potatoes, quartered
Salt and pepper to taste

Place stew meat, onion and margarine in Dutch oven; cook over medium heat until meat is browned. Add tomato paste, 1/2 cup water and sugar. Bring to a boil; reduce heat to simmer. May add small amount of water if sauce seems too thick. Simmer, stirring occasionally, for 2 hours. Add potatoes and seasoning; cook for 1 hour longer or until potatoes are tender. Yield: 4 servings.

Celine J. Adams, Pres.
Preceptor Alpha XP163
Sarasota, Florida

STIFADO (GREECE)

3 lb. beef cubes
3 lb. small onions, cut up
2 tbsp. oil
1 c. dry red wine
1 tsp. chopped garlic
2 tsp. salt
1 28-oz. can tomatoes, drained
2 tbsp. tomato paste
1/4 tsp. pepper
5 whole cloves
1 teaspoon cinnamon
1 bay leaf
1/4 c. sliced black olives

Pat beef dry with paper towels. Brown beef and 1/2 of the onions in oil. Add wine, stirring to mix. Mash garlic and salt to a paste; add to stew with remaining ingredients except olives. Cover; bring to a boil. Bake in preheated 325-degree oven for 1 hour and 30 minutes or until beef is tender. Add olives; serve with rice. Yield: 4-6 servings.

Grace Thompson
Preceptor Mu XP1360
Conway, Arkansas

MEXICAN GREEN CHILI

4 lb. pork, cut in bite-sized pieces
1 lg. onion, chopped
2 tbsp. oil

2 6-oz. cans chili salsa
2 4-oz. cans chopped hot chilies
6 4-oz. cans chopped mild chilies
2 cans Snappy Tom
2 13-oz. cans tomato juice
2 15-oz. cans tomato sauce and bits
4 1-lb. cans whole tomatoes, chopped

Simmer pork and onion in oil for 20 minutes; drain off excess oil. Combine all ingredients in large pan; cook over low heat for at least 3 hours. Serve on burritos, tacos, tostados or fried eggs.

Phyllis C. Groves, Treas.
Alpha Mu No. 1043
Thornton, Colorado

SLOW COOKER CHILE VERDE (MEXICO)

1 1/2 lb. boneless pork shoulder or beef chuck
Cooking oil
1 1-lb. 12-oz. can whole tomatoes, quartered
1/2 c. beef consomme
2 tbsp. lemon juice
1 med. clove of garlic, crushed
1/4 tsp. sugar
1 tsp. ground cumin
1/4 tsp. cloves
1 7-oz. can whole green chilies, cut in thin strips
1/3 c. chopped parsley
Salt to taste

Cut pork into 1 1/2-inch cubes. Brown on all sides in small amount of cooking oil. Drain off excess oil. Add tomatoes with tomato liquid and remaining ingredients. Bring to a boil. Place mixture in 3 1/2-quart electric slow cooking pot. Cook on Low for 6 to 8 hours.

Lourdes M. Wulfing
Zeta Delta No. 4466
Keokuk, Iowa

LABRADOR RABBIT STEW

1 3-lb. rabbit
1 lg. onion, diced
1 stalk celery, chopped
1 tbsp. salt
Dash of pepper
1 c. cubed carrots
1 c. cubed potatoes
1/4 c. flour

Wash and disjoint rabbit. Place in heavy kettle with onion, celery, salt and pepper. Add 6 cups boiling water; cover tightly. Simmer for 2 hours. Add carrots and potatoes; simmer until vegetables are tender. Mix flour and 1/2 cup water to a paste; stir into stew mixture. Cook, stirring, until thickened. Yield: 6 servings.

Dorothy Burton, W. and M. Chm.
Alpha No. 7214
Goose Bay, Labrador, Canada

Salads

In 15th and 16th Century Europe, medleys of vegetables and fruits were called "macedoines," after Macedonia, an ancient land long identified by the great racial variety of its inhabitants. Macedoines usually consisted of a salad of fresh herbs and greens, or a variety of cooked vegetables bound together in a savory sauce or gelatin mixture. In ancient Iran, salad vegetables including eggplant, cucumbers, cauliflower, beets, turnips and onions, were most often spicily pickled and served at almost every meal. Modern Persians still love these sour pickled salads for their traditional happy meaning — that a woman who craved them was soon to be blessed with a child.

Modern salads, a chilled medley of fresh lettuces, tomato, cucumber, onion and celery only began to appear regularly on restaurant and household menus with the advent of cool storage and refrigeration techniques in the mid-1800's. Now, of course, vegetables of all kinds can be shipped from far and near and still remain crisp, fresh, and full of vitamins and flavor. Happily though, a world of ideas has ensured that the definition of a salad goes far beyond that of a crisp mixture of green vegetables coated with a spicy, savory dressing. A light salad of this type often introduces a meal, while a larger one with additional diced meats, cheeses, pickles and relishes often becomes the meal in itself. Best of all, a salad is still a *macedoine,* a mixture of most any ingredients with compatible flavors and textures, whether it be a varicolored mixture of vegetables and fruits, or either of these embellished with nuts, sour cream, mayonnaise, cheeses, and other flavorful ingredients.

With roast, poultry, wildfowl, and lamb enjoy a cranberry salad, either frozen or in a gelatin base. Hot German Potato Salad flavored with bacon is delicious with pork roast, ham and cold fried chicken. Flaked salmon, tuna, and chicken each make excellent salads, hot or cold. And, they can be combined with ingredients chosen for the desired effect — Greek, Oriental, American, or Scandinavian. Beta Sigma Phis believe that is the truly wonderful thing about salads — that they can be just about anything the cook wants them to be and still be full of vitamins, flavor and fun.

FROG EYE SALAD

1 box Acini de Pepe macaroni
    or R and F soup macs
1 c. sugar
2 tbsp. flour
1/2 tsp. salt
1 3/4 c. pineapple juice
3 eggs, beaten
1 lg. can crushed pineapple, drained
1 can pineapple tidbits, drained
2 cans mandarin oranges, drained
1 sm. package miniature marshmallows
1 lg. carton whipped topping

Boil macaroni in salted water for about 25 minutes or until tender. Blanch and cool. Combine next 5 ingredients; cook over medium heat, stirring constantly, until thicken. Cool. Add cooled custard to cooled macaroni; let stand in refrigerator overnight. Add crushed pineapple, pineapple tidbits, oranges, marshmallows and whipped topping; blend well. Serve chilled.

Bonnie Barnes, Rec. Sec.
Xi Alpha Omega X1616
Hutchinson, Kansas

ARCTIC FREEZE

2 3-oz. packages cream cheese, softened
2 tbsp. mayonnaise
2 tbsp. sugar
2 c. cranberry sauce
1 c. crushed pineapple
1/2 c. chopped nuts
1/2 c. whipping cream, whipped

Blend cream cheese, mayonnaise and sugar together. Add next 3 ingredients; mix well. Fold in whipped cream. Pour into 8 1/2 x 4 x 2-inch loaf pan. Freeze for 6 hours or overnight. Let stand at room temperature for about 15 minutes before serving. Slice and serve on lettuce.

Margaret Gross, Corr. Sec.
Xi Sigma Alpha X4240
Dinuba, California

CRANBERRY RELISH MOLD

2 1/2 c. crushed pineapple
2 3-oz. packages cherry gelatin
3/4 c. sugar
1 to 2 tbsp. lemon juice
1 1/2 c. ground cranberries
1 sm. orange, ground
1 c. chopped celery
1/2 c. broken walnuts or pecans

Drain pineapple, reserving syrup. Combine gelatin and sugar; dissolve in 2 cups hot water. Add 1/2 cup cold water, lemon juice and reserved pineapple syrup. Chill until partially set. Add pineapple and remaining ingredients; turn into 2-quart mold. Chill until firm. Unmold to serve.

Nelda R. Kelley, Pres.
Beta Beta XP1570
Neodesha, Kansas

CREME DE MENTHE SALAD RING

1 3-oz. package lime gelatin
1 8 1/4-oz. can crushed pineapple
3 tbsp. Creme de Menthe
1 1/2 c. sour cream
1 c. diced pears
1 8-oz. carton plain yogurt
2 tsp. lime juice

Dissolve gelatin in 3/4 cup boiling water. Drain pineapple, reserving juice. Combine juice with Creme de Menthe; add enough water to equal 3/4 cup liquid. Add to gelatin. Chill until mixture starts to thicken. Add 1/2 cup sour cream; beat until light and well blended. Fold in pears and pineapple; pour into greased 4-cup ring mold. Chill until set. Unmold onto serving plate. Combine yogurt, remaining 1 cup sour cream and lime juice; blend well. Pour dressing into center of ring. Garnish with lime slices. Yield: 6 servings.

Mavalea Runyan
Exemplar Preceptor Alpha Zeta No. 1167
Shelbyville, Indiana

HAWAIIAN RAINBOW-HUED SALAD

1 29-oz. can cling peach slices
1 3-oz. package lemon gelatin
1 6-oz. package raspberry gelatin
1 3-oz. package orange gelatin
1 c. plain yogurt
1/2 c. chopped almonds

Drain peaches; reserve 1/3 cup syrup. Dissolve lemon gelatin in 1 cup boiling water; stir in reserved peach syrup. Chill until slightly thick. Place 16 peach slices in 10-cup mold. Pour gelatin over peaches; chill until set. Dissolve raspberry gelatin in 2 1/2 cups boiling water. Stir in 1 1/2 cups cold water. Chill until slightly thick. Pour over lemon layer. Refrigerate until set. Dissolve orange gelatin in 1/2 cup boiling water. Puree remaining peaches with yogurt in blender container. Stir into orange gelatin. Add almonds. Chill until slightly thick. Pour over raspberry layer. Chill for several hours. Yield: 12 servings.

Marta I. Garcia
Alpha Delta No. 7285
Wahiawa, Hawaii

PICO DE GALLO (MEXICO)

3 avocados, peeled and diced
1 tomato, diced
1/2 onion, diced
1 chile paten, diced (opt.)
1 c. vegetable oil
1/2 c. white vinegar
2 tbsp. pepper
2 tbsp. salt

Mix first 4 ingredients in salad bowl. Combine remaining ingredients; mix well; Pour enough oil mixture over salad to completely cover. Let stand, covered, in

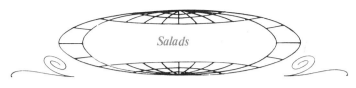

refrigerator for about 2 hours, stirring occasionally. Serve on warm flour tortillas or corn tortillas.

Nina S. Lefner, Rec Sec.
Pi Chi No. 4615
Lyford, Texas

CHINESE SALAD

1 c. slivered cooked chicken
1 c. slivered cooked ham
1 c. slivered celery
1 c. slivered green onion (opt.)
1 c. shredded Chinese cabbage (opt.)
1 pkg. ramen-type noodles
1/2 to 1 packet noodle seasoning
3 tbsp. oriental vinegar
1/2 to 1 tsp. sesame oil
2 tbsp. soy sauce
1/2 tsp. Accent
Salt and pepper to taste

Place first 5 ingredients in bowl. Soften noodles in boiling water for 3 minutes; cut into 2-inch lengths. Add to chicken mixture. Mix 1/4 cup boiling water with seasoning packet. Add remaining 5 ingredients; mix well. Pour dressing over salad at least 30 minutes to 1 hour before serving.

Drucilla Quesnel, Serv. Chm.
Alpha Zeta No. 1722
Port Angeles, Washington

HAWAIIAN SALAD

1 c. mayonnaise
1 tbsp. honey
2 tsp. prepared mustard
1 can pineapple chunks, drained
1   17-oz. can apricot halves, drained and halved
2 c. diced cooked ham
1/3 c. raisins
1/2 c. slivered almonds
Lettuce

Stir first 3 ingredients together for dressing; set aside. Combine pineapple, apricots, ham, raisins and 1/4 cup almonds in large bowl Spoon onto beds of lettuce. Pour dressing over all. Garnish with remaining almonds. Yield: 4 servings.

Lorraine Waxman
Delta Beta No. 1937
Williamsport, Pennsylvania

CRUNCHY TACO SALAD (MEXICO)

1 lb. hamburger
1 head lettuce
1 can red kidney beans, drained
1 sm. onion, diced
1 tomato, diced
1 avocado, diced
1 c. grated Cheddar cheese
1 1/2 c. mayonnaise

3 tbsp. mild taco sauce
1 pkg. Nacho chips, crushed

Brown hamburger; break up into small pieces. Drain; cool. Break lettuce into bite-sized pieces in large bowl. Add next 5 ingredients and hamburger; mix well. Combine mayonnaise with taco sauce. Add crushed chips and mayonnaise mixture just before serving. Toss well.

Lela Watson
Preceptor Theta XP819
Beatrice, Nebraska

PAM'S TACO SALAD (MEXICO)

1 lb. hamburger
1 can kidney beans, drained
1 pkg. taco seasoning mix
1 head lettuce, cut up
2 tomatoes, cut up
1 bunch green onions and tops, chopped
1/2 lb. shredded sharp Cheddar cheese
1 can black olives, halved
1/4 c. sour cream
1/4 c. Italian dressing
2 tsp. minced parsley
Dash of sugar
Freshly ground pepper
1 c. coarsely chopped corn chips

Brown hamburger; drain well. Cool. Mix hamburger, kidney beans and taco seasoning together. Add lettuce, tomatoes, onions, cheese and olives. Combine sour cream, Italian dressing, parsley, sugar and pepper; mix well. Add dressing and corn chips to salad mixture just before serving. Yield: 3-4 servings.

Pam German, Corr. Sec.
Theta Beta No. 7494
Dallas Center, Iowa

WURSTSALAT (GERMANY)

1/2 lb. bologna, thinly sliced and chopped
1/2 c. chopped Muenster cheese
3/4 c. thinly sliced radishes
1/2 c. chopped sweet pickle
1/4 c. chopped dill pickle
Chopped celery (opt.)
Chopped green pepper (opt.)
1 onion, chopped
5 tsp. vinegar
4 tbsp. oil
1 1/2 tsp. sugar
1/2 tsp. salt
1/8 tsp. pepper

Combine bologna, cheese, radishes, pickles, celery, green pepper and onion. Combine vinegar, oil, sugar, salt and pepper; mix well. Toss dressing over first mixture. Chill for about 30 minutes or longer. Serve with black bread, butter and beer. Yield: 3-4 servings.

Donna Thomas, Pres.
Xi Beta Delta X2294
Junction City, Oregon

Salads

BARBARA'S CRAB MOUSSE

1 env. unflavored gelatin
1 can cream of mushroom soup
1 3-oz. package cream cheese, softened
1 c. finely chopped celery
3 finely chopped green onions
1 c. mayonnaise
2 tbsp. lemon juice
1 can crab meat, drained and shredded

Soften gelatin in 3 tablespoons cold water. Heat soup, stirring until smooth; do not boil. Add gelatin; stir until gelatin is dissolved. Add remaining ingredients; mix well. Pour into mold; chill for at least 2 hours. Unmold; serve with crackers.

Barbara Rodrigues
Chi Omicron Chap.
Rancho Cordova, California

WEST INDIES SALAD

1 med. onion, chopped
1 lb. fresh lump crab meat
Salt and pepper to taste
1/2 c. Wesson oil
6 tbsp. cider vinegar

Spread half the onion in large bowl. Cover with crab and remaining onion. Season with salt and pepper. Combine oil, vinegar and 1/2 cup ice water; mix well. Pour over salad; marinate for 2 to 12 hours. Drain; toss lightly before serving.

Esther P. Still
Preceptor Laureate Alpha PL108
West Chester, Pennsylvania

CANTONESE WALNUT-LOBSTER SALAD (CHINA)

1 tbsp. melted butter
1 tbsp. soy sauce
1 c. California walnuts, large pieces and
    halves
1 c. diagonally sliced celery, chilled
1/2 c. sliced green onions, chilled
1 5-oz. can water chestnuts, drained,
    sliced and chilled
1 11-oz. can mandarin orange segments,
    drained and chilled
3 c. cooked lobster chunks, chilled
Sweet-Sour Dressing
Crisp watercress or salad greens

Combine butter, soy sauce and walnuts in skillet. Stir gently over low heat for about 10 minutes or until walnuts are lightly toasted. Remove and cool. Combine celery, onions, water chestnuts, mandarin orange segments and lobster. Add just enough Sweet-Sour Dressing to combine ingredients. Fold in walnuts. Pile onto crisp watercress. Serve with additional dressing, if desired. Yield: 6 servings.

Sweet-Sour Dressing

3 eggs, beaten
1/2 c. sugar
2 tbsp. all-purpose flour
2 tsp. seasoned salt
1/8 tsp. curry powder
1/3 c. strained lemon juice
1/3 c. cider vinegar
1 14 1/2-oz. can evaporated milk
1 tbsp. soft or melted butter

Combine eggs, sugar, flour, salt and curry powder; beat well. Blend in lemon juice and vinegar. Cook in

top of double boiler over boiling water for about 10 minutes or until mixture thickens, stirring frequently to keep smooth. Beat in evaporated milk and butter. Cool. Store in covered container in refrigerator. Yield: 3 cups dressing.

Photograph for this recipe on opposite page.

DELICIOUS HERRING SALAD (NORWAY)

1 1/4 tbsp. margarine
3 tbsp. all-purpose flour
1 1/4 c. milk
3/4 c. pickled beet juice
1 egg yolk, beaten
Dry mustard to taste
Pepper to taste
Sugar to taste
1/2 c. whipping cream, whipped
2 salted herring, cubed
2 cooked potatoes, cubed
2 to 4 pickled beets, cubed
2 apples, cubed
1 onion, cubed

Melt margarine in a saucepan. Stir in flour. Add milk and beet juice slowly, stirring constantly until blended. Stir small amount hot mixture into egg yolk; stir egg yolk into hot mixture. Cook, stirring, until thickened. Add mustard, pepper, sugar and whipped cream; blend in gently. Place next 5 ingredients on a serving dish. Pour sauce over all. Garnish with parsley and hard-boiled egg.

Beverly K. Tudor, Pres.
Preceptor Gamma Alpha XP1133
Port Neches, Texas

PINEAPPLE BOAT SALAD (PHILIPPINE ISLANDS)

2 fresh pineapples
2 1/2 c. chopped cooked shrimp or chicken
3/4 c. chopped celery
3/4 c. salad dressing
1 tsp. curry powder
1 banana, sliced
1/2 c. salted peanuts
1/2 c. coconut
1 can mandarin oranges, drained

Cut each pineapple in half, lengthwise, through green top, then in half again. Remove pulp from shells; drain shells upside down. Cube pineapple. Combine with shrimp and celery; cover. Chill. Mix salad dressing with curry powder; chill. Drain pineapple mixture just before serving. Toss with dressing, banana and peanuts. Fill shells with mixture; sprinkle with coconut. Garnish with mandarin oranges. Yield: 8 servings.

Judith S. Barney, Corr. Sec.
Xi Tau X2976
Lander, Wyoming

SHRIMP SALAD DELUXE

2 tbsp. unflavored gelatin
1 10-oz. can tomato soup
1 8-oz. package cream cheese, softened
2 c. mayonnaise
1 7-oz. can shrimp, rinsed and drained
1/2 tsp. salt
1/2 c. diced celery
1/2 c. diced green onions
1/2 c. diced pimento

Soak gelatin in 1/2 cup cold water. Heat soup. Beat in cream cheese; mix well. Add gelatin; mix well. Let cool until partially set. Fold in mayonnaise. Add shrimp, salt and vegetables; pour into mold. Chill until firm.

Jan Feeley
Alpha Mu No. 9648
Preeceville, Saskatchewan, Canada

SHRIMP-MACARONI SALAD

1 pkg. macaroni, cooked and drained
3 sm. cans deveined shrimp, drained
1 med. jar pimentos
1 lb. bell pepper, chopped
1 sm. jar sweet pickle relish
6 hard-boiled eggs, chopped
1/2 c. chopped onion (opt.)
1/2 c. chopped fresh tomatoes
Mayonnaise
Salt and pepper to taste
3 tsp. paprika
Juice of 1 lemon

Mix first 8 ingredients with enough mayonnaise to moisten well. Add salt, pepper and paprika; mix well. Add lemon juice just before serving; mix well.

Theda Duke McCrory, Corr. Sec.
Beta Epsilon No. 5436
Greenville, Mississippi

CRUNCHY LETTUCE SALAD

1 lb. Velveeta cheese, cubed
3 1/2 oz. evaporated milk
1 head lettuce, shredded
1 med. onion, diced
2 sm. tomatoes, chopped
1 avocado, diced
1 jalapeno pepper, chopped
1 6-oz. package corn chips

Melt cheese in milk over low heat, stirring frequently. Mix remaining ingredients together. Pour cheese mixture over all; mix well. Serve immediately.

Kay Dunlop
Xi Gamma Gamma X2914
Sioux City, Iowa

EGGPLANT SALAD (TURKEY)

2 or 3 eggplant
2 tbsp. olive oil
Juice of 1/2 lemon
Salt to taste
1 sm. onion, grated
Finely chopped garlic or garlic powder.

Broil whole eggplant until soft, turning frequently. Cut in half. Remove any dark or large seeds. Scoop out pulp; place in blender container. Add oil and lemon juice; blend well. Add salt, onion and garlic. Spread on platter; chill. Garnish with sliced tomatoes and black olives.

Georgia R. Clark, Rec. Sec.
Laureate Alpha PL 127
Springfield, Massachusetts

GERMAN SLAW

Sugar
1 lg. head cabbage, shredded
1 lg. onion, cut in thin slices
1/2 c. vinegar
3/4 c. salad oil
1 tbsp. salt
1 tsp. celery seed
1 tsp. dry mustard

Sprinkle 7/8 cup sugar over cabbage and onion. Let stand for several minutes. Combine 2 teaspoons sugar and remaining ingredients. Bring to a boil. Pour over cabbage mixture while boiling hot. Refrigerate in an airtight container for several hours for flavors to blend.

Virginia Kessinger, Pres.
Xi Delta Psi Chap.
Viburnum, Missouri

GREEK VEGETABLE SALAD

1 med. head iceberg lettuce, chopped
1 head curly endive, chopped
2 tomatoes, peeled and chopped
1/4 c. sliced pitted ripe olives
1/4 c. sliced green onion
2/3 c. olive or salad oil
1/3 c. white wine vinegar
1/2 tsp. salt
1/4 tsp. dried oregano leaves, crushed
1/8 tsp. pepper
3/4 cubed feta cheese
1   3-oz. can anchovy fillets, drained

Toss greens in large bowl or arrange on individual plates. Arrange tomatoes, olives and green onion over greens. Combine olive oil, vinegar, salt, oregano and pepper in jar. Cover; shake well. Pour over salad. Top with feta cheese and anchovies. Yield: 12 servings.

Charlotte Aber
Preceptor Alpha Alpha XP613
Durango, Colorado

SALAD NICOISE (GREECE)

1 c. cooked snap beans, chilled
2 tbsp. French dressing
1 lg. lettuce heart
1 clove of garlic
1 med. green pepper, sliced thin
3 med. tomatoes, sliced
12 pitted ripe olives
2 hard-boiled eggs, sliced
8 anchovy fillets
1   7-oz. can white tuna chunks
2 tbsp. chopped chives
2 tbsp. chopped parsley
3 tbsp. olive or salad oil
1 tbsp. red wine vinegar
1/2 tsp. salt
1/4 tsp. ground pepper
1/4 tsp. sugar

Marinate snap beans in French dressing for 1 hour in the refrigerator. Wash, dry and break lettuce into bite-sized pieces. Rub the inside of a salad bowl with garlic. Add lettuce. Arrange green pepper, tomatoes, beans, olives, eggs, anchovies and tuna over top of lettuce. Sprinkle with chives and parsley. Combine remaining ingredients. Pour over salad just before serving. Toss lightly but thoroughly. Serve as a main dish salad. Yield: 10-12 servings.

Photograph for this recipe above.

ISRAELI SALAD

1 carrot, shredded
2 tomatoes, cubed
2 green onions, cubed
1 cucumber, peeled and cubed
2 sm. radishes, shredded
1 green pepper, cubed

2 kosher dill pickles
2 tbsp. oil
Juice of 1 lemon
Salt and pepper to taste

Combine all ingredients and mix well.

Nan Lamb
Xi Gamma Phi X4805
Quantico, Virginia

CREAMY KOREAN SALAD

1 c. mayonnaise or salad dressing
1/3 c. catsup
1 med. onion, chopped
3/4 c. sugar
1 tbsp. Worcestershire sauce
1/4 c. vinegar
Fresh green spinach
1/2 can crumbled bacon bits
5 hard-boiled eggs, chopped
1 can bean sprouts, drained

Combine mayonnaise, catsup, onion, sugar, Worcestershire sauce and vinegar. Toss spinach, bacon, eggs and bean sprouts together. Pour dressing over all. Toss lightly until well coated.

Erla Johnson, Pres.
Xi Eta Chi X3922
Peoria, Illinois

LAYERED LETTUCE SALAD

1 head lettuce, cut up or shredded
1 1/2 c. chopped celery
1 bunch green onions, finely chopped
1 can water chestnuts, drained and sliced
1 green pepper, chopped
1   10-oz. package frozen peas, thawed
2 c. mayonnaise
2 tsp. sugar
Grated Parmesan Cheese

Place first 6 ingredients in layers in 9 x 13-inch pan. Do not mix. Combine mayonnaise and sugar; mix well. Spread dressing over top layer. Sprinkle with Parmesan cheese. Refrigerate for 24 hours. Garnish with crumbled bacon and chopped or sliced eggs, if desired. Cut into squares to serve.

Elinor Kennedy, Pres.
Preceptor Alpha Xi No. 1388
Joseph, Oregon

FRESH MUSHROOM-AVOCADO SALAD

1/2 lb. fresh mushrooms, thinly sliced
1 tbsp. lemon juice
1/4 c. chopped chives
1 c. bean sprouts, rinsed and dried
3 tbsp. salad dressing
1 avocado, sliced lengthwise
1/2 c. alfalfa sprouts

Salt
Freshly ground pepper

Place mushrooms in large salad bowl. Add lemon juice; toss well. Add remaining ingredients except salt and pepper; toss well. Season to taste. Chill before serving; toss again. Yield: 4 servings.

Linda J. Ransom, V.P.
Xi Gamma Theta X3516
Salem, Oregon

ITALIAN MUSHROOM-ARTICHOKE SALAD

1 lb. fresh mushrooms
1 6-oz. can pitted ripe olives
1 med. red onion, thinly sliced
1 6-oz. jars quartered marinated artichoke
    hearts, drained
2 tbsp. dried parsley flakes
1/3 c. Crisco oil
1/4 c. tarragon vinegar
1/2 tsp. garlic juice
1/4 tsp. hot sauce
Lettuce
Freshly ground pepper

Wash mushrooms; drain well. Trim ends; slice into medium plastic bowl. Slice olives into bowl. Add onion and artichoke hearts. Sprinkle parsley over vegetables. Combine oil, vinegar, garlic juice and hot sauce. Pour over vegetable mixture. Cover bowl; shake to mix. Refrigerate in covered bowl for at least 6 hours. Break lettuce into bite-sized pieces. Place on individual salad plates. Top with a generous portion of marinated vegetables; sprinkle with pepper.

Patricia A. Baum, Pres.
Scottsbluff City Council
Gering, Nebraska

BACON SALAD (HOLLAND) SPEKSLA

5 lb. potatoes, boiled and peeled
12 hard-boiled eggs
1 lb. lean bacon, fried crisp
1 head lettuce
1/4 c. sugar
1/2 c. vinegar
Salt and pepper to taste
3/4 c. bacon drippings

Mash hot potatoes thoroughly. Slice hot eggs; crumble fried bacon. Place first 3 ingredients in large bowl; mix well. Tear lettuce into bite-sized pieces; add to potato mixture. Combine sugar, vinegar, salt and pepper in skillet with hot bacon drippings. Mix well; pour over potato mixture. Serve hot as main dish. Dandelion greens or endive may be used in place of lettuce.

Patricia Ann Jasmann, Pres.
Preceptor Upsilon XP1458
Scottsdale, Arizona

OLD-FASHIONED GERMAN POTATO SALAD

6 med. potatoes
1/4 lb. bacon, cut into sm. pieces
1/4 green pepper, chopped
1 sm. onion, chopped
Salt and pepper to taste
2 tbsp. vinegar
2 tsp. sugar
3/4 c. salad dressing

Boil potatoes in skins in salted water until tender; drain. Fry bacon until crisp; drain on paper towel. Reserve 1 tablespoon bacon drippings. Peel and slice potatoes into bowl. Add bacon, green pepper and onion. Season with salt and pepper. Mix vinegar and sugar with salad dressing. Add reserved bacon drippings; stir well. Pour over potatoes; mix well. Serve warm.

Crystal Herold, Rec. Sec.
Zeta Chi No. 5650
Bradenton, Florida

IRISH POTATO SALAD

2 tbsp. vinegar
1 tsp. celery seed
1 tsp. mustard seed
8 med. to lg. potatoes, pared
2 tsp. sugar
1 tsp. salt
2 c. finely shredded cabbage
1   12-oz. can corned beef, chilled and cubed
1/4 c. finely chopped dill pickle
1/4 c. sliced green onion
1 c. mayonnaise
1/4 c. milk

Combine vinegar, celery seed and mustard seed; set aside. Cook potatoes in enough boiling salted water to cover for about 30 to 40 minutes. Drain and cube potatoes. Drizzle potatoes with vinegar mixture while still warm. Sprinkle with sugar and 1/2 teaspoon salt. Chill thoroughly. Add cabbage, corned beef, pickle and onion before serving. Combine mayonnaise, milk and remaining 1/2 teaspoon salt. Pour over corned beef mixture; toss lightly. Serve immediately.

Donna Mae Irsik
Delta Theta No. 9953
Perry, Oklahoma

SAUERKRAUT SALAD

1 lg. can sauerkraut
1/2 c. chopped onions
1/2 c. chopped green pepper
1/2 c. chopped celery
1 c. vinegar
4 tbsp. sugar

Mix first 4 ingredients together. Heat vinegar and sugar; pour over vegetables. Marinate for 2 hours or overnight.

Jeanette Hayes
Lambda Sigma No. 7808
Kissimmee, Florida

SEVEN-LAYER GREEN SALAD

1 head lettuce
1 c. chopped celery
1 c. chopped green pepper
1 sm. can green peas, drained
1/2 c. Parmesan cheese
Chopped green onions to taste
1 c. chopped cucumber
1 c. mayonnaise
1 tsp. sugar
Bacon bits

Cover bottom of large salad bowl with broken lettuce. Layer celery, green pepper, peas, Parmesan cheese, green onions and cucumber over lettuce. Top with more lettuce. Cover with mayonnaise; sprinkle with sugar. Cover top with bacon bits. Refrigerate overnight.

Savanna Hawks, Soc Chm.
Xi Beta Zeta X4098
Conover, North Carolina

WELL-DRESSED SPINACH SALAD

1 pkg. spinach
1 or 2 bell peppers, chopped
1 onion, chopped
1 or 2 tomatoes, chopped
2 hard-boiled eggs, cut up
1 or 2 avocados, diced
3 or 4 carrots, slivered
3 or 4 stalks celery, cut fine
1/4 c. Wesson oil
1/2 c. catsup
3 tbsp. wine vinegar
1/2 tsp. garlic salt
1/4 c. mayonnaise
1/4 c. cream
Pinch of salt

Place first 8 ingredients in a large bowl. Combine remaining ingredients; mix well. Pour over salad. Toss well and serve.

Ruby Mann, Alamo City Coun. Treas.
Preceptor Alpha Kappa XP620
San Antonio, Texas

AEGEAN SALAD BOWL WITH GREEN GODDESS DRESSING (GREECE)

Tender spinach leaves
Romaine greens
2 med. tomatoes, cut into 6 wedges each
1 med. cucumber, peeled and thinly sliced

1/2 c. Green Goddess dressing
1/4 lb. feta or provolone cheese, cubed (opt.)

Tear spinach leaves and salad greens into bite-sized pieces. Arrange in salad bowl. Add tomato wedges and cucumber slices. Toss lightly with Green Goddess dressing just before serving. Garnish with cheese. Yield: 4 servings.

Photograph for this recipe on page 40.

WHEAT GARDEN SALAD
(ARABIA) TABOULI

    1 c. fine-cracked wheat
    1 bunch green oinons, chopped
    2 lg. bunches parsley, chopped
    1/2 bunch mint, chopped
    4 lg. tomatoes, chopped
    Juice of 4 lemons
    1/2 c. olive oil
    Salt and pepper to taste

Soak wheat in water for several minutes. Squeeze dry. Combine all ingredients in order listed; mix well. Serve with fresh lettuce leaves, grape leaves or cabbage leaves. Yield: 6 servings.

Elaine Hamden
Xi Alpha Psi X2187
Kirkland Lake, Ontario, Canada

TOMATO-ONION AND CHILIES
SALAD (INDIA)

    2 tomatoes, chopped
    1/4 c. chopped onion
    1/4 c. chopped parsley
    3 tbsp. lemon juice
    1 tsp. crushed garlic
    1 tsp. salt
    2 green chili peppers, seeded and thinly sliced

Combine tomatoes, onion, parsley, lemon juice, garlic and salt in serving bowl. Toss until well mixed. Arrange chilies on top. Refrigerate for 1 hour.

Judith J. Van Dine
Gamma Pi No. 2320
Wellsville, New York

TOMATOES WITH SHRIMP
(BELGIUM) TOMATES AUX
CREVETTES

    4 lg. tomatoes
    2 c. (or more) cooked shrimp
    1 c. mayonnaise
    Salt and pepper to taste
    1/4 c. minced parsley

Cut a slice off top of each tomato and reserve. Hollow out each tomato with a spoon. Invert on plate to drain for 20 minutes. Combine shrimp and 3/4 cup mayonnaise. Sprinkle salt and pepper in each tomato shell. Fill with shrimp mixture. Spoon remaining mayonnaise over shrimp mixture; sprinkle with parsley. Place top on each tomato; chill. Serve on bed of lettuce.

Ingrid Gallett
Alpha No. 7483
Maisiers, Belgium

TURNIP SALAD (KOREA)
MOO SAENG CHAE

    2 c. finely shredded turnips
    1 c. finely shredded carrots
    3/4 tbsp. chopped leek or onion
    2 tsp. toasted ground sesame seed
    1 1/2 tsp. salt
    Vinegar to taste
    Pepper to taste
    Sugar

Toss first 5 ingredients together. Add vinegar, pepper, and a small amount of sugar; mix well.
This recipe is from Mrs. Syngman Rhee of Seoul, Korea.

Mrs. Norma Jordet Hoyt
International Honorary Member
Anchorage, Alaska

VEGETABLE SALAD WITH PEANUT
SAUCE (INDONESIA) GADO-GADO

    1 lb. fresh bean sprouts
    1/2 cabbage, thinly sliced
    1/2 lb. fresh green beans, cut thin diagonally
    Shredded lettuce
    Shredded carrots
    Tomato wedges
    3 med. cooked potatoes, sliced
    4 hard-boiled eggs, quartered
    1 clove of garlic, minced
    1 tbsp. oil
    1 sm. onion, sliced
    2 tbsp. chunky peanut butter
    1 tbsp. catsup
    1 tbsp. lemon juice
    1 tsp. sugar
    1 tsp. salt

Steam bean sprouts, cabbage and green beans separately in small amounts of water until tender crisp. Chill. Arrange on large platter. Garnish with lettuce, carrots, tomato wedges, potatoes and eggs. Chill. Saute garlic in oil until brown. Add onion; saute until tender. Add peanut butter and 1 cup water, stirring until smooth. Stir in catsup, lemon juice, sugar and salt. Chill. Serve over salad. Yield: 6 servings.

Jean G. Holroyd
Preceptor Psi XT581
Vancouver, Washington

Meats

European menus from the Middle Ages, also those from ancient Rome, show us that a balanced diet meant meat — plenty of it, and not much else. Bread was the standby staple, of course; but the use of fresh fruits and vegetables was almost unheard of. Yet, it seems that no one complained for lack of variety because almost no part of a cow, pig or lamb, from tip to toe, was considered inedible. Further variety in flavor was achieved through the use of vegetable and fruit sauces, while cooking methods varied the texture of the meat.

Today, the world's menus feature much more than meat, but most meals are planned around the meat, which is considered the main dish. The English seem to have developed the most skill at preparing succulent cuts of beef, especially sirloin served with Yorkshire pudding. They are also renowned for their beef and kidney pie, and for various liver dishes.

The Mid-Eastern cuisines have developed the finest ways of preparing mutton and lamb. At its best, a spring lamb is roasted whole on a spit, flavored by the smoke of fragrant branches resting on the glowing coals. They are also responsible for the delicious development of *shish kabob*, which is skewered lamb chunks dipped and basted in olive oil and garlic, then roasted over hot coals.

Veal, one of the specialties of the European continent, is a delicate meat which must be cooked and seasoned with care. Its tastiest preparation seems to be Austrian *Wiener Schnitzel*, served on a cloth or paper napkin. The schnitzel's bread crumb crust should be dry, crisp and brown, the meat very tender, and seasoned only with salt, pepper and lemon.

While German cooks probably prepare the best pork in Western cuisines, Oriental and Pacific cooks have developed what are probably the best of all pork recipes. Because both fuel and meat are scarce, Chinese cooks prepare their pork in small shreds, quickly stir-fried with crisp, colorful vegetables, or in a sweet-sour sauce with green peppers and pineapple. The mouth-watering Hawaiian version of pork is the pig roasted whole underground, to be featured in a festive *luau.* Philippine Islanders feature pork as *adobo* — chops, first simmered in a sauce of vinegar, bay leaves, garlic and peppercorn, then fried. They also enjoy barbecueing a whole pig that is stuffed with a combination of vegetables, rice, meat and seasonings.

Beta Sigma Phis want you to start enjoying the many international flavors there are for meat right away! With a wide world of recipes to serve, variety will be the spice of life for your mealtimes from now on.

BEEF TERIYAKI

1/3 c. Sake or dry Sherry
1/3 c. soy sauce
1/4 c. sugar
1 tsp. grated fresh ginger
   or 1/2 tbsp. ground ginger
1 clove of garlic, finely minced
1/4 lemon, thinly sliced
1 lb. lean beef shell or club
   steak

Combine Sake, soy sauce, sugar, ginger, garlic and lemon slices. Stir until sugar is dissolved. Cut steak into thin strips; add to marinade. Marinate for 15 minutes or longer. Drain. Cook briefly in hot skillet. The beef is best if eaten slightly rare. Yield: 4 servings.

Lynn Blanton
Xi Eta Phi X5119
Kansas City, Missouri

BELGIUM BEEF AND BEER

5 tbsp. flour
1 tsp. salt
1/2 tsp. pepper
2 lb. lean boneless chuck, cut
   into 1-in. cubes
1/4 c. salad oil
6 med. onions, sliced
1 lg. clove of garlic, finely
   chopped
1   12-oz. can beer
1 bay leaf
1/4 tsp. thyme
2 tbsp. chopped parsley

Combine flour, salt and pepper. Dredge beef cubes in seasoned flour. Heat oil in skillet. Add onions and garlic; saute until tender but not brown. Remove from skillet and reserve. Place beef in skillet; brown on all sides, adding more oil if needed. Place beef, reserved onion mixture, beer, bay leaf and thyme in casserole; cover. Bake in preheated 325-degree oven for 3 hours or until beef is tender. Remove bay leaf. Sprinkle with parsley. Serve with boiled potatoes. Yield: 4-6 servings.

Eula M. Wagner
Rho Phi Chap.
Englewood, Ohio

BRACIOLA (ITALY)

2 to 3 lb. round steak
Olive oil
Italian bread crumbs
3 onions, thinly sliced
1 lb. Romano cheese, diced
1 clove of garlic, thinly sliced
Salt and pepper to taste
1 lg. can whole tomatoes, diced
2 c. beef broth

Pound round steak between 2 pieces of waxed paper. Spread a thin layer of olive oil on one side steak.

Cover with bread crumbs. Arrange onions and cheese evenly over bread crumbs. Sprinkle garlic over top. Season with salt and pepper. Drain tomatoes; reserve juice. Spread tomatoes over all. Roll up steak; tie with string. Steak will be about 4 to 5 inches thick. Brown on all sides in frypan. Add reserved tomato juice and beef broth. Cook over medium heat for about 2 hours or until tender.

Patricia A. Bryan
Xi Phi X638
Monte Vista, Colorado

CHINESE BEEF AND PEA PODS

1   1-lb. beef sirloin steak 3/4 in.
   thick
3 tbsp. soy sauce
1 slice fresh gingerroot, crushed
1 clove of garlic, crushed
1   7-oz. package frozen Chinese
   snow peas
1/4 c. salad oil
1/4 lb. mushrooms, sliced
3 stalks Chinese cabbage, cut into
   1/4-in. slices
1 med. onion, sliced
1   8-oz. can water chestnuts,
   drained and sliced
1   5-oz. can bamboo shoots, drained
1   13 3/4-oz. can chicken broth
3 tbsp. cornstarch
1/2 tsp. salt
1/4 tsp. sugar

Cut steak diagonally into very thin slices. Combine 1 tablespoon soy sauce, gingerroot and garlic. Sprinkle on steak; toss. Marinate steak for 1 hour. Place frozen snow peas in colander; rinse with cold water until separated. Drain. Heat 2 tablespoons oil in large skillet or wok. Brown steak, turning once. Remove steak; keep warm. Add 2 tablespoons oil. Cook and stir mushrooms, cabbage, onion, water chestnuts and bamboo shoots for 2 minutes. Stir in snow peas and 1 cup chicken broth. Cover; cook for 2 minutes. Combine remaining chicken broth, cornstarch, 2 tablespoons soy sauce, salt and sugar; pour into skillet. Cook, stirring constantly, until mixture thickens and boils. Boil and stir for 1 minute. Add steak; heat through. Serve over chow mein noodles. Yield: 4 servings.

Nell Hodges, Pres.
Xi Alpha Tau X2447
Elkview, West Virginia

CHINESE BEEF AND VEGETABLES

2 stalks celery, cut diagonally
   in 1-in. pieces
3 tbsp. oil
1 c. shredded cabbage
2 lg. carrots, cut in thin strips
3 green onions, cut in 1-in. pieces
1 c. cooked roast beef, thinly sliced
1 beef bouillon cube

1 can bean sprouts, drained
1/4 c. soy sauce
1 peeled tomato, cut in sm. sections

Brown celery in oil in wok or electric skillet. Remove celery. Add cabbage, carrots and onions; saute until browned. Remove. Brown beef. Dissolve bouillon cube in 1 cup hot water; stir into beef. Add all ingredients except tomato. Simmer until heated through. Stir in tomato. Serve with rice. Yield: 4 servings.

Cheri Brown, Rec. Sec.
Xi Alpha Omicron X4628
Oxon Hill, Maryland

FINNISH MEAT PIE

1/2 lb. beef round steak, cubed
1 or 2 pork steaks, cubed
2 lg. carrots, diced
3 lg. potatoes, diced
1 lg. onion, chopped
Pastry for 2-crust pie
Salt and pepper to taste
Butter

Combine steaks and vegetables. Line pie pan with crust. Place steak mixture in pie shell. Season with salt and pepper. Dot with 3 or 4 pats of butter. Place second crust over steak mixture; seal edge. Make slits in top crust. Bake at 400 degrees for 45 minutes to 1 hour. Season with catsup after baking, if desired.

Pamela Sue Bristow, W. and M. Chm.
Xi Delta Theta X4713
Altus, Oklahoma

FRIED KOFTE – TAVADA KOFTE

3 slices stale bread
1/4 c. white wine
1 lb. beef
2 onions, grated
2 cloves of garlic
1 tsp. cayenne pepper
2 eggs
1 tbsp. chopped dill
3 tbsp. grated Gruyere cheese
Salt to taste
1/4 to 1/2 c. chicken fat

Soak bread in wine; squeeze dry and reserve wine. Process beef through food chopper 3 times. Add bread and process once more. Add remaining ingredients except chicken fat and reserved wine. Knead for 10 minutes. Wet palms of hands with reserved wine. Shape beef mixture into small balls. Heat chicken fat to sizzling point; add balls. Reduce heat to low. Cook for 25 to 30 minutes or until well browned on all sides. Serve hot with a border of plain pilaf.

Mrs. Thomas L. Lewalski, Librarian
Alpha No. 9534
Karamursel, Turkey

GOULASH STROGANOFF
(CZECHOSLOVAKIA)

1 lb. beef fillet, thinly sliced
Salt and pepper to taste
3 tbsp. butter
1 tbsp. minced onion
1/4 lb. fresh mushrooms, sliced
1 med. tomato, peeled and chopped
1/4 c. white wine
1 1/2 c. sour cream

Season beef with salt and pepper. Fry briefly in butter, browning slightly. Remove beef. Place onion and mushrooms in pan. Fry for 3 minutes. Add tomato and wine. Simmer for about 10 minutes or until tomato is soft. Add sour cream. Simmer until heated through and thickened. Add beef. Reheat, but do not boil. Serve with rice. Yield: 4 servings.

Ellen Barber
Alpha Alpha Sigma No. 6699
Dallas, Texas

GULYAS OVER NAKEDLI
(HUNGARY)

5 onions, chopped
5 tbsp. butter
2 tbsp. paprika
2 tsp. salt
1/2 tsp. pepper
3 lb. beef stew meat
1 can tomato sauce
1 clove of garlic, minced (opt.)
1/2 c. sour cream

Saute onions in 4 tablespoons butter for 15 minutes. Remove onions and set aside. Combine paprika, salt and pepper. Roll beef in mixture. Melt 1 tablespoon butter. Add beef and brown well. Return onions to beef; add tomato sauce and garlic. Cook over low heat for 3 hours, stirring frequently. Add sour cream. Heat but do not boil.

Dumplings

3 c. sifted flour
1 tsp. salt
Melted butter
2 eggs, beaten

Sift flour and salt into bowl. Add 1 tablespoon butter and 3/4 cup water to eggs. Stir into flour; beat until smooth. Drop batter from teaspoon into 2 quarts boiling salted water. Dumplings will rise to the top when done. Remove; drain. Pour 1/4 cup melted butter over dumplings. Serve with Gulyas.

Mary Minden, W. and M. Chm.
Xi Gamma Iota X2517
Paola, Kansas

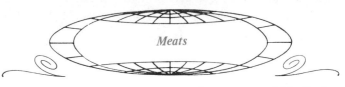
HUNGARIAN BEEF

1/2 c. onion flakes
5 tbsp. olive oil
2 tbsp. paprika
2 tsp. salt
1 tsp. caraway seed
1 tsp. marjoram leaves
1/2 tsp. instant garlic powder
1/4 tsp. freshly ground pepper
1/2 c. catsup
1 1/2 c. beef broth
3 lb. lean beef chuck, cut in
    1 1/2-in. cubes
1/4 c. flour
1 c. sour cream
Cooked broad noodles

Combine onion flakes and 1/3 cup water; let stand for 10 minutes to soften. Heat 2 tablespoons oil in skillet. Add softened onions; cook over low heat until lightly browned. Blend in paprika, salt, caraway seed, marjoram leaves, garlic powder and pepper. Stir in catsup and beef broth. Bring to a boil. Remove from heat; set aside. Heat 3 tablespoons oil in deep saucepan. Dredge beef with flour. Cook, several pieces at a time, until browned all sides. Add broth mixture. Bring to a boil. Reduce heat. Simmer for 2 hours and 30 minutes or until tender. Stir in sour cream just before serving. Serve over noodles.

Mrs. Madera Spencer
International Honorary Member
Montgomery, Alabama

HUNGARIAN GOULASH

1 1/2 lb. beef round steak, cubed
1/4 c. shortening
1 lg. onion, sliced
1 1/2 tsp. salt
1/2 tsp. pepper
1/8 tsp. allspice
1/8 tsp. ground cloves
1 16-oz. can tomatoes

Brown steak in shortening and cook onion until tender. Add remaining ingredients and 1/2 cup water. Cover; simmer for about 3 hours or until steak is tender, adding water, if needed. Serve over hot noodles or rice. Yield: 4-6 servings.

Pat Gohring, W. and M. Chm.
Xi Alpha Sigma X1179
New Castle, Indiana

BEEF LIVER CREOLE

1 lb. beef liver
3 tbsp. whole wheat or soy flour
Vegetable oil or chicken fat
1 1/4 c. sliced onions
1 1/2 c. canned tomatoes
1/2 c. diced celery

1 green pepper, thinly sliced
1/2 tsp. salt
Dash of cayenne pepper or paprika

Cut liver into thin slices. Dust with flour. Brown in oil. Add remaining ingredients. Cover; simmer for 20 minutes. Thicken gravy, if desired. Yield: 4-5 servings.

Carole Desormeau, Sec.
Xi No. 5445
Pierrefonds, Quebec, Canada

LIVER DUMPLINGS (GERMANY)

1/2 c. butter
3 eggs
1 sm. onion, finely chopped
2 tbsp. minced parsley
1/4 tsp. marjoram
1/4 tsp. thyme
Salt and pepper to taste
2 hard rolls, grated
1/2 lb. ground calf or beef liver
2 tbsp. melted butter
1 tbsp. flour
8 c. bouillon or water

Cream 1/2 cup butter in mixing bowl. Add eggs, 1 at a time, mixing well after each addition. Add onion, parsley, marjoram, thyme, salt, pepper and grated rolls to egg mixture; set aside. Brown liver in melted butter. Add liver and flour to egg mixture. Let stand for 1 hour. Shape into walnut-sized balls. Drop into hot bouillon. Cook for 15 minutes.

Barbara Treutle
Gamma Pi No. 8076
Salem, Massachusetts

CORNISH PASTIES

1 1/2 c. flour
1/2 tsp. baking powder
Salt
1/3 c. shortening
1/4 c. milk
1 egg, beaten
1 lb. diced beef sirloin
1 lg. onion, diced
3 or 4 potatoes, diced
Pepper to taste
4 tbsp. butter

Combine flour, baking powder and 1/2 teaspoon salt. Add shortening, milk and egg to make pastry. Divide into 4 balls. Roll out as for pie pastry. Combine sirloin, onion and potatoes. Season with salt and pepper to taste. Divide into fourths. Place filling on pastry rounds. Top each with 1 tablespoon butter. Fold pastry over; seal edges. Punch hole in top. Add 1 tablespoon water to each pasty. Bake at 350 degrees for 1 hour.

Jane Singleton, Pres.
Theta Iota No. 625.
Lawrence, Indiana

54

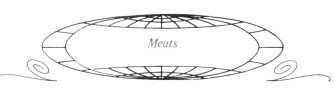

TASTY PASTIES

3 c. flour
3 tsp. salt
1 c. lard
3 potatoes, cubed
3/4 lb. beef, cut in 1/4-in. cubes
1/4 lb. pork, cut in 1/4-in. cubes
4 carrots, sliced
1 c. chopped onion
1/2 tsp. pepper
5 pats of butter

Stir flour and 1 1/2 teaspoons salt together; cut in lard with pastry cutter until mixture resembles coarse crumbs. Add 8 tablespoons water to flour mixture, 1 tablespoon at a time, mixing until dough holds together. Form into ball; chill slightly. Combine potatoes, meats, carrots and onion; season with pepper and remaining 1 1/2 teaspoons salt. Mix well. Divide dough into 5 portions. Roll out to 9-inch circle on lightly floured surface. Place 1 cup meat mixture on half of each circle; top with pat of butter. Fold pastry over filling; seal edge with tines of fork. Cut small slits for steam to escape. Place on ungreased baking sheet. Bake at 400 degrees for 45 minutes or until golden brown.

Erveen Serra, Serv. Chm.
Preceptor Theta No. 1649
Virginia, Minnesota

CORNED BEEF AND CABBAGE (IRELAND)

1 4 to 5-lb. corned beef brisket
1/2 tsp. Tabasco sauce
1 onion, sliced
1 bay leaf

1/2 tsp. dried rosemary
1 stalk celery
1 carrot, pared
1 parsley sprig
1 head green cabbage

Place brisket in large deep kettle; cover with cold water. Add Tabasco sauce, onion, bay leaf, rosemary, celery, carrot and parsley; cover. Bring to a boil; reduce heat. Simmer for 4 to 5 hours. Wash cabbage; cut into quarters. Skim excess fat from top of liquid 30 minutes before beef is done. Arrange cabbage on beef; cover. Simmer for 15 minutes or until cabbage is just crisp tender.

Emerald Sauce

1 c. corned beef stock
2 tsp. flour
1 tsp. horseradish
1/4 tsp. Tabasco sauce
1/4 c. chopped parsley
2 tbsp. sour cream

Pour stock into small saucepan. Combine flour with a small amount of cold water; stir into stock. Add horseradish and Tabasco sauce. Bring to a boil. Reduce heat; add parsley and sour cream. Do not boil. Serve with corned beef and cabbage. Yield: 6 servings.

Photograph for this recipe on this page.

COFFEE POT ROAST

1 3 to 5-lb. roast
Chopped onion to taste
Minced garlic to taste
1 c. tomato juice
1/2 c. red wine
1/2 c. soy sauce
1 1/2 c. strong coffee

Brown roast with onion and garlic until dark brown. Add tomato juice, wine, 1 1/2 cups water, soy sauce and coffee. Cover; simmer until roast is tender.

Judith Rynda
Beta Rho No. 8405
Bloomington, Minnesota

ITALIAN BEEF

1 3 to 4-lb. roast
5 tbsp. lemon juice
1 tbsp. oregano
1 med. onion, chopped
1 tbsp. salt
1 tbsp. pepper
Dash of garlic powder
5 bay leaves

Place roast with remaining ingredients in Crock-Pot on Low temperature. Cook for at least 8 hours or until roast is tender. Remove bay leaves. Tear meat into small pieces. Serve on Italian bread.

Paula Richerson, V.P.
Beta Kappa No. 872
Harrisburg, Illinois

PIZZAIOLA (ITALY)

1   3-lb. chuck roast
1/2 tbsp. oregano, crushed
1/2 tsp. garlic powder
1/2 tsp. salt
Dash of pepper
1   1-lb. can tomatoes or tomato
sauce

Place roast in roasting pan. Sprinkle with oregano, garlic, salt and pepper. Add tomatoes and 1/2 tomato can water. Cover with aluminum foil. Bake in preheated 350-degree oven for 1 hour. Remove roast from pan; slice thin. Serve sliced with pan juices.

Veronica Grossi, V.P.
Omega Xi No. 5859
Vista, California

GRANDMA'S SAUERBRATEN (GERMANY)

1   4 to 5-lb. beef roast
Vinegar
2 bay leaves
10 to 12 whole cloves
1 med. onion, sliced
9 or 10 gingersnaps, crushed
Sugar to taste (opt.)

Place roast in bowl. Cover completely with mixture of equal parts water and vinegar. Add bay leaves, cloves and sliced onion. Marinate overnight. Remove roast from marinade. Brown roast on all sides. Place in roaster. Bake at 350 degrees for 1 hour and 30 minutes. Baste with vinegar mixture. Remove roast to platter. Stir remaining vinegar mixture into roaster; add gingersnaps and sugar. Cook, stirring, until thickened. Strain. Return roast to gravy; marinate for 24 hours for best flavor.

Christine E. Snieg
Xi Iota No. 942
Milwaukee, Wisconsin

SPECIAL SAUERBRATEN (GERMANY)

1   4 to 5-lb. eye of round roast
1 tbsp. dry mustard
1 bay leaf
1 tsp. peppercorns
1 1/2 tsp. salt
1 1/2 tsp. poultry seasoning
1/2 tsp. tarragon leaves
1/2 tsp. instant minced garlic
2 tbsp. onion flakes
2 tbsp. light brown sugar
1 beef bouillon cube
1/2 c. red wine vinegar
2 tbsp. shortening
Flour
1/2 c. sour cream (opt.)

Place beef in a bowl. Mix mustard with 3 tablespoons water; let stand for 10 minutes. Combine mustard, next 10 ingredients and 1 cup water in saucepan. Bring to a boil; pour over roast. Cool. Cover; refrigerate for 24 to 48 hours, turning occasionally. Remove roast from marinade; wipe dry with paper towel, reserving marinade. Brown roast in shortening in Dutch oven. Pour in marinade; cover. Bake in preheated 325-degree oven for 3 hours to 3 hours and 30 minutes or until tender. Place roast on a platter. Strain pan juices and measure; place in saucepan. Blend 1 1/2 tablespoons flour with 2 tablespoons water for each cup pan juices. Stir into pan juices; cook for 1 minute or until thickened. Stir in sour cream. Yield: 8-10 servings.

Deana J. Wills
Beta Omega No. 6065
Scottsbluff, Nebraska

BEEF TENDERLOIN WITH SAUCE

1   2 1/2-lb. beef tenderloin roast
3 tbsp. butter
Salt and pepper to taste
1/4 c. chopped green onions
3/4 c. cooking Sherry
2 tbsp. soya sauce
1 tsp. dry mustard

Place roast in shallow roaster. Dot with 1 tablespoon butter. Season with salt and pepper. Bake, uncovered, in preheated 450-degree oven for 20 minutes. Saute onions in 2 tablespoons butter in frypan. Stir in remaining ingredients; heat through. Pour over roast. Bake for 10 minutes longer; baste. Bake for 15 minutes longer or until tender.

Judi Cherrington
Alpha Zeta Chap.
Victoria, British Columbia, Canada

LOBSTER-STUFFED TENDERLOIN OF BEEF

1   3 or 4-lb. whole beef tenderloin
2   4-oz. frozen lobster-tails
1 tbsp. melted margarine
1 1/2 tsp. lemon juice
6 slices bacon, partially cooked
1/2 c. sliced green onions
1/2 c. margarine
1/2 c. dry white wine
1/8 tsp. garlic salt

Cut beef tenderloin lengthwise to within 1/2 inch of bottom. Place frozen lobster-tails in boiling salted water to cover. Simmer for 5 minutes. Remove lobster from shells. Cut in half. Place lobster, end to end, inside beef. Combine margarine and lemon juice; drizzle over each lobster. Tie tenderloin together with string; place in pan on rack. Bake at 425 degrees for 30 minutes. Place bacon on top; bake for 5 minutes longer. Saute onions in margarine in saucepan. Add wine and garlic salt; heat. Slice roast; spoon on sauce.

Helene Tiute, V.P.
Xi Alpha Nu X1786
Richland, Washington

EGG NOODLES AND SAUERBRATEN (GERMANY)

1 c. red wine vinegar
3 c. beef bouillon
3 med. onions, sliced
2 carrots, sliced
1 stalk celery, chopped
Salt
1/4 tsp. freshly ground pepper
2 tbsp. light brown sugar
10 peppercorns
4 bay leaves
6 whole cloves
1 4-lb. beef rump roast
Flour
1/4 c. vegetable oil
1/2 c. dry red wine or beef bouillon
2/3 c. crushed gingersnaps
1 lb. medium egg noodles

Combine vinegar, 2 cups bouillon, onions, carrots, celery, 2 teaspoons salt, pepper, brown sugar, peppercorns, bay leaves and cloves in a large bowl. Place beef in bowl; cover. Marinate in refrigerator for 3 days, turning on second day. Remove beef from marinade, reserving 2 cups marinade and vegetables. Dry beef well; coat with flour. Brown slowly on all sides in hot oil in Dutch oven. Discard excess fat. Add reserved marinade, vegetables and wine; cover. Simmer for 2 hours and 30 minutes to 3 hours or until beef is tender. Remove beef to platter; keep warm. Strain juices into 4-cup measure; skim off fat. Add remaining 1 cup bouillon and enough water to make 4 cups. Return to Dutch oven; add gingersnaps. Heat until gravy boils, stirring constantly. Add 2 tablespoons salt to 4 to 6 quarts rapidly boiling water. Add noodles gradually so that water continues to boil. Cook, uncovered, stirring occasionally, until tender. Drain in colander. Toss with several tablespoons gravy. Arrange around roast on platter. Serve with gravy. Yield: 6-8 servings.

Photograph for this recipe above.

STEAK AND KIDNEY PIE (ENGLAND)

1 lb. beef kidney
1 lg. onion, sliced
1 lb. stewing beef or beef
   round steak, cubed
Butter or margarine
1 bouillon cube
1 tbsp. flour
1/2 tsp. salt
Dash of pepper
Dash of Worcestershire sauce
2 9-in. pie crusts
1 egg white

Clean and chop kidney into cubes. Saute onion and meats in a small amount of butter. Dissolve bouillon cube in 1/2 cup hot water; stir into meat mixture. Add flour, stirring well to thicken. Season with salt, pepper and Worcestershire sauce. Simmer for 20 minutes. Line pie pan with 1 pie crust. Fill with meat mixture. Top with second crust; seal edge. Cut 1-inch air vent in top crust. Glaze with egg white. Bake in 375-degree oven for 45 minutes.

Mrs. Annabel Campbell, Treas.
Gamma Theta No. 4536
Manotick, Ontario, Canada

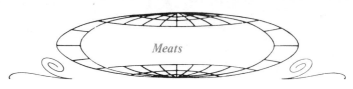

SOUTH AFRICAN CURRY

2 lb. round steak, cubed
2 tbsp. butter
2 tbsp. curry powder
1 lg. onion, diced
2 lg. apples, diced
1/2 lb. bacon, cut up
1 clove of garlic, minced
1 tsp. vinegar
Salt and pepper to taste
4 c. cooked rice

Place steak, butter, curry powder, onion, apples, bacon and garlic in heavy pan or electric skillet. Cook, stirring frequently, over low heat until mixture becomes dry. Add 2 cups water; simmer for at least 2 hours. Add vinegar; season with salt and pepper. Serve over rice with accompaniments of fruit chutney, coconut, bananas, almonds, mandarin oranges, raisins, crushed pineapple, tomatoes and cucumbers.

Kathryn Stevenson, City Coun. Rep.
Xi Lambda X1155
Idaho Falls, Idaho

STEAK CHOW MEIN

2 lb. round steak, cubed
2 lg. onions, diced
2 tsp. soy sauce
Salt and pepper to taste
1 tsp. chili powder
5 stalks celery, chopped
1/2 c. diced green pepper
2 cans bean sprouts
Chow mein noodles

Brown steak and onions together with soy sauce, salt and pepper. Cover; simmer for about 2 hours or until steak is tender. Remove from frypan; place in deep saucepan. Add chili powder and celery; cook for about 30 minutes. Add green pepper and bean sprouts. Simmer for at least 2 hours. Serve over chow mein noodles.

Eleanor Brooks
Zeta Tau No. 9196
Burlington, North Carolina

BEEF SUKIYAKI (JAPAN)

3 tbsp. oil
2 lb. round steak, thinly sliced
1 c. sliced mushrooms
1/2 c. sliced onion
1 bunch scallions, sliced
1 carrot, thinly sliced
1/2 red bell pepper, finely
    chopped
1 can water chestnuts, sliced
2 c. diagonally sliced celery
1 bunch watercress
1/2 c. soy sauce
1/3 c. Sherry or Sake

1/4 c. sugar
2/3 c. beef broth

Preheat electric frypan to 400 degrees. Add oil. Add steak, mushrooms and onion. Stir-fry until steak is browned. Push to one side of pan. Add remaining vegetables except watercress. Combine soy sauce, Sherry, sugar and broth; pour over all. Stir. Cook for about 3 minutes. Add watercress; cook for 1 minute longer. May be served over cooked rice or chow mein noodles, if desired. Yield: 4-6 servings.

Paula Pekar, Pres.
Xi Eta Xi X3979
Cocoa Beach, Florida

BAVARIAN FLANK STEAK (GERMANY)

1 flank steak
1 potato, shredded
1 tbsp. chopped onion
1 tbsp. chopped green pepper
1 tsp. chopped pimento
1 tsp. chopped parsley
1/2 tsp. salt
3 tbsp. shortening
1/2 can onion soup
Flour

Score flank steak on each side. Combine potato, onion, green pepper, pimento, parsley and salt; spread on steak. Roll up, starting at narrow end; tie securely or fasten with wooden picks. Brown in shortening. Pour off drippings; add soup. Cover. Simmer for 1 hour and 30 minutes to 2 hours or until tender. Remove steak to heated platter. Remove string before serving. Add enough water to cooking liquid to measure 1 1/2 cups. Thicken with flour for gravy. Yield: 4 servings.

Georgina Allee, Phone Chm.
Preceptor Eta Iota XP1598
Huntington Beach, California

CARNE ASADA

1 tbsp. rock salt
1/2 tsp. cumin seed
1/4 tsp. ground cloves
1 lb. flank steak
6 med.-sized ripe tomatoes, chopped
4 lg. green peppers, chopped
6 med. yellow peppers, chopped
5 med. onions, chopped
1 tsp. salt
Juice of 1 lemon

Combine rock salt, cumin and cloves; rub into both sides of steak. Pound with mallet, working seasoning in thoroughly. Let stand for 2 hours at room temperature. Combine remaining ingredients in large saucepan; cook for about 30 minutes or until onions are tender. Grill or broil steak to desired doneness; serve with sauce.

Jane Moraga
Beta Xi No. 1213
Brawley, California

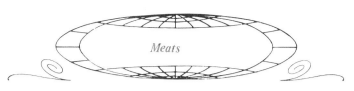

Meats

STEAK AU POIVRE (FRANCE)

6 tenderloin fillets 1 in. thick
2 tbsp. crushed peppercorns
2 tbsp. butter
1/2 c. Cognac
1 c. whipping cream
1 tbsp. flour

Season fillets with salt; sprinkle 1/2 teaspoon crushed peppercorns on each side of each fillet, pressing hard so pepper will adhere. Let stand for 30 minutes. Brown in hot butter; remove to hot serving plate. Discard butter; add Cognac to pan. Ignite. Add half the cream when flame dies out; boil slowly for 1 minute. Mix remaining cream with flour; add to pan. Bring to a boil; pour over fillets. Serve immediately.

Marzie Jennings, Corr. Sec.
Xi Pi Pi X4485
El Paso, Texas

BEEF-CABBAGE CASSEROLE (DENMARK)

1 lb. ground beef
1/4 c. minced onion
1 1-lb. can tomato sauce
1 tsp. salt
1/8 tsp. cinnamon
1/8 tsp. ground cloves
4 c. shredded cabbage

Brown beef with onion; drain off excess fat. Add tomato sauce, salt and spices; mix well. Place 2 cups cabbage in 2-quart casserole; add 1/2 of the beef mixture. Cover with remaining cabbage, then remaining beef mixture. Cover. Bake in preheated 350-degree oven for 45 minutes.

Mrs. Nola T. Durborow
Preceptor Xi Chap.
Collingswood, New Jersey

GREEK STUFFING BALLS

1/2 c. chopped onion
1/4 c. chopped celery
3/4 lb. ground chuck
3 chicken livers, diced
1 pkg. bread cubes
1/2 c. milk
3/4 tsp. poultry seasoning
2 eggs, well beaten
1 c. chicken or turkey broth

Saute onion and celery until lightly browned; remove from pan. Add ground chuck and chicken livers to pan; saute until browned. Return onion and celery to pan; add bread cubes and milk. Stir to loosen bits from bottom. Turn into mixing bowl. Add poultry seasoning and eggs. Season with salt and pepper. Shape into balls; place in greased shallow pan. Pour broth over each ball. Bake at 350 degrees for 45 minutes.

Carolyn T. Flaherty
Xi Alpha Pi Chap.
Hagerstown, Maryland

GERMAN SUMMER SAUSAGE

3 lb. hamburger
1 1/2 tsp. liquid smoke
1/4 tsp. garlic powder or garlic salt
3 tbsp. Tender-Quick
1 tsp. mustard seed
1/2 tsp. pepper
1/2 tsp. onion salt or onion powder

Mix all ingredients and 1 cup water together thoroughly; shape into 2 rolls. Wrap in foil with shiny side in; refrigerate for 24 hours. Poke holes in bottom of rolls with fork; place on rack in pan. Bake for 1 hour and 30 minutes at 350 degrees. Can be frozen.

Jody Weber
Eta Nu No. 10071
Royal City, Washington

ITALIAN BEEF CASSEROLE

2 pkg. frozen chopped broccoli
1 lb. ground beef chuck
1 8-oz. can mushrooms, drained
1 tbsp. salad oil
1 can cream of celery soup
1 c. sour cream
1 tsp. garlic salt
5 tsp. minced onion
1 6-oz. package sliced mozzarella cheese

Cook broccoli according to package directions just until pieces are separated; drain well. Brown beef and mushrooms in oil; spoon into 2-quart casserole. Stir in soup, sour cream, broccoli, garlic salt and minced onion. Cut cheese into strips; place on top of casserole. Do not cover. Bake in preheated 350-degree oven for 35 to 45 minutes. Yield: 4-6 servings.

Ernie Kay Smith
Alpha Mu Chi No. 9478
Madisonville, Texas

ITALIAN SPAGHETTI SAUCE

1 1/2 lb. hamburger
2 c. red or white wine
1 med. onion, chopped
1/2 c. chopped fresh parsley
1 leaf fresh sage, chopped
Leaves from 3-in. stem fresh rosemary, chopped
3/4 c. chopped thyme leaves
4 sm. cloves of garlic, chopped
Salt and pepper to taste
4 16-oz. cans tomato sauce
2 3-oz. packages dried mushrooms,
   simmered to soften

Brown hamburger; add wine. Bring to a boil. Add onion; cook until onion is tender. Add herbs, seasonings and tomato sauce; mix well. Add mushrooms and liquid. Simmer until thick and well blended.

Ruby Vogt
Preceptor Xi No. 523
Albany, Oregon

59

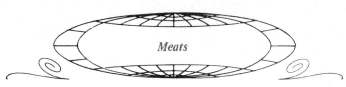

Meats

DANISH MEATBALLS
FRIKADELLER

    1 lb. lean ground beef
    1/2 lb. lean ground pork
    1/4 c. flour
    1 sm. onion, grated
    1 tsp. salt
    1/4 tsp. pepper
    2 eggs
    1 c. milk
    1 to 2 tbsp. butter or margarine

Combine beef, pork, flour, onion, salt and pepper; mix well. Add eggs, 1 at a time, mixing well after each addition. Add milk; mix well. Shape into irregular balls, using 3 to 4 tablespoons meat mixture for each ball. Melt enough butter in heavy skillet to coat bottom. Place balls in heated butter; fry until well browned, turning carefully. Serve with boiled red cabbage.

Anna M. Shaw, Soc. Com.
Xi Gamma Nu X1355
Garland, Texas

SWEDISH MEATBALLS IN GRAVY

    1/4 c. chopped onion
    6 tbsp. butter
    1 c. bread crumbs
    2 2/3 c. milk
    2 eggs, beaten
    2 lb. ground beef
    3 tsp. salt
    1/4 tsp. pepper
    2 tbsp. flour

Saute onion in 2 tablespoons butter in skillet. Soak bread crumbs in 2/3 cup milk. Add eggs, ground beef, sauteed onion, salt and pepper; mix well. Form into bite-sized meatballs. Melt remaining 4 tablespoons butter in skillet. Cook meatballs until brown. Remove meatballs; set aside. Stir flour into skillet; add remaining 2 cups milk. Cook, stirring constantly, until thickened. Return meatballs to gravy; simmer until serving time.

Ronnie Fagan, V.P.
Xi Alpha X196
Decatur, Georgia

KIMA (PAKISTAN)

    1 c. chopped onion
    1 clove of garlic, minced
    3 tbsp. butter, melted
    1 lb. ground beef
    1 tbsp. curry powder
    1 1/2 tsp. salt
    Dash of pepper
    2 tomatoes, diced
    2 potatoes, diced
    1 pkg. frozen peas

Cook onion and garlic in butter in electric frypan at 360 degrees until tender. Add ground beef; brown well. Stir in seasonings, tomatoes, potatoes and peas. Cover; reduce temperature to 250 degrees. Simmer for 25 minutes. Sprinkle with flaked coconut and serve with rice, if desired. Yield: 4-6 servings.

E. Grace Montague, V.P.
Xi Nu Exemplar X1892
Aberdeen, South Dakota

VENETIAN SMOKIE BAKE

    1 lb. ground beef
    1 sm. onion, chopped
    1/2 lb. smokie links, cut in 1/2-in. pieces
    2 8-oz. cans tomato sauce with
        tomato bits
    1 tsp. salt
    1 tsp. basil or oregano
    1 lb. lasagne noodles
    1 egg, well beaten
    1 c. ricotta cheese or cottage cheese
    1 2 1/2-oz. can sliced ripe olives
    1/2 lb. mozzarella cheese, thinly sliced

Brown beef with onion in skillet; pour off fat. Stir in smokie links, tomato sauce, 1 cup water, salt and basil; simmer, uncovered, for 20 minutes. Cook noodles according to package directions; drain. Combine egg, ricotta and olive slices. Arrange 1/2 of the noodles, 1/2 of the ricotta mixture, 1/2 of the mozzarella slices and 1/2 of the meat sauce in 2-quart oblong baking dish. Repeat layers, using remaining ingredients. Bake at 375 degrees for 30 minutes or until bubbly. Let stand for 5 to 10 minutes before serving.

Laura Ryan, 1st V.P.
Alpha Epsilon Kappa No. 7536
Pearland, Texas

CALORIE COUNTER'S MOUSSAKA

    1 lb. ground beef round steak
    1 med. onion, chopped
    5 c. peeled cubed eggplant
    1 16-oz. can tomatoes, chopped
    1/2 lb. fresh mushrooms, sliced
    1/4 c. snipped parsley
    1 clove of garlic, minced
    1/2 tsp. oregano
    1/2 tsp. rosemary, crushed
    1/4 tsp. cinnamon
    Salt and pepper to taste
    2 eggs
    1 8-oz. package diet cream cheese
    1 8-oz. carton plain yogurt

Cook beef and onion in skillet until beef is browned. Drain off fat. Add eggplant, tomatoes, mushrooms, parsley, garlic, oregano, rosemary and cinnamon; season with salt and pepper. Cook for 15 minutes, stirring occasionally. Turn into 9 x 13-inch baking dish. Place eggs, cheese, yogurt and dash of salt in blender container; blend until smooth. Pour over beef mixture.

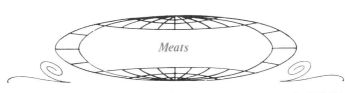

Bake at 350 degrees for 20 minutes or until lightly browned. Yield: 8 servings.

Mrs. Helen Maurer, Pres.
Preceptor Beta Beta XP608
Downey, California

EAST-WEST PINEAPPLE BEEF (HAWAII)

    1   13 -oz. can pineapple tidbits
    1 lb. ground leaf beef
    2 tbsp. finely chopped onion
    1/2 c. fine dry bread crumbs
    1 tbsp. chopped parsley
    1 tsp. garlic salt
    1/8 tsp. pepper
    1 egg
    2/3 c. milk
    1 tbsp. butter or margarine
    2 tbsp. cooking oil
    1/8 tsp. curry powder
    1/3 c. vinegar
    1/4 c. sugar
    1 tbsp. cornstarch
    1/8 tsp. salt
    1 tbsp. soy sauce

Drain pineapple, reserving juice. Combine beef with onion, bread crumbs, parsley, garlic salt, pepper, egg and milk until thoroughly blended. Cover; let stand for 1 hour or longer. Shape into 32 balls with 1 pineapple tidbit in center of each. Heat butter, oil and curry powder in skillet. Add meatballs. Brown slowly on all sides; drain off fat. Blend 1/2 cup reserved pineapple syrup, vinegar, sugar, cornstarch, salt and soy sauce together until smooth. Add sweet and sour sauce to meatballs. Cook over low heat, stirring gently, until sauce thickens and clears. Add remaining drained pineapple tidbits; heat for 5 minutes. Yield: 8 cocktail servings, 4 for entree.

Photograph for this recipe above.

MOUSSAKA KREAS (GREECE)

    1 clove of garlic, sliced
    2 tbsp. oil
    1 1/2 lb. lean ground beef
    1 bay leaf, crumbled
    1 tsp. ground sage
    1 tsp. salt
    1/4 tsp. pepper
    6 c. sliced potatoes
    1 c. sliced onions
    1 No. 2 1/2 can tomatoes

Brown half the garlic in oil in large skillet; remove garlic. Brown beef slowly with bay leaf and sage; stir in 1/2 teaspoon salt and pepper. Remove beef. Brown remaining garlic in drippings. Add potatoes; cook until brown, stirring frequently. Add onions and 1/2 teaspoon salt. Arrange layer of half the potatoes and half the tomatoes in 2 1/2-quart casserole. Add ground beef. Top with remaining potatoes and tomatoes; cover. Bake at 375 degrees for 1 hour. Sprinkle with paprika before serving. Yield: 8 servings.

Bettie Lou Plummer, Pres.
Exemplar Preceptor Alpha Tau XP1022
Independence, Missouri

CHEESY SPAGHETTI BAKE

1/2 lb. lean ground beef
1/4 c. chopped onion
1   15-oz. can prepared spaghetti
    sauce with mushrooms
6 to 7 oz. spaghetti
2 tbsp. butter
1 tbsp. flour
1/4 tsp. salt
3/4 c. evaporated milk
1/2 c. shredded American cheese
2 tbsp. grated Parmesan cheese

Brown beef and onion in skillet; drain off fat. Add spaghetti sauce; simmer for 10 minutes. Break spaghetti into fourths; cook according to package directions. Rinse and drain. Mix into sauce. Melt butter in saucepan; stir in flour and salt. Add milk and 1/3 cup water; mix well. Cook over medium heat until slightly thickened, stirring constantly. Add American cheese; stir until melted. Spread 1/2 of the spaghetti mixture in 10 x 6 x 2-inch baking dish; top with American cheese sauce. Add remaining spaghetti mixture; sprinkle with Parmesan cheese. Bake in 350-degree oven for 15 to 20 minutes or until heated through. Yield: 6 servings.

Nancy Stribling, V.P.
Xi Epsilon Upsilon X2721
Milan, Illinois

CAVATINI

1 lb. hamburger
1 clove of garlic, crushed
    or minced
1 med. onion, chopped
1 med. green pepper, chopped
1/4 to 1/2 lb. pepperoni, thinly
    sliced
1 sm. can mushrooms
1/4 lb. curly or spiral noodles
1/4 lb. wheel-shaped noodles
1   32-oz. jar spaghetti sauce with
    mushrooms
1/4 lb. mozzarella cheese, grated
1/4 lb. provolone cheese, grated
Grated Parmesan cheese

Brown hamburger; drain. Add garlic, onion and green pepper; cook until tender. Add pepperoni and mushrooms; set aside. Cook noodles according to package directions; drain. Add spaghetti sauce to hamburger mixture. Place half the noodles, meat sauce, mozzarella and provolone cheeses in layers in 9 x 13-inch baking dish; repeat layers. Top with Parmesan cheese. Bake at 400 degrees for 30 to 35 minutes. Let stand for 15 minutes before serving.

Jo Smith, Corr. Sec.
Sigma No. 1175
Beckley, West Virginia

EASY BEEF STROGANOFF

1   5-oz. package dumplets or
    noodles

1/2 c. minced onion
1/4 c. margarine
2 tbsp. flour
Salt and pepper to taste
2 lb. lean ground beef chuck
1   8-oz. can mushrooms
1 c. mushroom soup
1 c. sour cream
2 tbsp. minced parsley

Cook dumplets according to package directions; drain and set aside. Brown onion in margarine. Stir in flour, salt and pepper. Cook beef separately over low heat. Do not brown. Drain off fat; stir beef into onion mixture. Add dumplets, mushrooms, soup, sour cream and parsley. Place in greased casserole. Bake at 350 degrees for 35 to 45 minutes. This freezes well. Yield: 6-7 servings.

Margaret P. Eddy, Pres.
Xi Beta Theta X1914
Neodesha, Kansas

OVEN MOSTACCIOLI

1   8-oz. package mostaccioli noodles
1   28-oz. can tomatoes
1   8-oz. can tomato sauce
1   6-oz. can tomato paste
1 sm. onion, chopped
1 sm. green pepper, chopped
1 tsp. salt
1 tsp. sugar
1 tsp. dried basil
1/8 tsp. pepper
1 1/2 lb. ground beef
1 lg. bay leaf
1/2 c. grated Parmesan cheese
1   6-oz. package sliced mozzarella
    cheese

Cook mostaccioli in large amount of boiling salted water for about 7 minutes or until almost tender. Drain and set aside. Combine undrained tomatoes, tomato sauce, tomato paste, onion, green pepper, salt, sugar, basil, pepper and 1/2 cup water in blender container; blend well. Brown ground beef; drain off excess fat. Stir tomato mixture into ground beef; add bay leaf. Simmer for 30 minutes. Remove bay leaf; stir in mostaccioli. Pour into 9 x 13-inch baking dish; sprinkle with Parmesan cheese. Cover with foil. Bake at 350 degrees for 35 minutes. Remove foil; place mozzarella slices on top. Bake for 5 minutes longer.

Ruth Neppl
Xi Epsilon Rho X4845
Vincent, Iowa

RIGATONI ROMANO (ITALY)

1/2 lb. ground beef
1/2 lb. ground pork or pork
    sausage
1 onion, chopped
3 slices bacon, chopped
1 lg. can tomatoes, cut up

1 tsp. salt
1/4 tsp. pepper
1 6-oz. can tomato paste
1 tbsp. Sherry (opt.)
1 pkg. rigatoni noodles

Brown first 4 ingredients. Add next 3 ingredients; simmer for 1 hour, adding water, if needed. Add tomato paste and Sherry; simmer for 15 minutes longer. Cook noodles in salted water until tender, stirring frequently. Drain well. Pour meat sauce over noodles. Top with Parmesan cheese, if desired.

Dorothy Phillipson, W. and M. Co-Chm.
Xi Delta Mu X4081
Dowagiac, Michigan

CLASSIC LASAGNE (ITALY)

1 lb. ground beef
1/4 c. chopped onion
3 c. tomato sauce
1 6-oz. can tomato paste
1 tsp. leaf oregano
1 tsp. sweet basil
1 lb. lasagne noodles
1 lb. ricotta
2 c. milk
2 eggs, lightly beaten
2 tsp. (about) salt
1/2 lb. mozzarella cheese
Olive oil
Grated Parmesan cheese

Saute ground beef and onion; drain off excess fat. Add tomato sauce, tomato paste, oregano and basil; simmer for 1 hour. Sauce can be prepared ahead of time, refrigerated and reheated when needed. Cook noodles in rapidly boiling salted water to al dente stage. Drain; set aside. Cream ricotta with milk; add eggs and salt to taste. Dice mozzarella cheese into 1/2-inch cubes; add to ricotta mixture. Grease 9 x 13-inch baking dish with olive oil. Spoon part of the ricotta mixture over bottom of dish. Arrange layer of noodles in baking dish. Cover with ricotta mixture and meat sauce; sprinkle with grated cheese. Continue layers, ending with grated Parmesan cheese. Cover baking dish with foil. Bake at 350 degrees for 40 to 45 minutes. Remove foil; bake for 15 minutes longer. Yield: 6-8 servings.

Jeannette Cannon, Corr. Sec.
Eta Tau No. 9176
Fowler, Colorado

SIMPLE LASAGNE

1 onion, chopped
2 lb. ground beef
2 15-oz. cans tomato sauce
1 tsp. garlic powder
1 tsp. oregano
1 tsp. Italian seasoning
Salt and pepper to taste
1 lb. lasagne noodles

3/4 lb. Swiss cheese, cut up
3/4 lb. mozzarella cheese, cut up

Brown onion and ground beef. Add tomato sauce and next 4 ingredients; simmer for 20 minutes. Cook lasagne according to package directions; drain. Arrange half the lasagne in greased 9 x 13-inch pan; cover with half the ground beef mixture. Top with half the cheeses. Repeat layers; sprinkle top with additional seasoning, if desired. Bake at 350 degrees for 1 hour or until done.

Jan Berry
Alpha Nu No. 8975
Marshfield, Wisconsin

BIEROCKS (GERMANY)

1 box hot roll mix
1 lb. lean ground beef
1 med. onion, chopped fine
1 med. head cabbage, shredded
Salt and coarsely ground pepper to taste

Prepare roll mix according to package directions; let rise until doubled in bulk. Brown ground beef in large skillet; add onion and cabbage. Season with salt and pepper. Simmer until cabbage and onion are transparent and beef is crumbly. Roll out dough to make twelve 5-inch squares. Place about 1/3 cup beef mixture in center of each square. Bring corners to center; pinch seams together. Place, seam side down, on lightly greased cookie sheet; let rise for about 30 minutes. Bake in 375-degree oven for 30 minutes or until lightly browned. Serve hot.

Margery Brown, Treas.
Xi Sigma X673
Dodge City, Kansas

FLEISCHKUCHEL (GERMANY)

2 tbsp. (rounded) shortening
2 c. flour
Salt
1 egg, beaten
1/2 c. (about) warm milk
1 lb. hamburger
Pepper to taste
Onion to taste
1/4 c. diced green pepper
1 c. shredded med. Cheddar cheese
Vegetable oil for frying

Cut shortening into flour and 1/2 teaspoon salt as for pie dough. Combine egg and a small amount of milk; stir into flour mixture. Add enough milk to make a soft dough. Let stand for 30 minutes to 1 hour. Season hamburger with salt and pepper. Add onion, green pepper and cheese. Roll out dough thin; cut into 4-inch squares. Place about 1 tablespoon hamburger mixture on half the square. Fold over dough; press edges together firmly to seal. Drop into deep hot fat; fry until brown.

Sherrian Cobine, Treas.
Alpha Xi No. 3518
Lakeview, Oregon

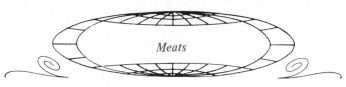

MEAT BISCUITS (GERMANY) FLEISAHBITTEL

1 pkg. dry yeast
2 tbsp. sugar
Salt
2 tbsp. shortening
1 c. milk, scalded
1 egg, well beaten
3 1/2 c. sifted flour
2 lb. lean ground beef
1 med. onion, chopped fine
1/2 med. head cabbage, chopped
1 tbsp. pepper

Dissolve yeast in 1/4 cup warm water; set aside. Combine sugar, 1 teaspoon salt, shortening and warm milk. Add egg and yeast; mix well. Add flour; mix well. Cover. Let rise for 2 hours or until doubled in bulk. Saute beef, onion, cabbage, pepper and 1 tablespoon salt. Roll out dough as for pie crust on lightly floured surface; cut into 5-inch squares. Fill center of each square with beef mixture. Fold corners to center; pinch seams to seal. Place squares, seam side down, on nonstick cookie sheet. Let rise for 20 minutes. Bake at 400 degrees until brown. Serve with salad or soup.

Carolyn J. Sharp, Treas.
Preceptor Beta Kappa XP1359
Maryville, Missouri

GROUND BEEF LUMPIA (PHILIPPINE ISLANDS)

4 to 5 lb. hamburger
1 med. onion, diced
1 clove of garlic, minced
2 tbsp. soy sauce
2 No. 303 cans bean sprouts,
   drained
Lumpia wrappers

Combine hamburger, onion and garlic; mix well. Add soy sauce and bean sprouts; mix thoroughly. Cut lumpia wrappers in half. Place about 1 tablespoon hamburger mixture onto wrapper. Start rolling from cut end; roll once and tuck in the ends. Seal ends together with cold water. Fry in deep fat at 350 degrees until browned.

Dotty Cline
Xi Eta Omicron No. 3427
Rantoul, Illinois

JAPANESE TACOS

1 bunch green onions, minced
4 cloves of garlic, minced
1 1/2 lb. ground beef
1 egg
Kikkoman soy sauce
1 1/2 tsp. Accent
1 pkg. won ton skins
Vegetable oil for frying

1/4 c. rice vinegar
2 tbsp. sesame oil

Combine onions, garlic and ground beef; mix well. Add egg, 1/4 cup soy sauce and 1/2 teaspoon Accent to beef mixture; mix well. Place 1 tablespoon beef mixture in center of each won ton skin; fold into a triangle, pressing edges to seal. Fry in 1/4-inch oil over medium heat until beef is done, turning to brown both sides. Combine 2/3 cup soy sauce, vinegar, sesame oil and remaining 1 teaspoon Accent; mix well. Serve with Japanese Tacos. May deep fat fry, if desired.

Shirley P. Babbitt
Xi Mu Epsilon Chap.
San Diego, California

WON TONS WITH DIPPING SAUCE

1 1/4 lb. ground round steak
1/4 lb. pork sausage
5 green onions, finely chopped
2 tbsp. dry onion soup mix
2 tbsp. soy sauce
1 pkg. won ton skins
Vegetable oil for frying

Combine all ingredients except won ton skins and oil. Place about 1 heaping teaspoon meat mixture in center of each won ton skin. Fold the skin around meat mixture. Dampen ends with water to seal. Fry in moderately hot deep oil until light golden brown. Drain.

Dipping Sauce

1/2 c. catsup
3 tbsp. soy sauce
1 tsp. chili sauce

Combine all ingredients; mix well. Serve with won tons.

Ethel Caffal
Xi Alpha Nu X3154
Kearny, Arizona

PINEAPPLE HAMBURGERS

1 lb. ground beef
Salt and pepper to taste
4 slices pineapple, well drained
1/4 c. (packed) brown sugar
1/4 c. catsup
4 tsp. mustard

Shape beef into 8 thin patties; season each patty. Place pineapple slices on 4 patties. Top with remaining patties; press edges together to seal. Combine remaining ingredients; set aside. Broil patties until brown. Turn patties; top with brown sugar mixture. Broil for 3 to 5 minutes longer or to desired doneness. Yield: 4 servings.

Sandy Reeder, Sec.
Epsilon Phi No. 7842
Ashland, Tennessee

PUERTO RICAN PINON

2 lb. ground round steak
1/2 tsp. meat tenderizer
10 lg. ripe bananas
Shortening
1/4 c. vegetable oil
2 cloves of garlic
2 lg. onions
1 green pepper
1 bay leaf
2 8-oz. cans tomato sauce
1/2 lb. sliced Swiss cheese
Grated Parmesan cheese

Sprinkle ground steak with tenderizer. Slice bananas lengthwise 1/4 inch thick. Fry in shortening until golden brown. Do not overcook. Place half the bananas in layer in a greased 12 x 12 x 3-inch pan. Brown ground steak in oil; crumble with fork. Combine garlic, onions, green pepper, bay leaf and tomato sauce in blender container; process until chopped. Add to steak mixture; simmer for 30 minutes. Cover bananas completely with Swiss cheese; sprinkle with Parmesan cheese. Spread all the meat sauce over cheese, then cover with Parmesan cheese. Place remaining bananas on top; top with layer of Swiss cheese. Bake at 500 degrees just long enough to soften cheese. Remove from oven; slice in squares. Spoon pan juices over each serving. Serve with rice and beans.

Elizabeth C. Brennan, Pres.
Xi Alpha X3938
Mayaguez, Puerto Rico

HOT TAMALES

1/2 lb. ground beef
1/2 lb. ground pork
1 lg. onion, chopped
3 tbsp. chili powder
1/2 tsp. red pepper
Salt and pepper to taste
Garlic salt to taste
1/4 c. chopped green pepper
5 cloves of garlic, minced
1 lg. potato, shredded
Yellow cornmeal
Corn shucks or paper towels,
    cut in half
1 can tomato sauce

Brown meats. Add onion, seasonings, green pepper and garlic; saute for 5 minutes. Add 2 quarts water; bring to a boil. Add potato; cook for 1 hour. Strain liquid from meat mixture. Reserve 1 cup liquid; pour remaining liquid in saucepan. Bring to a boil. Add enough cornmeal to make a thick mush. Boil corn shucks to soften or soak in water. Line corn shucks with layer of mush, beginning at edge of shuck. Place spoonful of meats mixture on mush; roll up tamale. Stack in pan. Combine reserved liquid with tomato sauce; pour over tamales. Steam for 1 hour. Yield: 6 servings.

Mrs. Sharon B. Dubard, Rec. Sec.
Xi Beta Delta X4011
Lake Charles, Louisiana

SICILIAN MEAT ROLL

2 eggs, beaten
3/4 c. soft bread crumbs
1/2 c. tomato juice
2 tbsp. snipped parsley
1/2 tsp. dried oregano, crushed
1/4 tsp. salt
1/4 tsp. pepper
1 sm. clove of garlic, minced
2 lb. lean ground beef
8 thin slices boiled ham
1 1/2 c. shredded mozzarella cheese
3 slices mozzarella cheese, halved
    and cut diagonally

Combine eggs, bread crumbs, tomato juice and seasonings. Stir in beef; mix well. Pat out meat to 12 x 10-inch rectangle on waxed paper. Arrange ham slices over beef mixture, leaving a small margin around edges. Sprinkle shredded cheese over ham. Roll up carefully, starting from short end and using paper to lift. Seal edges and ends. Place roll, seam side down, in 13 x 9 x 2-inch baking pan. Bake at 350 degrees for 1 hour and 15 minutes. Center of roll will be pink. Place cheese slices over top of roll; bake for 5 minutes longer or until cheese melts. Yield: 8 servings.

Clara E. Fruchtl, W. and M. Chm.
Preceptor Kappa XP416
Salunga, Pennsylvania
Joan Sladek, Rec. Sec.
Delta Eta Epsilon No. 9283
Mission Viejo, California

STROMBOLIS (ITALY)

1/2 lb. ground beef
1/2 lb. pork sausage
1 tbsp. finely chopped onion
1/3 c. catsup
2 tbsp. grated Parmesan cheese
1/3 tsp. garlic powder
1/4 tsp. fennel seed
1/8 tsp. ground oregano
6 lg. hard buns or hamburger buns
Garlic Spread
6 slices mozzarella cheese

Brown meats; drain off excess fat. Add next 6 ingredients; simmer for 20 minutes. Split buns; spread 1 teaspoon Garlic Spread on top of each bun. Divide meat mixture evenly on bottom buns; top with cheese and bun tops. Wrap in foil. Bake at 350 degrees for 15 minutes or until cheese is melted.

Garlic Spread

2 tbsp. soft butter
1/4 tsp. garlic powder
1/2 tsp. paprika

Combine all ingredients; mix well.

Linda Harris, Pres.
Kappa Psi No. 9317
Mount Vernon, Indiana

LADY'S THIGHS (TURKEY)
KADIN BUDU

2 med. onions, chopped
1 1/2 tbsp. butter
1 c. rice
3 tsp. salt
1 3/4 lb. lean ground beef
4 eggs
1/2 tsp. pepper
1 c. olive oil

Saute onions in saucepan in butter until lightly browned. Add 1 1/2 cups water, rice and 2 teaspoons salt; cook until rice is tender. Remove from heat; cool. Brown half the beef in separate saucepan over high heat until no juice remains. Add remaining beef; mix well. Add cooked rice, 2 eggs, pepper and remaining 1 teaspoon salt. Mix well for 5 minutes. Mold into egg-shaped pieces, then flatten. Beat remaining 2 eggs in a bowl; dip each pattie in egg. Fry in very hot olive oil, browning well on both sides. Yield: 6 servings.

Elizabeth J. Cornmesser
Xi Gamma Pi X3839
Security, Colorado

SPANISH BEEF-RICE DISH

1 lb. ground beef
1/2 c. chopped onions
1/2 c. chopped celery
3/4 c. Minute rice
1   6-oz. can tomato paste
2 tsp. salt
1/8 tsp. papper

Brown ground beef and onions in large frying pan. Drain off excess fat. Add remaining ingredients and 2 cups water; simmer for 20 to 25 minutes. Yield: 4 servings.

Barbara Price, Pres.
Beta Delta No. 3390
Christiansburg, Virginia

LAMB MOUSSAKA

3 med.-sized eggplant
1 c. butter
3 lg. onions, finely chopped
2 lb. ground lamb
3 tbsp. tomato paste
1/2 c. red wine
1/2 c. chopped parsley
1/2 tsp. cinnamon
Salt to taste
Freshly ground pepper to taste
6 tbsp. flour
1 qt. milk
4 eggs, beaten until frothy
Nutmeg to taste
2 c. ricotta cheese
1 c. fine bread crumbs
1 c. freshly grated Parmesan cheese

Peel eggplant; cut into 1/2-inch slices. Brown quickly in 1/4 cup butter. Set aside. Heat 1/4 cup butter in same skillet; cook onions until brown. Add lamb; cook for 10 minutes. Add tomato paste, wine, parsley, cinnamon, salt and pepper; simmer, stirring frequently, until all liquid is absorbed. Remove from heat. Melt 1/2 cup butter in saucepan; blend in flour. Bring milk to a boil; add to butter mixture gradually. Cook, stirring constantly, until thick and smooth. Cool slightly. Combine eggs, nutmeg and ricotta cheese; stir into white sauce. Sprinkle bottom of greased 11 x 16-inch pan lightly with bread crumbs. Arrange alternate layers of eggplant and lamb mixture in pan, sprinkling each layer with Parmesan cheese and bread crumbs. Pour ricotta cheese sauce over top. Bake in preheated 375-degree oven for 1 hour or until top is golden. Remove from oven; let cool for 20 minutes before serving. This dish is much tastier if made a day ahead and heated before serving. Yield: 8-10 servings.

Mary R. Neary
Xi Alpha Mu X4235
Annapolis, Maryland

STUFFED PEPPERS (TURKEY)
DOLMAS

6 green peppers or tomatoes
1 lb. ground lamb or beef
1 onion, chopped
1/4 to 1/2 c. rice
1 tsp. chopped mint
1 tsp. dillseed or dillweed
1 tbsp. tomato sauce or catsup
1 tsp. salt
Pepper to taste

Slice tops from green peppers; reserve tops for lids. Remove seeds and cores. Combine remaining ingredients for stuffing. Stuff peppers; cover with lids. Place in large saucepan with a small amount of water. Cook, covered, over low heat for 30 to 40 minutes or until done, adding water, if needed, to cover bottom of pan.

Kelly Nelson, Corr. Sec.
Xi Psi X1335
Potter, Nebraska

LAMB CURRY INDIENNE (INDIA)

1 med. onion, chopped
1 med. green pepper, chopped
2 tbsp. butter or margarine
2 c. cooked cubed lamb
2 1/2 c. chicken broth or bouillon
3 tbsp. lemon juice
1 c. prepared mincemeat
1 tbsp. salt
Dash of pepper
1 c. rice
1 tbsp. curry powder

all liquid from coconut; reserve liquid for Coconut Milk and discard coconut.

Photograph for this recipe on page 2.

Brown onion and green pepper in butter until crisp tender in large skillet. Add lamb, broth, lemon juice, mincemeat, salt and pepper. Bring to a boil. Add rice and curry powder; stir thoroughly. Cover tightly. Cook for about 30 minutes or until rice is tender and liquid is absorbed. Serve with coconut, diced green pepper and chopped filberts.

Photograph for this recipe above.

BENGAL CURRY

4 tbsp. margarine
1 med. onion, chopped
2 lb. lamb, cut into 1 1/2-in. cubes
2 c. chicken stock or bouillon
3 tbsp. chopped preserved ginger
2 to 2 1/2 tbsp. curry powder
2 tsp. salt
1 tsp. crushed dried mint flakes
1/4 tsp. ground cloves
1/8 tsp. pepper
1 c. Coconut Milk
1/2 c. flaked coconut
1/4 c. lime juice
2 tbsp. cornstarch
1/2 c. heavy cream

Melt 1 tablespoon margarine in large skillet over medium heat. Add onion; saute until transparent. Remove onion. Melt remaining 3 tablespoons margarine. Add lamb; brown on all sides. Stir in onion, chicken stock, ginger, curry powder, salt, mint, cloves and pepper; cover. Simmer for about 1 hour or until lamb is tender. Stir in Coconut Milk, coconut and lime juice. Mix cornstarch and 1/4 cup water together in small bowl. Stir into lamb mixture. Bring to a boil, stirring constantly, over medium heat. Boil for 1 minute. Stir in heavy cream just before serving. Heat; do not boil. Serve over hot cooked rice with curry accompaniments. Yield: 6-8 servings.

Coconut Milk

1   3 1/2-oz. can flaked coconut

Pour 1 1/2 cups boiling water over flaked coconut. Let stand for at least 2 hours or until cold. Drain, pressing

STRING KABOBS (TURKEY)
KAYTAN KEBABI

1 lb. leg of mutton
1 lg. onion, grated
1 bunch spring onions, chopped
1/4 tsp. mignonette salt
1/4 tsp. white pepper
1/4 c. dry white wine
1/4 tsp. nutmeg
1/2 tbsp. chopped dill
1/4 tsp. cinnamon
1/4 tsp. cloves
1 tbsp. grated coconut
2 tbsp. chopped parsley
2 tbsp. melted butter
1/4 tsp. chopped rosemary

Cut lamb into 3 x 1/2-inch strips. Place in bowl. Add onions, salt, pepper and wine; mix well. Let marinate for 12 hours. Combine remaining ingredients for sauce. Thread each piece of lamb on skewer. Grill for 3 minutes on one side; turn and grill for 2 minutes on other side, brushing with sauce frequently.

Marge Thomas, Dir. of Gifts
International Office
Kansas City, Missouri

MAKLUBI (ARABIA)

2 med. eggplant, peeled and sliced
Salt to taste
Oil
2 lb. lean lamb, cubed
Pepper to taste
1 med. onion, coarsely chopped
1 c. rice
1/2 c. whole almonds
1/2 c. pinenuts
2 tbsp. butter

Dry eggplant slices on paper towel. Season with salt. Fry in 1/2-inch oil until soft and slightly brown; drain. Season lamb cubes with salt and pepper. Place lamb in enough water to cover in a large saucepan. Add onion. Cook for 30 minutes or until tender. Remove lamb with slotted spoon; skim off fat from broth. Place lamb in flameproof casserole; add eggplant slices and rice. Measure lamb broth; add enough water to make amount liquid required to cook rice according to package directions. Pour over rice; cover. Simmer until rice is done. Brown almonds and pinenuts in butter; sprinkle over rice to serve.

Jane Nadosky, Rec. Sec.
Preceptor Gamma XP174
Centerville, Ohio

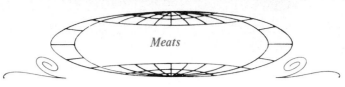

TURKISH SHISH KABOBS

1/2 c. dry onion flakes
2 lb. lamb shoulder or leg of lamb, cut in
   1-in. cubes
1 tbsp. ground cumin
1/2 tsp. pepper
1 1/2 tsp. rosemary, crushed
1/2 tsp. seasoned salt
1/2 c. olive oil
1/2 c. dry Sherry
1 1/2 tsp. salt

Soak onion flakes in 1/2 cup water for 5 minutes. Combine lamb cubes, onions, cumin, pepper, rosemary, seasoned salt and olive oil; toss until lamb is thoroughly coated. Stir in Sherry; let marinate for 2 hours or longer. Add salt just before broiling. Thread on skewers. Broil for 15 minutes or until done. Yield: 6 servings.

Betty Hood, Pres.
Xi Zeta Upsilon X1867
San Lorenzo, California

ROAST LAMB SHANKS
(ARMENIA) KOUZOU KZARTMA

4 lamb shanks
2 tomatoes, quartered
2 tsp. salt
1 tsp. paprika
2 potatoes, cut into lg. pieces

Wash lamb well; let stand in clean water for at least 15 minutes. Peel off membrane with sharp knife. Place in open roasting pan. Add tomatoes, salt, paprika and 2 cups water. Bake at 375 degrees for 30 minutes. Turn lamb over; bake for 30 minutes longer. Add potatoes; bake for 30 minutes. Turn potatoes and lamb; bake for 30 minutes longer. Serve with pan juices.

Virginia L. Fuller, Prog. Chm.
Preceptor Alpha Tau XP1524
Bend, Oregon

LAMB WITH YOGURT (GREECE)
ARNI ME YIAOURTI

1 rack of lamb
1/2 tsp. oregano
1/4 tsp. thyme
1 garlic clove, mashed
Salt and pepper to taste
Juice of 2 lemons
Dash of Cognac
1 tbsp. flour
1 c. yogurt
Dash of Brandy (opt.)

Bone rack of lamb, leaving eye of rib in 1 strip; trim off all fat. Combine oregano, thyme and garlic, rub rib eye thoroughly with oregano mixture. Season with salt and pepper; saturate with lemon juice. Place lamb and bones on rack with pan underneath to catch drippings.

Bones enrich the sauce. Sprinkle lamb with Cognac. Bake at 500 degrees for 20 to 25 minutes or until no longer pink. Mix flour and 2 tablespoons water together. Combine yogurt, flour mixture and Brandy; cook over very low heat, stirring constantly, for about 15 minutes. Add pan juices; blend well. Slice lamb; serve with sauce.

Mildred Burns, City Coun. Pres.
Laureate Epsilon PL 247
Alamosa, Colorado

LEG OF LAMB AND POTATOES

1 5 to 6-lb. leg of lamb
1 lemon
Salt and pepper to taste
Oregano to taste
2 tbsp. olive oil
Small potatoes, peeled and halved

Wash lamb; place in roaster. Squeeze lemon juice over top. Cut half the lemon rind in quarters; place in roaster. Season with salt, pepper and oregano; pour olive oil over top. Add 1 cup water to roaster; cover. Bake at 325 degrees for 2 hours. Baste; arrange potatoes around lamb. Cover; bake for about 1 hour longer or until done. Remove lamb; place on platter. Let stand for 15 minutes before slicing. Return potatoes to oven. Broil for about 15 minutes or until browned.

Geneveve Tallen
Preceptor Laureate Eta PL 206
Moberly, Missouri

SHOULDER OF LAMB AND
APRICOT STUFFING
(NEW ZEALAND)

1 tbsp. chopped onion
2 tbsp. butter or margarine
1/4 c. (heaping) fresh white bread crumbs
Salt and pepper to taste
1/2 tsp. minced parsley
1/2 tsp. sage
1 to 2 tbsp. milk
4 oz. chopped dried apricots
1 boned shoulder of lamb

Fry onion gently in butter. Add bread crumbs, salt, pepper and herbs. Stir in milk; mix in apricots. Stuff lamb shoulder. Roll up; tie securely with string. Place in pan; cover. Bake in 350-degree oven, allowing 30 minutes per pound. Uncover; bake for 30 minutes longer.

Lorna A. Ashton, Treas.
Xi Beta Omicron X4658
Squamish, British Columbia, Canada

Recipes on page 76 and 126

SYRIAN LEG OF LAMB

1   5-lb. leg of lamb
1 tsp. salt
2 cloves of garlic, minced
1/4 tsp. pepper
1/4 bay leaf, crushed
1/4 tsp. marjoram
1/4 tsp. sage
1/4 tsp. ginger
1/4 tsp. thyme
1 tbsp. olive oil

Wipe lamb with damp cloth. Cut gashes 1/4 inch long on top surface of lamb. Combine remaining ingredients except olive oil; rub into lamb so that all gashes are completely filled. Give leg of lamb a final coating of oil; place in baking pan. Bake in preheated 500-degree oven for 15 minutes. Reduce temperature to 350 degrees; bake for about 1 hour and 30 minutes longer or until done. Yield: 6-8 servings.

Sarah S. Dabdoub, City Coun. Rep.
Preceptor Laureate Alpha PL125
New Orleans, Louisiana

MOOSE COOKED IN WINE

1   5 to 6-lb. moose roast
Salt, pepper and garlic salt to taste
1 tbsp. oregano
1 onion, chopped
1/2 c. olive oil
1 1/2 c. dry wine
1 c. tomato juice
2 bay leaves
Juice of 1 lemon
1   4-oz. can mushrooms

Soak roast in cold water overnight. Drain well. Add seasonings, oregano, onion and olive oil. Bake, uncovered, in 350-degree oven for 1 hour. Add 4 cups water, wine, tomato juice and bay leaves; cover. Bake for 2 hours longer. Remove from oven; sprinkle with lemon juice. Add mushrooms; thicken pan juices to make gravy.

Myrna Jacques, 1st V.P.
Alpha Delta No. 8155
Grande Prairie, Alberta, Canada

POLYNESIAN KRAUT KABOBS

6 c. sauerkraut
1   20-oz. can pineapple chunks in
    juice
Brown sugar
1/2 c. catsup
2 tbsp. soy sauce
1 lb. frankfurters, cut into 1-in.
    pieces
2 med. green peppers, cut into chunks
2 tbsp. salad oil
1 c. chopped green onion

Recipe on page 121.

Drain sauerkraut, reserving 2 tablespoons liquid; set aside. Drain pineapple chunks, reserving juice. Combine 3 tablespoons brown sugar and 2 tablespoons reserved pineapple juice in small saucepan; stir in reserved sauerkraut liquid, catsup and soy sauce. Bring to a boil, stirring constantly. Reduce heat; simmer for 10 minutes. Thread pineapple chunks, frankfurters and green pepper chunks alternately on twelve 10-inch skewers. Place on rack of broiler pan; brush kabobs with sauce. Broil for 5 minutes, brushing occasionally with sauce. Turn kabobs; brush with sauce. Broil for 5 minutes longer or until franks are heated through. Heat salad oil in large skillet; add green onion and sauerkraut. Cook, stirring constantly, until onion is tender. Stir in 1/2 cup brown sugar and 1/2 cup reserved pineapple juice. Continue cooking until hot. Spoon hot sauerkraut mixture onto large serving platter; arrange kabobs on top. Garnish with parsley.

Photograph for this recipe on page 103.

ORIENTAL PORK CHOPS

4 lg. 3/4-in. thick pork chops
1   2-oz. can mushrooms
1 med. onion, thinly sliced
2 cans fancy Chinese vegetables
1/4 c. soy sauce
1 tsp. sugar
2 tbsp. lemon juice
1/2 tsp. ground ginger
1/4 tsp. garlic powder

Brown chops on both sides. Place in shallow baking dish. Drain mushrooms; reserve liquid. Add mushrooms to chops. Arrange onion and Chinese vegetables over chops. Combine reserved mushroom liquid with remaining ingredients; pour over chops. Bake at 350 degrees for 45 minutes. Serve with rice.

Jenny Tackett, Pres.
Xi Alpha Nu X4710
Lexington, Kentucky

ARABIAN PORK CHOPS

6 pork chops
Salt and pepper to taste
6 tbsp. rice
1 lg. onion, sliced
1 lg. tomato, sliced
1 bell pepper, cut into 6 wedges
2 cans tomato sauce
6 slices American cheese

Brown pork chops on both sides; place in baking dish. Season with salt and pepper. Place 1 tablespoon rice over each chop. Place onion slice over rice; add tomato slice. Season with salt and pepper. Add wedge of bell pepper. Mix tomato sauce with 2 cans water in saucepan; heat. Pour around pork chops. Cover. Bake at 375-degrees for 1 hour. Top with cheese. Bake until cheese melts.

Irene Bowman, Serv. Chm.
Preceptor Beta XP346
Eagle River, Alaska

CANTONESE PORK CHOPS (CHINA)

6 1-in. thick loin pork chops
2 tbsp. salad oil
1 30-oz. can apricot halves
2 to 3 tbsp. soy sauce
1 lg. clove of garlic, crushed
1/2 tsp. powdered ginger
1 8-oz. can water chestnuts,
   drained and sliced
5 scallions, sliced
2 c. diagonally sliced celery
Salt and pepper to taste

Brown chops on both sides in hot oil in large skillet. Pour off excess fat. Drain syrup from apricots into skillet. Add 1/2 cup water, soy sauce, garlic and ginger; cover. Simmer for 35 minutes, adding more water if necessary. Add water chestnuts, scallions and celery; cook for about 5 minutes longer or until celery is tender. Add apricots. Cook just until heated through. Season sauce with salt and pepper. Serve with parslied rice.

Photograph for this recipe above.

HAWAIIAN PORK CHOPS

1 lg. can pineapple slices
4 to 6 pork chops
Salt to taste
1/4 c. flour
1/2 c. shortening
1 tsp. sugar
1 tsp. lemon juice
1/4 tsp. cinnamon
1/4 tsp. nutmeg
1 tsp. cornstarch

Drain pineapple; reserve juice. Trim fat from chops; sprinkle with salt. Coat with flour. Brown in hot shortening. Drain fat from skillet. Add reserved juice, sugar, lemon juice and spices. Combine 1 tablespoon water and cornstarch; add to pork chops. Cook, stirring, until sauce is thickened. Top each chop with pineapple slice. Cook for 5 minutes longer.

Linda Lyons, Pres.
Alpha Theta No. 2781
Waynesville, North Carolina

SADDLE CHOPS

2 tbsp. butter
2 tbsp. lemon juice
2 tbsp. whiskey
2 tbsp. Worcestershire sauce
Dash of freshly ground pepper
8 med. pork chops
1/2 c. red currant jelly

Combine butter, lemon juice, whiskey, Worcestershire sauce and pepper in saucepan. Place over low heat; stir until butter is melted and well blended. Cool. Pour over chops; marinate for 30 minutes, turning once or twice. Remove chops from marinade; place on broiling pan. Broil on both sides. Combine remaining marinade with currant jelly. Heat just until jelly is dissolved. Pour over chops and serve.

Deborah Brown, W. and M. Chm.
Nu Zeta No. 6426
Collinsville, Illinois

SWEET-SOUR PORK AND PINEAPPLE (HAWAII)

1 1/2 lb. boneless lean pork
1/4 c. soy sauce
1 tbsp. Sherry
1 c. chicken broth
1 1-lb. 4-oz. can pineapple chunks
1/4 c. (packed) brown sugar
1 tbsp. cornstarch
1/3 c. vinegar
1/8 tsp. salt
1 sm. green pepper, cut in strips
1 med. onion, cut in eighths
1 lg. tomato, cut in sm. wedges

Trim excess fat from pork; cut into 2 x 1/2-inch strips or small cubes. Combine with 2 tablespoons soy sauce and Sherry, tossing well. Let stand for 1 hour. Drain and reserve any marinade. Brown pork slowly in 2 or 3 tablespoons fat rendered from pork trimmings. Discard fat. Add reserved marinade and 3/4 cup broth; cover tightly. Simmer for about 30 to 45 minutes or until pork is tender. Add remaining broth, if needed. Drain pineapple, reserving juice. Blend 1/4 cup juice with brown sugar, cornstarch, vinegar, remaining 2 tablespoons soy sauce and salt until smooth. Add to pork. Cook, stirring, until sauce thickens and clears. Add green pepper and onion; cover. Cook for several minutes until vegetables are just tender. Add tomatoes and drained pineapple chunks. Cook for several minutes longer.

Photograph for this recipe on page 61.

FILIPINO EGG ROLL

1 1/2 c. diced cooked pork
1 can bean sprouts, drained
1/2 c. sliced fresh mushrooms
1 clove of garlic, crushed
Pinch of curry powder
1 sm. onion, chopped
2 tbsp. soy sauce
2 tbsp. sweet rice wine
1 pkg. egg roll wrappers

Saute pork, bean sprouts, mushrooms, garlic, curry powder and onion in soy sauce and rice wine. Place 1 heaping tablespoon pork mixture in each wrapper. Roll, folding in ends. Dampen edge to seal. Deep fry until golden brown. Serve with hot Chinese mustard or sweet and sour sauce.

Debbie Smith
Beta Sigma Chap.
Kennewick, Washington

DUBLIN CODDLE (IRELAND)

8 thick slices ham or bacon
16 pork chipolata sausages
4 lg. onions, chopped
2 lb. potatoes, sliced
1/4 c. chopped parsley
Salt and pepper to taste

Cut ham into 2-inch chunks; place ham and sausages into pan of boiling water. Boil for 5 minutes; drain and reserve liquid. Arrange layers of onions and potatoes in ovenproof dish, sprinkling each layer with parsley and salt and pepper. Place ham and sausages on top. Pour enough reserved liquid in dish to barely reach top. Cover. Bake in preheated 350-degree oven for about 1 hour. Remove cover. Bake for about 1 hour longer or until liquid is reduced by half and potatoes are tender.

Mrs. Valerie P. Pye
England Omega No. 8541
Ipswich, Suffolk, England

HAM FUN BUN SANDWICHES

1 c. butter
3 tbsp. prepared mustard
1 sm. onion, minced
1 1/2 tsp. poppy seed
1 tbsp. Worcestershire sauce
16 hamburger buns
2 lb. cooked ham, thinly shaved
1 lb. Swiss cheese, thinly sliced

Blend butter with mustard, onion, poppy seed and Worcestershire sauce. Spread on both sides hamburger buns. Fill generously with ham and cheese. Wrap tightly in aluminum foil. Bake at 350 degrees for 30 minutes. Yield: 16 servings.

Maureen S. Tanner
Xi Alpha Tau X3475
East Brunswick, New Jersey

BAKED HAM IN WINE

1/2 tbsp. parsley flakes
1/2 tbsp. garlic powder
1 tbsp. dry mustard
6 tbsp. brown sugar
1/2 tsp. thyme
1/2 tsp. marjoram
1 tsp. ground cloves
1/4 c. herb wine vinegar
1 1/2 c. Sauterne
1 bay leaf
1 whole ham
Frosted Grapes

Combine all ingredients except bay leaf and ham. Place in pan or plastic bowl; add bay leaf. Place ham on bay leaf. Cover. Refrigerate for 4 days, turning twice daily. Bake ham in sauce at 300 degrees for 15 minutes per pound. Cool; chill and slice. Arrange on tray; decorate with Frosted Grapes.

Frosted Grapes

Grapes
Flavored gelatin

Wash grapes in water; drain. Shake in plastic bag with dry gelatin. Dry on paper towels on cookie sheet. Use lime gelatin for green grapes and cherry or raspberry gelatin for red grapes.

Helen Dolores McCabe, Soc. Chm.
Alpha Kappa Pi No. 8962
Robert Lee, Texas

HAWAIIAN-BAKED HAM

1 uncooked ham
1 1/2 c. flour
1 1/2 tbsp. dry mustard
1/2 c. (packed) brown sugar
1/2 tsp. cloves
1 tbsp. cinnamon
1/2 tsp. ginger
1/2 c. pineapple juice

Remove rind from ham; trim and wipe clean. Combine remaining ingredients; spread on all sides of ham. Wrap in brown paper as though wrapping a package. Place, folded side down, on unoiled shallow baking pan. Place in cold oven. Bake at 325 degrees for 20 minutes per pound. Remove from oven; cut paper away. The paste will adhere to paper.

Glaze

3/4 c. (packed) brown sugar
1/4 c. pineapple juice
Pineapple slices
Whole cloves
Candied cherries (opt.)

Combine brown sugar and pineapple juice; boil for 5 to 10 minutes. Garnish ham with pineapple; stud with cloves. Add cherries. Return ham to oven for 15 to 20 minutes, basting frequently with glaze.

Mrs. Glenn Durham, Corr. Sec.
Xi Iota X899
Harlan, Kentucky

RUSSIAN HAM

1   12-lb. (about) smoked ham
1/2 c. sugar
1 tsp. dry mustard
3 tbsp. mayonnaise
1   8-oz. package cream cheese, softened
1/2 c. cottage cheese
4 tsp. prepared mustard
7 hard-boiled egg whites

Trim rind and all but 1/4 inch fat from ham. Place ham, fat side up, on rack in shallow roasting pan. Combine sugar and dry mustard in small bowl; blend in mayonnaise to make a thick paste. Spread paste on top and sides of ham. Bake in preheated 350-degree oven for 1 hour. Increase oven temperature to 400 degrees; bake for about 30 minutes or until brown. Remove from oven; cool. Refrigerate, covered, until cold. Combine cheeses and prepared mustard in small mixer bowl; beat until smooth. Spread cheese mixture on top and sides of chilled ham. Press egg whites thru sieve; sprinkle on cheese mixture. Garnish with green pepper strips, black olives and sliced lemon leaves. Refrigerate ham for at least 1 hour before serving.

Norma Noland, Pres.
Xi Omicron X415
Kokomo, Indiana

HAWAIIAN PORK

3 green peppers, cut in 1-in. cubes
Vegetable oil
2 tbsp. flour
1 egg, beaten
1/2 tsp. salt
Pinch of pepper
1 lb. boneless pork, cut in 1-in. cubes
1/2 c. pineapple cubes
2 1/2 tbsp. cornstarch
2 1/2 tbsp. soy sauce
1/4 c. sugar
1/4 c. vinegar
1/4 c. pineapple juice

Saute green peppers in small amount of oil until tender. Remove from pan. Combine flour, egg, salt and pepper; coat pork cubes with mixture. Fry in oil. Cover; cook for 30 minutes. Add peppers and pineapple. Cover; cook for 15 minutes. Combine last 5 ingredients; add to pork mixture. Cook, stirring constantly, until thick and clear.

Dee Weybright, Pres.
Xi Rho Eta No. 3994
Santa Cruz, California

MARINATED PORK (JAPAN)

3/4 c. Kikkoman soy sauce
5 tbsp. sugar
1/4 c. Sake (opt.)
1/4 c. beef broth
1/2 tsp. pepper
1 tsp. ground ginger
2 cloves of garlic

1 tbsp. diced onion (opt.)
1/2 c. sesame seed
2   2-lb. pork tenderloins

Combine all ingredients except pork. Place pork in dish. Pour soy sauce mixture over pork; marinate for 3 hours at room temperature or for 12 hours in refrigerator, turning frequently. Bake at 350 degrees for 45 minutes or until done, turning and basting frequently. Cut in diagonal slices to serve. May cook over charcoal, if desired.

Candace Watanabe
Tau Iota No. 5245
Dallas, Texas

OKINAWAN PORK AND CABBAGE

1/2 c. sugar
1/2 c. soy sauce
1 1/2 lb. pork, cut in thin strips
1 med. head cabbage, chopped

Combine sugar, 1/2 cup water and soy sauce in large saucepan; add pork. Cook until tender. Add cabbage; cover. Cook until cabbage is tender.

Anna Marie Brehm, Corr. Sec.
Lambda No. 174
Cedar Rapids, Iowa

PANCIT (PHILIPPINE ISLANDS)

2 c. fresh pork, cut in 2-in. strips
2 cloves of garlic, minced
Ginger to taste
1 tbsp. oil
2 c. cooked chicken, cut in 2-in. strips
1 c. fresh shrimp, cut in 1-in. pieces
1/4 c. Chinese sausage, thinly sliced
2 celery stalks, slivered
1 med. onion, sliced lengthwise
2 tsp. MSG
2 tsp. paprika
1/4 c. soy sauce
2 boxes very thin egg noodles, cooked and
    drained
2 c. thinly sliced cabbage

Saute pork, garlic and ginger in oil in large saucepan until brown. Add chicken, shrimp and sausage; cook, stirring constantly to prevent scorching. Add celery, onion, MSG, paprika and soy sauce. Cook until onion and celery are tender. Add 2 cups water; simmer for 1 hour. Add noodles and cabbage; mix well. Cover; cook, stirring occasionally, until cabbage is soft. Do not overcook cabbage. Arrange on platter; garnish with sliced hard-boiled eggs and lemon slices. Serve with soy sauce.

Barbara E. Schindler, V.P.
Preceptor Alpha XP169
Kailua, Hawaii

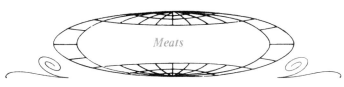

AMERICAN PORK PIE

3 lb. lean ground pork
3 tsp. salt
1 1/2 tsp. pepper
1/2 tsp. nutmeg
1/2 tsp. mace
2 1/4 tsp. cornstarch
Pastry for 2-crust pie

Combine all ingredients except pastry; add 2 1/2 cups water. Mix well. Simmer, covered, for 20 minutes. Uncover; simmer until liquid is almost evaporated but mixture is still juicy. Pour into pastry-lined pan; add top pastry. Prick top with fork. Bake at 425 degrees for 12 minutes. Reduce oven temperature to 350 degrees; bake for 35 to 40 minutes longer or until browned.

Theresa Levesque, V.P.
Xi Gamma X642
Lewiston, Maine

PORK ADOBO (PHILIPPINE ISLANDS)

1 2 to 3-lb. pork roast, cubed
Vegetable oil
3 tbsp. vinegar
3 cloves of garlic, minced
2 tbsp. Accent
1 tbsp. mixed pickling spices
1 tbsp. dry mustard
1 tbsp. ginger
1 tsp. paprika
1 tsp. curry powder
2 tbsp. soy sauce

Brown pork in small amount of oil in large skillet for about 15 minutes. Cover with enough water to almost cover pork. Add vinegar; bring to a boil. Add garlic, Accent, mixed spices, dry mustard and ginger; stir well. Cook, partially covered, for about 30 to 45 minutes or until water is almost evaporated. Uncover; add paprika, curry powder and soy sauce. Cook for about 10 to 15 minutes longer. Serve with rice, if desired. Yield: 4 servings.

Bobbi LeFevre, Treas.
Phi Alpha P2730
Charleston, West Virginia

PORK CHOW MEIN

1 lb. pork, cut in thin strips
3 tbsp. salad oil
3 c. thinly sliced celery
1 c. onion slices
1 c. sliced fresh mushrooms
2 1/2 tbsp. cornstarch
1 can beef broth
1/4 c. soy sauce
1 tbsp. brown gravy sauce (opt.)
1 1-lb. can bean sprouts, drained
1 5-oz. can water chestnuts, sliced

Cook pork in large skillet in 1 tablespoon hot salad oil for about 10 minutes or until tender. Remove from skillet; cook celery, onion and mushrooms in remaining salad oil for 2 to 3 minutes or until tender crisp, stirring frequently. Blend cornstarch and 1/4 cup water; add beef broth, soy sauce and brown gravy sauce. Stir into vegetables; add pork, bean sprouts and water chestnuts. Heat, stirring until thickened. Serve over chow mein noodles or hot rice. Yield: 4-5 servings.

Faye H. Stratton, Treas.
Xi Gamma Tau X4629
Appomattox, Virginia

PORK CHOP SUEY

1 lb. lean pork, diced
1 lb. fresh shrimp, diced
Soy sauce
1 lb. fresh mushrooms, chopped
Margarine
1 lg. head cabbage, chopped
3 to 4 tbsp. cooking Sherry
Cornstarch

Marinate pork and shrimp in 3 tablespoons soy sauce for 1 hour. Saute pork and shrimp in electric skillet until done; remove from pan and set aside. Saute mushrooms in small amount margarine until done; remove from pan and set aside. Add small amount margarine; saute cabbage until almost done. Return pork mixture and mushrooms to pan; mix well. Simmer for at least 30 minutes. Add Sherry and soy sauce to taste. Thicken with cornstarch. Serve on rice. Yield: 4-6 servings.

Addie Heck, Ext. Off.
Preceptor Lambda XP1575
Pleasant Grove, Alabama

BERRY-BARBECUED PORK ROAST

1 4 to 6-lb. pork loin roast
1 lb. fresh cranberries
1 c. sugar
1/2 c. barbecue sauce
1/2 c. orange juice

Place roast on rack in open roasting pan. Do not add water and do not cover. Bake in 325-degree oven for about 30 to 35 minutes per pound or until meat thermometer reads 170 degrees. Combine remaining ingredients in medium saucepan; stir until sugar is dissolved. Bring to a boil over medium heat; boil for 5 minutes without stirring. Baste roast with cranberry sauce during the last 20 minutes of roasting time. Serve remaining sauce with roast.

Christine Kryshak
Xi Alpha Upsilon X4438
Wisconsin Rapids, Wisconsin

Meats

CHINESE-BARBECUED PORK

1 3-lb. lean boneless pork loin roast
2 c. chicken stock
3 tbsp. Sherry (opt.)
1/3 c. thinly shredded preserved ginger
2 tbsp. brown sugar
1/4 c. soy sauce
2 cloves of garlic, crushed
Cornstarch

Trim excess fat from roast; place roast in roasting pan. Combine remaining ingredients except cornstarch; pour over roast. Cover. Bake at 350 degrees for 2 hours and 30 minutes or until roast is well done. Baste frequently with pan juices. Remove cover during last 30 minutes. Thicken pan juices with a small amount of cornstarch dissolved in water. Serve sliced pork with rice and gravy.

June Stella Willrich, Soc. Chm.
Gamma Beta No. 4411
Hamilton, Ontario, Canada

STUFFED PORK LOIN

4 tbsp. flour
Salt and pepper
1 3 to 4-lb. boneless loin roast
1/4 c. oil
2 1/2 c. dark rye bread crumbs
1 can beef consomme
2 eggs, beaten
2 tbsp. chopped parsley
3/4 c. minced onion
3 tsp. prepared mustard
1 clove of garlic, crushed
1 tbsp. Worcestershire sauce

Blend 2 tablespoons flour, 1/2 teaspoon salt and 1/8 teaspoon pepper together. Roll roast in flour mixture; brown in oil. Combine bread crumbs, 1/2 cup consomme, eggs, parsley, onion, 1 teaspoon mustard, garlic, dash of salt and 1/4 teaspoon pepper; spoon into roast cavity. Tie with string. Place in deep casserole. Add 1/4 cup water to remaining consomme; pour over roast. Cover tightly. Bake at 325 degrees for 2 hours and 30 minutes. Strain drippings from roast; add enough water to measure 2 cups liquid. Mix remaining 2 tablespoons flour in 1/4 cup water. Stir into drippings. Add remaining 2 teaspoons mustard and Worcestershire sauce. Bring to a boil. Reduce heat; simmer until thick. Yield: 4-6 servings.

Marsha Fahnenbruch
Kappa No. 7881
Pickering, Ontario, Canada

PORK LOIN ROAST WITH GRAVY

1 4 to 6-lb. pork loin center
rib roast
3 tbsp. flour
Salt and pepper to taste

Place roast, fat side up, on rack in open roasting pan. Insert meat thermometer in center or thickest part. Do not add water; do not cover. Bake in 325-degree oven until thermometer registers 170 degrees. Allow 30 to 35 minutes per pound for roasting a center loin, 35 to 40 minutes per pound for a half loin and 40 to 45 minutes per pound for an end roast. Remove roast from pan; place on carving board. Pour off all but 1/4 cup drippings, leaving brown particles in pan. Blend in flour; cook, stirring constantly, over low heat until mixture is lightly browned. Remove from heat. Add 2 cups water gradually, blending well after each addition. Return to heat. Bring to a boil; cook, stirring constantly, until thickened. Cook slowly for 3 to 5 minutes, stirring occasionally. Season with salt and pepper.

Photograph for this recipe on page 69.

SAUSAGE STUFFING BALLS

1 pkg. seasoned stuffing mix
1 lb. fresh pork sausage
1/2 c. finely chopped onion
1/2 c. finely chopped celery
1 egg, beaten
1/2 tsp. baking powder

Combine stuffing mix with 3/4 cup hot water. Break sausage into small pieces. Add to moistened stuffing mix. Stir in onion, celery, egg and baking powder until well mixed. Shape into balls, using 1/4 cup mixture for each ball. Place in baking pan. Cover with foil, securing tightly around pan. Bake in a 325-degree oven for 15 minutes. Remove foil; increase temperature to 350 degrees. Bake for 25 minutes longer or until sausage is done. Yield: 18 to 22 balls.

Photograph for this recipe on page 69.

SWEDISH SAUSAGE AND EGG CASSEROLE

1 lb. link sausage
8 slices fresh bread
4 eggs, beaten
2 1/2 c. milk
Pinch of salt
3/4 c. grated American cheese

Fry and drain sausage; cut into small chunks. Trim crusts from bread; cut into cubes. Combine eggs, milk and salt. Place bread cubes in 13 x 9-inch baking dish; add sausage and cheese. Pour egg mixture over top. Refrigerate overnight. Bake at 325 degrees for 35 minutes.

Phyllis Gorze, Pres.
Preceptor Theta XP1424
Minot, North Dakota

TOAD IN THE HOLE

1 lb. pure pork link sausages
1/4 c. beef drippings or clarified butter
2 eggs

Meats

1 c. milk
1 c. flour
1/4 tsp. salt

Prick sausages; simmer in water to cover for about 5 minutes. Drain. Pour beef drippings into a pie pan; place in preheated 450-degree oven to heat. Do not burn. Beat eggs in blender container or with electric mixer; Add remaining ingredients gradually. Beat until batter is very smooth. Remove pie pan from oven. Pour a thin layer of batter in pan. Arrange sausages over batter, then add remaining batter. Bake for 10 minutes. Reduce oven temperature to 350 degrees; bake for 20 minutes longer. Pudding should be puffed and golden brown. Serve at once. Yield: 2-3 servings.

Mrs. William H. Bass, Jr., Parliamentarian
Beta Psi No. 3650
Knoxville, Tennessee

BEERIBS SUPREME (CANADA)

1   10-oz. bottle chili sauce
1/2 c. catsup
1 c. finely chopped onion
1/4 c. lemon juice
1/4 c. vinegar
1 tbsp. brown sugar
1 tsp. salt
1 tsp. German-style mustard
2 cloves of garlic, chopped
2 dashes of Tabasco sauce
1 bay leaf
1 bottle ale or lager beer
4 lb. spareribs

Combine all ingredients except spareribs; simmer for 10 minutes. Brown spareribs on all sides in a frying pan. Place spareribs in shallow baking pan. Pour sauce over spareribs to cover. Cover with aluminum foil, shiny side down. Bake in preheated 350-degree oven for 1 hour. Serve with rice. Yield: 4-5 servings.

Helen McDonald, W. and M. Chm.
Xi Gamma Eta X3401
Lindsay, Ontario, Canada

COUNTRY RIBS INDONESIAN

6 lb. country-style pork ribs
4 onions, peeled and quartered
2 cloves of garlic
6 tbsp. soy sauce
3 tbsp. lemon juice
2 tbsp. (firmly packed) brown sugar
1 tbsp. coriander
1 tbsp. salt
2 tsp. ground cumin
1 tsp. cayenne pepper
1 tsp. freshly ground pepper
1 c. apricot jam

Place pork ribs in a single layer in shallow roasting pan. Cover with foil. Bake in preheated 350-degree oven for 1 hour. Combine onions, garlic, soy sauce, lemon juice, brown sugar, coriander, salt, cumin, cayenne pepper and pepper in blender container; cover. Blend until onions are chopped. Add jam; blend again until marinade is almost smooth. Pour marinade into large bowl; add ribs, coating on all sides with marinade. Cover. Refrigerate for several hours or overnight. Drain ribs; reserve marinade. Place ribs on rack in broiler pan, 5 inches from heating element. Broil for 20 minutes, turning every 5 minutes to brown on all sides. Heat reserved marinade until bubbly; spoon over ribs. Serve with rice; garnish with mandarin orange slices. Yield: 6-8 servings.

Jeanette Fehn, Pres.
Alpha Zeta No. 236
Elgin, Illinois

CHINESE SPARERIBS

3 lb. spareribs
Shortening
2 onions, chopped
Butter
1 c. diced celery
1 clove of garlic, minced
1 c. catsup
2 tbsp. vinegar
1/4 c. lemon juice
3 tbsp. Worcestershire sauce
1 tbsp. sugar

Brown spareribs in small amount shortening. Brown onions in small amount butter; add remaining sauce ingredients and 1 1/2 cups water. Pour sauce over spareribs. Bake at 375 degrees for 2 hours or until tender.

Joanne Newton, City Coun. Rep.
Xi Alpha Pi X4041
Rupert, Idaho

SWEET AND SOUR SPARERIBS

3 lb. spareribs, cut in serving-sized pieces
2/3 c. (packed) brown sugar
2 tbsp. cornstarch
2 tsp. dry mustard
1/3 c. vinegar
1 c. crushed pineapple
1/2 c. catsup
1/4 c. finely chopped onions
2 tbsp. soy sauce
Salt and pepper to taste

Arrange spareribs, meaty side up, in a single layer in a large shallow pan. Brown in 425-degree oven for 20 to 30 minutes; drain off fat. Combine 1/2 cup water and remaining ingredients, except salt and pepper, in a saucepan; stir until smooth. Cook over medium heat until thick and glossy, stirring constantly. Sprinkle salt and pepper over browned spareribs; spoon half the sauce over spareribs. Reduce oven temperature to 350 degrees. Bake for 45 minutes longer. Turn spareribs; cover with remaining sauce. Bake for 30 minutes longer or until well done. Yield: 4 servings.

Betty J. Smith
Omega Epsilon No. 5786
Morongo Valley, California

77

1 1/4 lb. lean pork, cut in 1-in. cubes
2 tbsp. shortening
2 tbsp. sugar
1 tbsp. cornstarch
1 tbsp. vinegar
1 1/2 c. Minute rice
1 lg. green pepper, cut into strips
1   13-oz. can pineapple chunks

Combine flour and salt; coat pork with flour mixture. Brown pork in shortening over medium heat. Cook, stirring constantly, for 20 minutes or until pork is tender. Combine sugar, cornstarch and vinegar; set aside. Add remaining ingredients and 1 1/2 cups water to skillet; bring to a boil, stirring to loosen particles on bottom of skillet. Add cornstarch mixture; cook, stirring, until slightly thickened. Cover; simmer for 5 minutes. Yield: 4 servings.

Suzanne G. Brown, W. and M. Chm.
Xi Rho X444
Woodburn, Indiana

BELGIAN RABBIT

1 frozen Pel rabbit, thawed
1/4 c. butter
1/2 to 3/4 can beer
2 sm. onions, quartered

Wash rabbit; remove fat. Soak in salted water for 30 minutes. Brown rabbit pieces in butter in Dutch oven or deep well. Mix in beer and onions. Cook for about 1 hour and 30 minutes or until tender.

Mrs. Lynn Aeck, North Houston Coun. Past Pres.
Xi Pi Upsilon X4551
Houston, Texas

HASENPFEFFER (GERMANY)

1   2 1/2-lb. pkg. frozen cut up rabbit
2 1/2 tsp. salt
6 tbsp. butter
1 med. onion
4 whole cloves
1 c. Port
1/4 c. lemon juice
12 peppercorns
Sprig of parsley
1/2 tsp. thyme
1 bay leaf
2   10 1/2-oz. cans beef bouillon
3 tbsp. flour
Currant jelly

Thaw rabbit. Rinse and pat dry with paper towels. Rub with 1 1/2 teaspoons salt. Saute rabbit in 3 tablespoons butter for about 20 minutes or until brown. Place in 3-quart casserole. Stud onion with cloves. Add onion, Port and lemon juice. Place peppercorns, parsley, thyme and bay leaf in cheesecloth bag; tie securely. Place in casserole. Pour in bouillon; cover. Bake in preheated 350-degree oven for 1 hour and 30 minutes. Discard onion and cheesecloth bag. Melt remaining butter in saucepan. Remove from heat; stir in

CANTONESE SPARERIBS AND KRAUT (CHINA)

6 lb. pork spareribs, cracked
Salt and pepper to taste
3 1/2 c. undrained sauerkraut
1/4 c. cornstarch
1/2 c. honey
1 c. chicken broth
1   20-oz. can crushed pineapple in syrup
1/2 tsp. ground ginger
1/2 tsp. garlic powder
4 tsp. soy sauce
1 med. onion, sliced
2 tbsp. salad oil
1 lg. apple, cored and sliced
1/2 green pepper, cut in sm. strips

Sprinkle spareribs on both sides with salt and pepper. Place in 2 shallow baking pans; cover. Bake in 325-degree oven for 1 hour. Drain sauerkraut juice into saucepan. Stir in cornstarch, honey, broth, undrained pineapple and seasonings. Cook, stirring constantly, for about 1 minute or until sauce boils. Pour 3 cups sauce over spareribs. Bake in 400-degree oven, uncovered, for 45 minutes or until spareribs are browned and tender. Saute sauerkraut and onion in oil in large skillet for 5 minutes. Add remaining pineapple sauce, apple and green pepper; cover. Cook over low heat for 5 minutes. Serve with spareribs. Yield: 6 servings.

Photograph for this recipe above.

SWEET-SOUR PORK AND RICE

2 tbsp. flour
1 tsp. salt

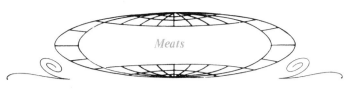
flour until smooth. Add 3 1/2 cups stock from rabbit. Bring to a boil; cook until thickened, stirring constantly. Serve rabbit with gravy and currant jelly. Yield: 4 servings.

Jean M. Branton
Delta Sigma Chap.
Shelby, North Carolina

STEWED RABBIT (BELGIUM)

1/4 c. butter
1/2 lb. lean pork side, thinly sliced
1 rabbit
Salt and pepper to taste
2 shallots, chopped or 1 med. onion, chopped
2 sprigs of thyme or 1/8 tsp. dried thyme
8 prunes
1 c. dry red table wine or 1/3 c. cider vinegar

Melt butter in heavy skillet. Saute pork in butter; remove when brown. Cut rabbit in serving pieces; dry thoroughly on paper towels. Season with salt and pepper. Brown in skillet on all sides. Return pork to skillet; reduce heat. Add shallots; cook slowly for 5 minutes. Sprinkle thyme over rabbit; place prunes in skillet. Add wine; cover. Simmer for 1 hour and 30 minutes. Add water, if needed. Serve sauce over rabbit.

Jeanette Layden
Zeta Omicron No. 2871
Hooperston, Illinois

BREAKFAST SAUSAGE CASSEROLE

8 slices bread, cubed
3/4 c. grated Cheddar cheese
2 lb. large round link sausage
4 eggs, beaten
2 3/4 c. milk
3/4 tsp. dry mustard
1 sm. can sliced mushrooms
1 can golden mushroom soup

Place bread cubes in greased 9 x 13-inch pan. Sprinkle cheese on top of bread. Fry link sausage; let cool. Dice sausage; place on top of cheese. Combine eggs, 2 1/4 cups milk, mustard and mushrooms; pour over sausage. Mix mushroom soup and remaining 1/2 cup milk together. Pour over top, spreading evenly. Cover with aluminum foil; refrigerate overnight. Remove foil. Bake at 325 degrees for 1 hour and 30 minutes. Yield: 12-14 servings.

Donna Dorsey Fries
Preceptor Epsilon XP499
Richwood, West Virginia

KIELBASA WITH RED CABBAGE

1 sm. red cabbage, coarsely shredded
1 sm. apple, peeled and diced
1 tbsp. lemon juice

Salt
1 sm. onion, chopped
1 tbsp. butter
1 tbsp. wine vinegar
1 lb. kielbasa sausage, cut in 1-in. chunks

Simmer cabbage with apple, 1/2 cup water, lemon juice and 2 teaspoons salt in covered 4-quart pan over medium heat for 15 minutes, stirring occasionally. Cook onion in butter in 10-inch skillet over medium heat until tender. Stir in cabbage mixture, 1 teaspoon salt, vinegar and sausage chunks. Reduce heat to low; cover. Simmer for 30 minutes or until sausage is cooked through. Yield: 4 servings.

Frances E. Brillian, W. and M. Chm.
Xi Delta X409
Rochester, New York

SICILIAN SAUSAGE BREAD

4 2/3 c. flour
2 tbsp. lard
1/4 tsp. salt
1/4 pepper
1 1/4 env. yeast
1 lb. Italian sweet sausage, skinned and fried
1/2 c. grated Italian cheese
8 oz. mozzarella cheese, chopped
3 tbsp. olive oil
1 tsp. oregano
2 cloves of garlic, minced

Combine flour, lard, salt, pepper, yeast and 1 1/8 cups warm water; work well until smooth. Place in large bowl; cover. Let rise in warm place for 2 hours or until doubled in bulk. Place on floured board; punch down. Divide into 2 pieces; press to 14 inches in diameter. Arrange sausage and cheeses on dough; sprinkle with olive oil, oregano, garlic and additional salt and pepper. Roll up dough; pinch edges together. Prick with fork 3 times; place on greased pan. Let rise for 30 minutes. Bake at 350 degrees for 40 minutes or until golden brown. Can be frozen. Yield: 6 servings.

Joanne Karczmarczyk
Alpha Beta No. 1580
Shelton, Connecticut

VEAL MARSALA (FRANCE)

1 lb. thin veal cutlets
1/4 c. butter
1/2 c. flour
1/2 c. Marsala or sweet Sherry
Salt and pepper to taste
1 lemon, sliced

Flatten veal; cut into 4-inch pieces. Heat butter. Dredge veal with flour; brown quickly in butter. Add Marsala; cover. Simmer for 10 to 15 minutes or until tender. Season with salt and pepper. Serve hot with lemon slices. Yield: 4 servings.

Gloria A. Dubuc
Xi Eta Mu X3532
Milan, Ohio

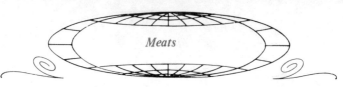
AUSTRIAN WIENER SCHNITZEL

6 veal cutlets or pork chops
Salt and pepper to taste
1/4 c. all-purpose flour
1 egg, beaten
Bread crumbs
1/2 c. oil

Pound veal to less than an 1/4-inch thickness. Season both sides with salt and pepper. Dredge with flour; dip into egg. Roll in bread crumbs. Heat oil in large frying pan. Fry one side on medium heat until golden brown. Turn over; fry other side. Do not turn a second time. Drain on paper toweling. Schnitzel must be crisp and free of all extra grease. Transfer to a warm platter; garnish with lemon slices and fresh parsley. Serve immediately. Yield: 6 servings.

Emmy Reynolds, Rec. Sec.
Xi Epsilon X1236
Gulfport, Mississippi

VEAL CUTLET PARMESAN (ITALY)

8 4 to 5-oz. veal cutlets
Salt to taste
1 egg, beaten
1 1/2 c. dry bread crumbs
Vegetable oil
1 1/2 c. tomato sauce
1/2 tsp. oregano
Dash of garlic salt
1/4 c. grated Parmesan cheese
8 slices mozzarella cheese

Sprinkle cutlets lightly with salt. Dip in egg, then in bread crumbs. Shake off excess crumbs so that coating will not be too thick. Brown cutlets in hot oil in skillet; place in buttered baking dish. Heat tomato sauce with oregano and garlic salt. Pour over cutlets; sprinkle Parmesan cheese on top. Cover. Bake in 350-degree oven for 30 to 35 minutes. Uncover; place 1 slice mozzarella cheese on each cutlet. Return to oven; bake for 5 to 8 minutes longer or until cheese is melted. Serve immediately. Yield: 8 servings.

Sherry Landers
Eta Mu No. 8856
Stratford, Ontario, Canada

VEAL PICCATA (ITALY)

4 pieces of scallopini of veal
2 tbsp. flour
4 tbsp. Fleischmann's corn oil margarine
1 clove of garlic, crushed
1/4 c. dry vermouth
1 tbsp. lemon juice
1/2 lemon, sliced

Pound veal with wooden mallet until 1/8 inch thick. Dredge lightly with flour, shaking off excess. Melt 3 tablespoons margarine in skillet; add garlic. Cook until golden brown; discard garlic. Place veal in skillet. Cook quickly for about 1 to 2 minutes on each side or just

until brown. Remove onto serving dish. Add remaining margarine, vermouth and lemon juice. Simmer for 3 minutes, scraping bottom of pan to loosen drippings. Pour sauce over veal. Garnish with lemon slices. Yield: 4 servings.

Photograph for this recipe on page 50.

VEAL CUTLETS IN CREAM (FRANCE) ESCALOPES DE VEAU A LA CREME

1 1/2 lb. veal cutlets
1/4 c. flour
1 1/4 tsp. salt
1/8 tsp. white pepper
1/4 c. butter
3/4 c. heavy cream
2 tbsp. lemon juice

Cut veal into 6 pieces; pound thin. Dip veal into mixture of flour, salt and pepper. Melt butter in skillet over low heat; saute veal on both sides for about 10 minutes or until tender but not brown. Transfer to hot platter. Stir cream and lemon juice into skillet. Cook over high heat for 3 minutes, scraping browned bits from skillet. Pour over veal. Yield: 6 servings.

Faye Reed, Corr. Sec.
Xi Alpha Zeta X5008
Fairfield, Connecticut

BREADED VEAL CUTLET (GERMANY) WIENER SCHNITZEL

2 lb. veal cutlets, 1/2 in. thick
1/4 c. flour
1 tsp. salt
1/4 tsp. pepper
1 egg, slightly beaten
1 tbsp. milk
1 c. fine dry bread crumbs
4 to 5 tbsp. butter
Lemon juice

Cut veal into 6 pieces; coat with mixture of flour, salt and pepper. Combine egg and milk; dip cutlets into egg mixture. Coat with bread crumbs; let stand for 5 to 10 minutes to seal coating. Melt butter in large heavy skillet. Add cutlets; cook over medium heat for about 20 minutes or until browned and tender. Remove cutlets to warm serving platter; sprinkle with lemon juice. Top each portion with a fried egg.

Ellen J. Packey, City Coun. Rep.
Preceptor Beta XP346
Anchorage, Alaska

JELLIED VEAL (SWEDEN) KALVSYLTA

1 veal knuckle
1 onion, chopped
10 peppercorns

Meats

1 bay leaf
Salt to taste

Boil veal knuckle, onion, peppercorns and bay leaf gently in enough water to cover. Season with salt. Cook until meat falls from bones. Cut all meat from bone and chop. Strain juice; add chopped meat. Pour into mold; chill until firm. Slice to serve.

Mrs. Deanne Fortney
Beta Pi No. 2327
El Dorado, Kansas

VEAL A LA CREME (BELGIUM)

3 lb. veal steak
1 lb. button mushrooms
1/4 c. (or more) butter
Salt to taste
1 c. cream
3 tbsp. Cognac
Fresh-ground pepper to taste

Saute veal and mushrooms in butter over medium heat. Add salt. Remove veal. Stir cream into pan juices; add Cognac. Grind pepper over veal; pour sauce over top. Yield: 6 servings.

Gladys Garner, Pres.
Laureate Theta PL230
Saint Catharines, Ontario, Canada

PAPRIKA SCHNITZEL (AUSTRIA)

3 tbsp. butter
Paprika
3 onions, sliced
1 1/2 lb. thin veal round steaks
1/4 c. seasoned flour
1/2 c. thick sour cream

Melt butter in frying pan; add enough paprika to make a reddish color. Add onions; saute until tender. Shake steaks in flour in a plastic bag until well coated. Brown steaks in frying pan; add sour cream slowly. Cover; simmer for about 30 minutes or until tender. Add more water, if needed, stirring constantly.

Julie Ann M. Prahler, V.P.
Xi Tau Chap.
Detroit, Michigan

VEAL PARMESAN

Flour
Salt, pepper and oregano to taste
1 egg
1/4 c. light cream
1/3 c. dry bread crumbs
1/3 c. grated Parmesan cheese
2 tbsp. minced parsley
4 to 6 pieces cubed veal steak
2 tbsp. butter
Crushed garlic to taste
1 c. spaghetti sauce
2 tbsp. dry white wine
4 to 6 slices mozzarella cheese

Combine flour, salt, pepper and oregano. Beat egg and cream together. Combine bread crumbs, Parmesan cheese and parsley. Dredge veal with flour; dip in egg mixture. Coat with cheese mixture. Brown slowly in butter with crushed garlic. Pour spaghetti sauce and wine around veal; place 1 slice mozzarella cheese on top of each cutlet. Bake in 325-degree oven for 30 to 40 minutes or until veal is tender and cheese is lightly browned.

Linda Cleland, Past Pres.
Gamma Epsilon Chap.
Burlington, Iowa

VEAL SCALOPPINE WITH MARSALA

1 1/2 lb. boneless veal steak
All-purpose flour
Salt and freshly ground pepper to taste
2 tbsp. vegetable oil
1 tbsp. butter
1/2 lb. fresh mushrooms, sliced thin
1 clove of garlic, minced
6 to 8 scallions, chopped
2 tbsp. minced fresh parsley
1 tsp. dried basil
1 c. chopped peeled and seeded tomatoes
1/2 c. Marsala or Sherry

Pound veal until thin; cut into 2-inch squares. Dredge with flour seasoned with salt and pepper. Heat oil and butter together in skillet; brown veal on all sides. Place in casserole. Add mushrooms, garlic and scallions to skillet; cook until limp. Add remaining ingredients to skillet; stir well. Pour mixture over veal; cover. Bake in preheated 350-degree oven for 45 minutes. Yield: 4 servings.

Katherine Krenitsky
Kappa Omicron No. 8089
Stroudsburg, Pennsylvania

VEAU CORDON BLEU

6 thin veal steaks
6 thin ham slices
6 thin slices Gruyere or Swiss cheese
Seasoned flour
1 egg, beaten
Packaged dry bread crumbs
1/4 c. butter
2 tbsp. oil

Pound steaks to about 1/8-inch thickness. Top each steak with 1 slice ham and 1 slice cheese. Fold steaks in half; secure with toothpicks. Dip in flour and egg, then drudge with bread crumbs. Refrigerate for 1 hour. Heat butter and oil in large frying pan. Cook steaks, turning occasionally, until cooked through. Drain well; remove toothpicks. Yield: 3 servings.

Roberta Huisman
Xi Epsilon Omega Chap.
Centerville, Iowa

Seafood

Around the world, fish and seafood hold an important place on the menu, or they are the mainstay of some cuisines, and then considered almost a gourmet treat in others — depending on availability. In Scandinavian countries, for example, seafood is abundant but the winters are long and harsh. As a result, Scandinavian cooks excel in the preparation of pickled and salted fish. In the Mediterranean, most seafood is cooked fresh, and flavored with wine, lemon and the herbs popular to the region. Fresh seafood is also plentiful in the coastal areas of Mexico and South America, where it is seasoned with green peppers and chilies, or coconut.

Seafood that is uncommon and expensive by Western standards is ordinary fare in Japan and Hawaii. An Oriental favorite, Seafood Tempura, is thought to have been introduced by Jesuit missionaries to Japan in the 1500's. The name is derived from a Portugese phrase meaning "Lenten Days," the time when Christians do not eat meat or poultry. Pacific Islanders also have a unique variety of recipes for seafood, including baked, dried and raw. If their shark fin soup seems unusual to Western palates, then the Spanish custom of cooking and serving squid in its own ink may be a surprise to Oriental tastes!

Freshwater fish is plentiful in Canada, America, the mid-European countries, and the interior, mountainous areas of other countries. Freshwater fisherman have definite but varying opinions on how to cook these fish for best results. European fishermen say fresh lake and stream trout should only be grilled above an outdoor campfire and basted with butter and lemon juice while cooking. However, the use of herbs, peppers, onions, and piquant sauces with fish is as varied as there are cooks in the world, and all would claim their recipe to be the very best.

Beta Sigma Phis over the world include seafood in their menu plans because most varieties are high in nutrition and low in calories. And, if seafood is available locally, it can be a real budget saver. Fish and seafood prepared to reflect the flavors from many lands are new and imaginative ways to add variety to your meal plan.

DRESSED COD FILLETS

1 lb. cod fillets
1 1/2 c. soft bread crumbs
1 tsp. savory
2 tsp. grated onion
1 tsp. salt
1/8 tsp. pepper
2 tbsp. butter
1 egg, beaten
Flour

Wipe thinly cut fillets with a damp cloth. Mix bread crumbs, savory, onion, salt and pepper together; rub in butter. Add egg. Place thin layer of crumb mixture on each fillet; roll up as for jelly roll. Secure with a toothpick. Coat fish rolls with flour; brown in hot fat. Arrange browned fish rolls in a 1 1/2-quart casserole. Bake in 350-degree oven until heated through and fish flakes easily when tested with fork.

Agnes Murphy
Xi Delta Chap.
Saint John's, Newfoundland, Canada

FISH PLAKI (GREECE)

1 med. onion, sliced
1 clove of garlic, minced
2 med. tomatoes, sliced
1 c. chopped parsley
1/2 c. Fleischmann's corn oil margarine
2 lb. frozen fish fillets, thawed
1/2 tsp. salt
1/2 tsp. oregano
1/4 tsp. pepper
1/2 c. bread crumbs

Saute onion, garlic, tomatoes and parsley in 1/4 cup margarine in a large skillet. Set aside. Arrange fillets in 13 x 8 x 1-inch baking dish. Sprinkle with salt, oregano and pepper. Arrange sauteed mixture over fillets. Sprinkle bread crumbs evenly over all. Dot with remaining margarine. Bake, covered, at 350 degrees for 35 to 40 minutes or until fillets are fork tender. Yield: 6-8 servings.

Photograph for this recipe on page 50.

ORIENTAL TUNA CHOP SUEY

1/4 c. Fleischmann's corn oil margarine
1 c. sliced celery
1 med. onion, sliced
1 med. green pepper, cut in strips
1 clove of garlic, minced
1 8-oz. can bamboo shoots, drained
1 8-oz. can water chestnuts, drained and sliced
1 tbsp. soy sauce
1/2 tsp. salt
2 tbsp. cornstarch
2 7-oz. cans tuna, drained and flaked
Cooked rice

Melt margarine over medium heat in a large skillet. Saute celery, onion, green pepper, garlic, bamboo shoots and water chestnuts. Mix 1 1/4 cups water, soy sauce and salt into skillet. Combine cornstarch with 1/4 cup water; add slowly to skillet, stirring constantly. Simmer until thickened. Fold in tuna; heat through. Serve over rice. Yield: 6 servings.

Photograph for this recipe on page 50.

KABOBS ORVIETO (ITALY)

1/2 c. Ruffino Orvieto Secco white wine
1/3 c. salad oil
2 tbsp. fine dry bread crumbs
1/2 tsp. salt
1/4 tsp. marjoram, crushed
1 lb. fresh or frozen flounder fillets, cut in half lengthwise
1 med. zucchini, cut into 8 slices
8 cherry tomatoes

Combine wine, oil, bread crumbs, salt and marjoram in bowl. Add fish; coat with wine mixture. Marinate in refrigerator for at least 30 minutes. Remove fish from marinade; reserve liquid. Roll up fish. Thread onto four 10-inch skewers with zucchini and cherry tomatoes. Grill about 4 inches from source of heat for about 10 to 12 minutes or until fish flakes easily when tested with fork, brushing occasionally with reserved marinade and turning once. Serve immediately. Yield: 4 servings.

Photograph for this recipe below.

STUFFED FISH FILLETS

4 oz. chopped onion
1/2 c. chopped celery
1/2 c. onion bouillon
1 c. drained mushrooms
2 slices bread, crumbled
1 tsp. salt
1/4 tsp. pepper
1 1/2 lb. cod fillets

Cook onion and celery in onion bouillon for 5 minutes or until tender. Add mushrooms, bread crumbs, salt and pepper; mix well. Divide into 4 equal parts. Sprinkle fish with additional salt and pepper; spread crumb mixture over fish fillets. Roll up; secure with toothpicks. Place in nonstick pan. Bake at 375 degrees for 15 minutes or until done. Garnish with lemon slices. Yield: 4 servings.

Mrs. Sally Barker
Beta Delta Chap.
Sidney, Ohio

FISH IN MARINADE

1 c. apple cider vinegar
2 c. water
1/2 c. (or less) sugar
1 tsp salt
2 bay leaves
10 peppercorns
1 1/2 c. catsup
2 lb. fish fillets
2 eggs, beaten
Bread crumbs
Cooking oil
2 lg. onions, sliced

Combine first 6 ingredients in medium saucepan; simmer for 15 minutes. Cool. Add catsup; mix well. Dip fish fillets in eggs; roll in bread crumbs. Fry in hot oil on both sides until brown. Arrange in shallow dish; cool. Saute onions in oil; place over fish. Pour vinegar mixture over fish and onions. Marinate for 6 hours in refrigerator. Serve cold.

Marija Pascuzzi
Xi Omicron X868
Bluefield, West Virginia

CANADIAN FISH SOUFFLE

3 tbsp. butter
3 tbsp. flour
1 c. scalded milk
3 eggs, separated
1 c. flaked cooked fish
1/2 tsp. salt
Pepper to taste

Melt butter in top of double boiler; blend in flour. Add milk gradually; cook, stirring, until thick. Stir slowly into beaten egg yolks. Return to heat; cook for 1 minute, stirring constantly. Cool. Add fish and sea-sonings. Fold in stiffly beaten egg whites. Turn into a greased casserole. Bake at 300 degrees for about 45 minutes. Serve at once. Yield: 5-6 servings.

Margaret M. Madden
Xi Alpha X1713
Saint John's, Newfoundland, Canada

HADDOCK IN SAUCE

2 lb. haddock
Lawry's salt to taste
2 c. milk
1 onion, quartered
1/2 c. butter
1/2 c. flour
1 egg yolk, beaten
Pepper to taste
Buttered bread crumbs

Cook fish in small amount of salted water until tender. Drain off liquid, reserving 1/2 of the liquid. Flake fish; season with salt. Place in buttered casserole. Heat milk and onion together. Remove onion. Melt butter; stir in flour. Add reserved fish liquid and egg yolk, blending well. Stir in milk to make smooth sauce. Season with salt and pepper. Pour sauce over fish. Sprinkle top with bread crumbs. Bake at 350 degrees until bubbly.

Marsha Blaisdell, Pres.
Alpha Upsilon Chap.
Rockland, Maine

PSARI PLAKI

1 4-lb. bass or snapper
Juice of 1 lemon
Salt to taste
2 lg. onions, sliced lengthwise
3/4 c. olive oil
2 tbsp. chopped parsley
3 stalks celery, chopped
1 lg. carrot, sliced
1 sm. green pepper, chopped
1 No. 2 can tomatoes
Pepper to taste

Clean fish thoroughly. Sprinkle with lemon juice and salt; let stand for 30 minutes. Arrange in baking pan. Fry onions in oil for 5 minutes; add parsley, celery, carrot and green papper. Cook over high heat for 5 minutes. Add tomatoes; season with salt and pepper. Cover; cook over medium heat for 20 minutes. Add 1/4 cup water; cook for 10 minutes longer, stirring occasionally. Pour over fish. Bake at 400 degrees for 35 minutes. Serve very hot.

Hazel E. Clay, V.P.
Preceptor Alpha XP126
Stevensville, Montana

SALMON CREPES (FRANCE)

Flour
3/4 tsp. salt
2 eggs
1 c. milk
Butter
Dash of pepper
1/4 tsp. leaf tarragon, crumbled
1 1/2 c. light cream
2 egg yolks
1   1-lb. can salmon, drained, boned
    and flaked
1 tbsp. freeze-dried chives
1 tbsp. lemon juice
3 tbsp. grated Parmesan cheese

Combine 3/4 cup sifted flour and 1/4 teaspoon of salt in bowl. Beat eggs until blended in small bowl; stir in milk. Beat into flour mixture until smooth. Melt 1 tablespoon butter in saucepan; stir into batter. Cover and chill for 2 hours. Heat 7-inch frying pan until drops of water sizzle. Grease pan lightly with butter. Measure 2 tablespoons batter into pan, tilting pan so batter covers bottom. Bake crepe for 1 to 2 minutes or until brown; turn and bake for 1 minute. Repeat, buttering pan before each crepe. Melt 3 tablespoons butter in saucepan; blend in 3 tablespoons flour. Cook, stirring constantly, until bubbly. Stir in remaining 1/2 teaspoon salt, pepper, tarragon and cream. Cook until sauce thickens and boils for 1 minute. Beat egg yolks slightly in small bowl; stir in about half the hot sauce, then stir back into remaining sauce in pan. Cook for 1 minute longer; remove from heat. Blend 3/4 cup sauce with salmon and chives in bowl; stir in lemon juice. Place heaping teaspoon of salmon mixture on each crepe; roll up jelly roll fashion. Place in single layer in a buttered baking dish. Pour remaining sauce over crepes; sprinkle with cheese. Bake at 400 degrees for 10 minutes or until bubbly. Garnish with parsley.

Debi Gillott
Delta Omega No. 9967
Victoria, British Columbia, Canada

SALMON DIABLE

3/4 c. sour cream
1/4 c. dry Sherry
1 tbsp. lemon juice
1 tsp. Worcestershire sauce
1/2 tsp. dry mustard
1 tbsp minced onion
2 eggs, slightly beaten
1   1-lb. can salmon
1/3 c. cracker crumbs
1/4 c. minced parsley

Combine sour cream, Sherry, lemon juice, Worcestershire sauce, mustard, onion and eggs. Stir in salmon, cracker crumbs and parsley. Spoon into 6 greased seafood baking shells. Garnish tops with lemon slices and paprika. Bake at 350 degrees for 30 minutes.

Marcia Preston
Beta Omicron No. 1304
Clear Lake, Iowa

SALMON AND POTATO FRITTERS (LAPLAND)

2   7-oz. cans salmon
3/4 c. mashed potatoes
3 tbsp. grated onion
1 tbsp. lemon juice
1 tbsp. chopped parsley
1 tsp. salt
1/2 tsp. freshly ground pepper
1 egg, beaten
3/4 c. fresh bread crumbs
Cooking oil

Drain and mince salmon. Combine with remaining ingredients except oil. Chill. Remove from refrigerator; place mixture on floured board. Pat flat. Form into 2-inch fritters. Pour enough oil in fryer to cover fritters; heat to 375 degrees. Deep fry fritters until golden brown. Drain well and serve. Fritters may be frozen until ready to deep fry.

Barbara Schroer
Xi Lambda Rho X2821
Orland, California

SALMON ROLL (CANADA)

2 c. flour
4 tsp. baking powder
Salt
1/3 c. shortening
7/8 c. milk
1   15-oz. can salmon
1/4 c. chopped onion
2 tbsp. chopped green pepper
2 tbsp. chopped celery
2 tbsp. catsup
1/2 tsp. dry mustard
1 egg, beaten
Pepper to taste

Sift flour with baking powder and 1 teaspoon salt into bowl; cut in shortening until fine crumbs are formed. Add milk; stir with fork to make a soft dough. Turn dough onto lightly floured surface; knead gently for 8 to 10 times. Roll into a 10 x 12-inch rectangle. Remove skin from salmon; mash with juices. Mix salmon with onion, green pepper, celery, catsup, mustard and egg; season with salt and pepper. Spread to within 1/2 inch of the edges of biscuit rectangle. Roll up as for jelly roll, starting from the longer side. Moisten edge and seal. Place on a greased baking sheet, tucking ends under. Bake in 425-degree oven for 25 to 30 minutes. Serve with cheese sauce, if desired.

Lorraine Fenton, Publ. Chm.
Xi Gamma X399
Tolland, Connecticut

BAKED RAINBOW TROUT

Flour
Salt and pepper to taste

1   3 or 4-lb. rainbow trout
3 tbsp. butter
1 c. cream

Combine small amount of flour, salt and pepper. Dredge trout with flour mixture. Melt butter in roaster. Place trout in roaster. Bake at 375 degrees until golden brown. Pour cream over trout; bake for 20 minutes longer.

Barbara Biddulph
Alpha No. 8023
Whitehorse, Yukon Territory, Canada

BROILED TROUT (GREECE)
PSARI ME OREGANO

2 lg. trout, filleted
Salt and pepper to taste
1/4 c. butter
2 lemons
Oregano to taste

Place fish on broiler pan. Season with salt and pepper. Dot with butter; squeeze juice of 1 lemon over fillets. Sprinkle with oregano. Broil at 400 degrees until fish begins to brown lightly. Baste with juice of remaining lemon and butter as needed. Remove to hot platter. Dot with any remaining butter; sprinkle with oregano. Serve hot. May garnish with lemon slices, if desired.

Angeline K. Russo, Treas., W. and M. Chm.
Xi Gamma Eta X3733
Auburn, New York

TUNA-STUFFED SHELLS

1   4-oz. package conchiglioni or
    20 jumbo macaroni shells
1   6 1/2 or 7-oz. can tuna, drained
    and flaked
1 c. soft bread crumbs
1 egg, beaten
1/4 c. chopped onion
1 tsp. lemon juice
4 tbsp. snipped parsley
1 can cream of celery soup
1/2 c. milk
Paprika
Parmesan cheese to taste

Cook shells in salted boiling water for 15 to 20 minutes until al dente. Drain; rinse in cold water. Combine tuna, bread crumbs, egg, onion, lemon juice and 2 tablespoons parsley; fill each shell with 1 tablespoon filling. Arrange in 8 x 11-inch baking dish. Heat soup, milk and remaining 2 tablespoons parsley in saucepan; pour over shells. Sprinkle with paprika and Parmesan cheese. Cover. Bake at 350 degrees for 20 minutes. Yield: 5 servings.

Barbara Lukehart, Librarian
Iota Mu No. 6812
Montoursville, Pennsylvania

TURBOT IN CHAMPAGNE

1/2 c. butter
2 tbsp. olive oil
2 shallots, finely chopped
1/4 lb. mushrooms, sliced
4 turbot fillets
6 tbsp. fish stock
1/2 c. (about) Champagne
Salt and white pepper
2/3 c. heavy cream
1 tbsp. cornstarch

Melt half the butter in a large shallow saucepan; add olive oil. Saute shallots until transparent; add mushrooms. Cook until tender. Remove vegetables with slotted spoon; add remaining butter. Saute turbot until golden. Return mushrooms and onions; add fish stock and half the Champagne or enough to barely cover fillets. Season with salt and pepper; simmer until tender. Remove turbot to a serving dish. Add cream to liquid in pan; heat without boiling until cream is warm. Mix cornstarch with small amount of water; add to sauce. Cook, stirring constantly, until smooth. Add remaining Champagne; stir until sauce is warm. Pour over fish.

Pam Kloski, Treas.
Xi Tau Phi No. 5086
Vallejo, California

NEWFOUNDLAND FLIPPER PIE

2 seal flippers
1 tsp. soda
4 slices salt pork
2 onions, chopped
2 carrots, diced
1 turnip, diced
1 parsnip, diced
5 potatoes, diced
Salt
1/4 tsp. pepper
2 c. flour
4 tsp. baking powder
1/2 c. shortening

Soak flippers in soda and water to cover for 3 minutes. Remove white fat from flippers; wash. Cut into serving pieces. Fry salt pork slices in a heavy pot; remove pork slices. Brown flipper pieces in hot fat; add 1 cup water. Reduce heat; simmer until almost tender. Add chopped vegetables, except potatoes; add 1 cup water. Boil for about 30 minutes. Add potatoes, 1 teaspoon salt and pepper; cook for 15 minutes longer. Place in casserole. Sift flour, baking powder and 1/2 teaspoon salt together; cut in shortening. Add 1/2 cup water, blending to make a stiff dough. Roll out; place over casserole. Bake at 450 degrees for 20 minutes or until lightly browned. Yield: 6 servings.

Marilyn Whitehead
Mu No. 6898
Dartmouth, Nova Scotia, Canada

NA MA SU (JAPAN)

3 cucumbers, thickly sliced
2 carrots, thinly sliced
2 lg. onions, thinly sliced
3 stalks celery, thickly sliced
1/2 c. (packed) brown sugar
3/4 c. white vinegar
1 tbsp. salt
1 tsp. MSG
1 can abalone

Place vegetables in a shallow glass dish. Mix brown sugar, vinegar, salt, MSG and 1 cup water in saucepan; bring to a boil. Pour over vegetables. Cover and refrigerate overnight. Slice abalone into long thin slivers; add to vinegar mixture. Toss until well coated. Drain and arrange on serving dish.

Gail Bishop, V.P.
Xi Alpha Alpha X3445
Rockville, Maryland

ITALIAN BAKED CLAMS

2 onions, diced
1/4 c. butter
1 tbsp. olive oil
1 can minced clams with juice
1 can white clam sauce
Salt and pepper to taste
Flavored bread crumbs
Grated Parmesan cheese
Paprika

Saute onions in butter and olive oil. Combine onions, clams, clam sauce, salt and pepper in a large bowl. Add equal amounts of bread crumbs and Parmesan cheese until mixture is firm but moist. Spoon into clam shells; sprinkle with paprika. Bake at 350 degrees for 15 minutes.

Rosemarie Vorburger
Preceptor Mu XP922
Huntington, New York

MAINE-STUFFED CLAMS

1 sm. onion, grated
2 cans minced clams
3 c. saltine cracker crumbs
1/2 c. melted butter
1 tbsp. Worcestershire sauce
2 tbsp. Sauterne
1/2 tsp. Tabasco sauce
Freshly ground pepper to taste

Combine all ingredients; mix well. Place in scallop shells. Dot with additional butter. Place on cookie sheet. Bake at 350 degrees for 30 minutes or until brown. May use 1 pint fresh clams and grind, if desired.

Ann Marie Therrien, Prog, Chm.
Preceptor Mu XP1617
Springvale, Maine

CRAB QUICHE

1 stick or 1/2 pkg. pie crust mix
4 eggs
2 c. light cream
1/3 c. minced onion
1 tsp. salt
1/8 tsp. cayenne pepper
1 7 1/2-oz. can crab meat, drained and
    cartilage removed
1 c. shredded Swiss or mozzarella
    cheese
Snipped parsley to taste

Prepare pastry for one 9-inch pie crust according to package directions. Beat eggs until blended; stir in cream, onion, salt and cayenne pepper. Pat crab meat dry with paper towels; sprinkle crab meat and cheese in pastry-lined pie pan or quiche pan. Pour egg mixture over top. Sprinkle with parsley. Bake in preheated 425-degree oven for 15 minutes. Reduce oven temperature to 300 degrees. Bake for 30 minutes longer or until knife inserted 1 inch from edge comes out clean. Let stand for 10 minutes before cutting into wedges to serve.

Olivia Brand
Xi Beta Lambda Chap.
Chambersburg, Pennsylvania

CRAB SAINT JACQUES (FRANCE)

1/4 c. chopped onion
1 4-oz. can chopped mushrooms
4 tbsp. butter
1 can cream of chicken soup
1/2 c. dry vermouth
1/2 tsp. minced parsley
1 7-oz. can crab meat, flaked
2 tbsp. shredded Swiss cheese
2 tbsp. Parmesan cheese
1/3 c. bread crumbs

Brown onion and mushrooms in 3 tablespoons butter. Remove from heat. Combine soup and vermouth; bring to a boil. Add half the sauce to onion mixture. Spoon equally into 4 buttered baking seashells or 6 ramekins. Top with parsley and crab meat. Spoon on remaining sauce. Combine cheeses and bread crumbs; sprinkle over tops. Drizzle remaining 1 tablespoon melted butter over tops. Bake in preheated 450-degree oven for 10 minutes or until browned.

Charlene Giesinger, Ext. Off.
Alpha Rho No. 3057
Chesapeake, Virginia

CANADIAN LOBSTER PIE

2 c. chopped lobster
Melted butter
2 tbsp. flour

1 1/2 c. light cream
Salt and pepper to taste
4 egg yolks, well beaten
Pastry for 1-crust pie

Saute lobster in 1/4 cup melted butter until heated through. Melt 6 tablespoons butter in saucepan; stir in flour until smooth. Add cream, salt and pepper; cook, stirring constantly, until smooth and thickened. Stir small amount hot mixture into egg yolks, then stir back into sauce. Add lobster; turn into casserole. Cover with pie crust. Bake at 375 degrees until crust is browned.

Elizabeth O'Rourke
Xi Delta Kappa X4321
Kemptville, Ontario, Canada

OYSTERS LINGUINI

2 tbsp. minced garlic
1 1/2 c. chopped green onions
3 tbsp. olive oil
1   15-oz. can peeled crushed
    tomatoes
2 tbsp. sugar
2 tsp. salt
1 tsp. pepper
2 doz. oysters
1 c. oyster liquid
12 oz. cooked linguini
12 oz. grated Cheddar cheese

Saute garlic and green onions in olive oil; add tomatoes. Simmer for 15 minutes. Add 2 tomato cans water, sugar, salt and pepper; simmer for 1 hour. Add oysters and oyster liquid; simmer for 1 hour longer. Arrange alternate layers of linguini, oyster mixture and cheese in casserole, ending with remaining cheese. Bake at 400 degrees for 30 minutes. Yield: 6 servings.

Francesca B. Cusimano, Rec. Sec.
Beta Alpha No. 9023
New Orleans, Louisiana

SHRIMP ENCHILADAS (MEXICO)
ENCHILADAS CON CAMARONES

1/4 c. cooking oil
2 lb. small shrimp, shelled and
    deveined
1/2 c. thinly sliced onions
1 green pepper, cut in thin slices
1   8-oz. can tomato sauce
1 clove of garlic, minced
Salt and pepper to taste
12 tortillas

Heat oil in large skillet. Saute shrimp, onions and pepper for 5 minutes, stirring frequently. Drain off excess oil. Add tomato sauce and garlic. Season with salt and pepper. Cook just until heated through. Fry tortillas according to package directions until lightly browned

and tender. Spoon shrimp mixture in center of each tortilla; roll up. Arrange in serving dish. Spoon remaining sauce over top. Garnish with several whole shrimp. Yield: 6-8 servings.

Photograph for this recipe on page 82.

BATTER-FRIED SHRIMP

2 eggs
1/2 c. milk
1 c. all-purpose flour
1 tsp. baking powder
1 tsp. salt
2 tsp. cooking oil
2 lb. fresh or frozen whole shrimp
Oil or shortening for frying
Orange Sauce
Grape-Horseradish Sauce
Plum Hot

Beat eggs and milk together until frothy. Sift flour, baking powder and salt together. Add to egg mixture. Add oil; beat until mixture is smooth and well blended. Set aside. Remove shells from shrimp, leaving tails. Cut partway through lengthwise along outside curve. Lift out vein. Wash shrimp and flatten to stay open. Drain well on paper towels. Place enough oil to more than cover shrimp in a deep-fat fryer or kettle. Heat to 375 degrees. Dip shrimp into batter, one at a time. Fry, several at a time, for about 4 minutes or until golden brown and puffy. Drain on paper towels. Serve immediately with Orange Sauce, Grape-Horseradish Sauce or Plum Hot.

Orange Sauce

1 c. sweet orange marmalade
1 clove of garlic
1 piece of whole gingerroot or
    1/2 tsp. ground ginger

Combine all ingredients in a saucepan; cook over low heat, stirring constantly, until mixture bubbles. Remove garlic and gingerroot. Yield: 1 cup.

Grape-Horseradish Sauce

1 c. grape jelly
1 tbsp. prepared horseradish
1/4 c. catsup

Combine all ingredients. Yield: 1 cup.

Plum Hot

1 c. plum preserves
1 or 2 cloves of garlic, finely
    minced
2 tsp. soy sauce
1/4 tsp. pepper

Combine all ingredients in a saucepan. Cook over low heat, stirring occasionally, for at least 5 minutes or until garlic is cooked. Remove from heat; cool slightly. Yield: 1 cup.

Photograph for this recipe on page 35.

SPECIAL COQUILLES SAINT JACQUES (FRANCE)

1 1/2 lb. scallops
2 sprigs of fresh thyme or 1/2 tsp. dried thyme
1 bay leaf
1 sprig of parsley
8 peppercorns
Salt to taste
1/2 c. dry white wine
7 tbsp. butter
3 tbsp. flour
2 egg yolks, lightly beaten
1 tsp. lemon juice
Cayenne pepper to taste
Parmesan cheese to taste

Combine first 7 ingredients and 1/2 cup water; bring to a boil. Cover; simmer for 2 minutes. Strain off liquid and reserve. Let scallops cool; cut into small pieces. Melt 2 tablespoons butter; stir in flour until blended. Add reserved scallop liquid, stirring vigorously. Remove sauce from heat; beat with an electric beater, adding remaining butter slowly. Beat in egg yolks, lemon juice and cayenne pepper. Continue beating until cool. Spoon small amount of sauce mixture into 12 to 16 small scallop shells or 6 to 8 large shells. Top with scallops. Cover with remaining sauce; sprinkle with Parmesan cheese. Bake in preheated 400-degree oven for 5 to 10 minutes or until golden brown.

Cathy Nash, V.P.
Beta Beta No. 9632
Sparks, Nevada

PRAWNS AND PINEAPPLE (SOUTH SEAS)

1 1/2 lb. fresh prawns
1/4 c. Sherry
Soy sauce
1 tbsp. lemon juice
1/2 tsp. ginger
1 tsp. dry mustard
3/4 c. sifted flour
Salt
1/4 tsp. baking powder
1 egg
Peanut or sesame oil
1   1-lb. 4-oz. can pineapple slices
1/3 c. (packed) brown sugar
1/3 c. vinegar
1/2 tsp. monosodium glutamate
1 tbsp. cornstarch
2 tbsp. chopped onion

Shell and devein prawns, leaving on tails. Butterfly prawns by splitting along back curve cutting almost to inner edge; open and press flat. Combine with Sherry, 1/4 cup soy sauce, lemon juice, ginger and mustard; cover. Refrigerate for several hours, turning 2 or 3 times in marinade. Drain well. Combine sifted flour, 1/2 teaspoon salt, baking powder, egg and 3/4 cup water; beat until smooth. Hold prawn by tail, then dip in batter, draining off excess batter. Drop several at a time in 2 or 3 inches of hot oil. Fry, turning until golden brown. Lift out; drain on absorbent paper. Keep hot until all are cooked. Drain pineapple, reserving juice. Combine reserved juice with brown sugar, vinegar, 1 tablespoon soy sauce, monosodium glutamate, 1/8 teaspoon salt and cornstarch until smooth. Heat, stirring, until sauce boils and thickens. Add halved pineapple slices and onion. Heat for 5 minutes. Combine prawns with hot pineapple sweet-sour sauce.

Photograph for this recipe on page 61.

BATTER-FRIED SHRIMP WITH PINEAPPLE (CHINA) PO LOHO

1 c. sifted flour
1 tsp. baking powder
1 1/2 tsp. salt
1 egg, beaten
1/2 c. beer
1 lb. shrimp, shelled and deveined
Cooking oil
1 tbsp. cornstarch
1 tbsp. sugar
1/4 c. vinegar
1/2 c. pineapple juice
1 c. drained pineapple chunks

Sift flour, baking powder and 1/2 teaspoon salt into a bowl. Beat in egg and beer. Dip shrimp in batter, coating well. Heat oil to 370 degrees; fry shrimp until browned. Drain and keep warm. Combine cornstarch, sugar and remaining salt with vinegar; add pineapple juice. Cook over low heat, stirring constantly, until thickened. Arrange shrimp and pineapple on a dish; pour sauce over all. Serve with cooked rice. Yield: 4-6 servings.

A. J. May Kobold
Epsilon Gamma Chap.
Sierra Vista, Arizona

SHRIMP EGG ROLLS

1 c. sifted flour
3 eggs
2 c. minced cooked shrimp
1 c. finely chopped celery
1/4 c. minced bamboo shoots
1/4 c. minced water chestnuts
1 tbsp. finely chopped onion
1 qt. corn oil
1/2 tsp. salt
1/4 tsp. Accent

Combine flour, 1 cup water and 2 eggs. Beat at low speed of electric mixer for 5 minutes. Set aside for at least 15 minutes. Mix shrimp, celery, bamboo shoots, water chestnuts, onion, 2 tablespoons corn oil and seasonings thoroughly. Heat heavy 6-inch skillet until drop of water will sizzle. Grease lightly with corn oil before cooking each skin. Hold skillet off heat; pour 2 to 3 tablespoons batter into pan, moving and tilting pan while pouring. Pour excess back into bowl of bat-

ter; return skillet to heat. Batter will set very quickly. Cook just until set and edge curls slightly. Turn out onto dry dish towel until ready to roll. Place about 2 tablespoons filling in center of each skin; brush edge with beaten egg. Fold nearest edge over filling; fold over sides about 1 inch. Roll skin; seal with beaten egg. Pour enough of remaining corn oil into deep fryer or skillet to fill 1/3 full. Heat over medium heat to 375 degrees or until 1-inch square cube of bread turns brown in 10 seconds. Add several egg rolls slowly; fry until lightly browned on all sides, turning as needed. Drain on absorbent paper. Repeat with remaining rolls. Yield: 15 egg rolls.

Linda Epperson, Treas.
Epsilon Theta No. 7638
Brevard, North Carolina

SCAMPI A LA CREME (ENGLAND)

1/4 c. butter or margarine
1/2 lb. fresh mushrooms, chopped
1 1/2 lb. scampi, peeled and deveined
3 tbsp. minced parsley
2 tbsp. flour
1 8-oz. carton sour cream
1/4 c. dry white wine
2 tbsp. rum
Juice of 1/4 lemon
1/2 tsp. salt
1/4 tsp. pepper
1/4 c. (about) Cognac

Melt butter in large frypan; saute mushrooms and scampi with parsley until mushrooms are tender and scampi is pink. Add flour to sour cream; add to scampi mixture. Stir until smooth and hot over low heat. Add wine, rum, lemon, salt and pepper. Simmer for about 3 to 5 minutes. Add Cognac and ignite. Serve over rice. Yield: 3-4 servings.

Betty Hagen
Upsilon Gamma No. 5378
Houston, Texas

SCAMPI GRILLETTATO

24 lg. scampi, peeled and deveined
1/2 c. finely chopped onions
2 cloves of garlic, finely chopped
1/4 c. olive oil
1/4 c. melted butter
Salt to taste
1/2 tsp. cracked pepper
1/2 tsp. dried parsley
Juice of 2 lemons
1/4 c. dry bread crumbs

Boil scampi for 5 minutes. Saute onions and garlic in olive oil and butter. Add salt, pepper, parsley and lemon juice. Remove scampi from boiling water; add to sauteed mixture. Cook, stirring constantly, for

about 2 minutes. Add bread crumbs; toss until liquid has been absorbed.

Sara Pitcher, Serv. Chm,
Preceptor Alpha Mu XP470
San Jose, California

SHRIMP AMANDINE

1 1/2 c. diagonally sliced carrots
2 tbsp. salad oil
1 tbsp. minced onion
1 9-oz. package frozen French-cut green beans
1 10-oz. package frozen cauliflower, thinly sliced
1 8-oz. can water chestnuts, thinly sliced
1 12-oz. package frozen shrimp
2 tbsp. soy sauce
2 tsp. chicken stock base
2 tsp. cornstarch
1/2 tsp. garlic powder
1 2-oz. package sliced unsalted almonds, browned

Stir-fry carrots in hot salad oil in large skillet or wok for 3 minutes. Add onion, green beans, cauliflower and water chestnuts. Cook for 2 minutes longer. Saute shrimp in 1 tablespoon soy sauce; add to vegetables. Combine 1 cup water, chicken stock base, cornstarch, garlic powder and remaining soy sauce; stir into shrimp mixture. Cook, stirring, until mixture thickens and vegetables are crisp tender. Sprinkle with almonds. Serve with steamed or fried rice.

Marjorie Gilbertson, Pres.
Nu Omicron No. 8681
Rock Port, Missouri

SHRIMP CANTONESE DELIGHT

3/4 lb. shrimp
2 tbsp. butter or margarine
2 c. sliced onion
2 c. diagonally sliced celery
1/2 lb. spinach leaves
1 16-oz. can Chinese vegetables, drained
1/4 c. soy sauce
1/4 tsp. pepper
1 1/4 c. chicken broth
2 tbsp. cornstarch

Saute shrimp in butter in large skillet for 1 minute or until shrimp are pink. Add onion and celery. Cook, stirring, for 2 minutes. Add spinach and Chinese vegetables. Cover; cook for 1 minute. Blend soy sauce, pepper, chicken broth and cornstarch together; stir into skillet. Cook, stirring, for about 2 minutes or until sauce is clear and thickened. Serve over rice.

Cherie Shallock, Corr. Sec.
Xi Iota Nu X4770
Bolingbrook, Illinois

Poultry

Cooks the world over have been so inspired by the delicate flavor of poultry
that many cultures have had to create strict dietary laws limiting its use.
Some foods are markedly regional — such as lamb in the Middle East or rice
in the Orient — but not so with poultry. It is used as commonly in the Orient
as it is in South America or Israel, and most food fanciers would agree that it
is responsible for more imaginative cooking than almost any other food.
Wildfowl were probably the earliest popular poultry because they were abun-
dantly available without domestication. However, archeological study shows
us that the turkey had already been domesticated in South America in pre-
historic times — then its popularity spread to Europe, the Middle East and
India by Medieval times. By 200 B.C., chicken was a mainstay in the Chinese
diet, just as it is today, as well as in India where the cow is sacred, the pig
considered unclean, and sheep not suited to the climate. Because chickens
are also highly valued for their eggs, they were often not eaten until their
laying capabilities were over. These, of course, were not the young, tender
chickens the world is familiar with today, which is probably why most classic poultry dishes, both plain and fancy, call for long cooking in a liquid.
Today, however, this has changed, and we roast, grill and broil poultry to
enjoy its truly melt-in-the-mouth texture.

Game birds and wildfowl are still prized where they are abundant for their
delicate, yet savory meat. Like classic poultry recipes, those for game birds
and wildfowl usually call for long, moist cooking. Interestingly enough, in
Medieveal Europe, it was customary to enclose four and twenty blackbirds in
a pastry shell, to be baked quickly so that they would fly out as the pie was
sliced. The Canadian, English, and European cuisines have produced the
most memorable recipes for wild birds, while the most popular waterfowl
dishes were developed in China and South America.

Smart Beta Sigma Phi homemakers have found that a poultry dish is almost
always the cook's wisest choice — everyone likes poultry, which can include
anything from the dependable chicken to the extraordinary pheasant.
Chicken and other poultry favorites are always an excellent buy; wildfowl is
even thriftier if there is a hunter in the house. With a world of poultry dishes
here at your fingertips, there is every reason to depend on them more and
more in your meal planning.

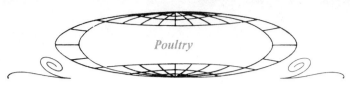

TANDOORI CHICKEN

1 tbsp. paprika
1 tsp. coriander
1/2 tsp. ground cardamom
1/2 tsp. salt
1/2 tsp. onion powder
1/4 tsp. garlic powder
1/4 tsp. cayenne pepper
1/4 tsp. ground cinnamon
1/8 tsp. chili powder
Dash of turmeric
1 tbsp. lemon juice
2 tbsp. corn oil
1 2 1/2-lb. broiler, halved

Mix first 10 ingredients together; stir in 2 tablespoons water and lemon juice. Add corn oil. Brush mixture on all sides of chicken; cover. Refrigerate for about 4 hours. Place chicken, skin side down, on rack in broiler pan. Broil 4 inches from source of heat for 15 to 20 minutes. Turn chicken, skin side up. Broil for about 15 minutes or until chicken is fork-tender and browned. Yield: 4 servings.

Photograph for this recipe on page 2.

INTERNATIONAL DATE-LINE CHICKEN

1/4 c. butter or margarine
3 lg. chicken breasts, skinned and halved
1 can chicken broth
1 tbsp. minced onion
1 tsp. salt
1/2 tsp. curry powder
1/8 tsp. pepper
1 can mandarin oranges
2 tbsp. cornstarch
1 tsp. lemon juice
1 c. thinly sliced green pepper
1 c. pitted dates, halved

Melt butter in large skillet; cook chicken slowly until golden brown. Combine chicken broth, onion, salt, curry powder and pepper; pour over chicken. Cover; simmer for 45 minutes or until done. Remove chicken to warm serving platter. Drain oranges, reserving syrup. Combine syrup, cornstarch and lemon juice; stir into pan juices. Cook, stirring constantly, until thickened. Add green pepper slices and dates; simmer for 3 to 4 minutes longer. Add orange segments; heat through. Serve hot over chicken breasts. Yield: 6 servings.

Virginia Docking
Honorary Member
Topeka, Kansas

SPANISH ARROZ CON POLLO

1 2 1/2 to 3-lb. chicken, disjointed
Seasoned flour
1/3 c. vegetable oil

1 med. onion, chopped
1 clove of garlic, minced
1 c. rice
Pinch of saffron
3 1/2 to 4 c. stewed tomatoes
1 green pepper, chopped
1 tsp. salt

Dredge chicken with seasoned flour; brown in hot oil. Arrange in 3-quart casserole. Saute onion and garlic until soft in remaining oil in frypan. Add to chicken. Sprinkle rice and saffron around chicken. Pour tomatoes over top. Add green pepper and salt. Cover tightly. Bake at 350 degrees for 1 hour. Yield: 4-6 servings.

M. Helen Maffuid, Rec. Sec.
Xi Beta Theta X2353
Glens Falls, New York

CHICKEN WITH BAMBOO SHOOTS (CHINA)

4 chicken breasts, cut in bite-sized pieces
2 tbsp. soy sauce
1 tbsp. cornstarch
1/8 tsp. sugar
6 tbsp. peanut oil
1 sm. sweet green pepper, chopped
1 sm. sweet red pepper, chopped
1/2 c. bamboo shoots, minced

Combine chicken, 1 tablespoon soy sauce, cornstarch and sugar; mix well. Fry chicken mixture in peanut oil for 5 minutes. Remove chicken from pan. Add peppers and bamboo shoots to oil in pan; cook for 2 minutes. Add remaining 1 tablespoon soy sauce; return chicken to pan. Remove from heat. Serve hot with rice.

Sue Ann Knebel
Xi Gamma Phi X2930
Belton, Missouri

CHICKEN BREASTS WITH GREEN CHILIES

1/4 c. butter
1/4 c. peanut oil
6 boned chicken breasts, cut into 3 or 4 pieces
Salt
Pepper to taste
1 lg. onion, thinly sliced
20 to 22 canned whole green chilies
2/3 c. milk
2 c. sour cream
1/4 lb. grated Cheddar cheese

Heat butter and oil in frypan; saute chicken fillets for 2 minutes on one side and 1 minute on other side. Drain on paper towels. Season with salt and pepper. Add onion and 1/2 cup water to pan; bring to a boil. Cook until onion is soft and water has evaporated. Set aside 9 chilies. Cut remaining chilies into strips; add to

onion. Cover; cook over medium heat for 5 minutes. Place 9 reserved chilies, milk and 1/2 teaspoon salt in blender container; blend until smooth. Add sour cream; blend well. Arrange half the chicken in 10 x 13-inch casserole. Cover with half the chilies and onion mixture. Spread with half the sauce. Repeat layers. Sprinkle with cheese. Bake at 350 degrees until bubbling. Yield: 6-8 servings.

Lois Marquardt, Pres.
Preceptor Beta XP246
Laramie, Wyoming

CHICKEN IN CREAM

    1   2 1/2-oz. jar dried beef
    3 lg. boneless chicken breasts or cutlets
    3 slices bacon, halved
    1 can cream of mushroom soup
    1   8-oz. carton sour cream
    3/4 tsp. dried oregano, crushed

Place dried beef in sieve; rinse under cold water to remove excess salt. Dry on paper towel. Shred coarsely; spread in 12 x 8 x 2-inch dish. Pull skin from chicken breasts; cut each breast in half. Place in a single layer over beef in dish. Top each with half slice of bacon. Bake in preheated 350-degree oven for 30 minutes. Combine soup, sour cream and oregano in medium bowl; spoon over chicken. Stir to mix with juices in dish. Bake for 30 minutes longer or until chicken is tender. Yield: 6 servings.

Judy Schiltz, Treas.
Xi Epsilon Upsilon X2721
Moline, Illinois

CHICKEN CUTLET WITH SHRIMP

    4 chicken breast halves
    Garlic salt to taste
    1/4 c. chopped green onions with tops
    1   4 1/2-oz. can shrimp, rinsed and drained
    1/4 c. margarine
    Paprika

Remove skin from chicken. Cut and pull meat away from bones, keeping meat in one piece. Pound between waxed paper to form a thin cutlet, 1/4 inch thick. Sprinkle cutlet with garlic salt. Place equal amounts of onions and shrimp on each cutlet. Divide margarine into fourths, then cut each piece again. Place 2 pats margarine on each cutlet. Roll cutlet up and secure with toothpicks. Sprinkle with paprika. Place in baking dish. Bake at 400 degrees until chicken is done.

Donna Meerdink, Pres.
Eta Mu No. 6595
Muscatine, Iowa

GLAZED CHICKEN (SPAIN)

    1/3 c. pine nuts
    2 tbsp. olive oil
    2/3 c. finely chopped shallots
        or scallions

Pimento-stuffed olives
3 tbsp. chopped parsley
1/2 tsp. grated lemon peel
4 lg. skinned chicken breasts,
    halved and boned
1 c. chicken stock
2 env. unflavored gelatin
1 c. heavy cream
Cooked asparagus tips
3/4 c. mayonnaise

Saute pine nuts in olive oil in large skillet until lightly browned. Add 1/3 cup shallots; saute until tender but not browned. Stir in 1/2 cup chopped olives, chopped parsley and lemon peel. Place each chicken piece between 2 sheets waxed paper; flatten with rolling pin. Place about 1 1/2 tablespoons olive mixture in center of each chicken piece; roll up. Secure with wooden picks. Place in large skillet with remaining 1/3 cup shallots and stock; cover. Simmer for 15 minutes, turning chicken once. Remove chicken; cool. Cover and chill. Boil liquid in skillet until reduced to 1/2 cup. Soften 1 envelope gelatin in cream; add to reduced liquid. Heat until gelatin dissolves. Remove wooden picks from chicken. Place chicken breasts on rack over a tray. Place cream mixture over bowl of ice; stir until consistency of unbeaten egg white. Spoon over chicken. Chill chicken until glaze sets. Repeat glazing and chilling until all glaze is used. Any glaze left in pan under rack may be reheated and chilled to proper consistency for glazing. Soften remaining envelope gelatin in 1/2 cup water. Heat until dissolved; cool. Dip olive slices and parsley sprigs for garnish in clear gelatin; arrange on chicken. Spoon remaining gelatin over chicken breasts; chill. Arrange chicken breasts, asparagus and additional whole olives in lettuce-lined dish. Mix mayonnaise with 1/4 cup chopped olives; serve with chicken.

Photograph for this recipe below.

Poultry

CHICKEN DIVAN

4 whole chicken breasts
2 bunches fresh broccoli, partially cooked
2 cans cream of chicken soup
1 c. mayonnaise
2 tsp. lemon juice
1 tsp. poultry seasoning
3 to 4 tbsp. Sherry (opt.)
1/2 c. bread or cracker crumbs
1/4 c. margarine, melted
1/2 c. grated sharp cheese

Simmer chicken until almost tender. Remove skin and bones. Place broccoli in large shallow casserole; add chicken. Combine next 5 ingredients; spread sauce over top. Combine remaining ingredients; sprinkle over top. Bake at 350 degrees for 30 to 40 minutes or until crumbs are browned. Yield: 8 servings.

Emma R. M. Gilarde
Preceptor Alpha Delta XP811
Daytona Beach, Florida

CHICKEN MARENGO SUPREME

2 lb. boned and skinned chicken breasts
1 clove of garlic, crushed
2 c. chicken stock
4 med. peeled tomatoes, chopped
1/2 c. diced celery
1/2 bay leaf
1 tbsp. chopped parsley
1/2 tsp. mixed herbs
2 tsp. Sherry extract
Salt and pepper to taste
2 c. sliced mushrooms
1 4-oz. jar pearl onions, drained

Cut chicken into 1 1/2-inch pieces. Brown chicken and garlic in nonstick skillet; remove chicken. Add stock, tomatoes, celery and bay leaf. Bring to a boil; simmer for 30 minutes. Add parsley, mixed herbs, Sherry extract, salt and pepper; cook for 5 minutes. Pour sauce into blender container or food processor; process until smooth. Return to skillet. Add more stock if sauce is too thick. Stir in mushrooms and onions. Simmer for 10 minutes. Pour over chicken; serve hot. Yield: 4 servings.

Dawn Tomesello
Alpha Upsilon No. 10137
Buffalo, Wyoming

CHICKEN MARSALA

5 tbsp. butter
8 1/4-in. thick slices chicken breast
1/8 tsp. pepper
8 thin slices prosciutto ham
8 oz. mozzarella cheese, cut into 8 slices
1/2 c. Marsala wine
1/2 c. chopped parsley

Heat butter in large skillet; saute chicken slices in single layer until golden on both sides, adding more butter if needed. Remove chicken; keep warm until all

chicken is browned. Return to skillet; sprinkle with pepper. Place 1 slice proscuitto and 1 slice cheese on each slice of chicken. Pour wine over all; cook for 3 to 5 minutes or until heated through and cheese is melted. Sprinkle with parsley. May serve with rice or buttered noodles.

Carol Ann Vale, Pres.
Lambda Beta No. 9529
Crown Point, Indiana

CHICKEN AND SNOW PEAS (JAPAN)

1/4 c. soy sauce
1 tsp. sugar
3 tbsp. cooking Sherry
2 tsp. cornstarch
1/2 tsp. ground ginger
1 lb. chicken breasts
1/4 c. vegetable oil
1 10-oz. package snow peas
2 tbsp. sliced green onions

Combine soy sauce, sugar, Sherry, cornstarch and ginger. Blend and set aside. Remove skin and bone from chicken; cut into bite-sized pieces. Preheat wok or large pan over high heat for 2 minutes. Add oil; continue heating for 1 minute. Add chicken pieces; stir-fry for 2 minutes or until chicken is white. Push up on side of wok. Add peas and onions; stir-fry for about 3 minutes. Push to side. Add soy sauce mixture to center; boil for 1 to 2 minutes or until thickened. Stir in chicken and peas until well mixed and heated through. Serve over hot rice. Yield: 2-3 servings.

Betsy Grier, Pres.
Gamma Gamma No. 4956
Brookings, Oregon

CHICKEN A LA SUISSE (FRANCE)

6 whole chicken breasts, skinned and boned
6 slices Swiss cheese
6 slices ham or dried beef
3 tbsp. flour
1 tsp. paprika
6 tbsp. butter
1 chicken bouillon cube
1/2 c. dry white wine
1 tbsp. cornstarch
1 c. half and half

Spread chicken breasts flat; fit cheese slice and ham slice over breast. Roll up; fasten with toothpick. Combine flour and paprika; roll breasts in flour mixture. Brown in melted butter. Place breasts in casserole. Dissolve bouillon cube in wine; pour over breasts. Bake at 350 degrees for 1 hour. Remove chicken; place on platter. Blend cornstarch and half and half together until smooth. Add to liquid from casserole.

96

Cook, stirring, until thickened. Spoon over chicken. Garnish with parsley. Yield: 6 servings.

Hazel Breeding, Sec.
Laureate Gamma PL201
Marysville, Kansas

CHICKEN ROSÉ (FRANCE)

2 chicken breasts, skinned and boned
3 tbsp. flour
6 tbsp. Fleischmann's corn oil
    margarine
Rosé wine
3/4 c. sliced mushrooms
2 tbsp. chopped parsley

Dredge chicken with flour. Melt margarine in skillet. Brown chicken quickly on both sides. Cover; reduce heat. Cook until chicken is tender. Pour in enough wine to cover bottom of pan. Add mushrooms and parsley. Simmer for 5 minutes, stirring occasionally. Serve sauce over chicken.

Photograph for this recipe on page 50.

EASY CHICKEN CORDON BLEU (FRANCE)

4 whole chicken breasts
Salt to taste
8 pieces thinly sliced ham
8 slices Swiss cheese
1/2 c. flour
1 egg, beaten
1 c. cracker crumbs
Vegetable oil

Remove skin and bone from chicken; cut in half. Place between 2 pieces of waxed paper, one piece at a time. Pound with rolling pin until well flattened. Remove from paper; sprinkle inside with salt. Place 1 slice ham and 1 slice cheese at one end of each breast; fold breast in half. Secure with a toothpick. Roll chicken in flour, then into egg beaten with 2 tablespoons water. Roll in cracker crumbs. Fry in hot oil, browning well on both sides. Serve immediately.

Lynn Weed, Pres.
Preceptor Alpha Pi XP978
Everett, Washington

CHICKEN PARMIGIANA

4 whole skinned boned chicken breasts
1/3 c. butter
1 egg
1 c. seasoned bread crumbs
1   15 1/2-oz. jar Ragu spaghetti sauce
2 cloves of garlic, minced
1/2 tsp. thyme
1/2 tsp. oregano
1 pkg. mozzarella cheese

5 oz. grated Parmesan cheese
Cooked spaghetti

Cut chicken breasts in half. Rinse in cold water; pat dry. Pound with mallet until 1/4 inch thick. Heat butter in skillet. Beat egg in medium bowl. Dip chicken in egg, then into bread crumbs to coat. Saute chicken in butter until browned. Pour spaghetti sauce over chicken; add garlic, thyme and oregano. Bring to a boil; cover. Reduce heat; simmer for 30 minutes. Place a slice of mozzarella cheese on each piece of chicken; cook for 5 minutes longer. Sprinkle Parmesan cheese on top. Cover; cook until cheese melts. Serve over spaghetti.

Cindy Hummel
Epsilon Gamma No. 10189
Sierra Vista, Arizona

PETER PAN CHICKEN (AFRICA)

3 chicken breasts, split
3 tbsp. butter
1/3 c. chopped scallions or green
    onions
1 lg. tomato, diced
1 1/2 c. chicken broth
3 tbsp. chili sauce
1 tsp. paprika
3/4 tsp. salt
1 bay leaf
1/2 c. smooth peanut butter

Brown chicken in butter in large skillet; drain off fat. Add scallions, tomato, 1 cup chicken broth, chili sauce, paprika, salt and bay leaf. Simmer, covered, for 25 minutes or until chicken is tender. Move chicken to side of pan. Discard bay leaf. Blend peanut butter and remaining broth into pan liquid; cook for 5 minutes longer. Serve with rice. Yield: 6 servings.

Photograph for this recipe below.

JADE CHICKEN

2 lg. chicken breasts
2 c. sliced fresh mushrooms
3 tbsp. light salad oil
1 tbsp. butter
2 c. diagonally sliced celery
1 or 2 bell peppers, cut in chunks
1 13 1/2-oz. can pineapple tidbits
1/2 c. dry white wine
1/4 c. soy sauce
1/2 tsp. ginger
2 tbsp. cornstarch or flour
1/2 c. sliced green onions
1/2 c. chopped cashews

Remove skin and bones from chicken breasts; cut into 1 1/2-inch chunks. Saute mushrooms in oil and butter in large skillet. Add celery and peppers; cook for 2 or 3 minutes, stirring constantly. Add chicken; cook for several minutes or until creamy white. Drain pineapple; reserve juice. Mix reserved juice, wine, soy sauce, ginger and cornstarch together; add to skillet. Cook for 2 to 3 minutes or until sauce thickens. Fold green onions, pineapple and chopped cashews into chicken mixture; heat through. Serve over rice. Yield: 6 servings.

Ann Frick, Treas.
Iota Epsilon No. 7440
Wawaka, Indiana

CLASSIC CHICKEN KIEV

4 lg. boned chicken breasts, skinned and
    halved lengthwise
Salt to taste
1 tbsp. chopped green onion
1 tbsp. snipped parsley
1 stick butter or margarine, chilled
All-purpose flour
1 or 2 eggs, beaten
1/2 to 1 c. fine bread crumbs

Place chicken pieces, boned side up, between 2 pieces of clear plastic wrap. Work out from center, pounding to form cutlets not quite 1/4 inch thick. Peel off wrap; sprinkle with salt, onion and parsley. Cut butter into 8 pieces; place 1 piece at end of each cutlet. Roll as for jelly roll, tucking in sides. Press end to seal well. Coat each roll with flour; dip in mixture of 1 tablespoon water and eggs. Roll in bread crumbs. Chill in refrigerator for at least 1 hour. Fry rolls in deep fat at 375 degrees for about 5 minutes or until golden brown.

Cynthia King
Sigma Lambda No. 10163
Inverness, Florida
Joy Brown, Rec. Sec.
Delta Rho No. 6525
Rome, Georgia

CRAB-STUFFED CHICKEN KIEV

4 lg. boned chicken breasts, skinned and halved
4 tbsp. butter or margarine

1/4 c. all-purpose flour
3/4 c. milk
3/4 c. chicken broth
1/3 c. dry white wine
1/4 c. chopped onion
1 7 1/2-oz. can crab meat, drained and flaked
1 3-oz. can chopped mushrooms, drained
1/2 c. coarsely crumbled saltine cracker crumbs
2 tbsp. snipped parsley
1/2 tsp. salt
Dash of pepper
1 c. shredded Swiss cheese
1/2 tsp. paprika

Place one piece chicken, boned side up, between 2 pieces waxed paper. Working from center out, pound meat lightly with meat mallet to make 8 x 5-inch cutlet, 1/8 inch thick. Repeat with remaining chicken; set aside. Melt 3 tablespoons butter in saucepan; blend in flour. Add milk, chicken broth and wine all at once; cook, stirring until mixture thickens and bubbles. Set aside. Cook onions in remaining tablespoon butter until tender but not brown. Stir in crab, mushrooms, cracker crumbs, parsley, salt and pepper. Stir in 2 tablespoons wine sauce. Top each chicken piece with 1/4 cup crab mixture. Fold sides in; roll up. Place, seam side down, in 12 x 7 1/2 x 2-inch baking dish. Pour remaining wine sauce over all. Bake, covered, in 350-degree oven for 1 hour or until chicken is tender. Uncover; sprinkle with cheese and paprika. Bake for 2 minutes longer or until cheese melts. Yield: 8 servings.

Marilyn Harder, V.P.
Xi Beta Psi X2856
Palouse, Washington

ROLLED CHICKEN WASHINGTON

1/2 c. finely chopped mushrooms
2 tbsp. butter or margarine
2 tbsp. flour
1/2 c. light cream
Salt
Dash of cayenne pepper
1 1/4 c. shredded sharp Cheddar cheese
8 chicken breast halves, boned and skinned
2 eggs, slightly beaten
Milk
3/4 c. bread crumbs

Cook mushrooms in butter for 5 minutes; blend in flour. Stir in cream; add 1/4 teaspoon salt and pepper. Cook, stirring until thickened. Stir in cheese; cook until cheese melts. Turn into pie plate; chill. Cut into short sticks. Pound chicken to flatten; sprinkle with salt. Place cheese stick on each piece of chicken; tuck in sides. Roll as for jelly roll, pressing well to seal. Combine eggs and small amount of milk. Dip chicken rolls in eggs; roll in bread crumbs. Chill for at least 1 hour or overnight. Place in shallow baking dish. Bake at 250 degrees for 1 hour and 30 minutes to 2 hours.

Janie McCord, Pres.
Gamma Lambda No. 2552
Mexico, Missouri

CHICKEN IN WHITE WINE
COQ AU VIN BLANC

5 lb. chicken breasts
1/4 c. flour
2 tsp. salt
1/2 tsp. freshly ground pepper
1/4 c. oil
3/4 c. chopped onion
1/2 c. grated carrot
2 cloves of garlic, minced
2 tsp. finely chopped bay leaves
3 tsp. minced parsley
1/4 tsp. thyme
3 c. dry white wine
2 whole cloves
18 sm. white onions
3/4 lb. mushrooms, sliced
3 tbsp. butter

Dip chicken in mixture of flour, salt and pepper. Heat oil in deep skillet; brown chicken. Add chopped onion, carrot and garlic; cook for 10 minutes, stirring frequently. Add bay leaves, parsley, thyme and wine. Bring to a boil; cook over medium heat for 10 minutes. Insert cloves in 2 of the onions. Saute mushrooms and all onions in butter. Add mushrooms and onions to chicken mixture; cover. Cook over low heat for 20 minutes or until chicken is tender.

Janet M. Cornwall, Soc. Com.
Eta Iota Chap.
Burlington, Ontario, Canada

SPICY FRUITED CHICKEN

2 lb. chicken breasts and legs
1 tbsp. flour
1 8 3/4-oz. can fruit cocktail
1/2 c. chicken consomme
1/8 tsp. salt
1/4. tsp. turmeric
1/8 tsp. dry mustard
1/8 tsp. ground mace
1/8 tsp. ground cardamom
1/8 tsp. ground ginger

Dust chicken with flour; place chicken and fruit cocktail in 1 1/2-quart baking dish. Combine consomme, salt and spices; pour over chicken. Cover with foil. Bake in preheated 350-degree oven for 1 hour or until tender. Serve over rice. Yield: 6 servings.

Judith O'Neil, Rec. Sec.
Nu No. 5860
Keene, New Hampshire

CHICKEN CASSEROLE WITH
OLIVE SAUCE

1 chicken, disjointed
6 tbsp. butter
1 tsp. paprika
1/8 tsp. pepper
1/2 tsp. salt
1 sm. jar sliced mushrooms

1 tbsp. flour
1/2 c. evaporated milk
1 can cream mushroom soup
3/4 c. sliced olives

Brown chicken in butter in large frying pan. Arrange chicken in 2-quart buttered casserole. Sprinkle with paprika, pepper and salt. Cook mushrooms in pan drippings until lightly browned. Stir in flour. Add milk, soup and 1 cup water; cook, stirring, until heated through. Add olives. Pour over chicken. Bake, covered, at 350 degrees for 35 minutes or until chicken is tender. Uncover; bake for 15 minutes longer. Serve over rice.

Debbie Alewine, V.P.
Phi Alpha Zeta P2780
Rock Hill, South Carolina

CHICKEN LIVERS PAGLIACCI (ITALY)

1 packet chicken broth or golden seasoning
  and broth mix
1 lb. chicken livers, cut in thirds
1 c. sliced mushrooms
1 tbsp. Worcestershire sauce
1 tsp. salt
1/2 tsp. pepper
1/2 clove of garlic, minced
2 c. buttered cauliflower or creamed potatoes

Combine chicken broth mix and 1 cup boiling water; stir until broth is dissolved. Brown chicken livers on all sides over moderate heat in nonstick skillet. Reduce heat to low; add mushrooms, chicken broth, Worcestershire sauce, salt, pepper and garlic. Cook over low heat for 10 minutes or until livers are done. Serve over cauliflower or potatoes. Garnish with parsley. Yield: 2 servings.

Loyce Coleman
Xi Zeta Omega X2123
Nederland, Texas

CHICKEN MOLE

1 2 1/2-lb. fryer, disjointed
Oil
1 onion, chopped
1 green pepper, chopped
1 garlic clove, minced
2 8-oz. cans tomato sauce
1 to 2 tsp. chili powder
1 tsp. salt
1/4 tsp. Tabasco sauce
2 whole cloves
1/2 oz. unsweetened chocolate
1 jar sm. cooked onions

Coat chicken pieces with oil; brown in skillet. Remove chicken. Add onion, green pepper and garlic; cook for 3 minutes. Add tomato sauce, chili powder, salt, Tabasco sauce, cloves and chocolate; stir to melt chocolate. Return chicken to skillet; cover. Simmer for 30 minutes. Garnish with onions. Yield: 4 servings.

Myra Mauterer, Past Pres.
Xi Alpha Lambda X374
Eldorado, Illinois

CHICKEN IN ORANGE-ALMOND SAUCE (SOUTH AFRICA)

1 fryer, disjointed
Salt
6 tbsp. butter
1/4 c. flour
Pinch of cinnamon and ginger
1 1/2 c. orange juice
2 oz. blanched sliced almonds
2 oz. seedless raisins
2 oranges, peeled and sectioned

Remove skin and bones from chicken; sprinkle with 1/4 teaspoon salt. Melt butter in pan; brown chicken lightly. Remove from pan. Combine flour, a pinch of salt, cinnamon and ginger; blend into butter to make a smooth paste. Add orange juice. Cook, stirring constantly, until sauce bubbles and begins to thicken. Return chicken to pan; add almonds and raisins. Cover; cook over low heat for 30 minutes or until chicken is tender. Add orange segments; heat through. Yield: 4 servings.

Margaret Thomas
Pi No. 2725
North Vancouver, British Columbia, Canada

CHICKEN ORIENTAL

4 c. cooked cubed chicken
2 lg. cans chow mein noodles
2 cans cream of mushroom soup
3/4 c. cashews
1 tbsp. soy sauce

Combine all ingredients; spread in buttered 9 x 13-inch pan. Add small amount water if mixture seems dry. Bake at 350 degrees for 30 minutes.

Pamela Hartman
Theta No. 10367
Mystic, Connecticut

CHICKEN IN PIQUANT SAUCE

1 fryer, disjointed or 8 pieces of chicken
1 pkg. onion soup mix
1 bottle red Russian dressing
1 sm. jar apricot preserves

Place chicken pieces in shallow casserole. Sprinkle onion soup mix over chicken. Pour dressing over all. Top with preserves. Bake in 350-degree oven for 1 hour and 30 minutes.

Llvene Gement, Treas.
Xi Alpha Beta X4724
Greenwood, Mississippi

CHICKEN SAUTE

3 tbsp. margarine
1/4 c. flour
2 tsp. salt
1/4 tsp. pepper
1/4 tsp. thyme
1   2 to 2 1/2-lb. frying chicken, disjointed
4 green onions, chopped
1/4 lb. mushrooms, sliced
1/2 c. Sherry
2 med. tomatoes, diced

Heat margarine in heavy skillet; mix flour, salt, pepper and thyme in paper bag. Coat chicken in flour mixture; brown thoroughly in margarine in skillet. Add onions and mushrooms. Cover; simmer for 3 minutes. Pour Sherry over chicken; simmer for 5 minutes. Sprinkle tomatoes over chicken; cook for 1 hour over low heat. Serve hot.

Pat Hudsonpillar, V.P.
Tau Eta No. 5242
Edinburg, Texas

CHICKEN WITH SQUASH (MEXICO) POLLO CON CALABAZAS

1 fryer, disjointed
1 tbsp. shortening
2 med. squash, cubed
4 ears of corn, quartered
2 cloves of garlic, minced
1 tsp. salt
1 tsp. pepper
1   12-oz. can whole kernel corn

Fry chicken in shortening until brown; add squash. Add ears of corn, garlic, salt and pepper. Cook until soft and tender. Add whole kernal corn; heat for 5 minutes.

Mrs. Bonnie Brown
Alpha Rho Sigma No. 10525
Raymondville, Texas

CHICKEN-TORTILLA PIE

1   3-lb. chicken, cooked
2 sm. onions, diced
1 sm. can Ortega green chilies, chopped
1/2 c. margarine
1 can cream of chicken soup
1 can cream of mushroom soup
1 can evaporated milk
1 c. chicken broth
1 sm. can olives, diced
12 corn tortillas, torn into bite-sized pieces
1 lb. sharp Cheddar cheese, grated

Bone and cut chicken into bite-sized chunks. Brown onions and chilies in margarine; add soups and milk. Simmer for about 10 minutes, stirring frequently. Combine all ingredients in large bowl; mix well. Turn into baking dish. Bake at 350 degrees for 45 minutes. Yield: 10 to 12 servings.

Barbara Hanson, Jr. Past Pres., W. and M. Com.
Xi Xi Beta X3186
Lakewood, California

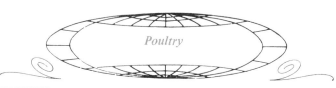

Poultry

CHICKEN VOL-AU-VENTS

6 chicken thighs
2 tbsp. margarine
1 chicken bouillon cube
3 tbsp. flour
1/4 tsp. salt
1/4 tsp. paprika
Pepper to taste
1 c. light cream
1 6-oz. can sliced mushrooms, drained
1/4 c. dry white wine
6 brown and serve sausages
1 10-oz. package frozen patty shells, thawed

Brown chicken on both sides in margarine in medium skillet. Dissolve bouillon cube in 1/2 cup hot water; add to chicken. Cover; simmer for 20 to 30 minutes or until tender. Remove chicken from broth. Cool; remove bones carefully. Measure broth from skillet; add enough water to equal 1 cup liquid. Return to skillet. Combine flour, salt, paprika and pepper; stir in cream. Add to chicken broth; cook, stirring constantly, until mixture thickens and bubbles. Stir in mushrooms and wine. Place a sausage in bone cavity of each thigh. Roll each thawed patty shell to a 6-inch square on lightly floured surface. Place stuffed thigh in center of each square. Top with 2 tablespoons mushroom sauce. Fold pastry over; seal center seam. Fold ends to center; seal. Place, seam side down, in 13 1/2 x 8 3/4 x 1 3/4-inch baking dish. Brush with additional cream. Bake at 400 degrees for 30 minutes or until golden brown. Heat remaining sauce; serve with vol-au-vents.

Margaret Pritchard, Pres.
Xi Pi X412
Fresno, California

EASY CHICKEN SKILLET

1 can cream of chicken soup
1 can cream of celery soup
1 soup can water
1 1/3 c. instant rice
1 12-oz. can chicken or 1 1/2 c. cooked chicken
1 3-oz. can chow mein noodles

Combine all ingredients except noodles in a large skillet; stir to mix. Bring quickly to a boil; cover. Reduce heat; simmer for 7 minutes. Remove from heat; stir. Serve with noodles. Yield: 4-6 servings.

Mrs. Ann L. Shetler
Mu Phi No. 6053
Brewster, Ohio

CHINESE PINEAPPLE-CHICKEN

2 lb. chicken thighs, breasts or wings
2 eggs, beaten
1 c. flour
Vegetable oil
3/4 c. sugar
1/4 c. pineapple juice
1/2 c. vinegar
1 tsp. Accent
1/2 tsp. salt
3/4 c. catsup
1 tsp. soy sauce
Pineapple chunks

Dip chicken in egg, then flour. Brown in oil; place in baking dish. Combine remaining ingredients except pineapple chunks; spoon over chicken. Place pineapple chunks on top. Bake at 350 degrees for 1 hour.

Debbie Linder, Sec.
Gamma Alpha Chap.
Astoria, Oregon

CHINESE-FRIED CHICKEN WITH WALNUTS

1 lb. boneless chicken or cubed chicken fillets
1 egg white
2 tbsp. cornstarch
2 c. walnuts
Oil for frying
6 tbsp. peanut oil
2 slices ginger
1 tbsp. wine
1 tsp. sugar
2 tbsp. soy sauce

Cut chicken into 1/2-inch cubes; mix with unbeaten egg white and 1 tablespoon cornstarch. Blanch walnuts in boiling water for 15 minutes; drain immediately. Skins will come off easily. Heat oil for frying; fry walnuts until light brown. Walnuts burn easily so must be removed from oil as soon as color changes. Heat peanut oil; add ginger and chicken cubes. Fry for several minutes or until chicken is lightly browned. Add wine, sugar and soy sauce. Fry for several minutes longer. Combine remaining 1 tablespoon cornstarch with 1 tablespoon water; stir into chicken mixture. Cook, stirring, until thickened.

Barbara Jean Wong, V.P.
Xi Beta Zeta Chap.
San Francisco, California

FRIED CHICKEN DRUMSTICKS (THAILAND)

8 chicken drumsticks
1 tsp. garlic salt
1/2 tsp. pepper
1 tbsp. soy sauce
Vegetable oil
1/2 c. flour
1 tbsp. coarsely chopped green onion

Marinate drumsticks with garlic salt, pepper, soy sauce and 1 tablespoon oil for 2 hours. Dredge drumsticks with flour. Fry 4 drumsticks at a time in 2 cups hot oil for 3 minutes and 30 seconds. Drain thoroughly on paper towels. Garnish with green onion.

Beth Veohonqs
Kappa Delta No. 4660
Flora, Illinois

101

GREEK-STYLE STEWED CHICKEN – KAPAMA

1 lg. chicken, disjointed
Juice of 1/2 lemon
2 tsp. cinnamon
Salt and pepper to taste
1/2 c. butter
1/2 c. tomato paste
1/4 c. wine

Sprinkle chicken with lemon juice; dust with cinnamon, salt and pepper. Brown chicken in butter. Combine tomato paste with 1 1/2 cups boiling water in large deep pot; bring to a boil. Reduce heat; place chicken carefully in tomato sauce. Pour butter from skillet through strainer and over chicken; add wine. Cook on low heat for about 1 hour or until chicken is tender, stirring occasionally, being careful not to tear chicken. Serve over macaroni, spaghetti or rice and sprinkle with grated kefalotiri cheese or top with browned butter, if desired.

Pat Kandis. Soc. and Serv. Chm.
Preceptor Gamma Kappa XP1201
Victoria, Texas

HAWAIIAN CHICKEN

2/3 c. flour
1/2 tsp. salt
1/2 tsp. Accent
1/2 tsp. celery salt
1/2 tsp. garlic salt
Dash of nutmeg
1   2 1/2 to 3-lb. chicken, disjointed
1/4 c. butter or margarine
2 tbsp. cooking oil
1   20-oz. can pineapple tidbits
1/4 c. soya sauce
2 tbsp. brown sugar

Combine flour, salt, Accent, celery salt, garlic salt and nutmeg in paper bag. Shake chicken in bag until well coated. Heat butter and oil in frypan; brown chicken. Arrange chicken in roasting pan or casserole. Combine syrup from pineapple with soya sauce and brown sugar; pour over the chicken. Cover. Bake at 350 degrees for 1 hour to 1 hour and 30 minutes, basting frequently. Saute pineapple tidbits in frypan; place on chicken 15 minutes before chicken is done.

Patricia Edwards, Rec. Sec.
Xi Gamma Iota X3430
Kitchener, Ontario, Canada

HONEY-CURRIED CHICKEN

1/3 c. butter
1/2 c. honey
1/4 c. prepared mustard
2 tsp. curry powder
1 sm. chicken, disjointed

Place 2 layers of foil in broiler pan. Melt butter in broiler pan; add honey, mustard and curry powder.

Blend well. Coat chicken on both sides with honey mixture, turning boney side down in pan. Bake in preheated 375-degree oven for 45 minutes, basting frequently. Turn; bake for 15 minutes longer or until tender.

Evelyne MacMillan, Corr. Sec.
Epsilon Lambda No. 10620
Votimo, British Columbia, Canada

ITALIAN-BAKED CHICKEN AND POTATOES

1 chicken, disjointed
4 med. peeled potatoes, quartered
1 onion, diced
3 tbsp. cooking oil
3 tbsp. oregano
1 tsp. salt
1/2 tsp. pepper

Place chicken in roasting pan. Arrange potatoes around chicken. Sprinkle remaining ingredients over chicken and potatoes; cover. Bake in preheated 350-degree oven for 1 hour.

June Dowd
Zeta Kappa No. 3685
Allentown, Pennsylvania

NEWFOUNDLAND-FRIED CHICKEN

1 egg, beaten
1/4 c. milk
Meaty chicken pieces
Coating Mixture
Oil for frying

Combine egg and milk; dip dried chicken in egg mixture. Dredge with Coating Mixture. Fry in 375-degree oil until brown, turning once. Drain on paper towels; place in baking pan. Bake at 300 degrees for 40 to 45 minutes or until chicken is tender. Serve hot or cold.

Coating Mixture

1 1/2 c. flour
1 tsp. dry mustard
1 tsp. turmeric
1 tsp. garlic powder
1 tsp. onion salt
1 tsp. curry powder
1 tsp. ground sage or savory
1 tsp. pepper
1 tsp. ground cloves
1 1/2 tsp. salt

Combine all ingredients in plastic bag; mix thoroughly. This keeps well and can be used as needed.

Mrs. Doris M. Richards
E'ta Eta Chap.
Windsor, Ontario, Canada

Recipe on page 71.

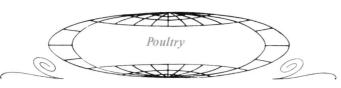
CHICKEN PAPRIKA WITH MUSHROOMS (HUNGARY) CSIRKE PAPRIKAS GOMBA

1 med. onion, chopped
2 tbsp. shortening
1/4 lb. mushrooms, cooked and chopped
3 1/2 lb. chicken, disjointed
2 tbsp. flour
1/4 tsp. salt
1/4 tsp. pepper
1/2 tsp. paprika
1 bay leaf
1 c. sour cream
1 1/2 c. tomato juice
1/2 tsp. vinegar
Dumplings

Brown onion in shortening; add mushrooms. Sprinkle chicken with flour. Add chicken to onion mixture; cook until browned. Add salt, pepper and paprika. Add bay leaf. Stir in sour cream and tomato juice slowly. Add vinegar. Cover; simmer for 45 minutes or until chicken is tender. Remove bay leaf just before serving. Serve with Dumplings.

Dumplings

3 eggs, beaten
3 c. flour
1 tbsp. salt
1/4 tsp. baking powder

Combine all ingredients; add 1/2 cup cold water. Beat with spoon. Drop by teaspoonfuls into boiling salted water; cook until dumplings rise to top. Drain and rinse in cold water.

Karen Lynn Ewing
Phi Delta Theta Chap.
Huntingdon, Pennsylvania

SPECIAL CHICKEN PAPRIKAS

1/4 c. butter or margarine
6 chicken legs
6 chicken thighs
1 sm. onion, sliced
1 lb. fresh mushrooms, sliced
3 to 4 tbsp. Hungarian paprika
2 tbsp. flour
1 1/4 tsp. salt
1 10 1/2-oz. can chicken broth
1 c. sour cream
2 egg yolks
1 to 2 tsp. lemon juice

Melt butter in Dutch oven. Brown chicken pieces on all sides, adding more butter if needed. Remove chicken; set aside. Fry onion and mushrooms just until soft. Stir in 2 tablespoons paprika, flour and salt; add broth and 1/2 cup water gradually. Bring to a boil, stirring constantly. Return chicken to Dutch oven; reduce heat. Cover; simmer for 30 to 40 minutes or until

Recipe on page 184.

chicken is tender. Combine sour cream, remaining paprika, egg yolks and lemon juice in small bowl; mix well. Remove chicken to warm serving platter; keep warm. Stir sour cream mixture gradually into pan liquid. Heat, but do not boil, for about 5 minutes, stirring constantly. Pour sauce over chicken. Sprinkle with parsley; serve with noodles, if desired. Yield: 6 servings.

Carolyn Knox
Beta Nu No. 7426
Kingston, Idaho

CIRCASSIAN CHICKEN (MIDDLE EAST) SHERKASIYA

1 chicken
3 oz. shelled almonds
3 oz. shelled walnuts
3 oz. shelled hazelnuts
1/8 tsp. paprika
Dash of cayenne
Salt to taste
2 onions, chopped
Butter
Cooked rice

Boil chicken until tender; reserve stock. Pound nuts in mortar with paprika, cayenne and salt. Fry onions in butter; add pounded nuts and a small amount chicken stock. Cook until thick. Cut chicken into 4 pieces; arrange in center of dish of hot rice. Pour sauce over chicken and rice.

Janet McDaniel
Xi Nu No. 1223
Weiser, Idaho

CHICKEN WITH SAFFRON RICE (URUGUAY)

1 chicken, disjointed
1/4 c. oil
1 med. onion, finely chopped
1 green pepper, finely chopped
2 med. carrots, finely chopped
1 med. tomato, chopped
1 tbsp. minced parsley
1 tsp. garlic (opt.)
1 tsp. oregano
Salt and pepper to taste
1 env. Spanish saffron
1 c. long grain rice

Fry chicken in oil until brown; set aside. Fry onion until tender; add green pepper and carrots. Cook on medium heat until tender. Add tomato and next 4 seasonings. Simmer for 10 minutes. Add 3 cups boiling water and saffron. Cook for 5 minutes. Add rice; cook on medium heat for about 15 minutes or until rice is tender. Remove from heat; let stand for 5 minutes. Serve with cheese, if desired.

Raquel Munilla
Epsilon Chi No. 8401
Doraville, Georgia

CHICKEN WITH WILD RICE

1 lb. fresh mushrooms, sliced
Butter
2 6-oz. packages wild rice or long grain rice
Chicken broth
1 c. sour cream
1 15-oz. can cream of mushroom soup
2 3-lb. chickens, cooked and chopped
1 8-oz. can water chestnuts, chopped

Saute mushrooms in small amount butter; set aside for top. Cook rice according to package directions for firm rice, using chicken broth for liquid. Blend sour cream and mushroom soup together. Combine chicken, rice, cream mixture and water chestnuts. Turn into casserole. Top casserole with mushrooms. Bake at 350 degrees for 1 hour. Chopped almonds may be substituted for water chestnuts, if desired. Yield: 8 servings.

Kathy Cousins
Alpha Kappa Nu. 7135
Old Town, Maine

SPANISH CHICKEN WITH AN ITALIAN TWIST — PAELLA

4 Italian sausages
1/4 c. olive oil
1 3-lb. fryer, disjointed
1 c. chopped onion
1 clove of garlic, minced
1 1/2 c. long grain rice
1 8-oz. can tomato sauce
1 3/4 c. chicken broth
1 tsp. leaf oregano, crumbled
1 tsp. salt
1/4 tsp. pepper
1/4 tsp. powdered saffron
1/2 lb. shelled fresh shrimp, deveined
1 box frozen Italian green beans
1 4-oz. jar pimento strips

Parboil sausages in water to cover for 10 minutes; drain. Cut into 1/4-inch slices; set aside. Heat oil in large deep skillet or paella pan. Brown several chicken pieces at a time; set aside. Saute onion and garlic in same skillet for about 5 minutes or until tender. Add rice, tomato sauce, chicken broth, 2 cups water, oregano, salt, pepper and saffron. Bring to a boil. Pour rice mixture into 13 x 9 x 2-inch baking dish; place chicken on top. Cover with aluminum foil. Bake in 400-degree oven for 30 minutes. Add shrimp and sausages; cover. Bake for 20 minutes longer or until chicken, rice and shrimp are done. Cook green beans according to package directors; drain well. Fluff up rice mixture; stir in pimentos. Arrange green beans around edges of baking dish to serve. Yield: 6 servings.

Patsy Bruce
Alpha Psi No. 6448
Winshahe, British Columbia, Canada

SWEDISH CHICKEN-RICE BAKE

1 can cream of chicken soup
1 can cream of celery soup
1 can onion soup
1 pkg. Uncle Ben's wild rice mix
1 sm. jar pimento, chopped
1/2 c. chopped black olives
1 2-lb. chicken, disjointed

Combine first 6 ingredients with 1 1/3 soup cans water; pour into 9 x 13-inch baking dish. Arrange chicken pieces on top. Bake, uncovered, at 350 degrees for 2 hours.

Phyllis Gorze, Pres.
Preceptor Theta XP1424
Minot, North Dakota

CHICKEN ESSEX (ENGLAND)

4 c. chopped cooked chicken
1/2 lb. fresh mushrooms, sliced
2 c. uncooked elbow macaroni
1 can mushroom soup
1 can cream of chicken soup
1 14-oz. can chicken broth
1 sm. onion, finely chopped
1/2 green pepper, finely chopped
1 2-oz. jar pimentos, diced
1 sm. can water chestnuts, thinly sliced
1/2 lb. Cheddar cheese, grated
1/2 tsp. salt

Combine all ingredients; mix well. Turn into 9 x 13-inch pan. Cover with foil. Refrigerate overnight. Remove foil. Bake in 350-degree oven for 1 hour.

Marge Andersen, Pres.
Preceptor Alpha Iota XP1531
Council Bluffs, Iowa

CHICKEN-SPAGHETTI PARMESAN (ITALY)

1 4-lb. hen
1 sm. onion, chopped
3/4 c. chopped green pepper
3/4 c. chopped celery
2 tbsp. bacon drippings
1 sm. jar pimento strips
1 sm. can sliced mushrooms
Salt and pepper to taste
1 sm. package extra thin spaghetti
1 clove of garlic
6 Ritz crackers, crumbled
1 c. Parmesan cheese
Paprika

Stew hen in 3 quarts water; remove chicken. Reserve broth. Cool and chop chicken. Saute onion, green pepper and celery in bacon drippings. Remove from heat; add chicken, pimento, mushrooms, salt and pepper. Place in baking dish. Cook spaghetti in reserved broth with garlic. Add spaghetti to chicken mixture, using just enough broth to make juicy. Sprinkle cracker

Poultry

crumbs, Parmesan cheese and paprika on top. Bake, covered, at 350 degrees for 40 minutes or until bubbly.

Jody Quincey, Treas.
Xi Iota Upsilon Chap.
Fort Lauderdale, Florida

SPANISH CHICKEN

    1   4 to 5-lb. stewing hen, disjointed
    1   16-oz. package long spaghetti
    Butter
    3 lg. onions, finely chopped
    4 sweet green peppers, finely chopped
    2 sweet red peppers, finely chopped
    1   20-oz. can tomato juice
    1 lb. sharp Cheddar cheese, grated
    3 tsp. curry powder
    2 tsp. chili powder
    3 tsp. salt

Place chicken in kettle; cover with cold water. Bring to a boil. Reduce heat; simmer for about 3 hours or until tender. Remove chicken; reserve broth. Remove skin and bones. Cook spaghetti in reserved broth until tender; drain well. Toss spaghetti in butter to prevent sticking. Combine vegetables. Place alternate layers of spaghetti, chicken pieces and vegetables in roasting pan or large casserole. Repeat layers until all ingredients are used. Combine remaining ingredients in saucepan; cook, stirring, until cheese is melted. Pour sauce over chicken mixture. Bake at 325 degrees for 30 to 45 minutes or until heated through. Yield: 8-10 servings.

Wendy Ritchie
Epsilon Kappa Chap.
Abbotsford, British Columbia, Canada

PHILIPPINE-STYLE PICKLED CHICKEN

    1 chicken, cooked and boned
    6 sweet pickles, chopped fine
    1 med. onion, sliced thin
    1 can green beans
    1 1/2 c. catsup
    1 clove of garlic, minced
    1 tsp. salt
    2 tbsp. vinegar
    1/4 c. sweet pickle juice

Cut chicken into bite-sized pieces. Combine all ingredients in Dutch oven. Cook over low heat for 30 to 40 minutes or until chicken is tender and broth thickened. Serve with rice. Yield: 6 servings.

Joyce Mason
Xi Beta Xi Chap.
Little Rock, Arkansas

VELVETY CHICKEN (FRANCE)

    2 pkg. frozen artichoke hearts
    1 pt. fresh mushrooms, sliced
    2 tbsp. margarine
    2 c. cooked cubed chicken
    1 env. chicken gravy mix
    1 c. shredded process Swiss cheese
    1 tbsp. dry Sherry
    1/2 c. bread crumbs
    1 tbsp. butter or margarine

Cook artichokes according to package directions; drain. Saute mushrooms in margarine. Combine artichokes, mushrooms and chicken in casserole. Prepare gravy mix according to package directions; remove from heat. Add cheese; stir until melted. Stir in Sherry. Pour over chicken in casserole. Sprinkle bread crumbs over top; drizzle with melted butter. Bake in 350-degree oven until bubbly and heated through.

Brenda Henningsen, Soc. Chm.
Xi Beta Pi X4829
Phoenix, Arizona

SPAGHETTI WITH CHICKEN CREOLE

    3 lb. chicken pieces
    Salt
    3 slices bacon, diced
    2 tbsp. salad oil
    2 c. chopped onion
    1 clove of garlic, minced
    1 1/2 c. chopped celery
    1 med. green pepper, diced
    2 tbsp. flour
    1   28-oz. can tomatoes
    1   8-oz. can tomato sauce
    1/2 tsp. thyme leaves, crushed
    1 tbsp. chili powder
    2 bay leaves
    1/2 tsp. Tabasco sauce
    2 tbsp. Worcestershire sauce
    1 tbsp. dark brown sugar
    1   10-oz. package frozen cut okra, thawed
    12 oz. spaghetti

Sprinkle chicken lightly with salt. Cook bacon until crisp in Dutch oven or large skillet; drain on paper towels. Add oil to drippings; brown chicken. Remove chicken; set aside. Add onion and garlic. Saute until onion is soft. Stir in celery and green pepper. Saute for 3 minutes. Blend in flour, tomatoes, tomato sauce, 2 1/2 teaspoons salt, seasonings and brown sugar; stir until smooth. Add chicken and okra. Bring to a boil; cover. Simmer for 25 to 30 minutes or until chicken is tender. Remove bay leaves. Cook spaghetti in 1 1/2 tablespoons salt and 4 to 5 quarts rapidly boiling water until done. Drain in colander. Place spaghetti in deep serving platter. Spoon sauce and chicken on top. Sprinkle with bacon. Yield: 6 servings.

Photograph for this recipe on page 92.

107

SOUR CREAM-CHICKEN ENCHILADAS (MEXICO)

3 1/2 c. sour cream
3 5-oz. cans boned chicken
2 4-oz. cans mushroom stems and pieces, drained
1 4-oz. can green chilies, drained
1/3 c. onion flakes
1 tsp. chili powder
1/2 tsp. salt
1/2 tsp. garlic powder
1/4 tsp. pepper
Salad oil
12 corn tortillas
1/3 lb. Cheddar cheese, grated

Spread 1 cup sour cream in 13 x 9-inch baking pan one hour before serving; set aside. Flake chicken in 2-quart saucepan. Add 1 cup sour cream, mushrooms, green chilies, onion flakes, chili powder, salt, garlic powder and pepper; cook over low heat just until heated through, stirring constantly. Pour about 1/2 inch salad oil in skillet. Fry 1 tortilla over medium heat until soft. Remove from oil; fill along center with 1/4 cup chicken mixture. Fold sides over filling; place, seam side down, in sour cream in baking dish. Repeat 11 times. Spread enchiladas with remaining sour cream; sprinkle with cheese. Bake in preheated 450-degree oven for 8 minutes or until cheese is melted. Yield: 6 servings.

Jackie Shira, Pres.
Preceptor Alpha XP189
Fairbanks, Alaska

WARSAW CHICKEN

1 3-lb. chicken
2 tbsp. butter
3 tbsp. flour
2 tbsp. lemon juice
1 tbsp. parsley

Cook chicken in boiling salted water until tender. Remove chicken; reserve 1 3/4 cups broth. Remove skin and bones; cut chicken into bite-sized chunks. Melt butter in saucepan; stir in flour to make a smooth paste. Stir in reserved chicken broth and lemon juice; cook to make a thin sauce. Add chicken; pour into serving dish. Sprinkle parsley over top; serve.

Cheri Neal, V.P.
Alpha Omicron Sigma No. 10155
Plano, Texas

CORNISH HENS AND RICE CASSEROLE

1 1/2 c. rice
2 tbsp. butter or margarine
1/2 c. chopped green pepper
1/2 c. chopped celery
1/2 c. chopped onions
2 chicken bouillon cubes
1/2 tsp. parsley flakes

2 pinches of rosemary
1 sm. can evaporated milk
2 or 3 Cornish hens, halved
Salt and pepper to taste

Brown rice in 1 tablespoon butter; set aside. Saute green pepper, celery and onions in remaining butter in large skillet until transparent. Add 3 cups water and bouillon cubes; stir until bouillon cubes are dissolved. Stir in parsley, rosemary, milk and rice; pour into large casserole. Season Cornish hens with salt and pepper; place over rice mixture. Cover with foil. Bake at 350 degrees for 45 minutes. Uncover; bake for 10 minutes longer or until hens are tender and browned. Garnish with sliced almonds, if desired.

Sammie P. Jester, Rec. Sec.
Xi Kappa Chi Chap.
Lancaster, California

NORMANDY-STYLE DUCKLING (FRANCE) CANETON A LA NORMANDIE

1 4-lb. duckling, disjointed
5 tbsp. butter
3/4 tsp. salt
1/8 tsp. pepper
6 med. apples
1/2 c. apple Brandy

Rinse duckling pieces; pat dry. Cut away and discard excess fat. Heat 2 tablespoons butter in large skillet. Sprinkle duckling pieces with salt and pepper. Add duckling to skillet; brown on all sides, turning with tongs. Pour off fat as it collects. Quarter, core, pare and slice apples. Melt remaining butter; saute apple slices. Place thin layer of apple slices in buttered 3-quart casserole. Arrange duckling over apples, plumpest pieces on top. Surround with remaining apple slices. Discard fat from skillet; add apple Brandy to same skillet. Stir over low heat to loosen particles; heat until steaming. Pour over duckling. Cover tightly. Bake at 350 degrees for about 2 hours or until duckling is tender. Serve in casserole. Yield: About 3 servings.

Margaret Nelson, Pres.
Xi Gamma Chi No. X1468
Baytown, Texas

ROASTED GAME HENS (SPAIN)

4 Cornish game hens
Salt and pepper
1 lb. small fresh mushrooms
Pimento-stuffed olives
Bacon slices
1/2 tsp. paprika
4 tbsp. butter or margarine
1/3 c. chopped filberts
1/3 c. finely chopped onion
1 c. rice

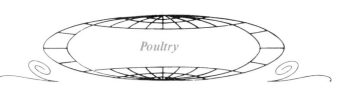

350 degrees for 1 hour or until pheasant is tender, turning occasionally.

Judy Thiesse
Delta No. 478
Mitchell, South Dakota

TURKEY AND HAM CASINO

1 c. chopped onions
1 c. chopped green peppers
1/4 c. butter or margarine
1/2 c. all-purpose flour
2 c. milk
1 3/4 c. chicken broth
1/4 c. dry Sherry
1 4-oz. can sliced mushrooms, drained
2 c. coarsely chopped cooked turkey or chicken
2 c. coarsely chopped ham
1 to 2 tbsp. chopped pimento
1 8-oz. can water chestnuts, drained and
   sliced
1 tsp. salt
1/2 tsp. pepper

Saute onions and green peppers in butter in Dutch oven or electric frypan until tender. Add flour; blend in smoothly. Add milk, broth and Sherry; cook, stirring constantly, until mixture comes to a boil. Add mushrooms, turkey, ham, pimento, water chestnuts, salt and pepper; bring to boiling point. Reduce heat; simmer for 5 minutes or until heated through. Pour into serving dish or chafing dish. Serve over rice. Yield: 12 servings.

Elaine Saladini
Delta No. 246
Morgantown, West Virginia

VIVA LA TURKEY TORTILLA (MEXICO)

1 can cream of chicken soup
1 can cream of mushroom soup
1 c. milk
1 onion, grated or chopped
1 can green chile salsa
12 corn tortillas, cut in 1-inch strips
1 lb. sliced turkey or chicken white meat
1 lb. Cheddar cheese, grated
1 sm. jar black olives

Combine soups, milk, onion and salsa. Arrange a layer of tortillas in buttered 9 x 13-inch baking dish. Add a layer of turkey and a layer of soup mixture. Repeat layers, using all ingredients and ending with soup mixture. Top with cheese; garnish with black olives. Let stand in refrigerator for 24 hours. Bake at 300 degrees for 1 hour and 30 minutes or until heated through and bubbly. Yield: 8 servings.

Helen Wilkinson, Philanthropic Chm.
Xi Beta Mu No. X838
San Bernardino, California

2 c. cold chicken broth
1/2 c. grated Swiss cheese

Sprinkle insides of game hens with salt and pepper. Toss mushrooms with 2/3 cup whole olives. Stuff into body of hens. Fasten openings with poultry pins; tie legs together. Place 1/2 slice bacon on each hen. Place hens in roasting pan. Bake in 450-degree oven for 20 minutes. Remove bacon. Combine paprika with fat in roasting pan; brush on hens. Reduce oven temperature to 350 degrees; bake for 30 minutes longer or until hens are lightly browned and tender. Melt 2 tablespoons butter in heavy saucepan. Add filberts; saute until lightly browned. Remove filberts with slotted spoon; set aside. Add remaining butter, onion and rice to saucepan. Cook, stirring occasionally, until rice turns opaque. Add broth; bring mixture to a boil. Cover pan tightly. Simmer for 12 to 14 minutes or until rice is tender and all liquid is absorbed. Stir in cheese, 1/4 cup chopped olives and reserved filberts. Place rice mixture on serving platter. Arrange hens on top. Garnish with whole olives.

Photograph for this recipe above.

BARBECUED PHEASANT

1 pheasant, disjointed
2 med. onions, sliced
1 c. catsup
2 tbsp. vinegar
1/4 c. Worcestershire sauce
1 tsp. chili powder
1 tsp. salt

Place pheasant in shallow pan; cover with onion slices. Bake in 400-degree oven for 30 minutes. Combine remaining ingredients and 2 cups water in saucepan; bring to boiling point. Pour over pheasant. Bake at

Cereal, Cheese, Egg and Pasta

Most experts agree that it was the appearance of vast fields of wild grain (cereals) such as rice and wheat that brought man out of caves and into villages. From these ancient villages grew all the world's great civilizations — and with them, the world's great cuisines. Even after many thousands of years, rice is still the staple food in the Orient, India and parts of Europe and the Middle East. Corn is the staple in many parts of Africa and the Americas, while northern Europe depended solely on oats, buckwheat, barley and rye before wheat became common. Moreover, without wheat, there would be no Italian pasta, no German dumplings or noodles, and no Chinese egg rolls — each a cornerstone in its own cuisine.

Italian pasta comes in many shapes and sizes, and serves just about as many purposes. Large pasta tubes can be stuffed with meat, vegetable, or cheese mixtures, while the smaller types can be served alone with a pat of butter, or with a savory sauce. Today, cooks use pasta in dishes that are not at all Italian in flavor because it stretches the flavor and nutrition of foods when used in soups, stews, casseroles and salads. Eggs and cheese are two nutritious and flavorful foods that cooks use for seasoning and garnish but sometimes overlook as excellent entrees. Often, too, they are served together, as in a cheese souffle or in the custard-like French *quiche.* Alone, they can be appetizers, as in cheeseballs or pickled eggs; but as an entree, cheese becomes Swiss fondue or Welsh Rarebit, while eggs can be scalloped, made into egg salad, or served as stuffed eggs. Even better, dishes like these make perfect quick and easy suppers! Cheese and eggs both can be combined with pasta or cereals for another array of entrees and side dishes.

Because cereals, cheese, eggs, and pasta offer such unlimited variety to mealtime, Beta Sigma Phi cooks believe they all hold an important place in any menu around the world. Don't overlook any of them!

BRITISH CHEESE PUDDING

1 c. fresh fine bread crumbs
1 1/2 c. grated Cheddar cheese
1 1/4 c. milk
3 tbsp. butter
2/3 c. cream or milk
Dash of dry mustard
Salt and pepper to taste
3 eggs, lightly beaten

Combine bread crumbs and cheese in bowl. Heat milk with 1 1/2 tablespoons butter, cream, mustard, salt and pepper; do not boil. Beat hot milk mixture into eggs. Strain into bread crumb mixture; set aside for 15 to 20 minutes. Grease a 1-quart souffle dish with remaining 1 1/2 tablespoons butter. Pour cheese mixture into dish. Bake at 375 degrees for about 45 minutes or until puffed and golden brown. Serve immediately.

Paula Mabley
Preceptor Tau XP640
Belleville, Illinois

CHEESE-EGG FONDUE

8 slices firm bread, crust removed
1/2 c. butter
1/2 lb. Cheddar cheese, grated
1/2 tsp. salt
2 c. milk
4 eggs, beaten

Cut bread into 1-inch cubes; place in buttered 1 1/2-quart casserole. Combine butter, cheese, salt and milk in saucepan; heat over low heat until cheese is melted. Remove from heat. Add eggs slowly, stirring constantly. Pour over bread cubes. Refrigerate overnight. Bake at 350 degrees for 1 hour and 15 minutes.

Geneva Reves, W. and M. Chm.
Gamma Omicron No. 6301
Rogers, Arkansas

EASY CHILES RELLENOS

1 28-oz. can whole green chilies
1/2 lb. Monterey Jack cheese, grated
1/2 lb. Cheddar cheese, grated
Paprika
5 eggs, beaten
1/4 c. flour
1 1/4 c. milk
Salt and pepper to taste
Tabasco sauce to taste

Slit and wash chilies, removing seeds. Stuff chilies with Jack cheese. Place in baking dish. Add Cheddar cheese; sprinkle with paprika. Beat eggs, flour, milk and seasonings together; pour over chilies. Sprinkle with paprika. Bake at 350 degrees for 45 minutes or until knife inserted near edge comes out clean.

Cheryl Butcher, Pres.
Xi Alpha X125
La Junta, Colorado

COTTAGE CHEESE BALLS (CZECHOSLOVAKIA)

1 lb. dry cottage cheese
4 eggs, lightly beaten
1/2 c. flour
1 tsp. salt
1/2 c. butter
3 tbsp. cracker or bread crumbs

Combine first 4 ingredients; mix well. Shape into small balls, adding more flour if needed to hold mixture together. Drop carefully into rapidly boiling water; cook for about 10 minutes. Strain carefully. Brown butter; add crumbs. Season with salt to taste, if desired. Sprinkle generously over cheese balls; serve hot.

Doris G. Guidon
Preceptor Laureate Gamma PL140
Seattle, Washington

SOUR CREAM ENCHILADAS (MEXICO)

2 cans cream of chicken soup
1 c. sour cream
2 sm. cans green chilies, chopped
12 corn tortillas
1 1/2 c. grated Cheddar cheese
1 med. onion, chopped

Heat soup; add sour cream and green chilies. Fry tortillas; sprinkle a small amount of cheese and onion on each tortilla. Top with 2 tablespoons cream mixture. Roll up; place in 9 x 13-inch pan. Pour remaining cream mixture over top; sprinkle with remaining cheese. Cover with foil. Bake at 350 degrees for 15 to 20 minutes.

Judy Braten
Xi Omicron X2490
Powell, Wyoming

ENGLISH MONKEY

2 tbsp. butter
2/3 c. milk
2/3 c. fresh fine bread crumbs
1 c. grated cheese
1 egg, beaten
Salt and pepper to taste
Prepared mustard to taste
Worcestershire sauce to taste
4 slices toast
1 tomato, sliced

Melt butter; add milk and bread crumbs. Heat until hot. Remove from heat; stir in cheese and egg. Add all seasonings. Cook, stirring, until thick and creamy. Pour over toast; top with tomato slice. Yield: 4 servings.

Claudia Holland, Pres.
Zeta Lambda No. 8997
Havelock, North Carolina

FAMILY PIEROGI

3 c. flour
1 tsp. baking powder
3 eggs
1 8-oz. carton sour cream
6 to 8 med. potatoes
1/4 lb. sharp cheese, chopped
Dash of turmeric
1/2 c. butter or margarine
1 onion, chopped

Mix first 4 ingredients; knead until smooth. Refrigerate for 1 hour. Boil potatoes; drain. Add cheese and turmeric. Mash as for mashed potatoes. Chill. Roll out dough; cut into squares. Place a small amount of potato filling in center of each square; pinch into small envelopes. Boil in salted water for about 5 minutes or until done; drain. Melt butter; add onion. Pour over top.

Barbara Bonner
Kappa Omicron No. 8089
East Stroudsburg, Pennsylvania

TRIANGLE PIEROGI (POLAND)

2 c. flour
1 egg
1 egg yolk
2 tbsp. sour cream
Salt
1 tsp. butter (opt.)
1 c. (heaping) mashed potatoes
1 c. (scant) dry cottage cheese
Minced chives or green onion to taste
Pepper to taste

Combine first 4 ingredients; add scant 1/4 teaspoon salt and butter. Mix well. Knead into soft, pliable dough. Roll out thin on board. Cut into 2-inch squares. Combine potatoes, cottage cheese and chives; season with salt and pepper. Place small spoonful of filling a little to one side of square; fold over and pinch edges together into a triangle. Drop into boiling, salted water carefully; cook for about 5 minutes until dumplings float to top. Remove with slotted spoon. Serve with additional sour cream.

Lorraine Belk, City Coun. Rep.
Omicron Mu No. 9331
Joplin, Missouri

SMALL GREEK CHEESE PIES

6 oz. cream cheese, softened
1 egg
1 c. crumbled feta cheese
1 tbsp. chopped parsley
1 10-oz. package frozen patty shells
2 tbsp. milk

Beat cream cheese with electric beater until smooth. Add egg; beat well. Add feta cheese and parsley; beat until well combined. Chill for at least 1 hour. Thaw patty shells at room temperature for 15 to 20 minutes or until soft. Roll each patty shell to a 4 1/2 x 8 1/2-inch rectangle on floured pastry cloth. Place 1/4 cup cheese mixture on half of each rectangle. Fold tops of rectangles over bottoms to form square pies. Seal with milk; brush tops with milk. Place pies on cookie sheet. Place in preheated 450-degree oven. Reduce heat immediately to 400 degrees. Bake for 20 to 25 minutes or until well browned and puffed.

Betty B. Baccus, Corr. Sec.
Alpha Gamma No. 2238
Columbus, Georgia

NANNY'S CHEESE PIE
(ENGLAND)

Pastry for 9-in. deep-dish pie
1 egg white
6 slices bacon, crisply fried
3/4 c. diced ham
3/4 c. sliced fresh mushrooms
8 oz. Swiss cheese, diced
1 1/2 c. cream, scalded
3 eggs, beaten
1/2 tsp. salt
1/4 tsp. nutmeg
1/8 tsp. white pepper

Brush pastry with egg white. Crumble bacon into pie crust. Saute ham lightly in bacon drippings; drain. Place over bacon. Add mushrooms and cheese. Cool cream slightly. Add cream to eggs; add salt, nutmeg and pepper. Beat well. Pour into pie pastry. Bake in preheated 375-degree oven for 35 to 40 minutes or until top is light golden brown and knife inserted 1 inch from edge comes out clean. Remove from oven. Let stand for at least 10 minutes before serving. Yield: 6 servings.

Jean L. Allen, Corr. Sec.
Alpha Alpha No. 9634
Jacksonville, Florida

SWISS CHEESE PIE

2 tbsp. flour
1 1/2 to 2 tbsp. butter
3/4 c. milk
Salt to taste
3 eggs
2 c. grated Swiss cheese
2/3 c. cream
1 unbaked pastry shell

Combine flour and butter in saucepan over low heat; stir until smooth. Add milk and salt; cook, stirring, until thickened. Cool for about 10 minutes. Beat in 1 beaten egg at a time. Add cheese and cream. Pour into pastry shell. Bake at 400 degrees for 15 minutes. Reduce oven temperature to 375 degrees. Bake for 30 minutes longer or until knife inserted comes out clean. Serve hot.
This is traditionally served on New Year's Day in Switzerland.

Margaret M. Fisher, V.P.
Preceptor Beta Kappa XP1359
Maryville, Missouri

pan with foil; refrigerate overnight. Bake at 350 degrees for 50 minutes. Remove foil; bake for 10 minutes longer. Cool for several minutes before serving. Bacon, sausage or ham may be added for variation, if desired.

Charlene Johnson, Treas.
Phi Nu P2783
Baltic, South Dakota

BASQUE PIPERADE (FRANCE)

3 med. onions
3 lg. green or red bell peppers
4 med. tomatoes
1/3 to 1/2 c. oil
1 clove of garlic, mashed
1 tbsp. chopped parsley or 1/2 tsp.
   dried parsley flakes
8 eggs
Salt and pepper to taste

Peel and thinly slice onions; cut peppers in 1/2-inch strips lengthwise. Chop tomatoes into 1/2-inch cubes. Heat oil in skillet; add onions. Cook over medium heat until golden brown. Add peppers; cook for about 5 minutes or until soft. Add tomatoes; cover. Cook over low heat for 30 minutes, stirring occasionally. Add garlic and parsley; cook for 15 minutes longer. Break eggs into bowl; beat vigorously with whisk or fork until frothy. Season with salt and pepper. Stir eggs into vegetables with wooden spoon; cook over low heat, stirring until soft scrambled. Remove to heated platter; serve with buttered French or Italian bread. Yield: 4 servings.

Grace Clayton, 2nd V.P.
Xi Theta Psi X2315
Anaheim, California

TABASCO CHEESE SOUFFLE

1 1/2 c. milk
1/4 c. butter or margarine
1/4 c. flour
1 tsp. salt
1/2 tsp. Tabasco sauce
1/2 lb. sharp American cheese
6 eggs, separated

Heat, do not scald, milk. Melt butter in double boiler. Stir in flour, milk, salt and Tabasco sauce. Cook, stirring constantly, until mixture is smooth and thickened. Slice cheese thinly into mixture; stir until cheese melts and sauce is smooth. Beat egg yolks with fork. Stir in a small amount of cheese sauce, then stir mixture back into remaining cheese sauce. Cool slightly. Beat egg whites until stiff, but not dry. Fold gradually into cheese sauce. Pour into ungreased 2-quart casserole to 1/4 inch from top. Make shallow ring in souffle about 1 inch from edge with teaspoon. Bake in 300-degree oven for 1 hour and 30 minutes or until top is golden brown. Serve immediately. Yield: 6 servings.

Photograph for this recipe above.

BAKED EGG STRATA

8 slices bread, cubed
1 lb. grated Velveeta cheese
8 eggs
2 tsp. salt
2 tsp. dry mustard
4 c. milk
Paprika

Place bread in buttered 9 x 13-inch pan; top with cheese. Beat eggs with salt, mustard and milk; pour over bread and cheese. Sprinkle with paprika. Cover

CHEESY EGG BAKE

2 cans cream of chicken soup
1 c. milk
4 tsp. instant minced onion flakes
1 tsp. prepared mustard
1 8-oz. package shredded process
   Swiss cheese
12 eggs
12 1/2-in. thick slices French bread,
   buttered and halved

Combine soup, milk, onion flakes and mustard in saucepan; cook, stirring, until heated through. Remove from heat; stir in cheese until melted. Pour 1 cup sauce into each of two 10 x 6 x 1 3/4-inch baking dishes. Break 6 eggs into sauce in each casserole. Spoon remaining sauce carefully around eggs. Stand French bread slices around edges of casseroles with crusts up. Bake in 350-degree oven for 20 minutes or until eggs are set. Garnish with snipped parsley. Yield: 12 servings.

Virginia D. Holsinger
Xi Kappa X938
Harrisonburg, Virginia

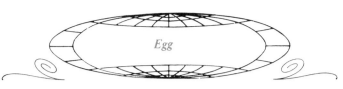

Egg

HUEVOS RANCHEROS AMERICANO

1/4 c. chopped onion
2 tbsp. chopped green pepper
1 lg. clove of garlic, minced
1 tsp. chili powder
2 tbsp. butter
1 can tomato soup
1/4 c. sliced ripe olives (opt.)
Dash of Tabasco sauce
4 to 6 strips fried bacon, crumbled
3 to 6 cooked link sausages, cut in
    pieces
4 potatoes, diced and fried
8 eggs
Salt and pepper to taste
Shredded Cheddar cheese

Cook onion, green pepper, garlic and chili powder in butter in saucepan until vegetables are tender. Stir in soup, 1/3 cup water, olives and Tabasco sauce. Heat; stirring occasionally. Spoon 3 tablespoons soup mixture into each of 8 individual shallow baking dishes; add pieces of bacon, sausages and a spoonful of fried potatoes. Break egg into each dish. Season with salt and pepper. Bake at 350 degrees for 12 to 15 minutes or until eggs are set. Sprinkle cheese over eggs.

Jo Ann Witte, Sec.
Preceptor Beta Epsilon XP1303
Naperville, Illinois

BAKED MUSHROOM-CHEESE OMELET

1/2 c. chopped onion
1/2 c. diced green pepper
1/2 lb. fresh mushrooms
1/4 c. margarine
8 eggs
1 c. milk or water
1 tsp. salt
1/2 tsp. oregano leaves, crushed
1/8 tsp. pepper
3/4 c. shredded Monterey Jack cheese

Saute onion, green pepper and mushrooms in margarine; remove from heat. Beat eggs with milk, salt, oregano and pepper; stir in mushroom mixture and cheese. Pour into buttered 10-inch pie pan or quiche pan. Bake in preheated 325-degree oven for 40 minutes or until knife inserted in center comes out clean. Cut in wedges. Serve with oregano-seasoned tomato sauce.

Bev Nelson, Pres.
Preceptor Beta Theta XP1473
Bellevue, Washington

DESSERT OMELET

8 eggs, separated
2 tbsp. sugar
1/2 tsp. salt
1 tsp. vanilla extract

Butter
1/2 c. French mirabelle preserves

Beat egg yolks until light and frothy with sugar, 1/4 teaspoon salt, 2 tablespoons water and vanilla. Add remaining 1/4 teaspoon salt to egg whites; beat until stiff. Fold into yolks. Melt small amount of butter in heavy 10-inch skillet over low heat. Rotate pan to spread butter evenly over bottom. Add egg mixture. Cook slowly for 8 to 10 minutes or until brown on bottom and well puffed. Place skillet in preheated 350-degree oven for 10 to 12 minutes or until omelet is dry and firm in center. Remove from oven; spread 1/2 of the omelet with preserves. Fold over; turn out onto warm platter. Yield: 6 servings.

Ruth Pullen, Sec.
Preceptor Xi Xp395
Lakewood, Colorado

SPANISH OMELET – TORTILLA A LA ESPANOLA

1/2 c. oil
1 lb. sliced potatoes
1/2 lb. sliced green onions with tops
4 eggs
1/4 tsp. salt
Dash of pepper

Heat oil in skillet over medium heat; add potatoes and onions. Cover; cook until soft, stirring frequently. Remove from pan with slotted spoon. Drain off all but 1 tablespoon oil. Beat eggs and seasonings; stir potatoes and onions into egg mixture. Pour into skillet. Cook over low heat until set; invert dish over skillet, then turn over. Slide omelet back into skillet, browned side up. Cook for 2 minutes longer. Serve immediately. Yield: 4 servings.

Denise Frederick
Xi Beta Upsilon X4344
Kingsport, Tennessee

BASIC QUICHE LORRAINE (FRANCE)

1   9-in. pie shell
1 c. diced cheese
6 strips cooked bacon, crumbled
3 eggs, well beaten
Salt and pepper to taste
1 1/4 c. milk
1 tbsp. grated onion

Bake pie shell at 350 degrees for 10 minutes. Sprinkle cheese and bacon into pie shell. Combine remaining ingredients; pour carefully into pie shell. Bake at 350 degrees for 30 minutes or until knife inserted near center comes out clean. Cool for 5 minutes before serving.

Jean Matheson, Sec.
Xi Mu X1773
Augusta, Maine

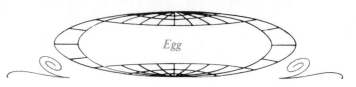
QUICHE FLORENTINE (FRANCE)

1   10-in. pastry shell
1 egg white, slightly beaten
2 tbsp. minced onion
1/4 c. butter
3 tbsp. flour
1/2 tsp. salt
1/8 tsp. pepper
1 c. milk
4 eggs, beaten
1   10-oz. package frozen chopped
    spinach, thawed and drained
1/2 c. finely chopped ham or bacon
1/2 c. shredded Swiss cheese

Brush pastry shell with egg white. Bake in 450-degree oven for 5 to 8 minutes or until pastry begins to change color. Saute onion in butter until tender; blend in flour, salt and pepper. Add milk; cook, stirring until smooth and thickened. Add a small amount hot mixture gradually to eggs; return to saucepan. Cook for 1 minute. Remove from heat; stir in spinach, ham and cheese. Pour into pastry shell. Bake in preheated 375-degree oven for 30 to 40 minutes or until knife inserted near center comes out clean.

Suzan Elizabeth McIntire, Ext. Off.
Iota Psi No. 9349
Paola, Kansas

HEARTH AND HEATHER QUICHE (SCOTLAND)

3/4 c. sifted all-purpose flour
1 tsp. salt
1/3 c. shortening
1/2 c. rolled oats

1/2 lb. Swiss cheese, grated
6 slices bacon, cooked and
    crumbled
1   14 1/2-oz. can evaporated milk
4 eggs
1/8 tsp. white pepper
1 tsp. chopped chives
Dash of nutmeg

Sift flour and 1/2 teaspoon salt together; cut in shortening until mixture resembles coarse crumbs. Stir in oats. Sprinkle 4 or 5 tablespoons cold water by tablespoons over mixture; stir lightly with fork until just dampened. Form into ball. Turn out on lightly floured board. Roll to form a 13-inch circle. Fit loosely into pie plate; Fold edges under; flute. Sprinkle cheese in pie shell; top with bacon. Combine milk, eggs, 1/2 teaspoon salt, pepper, chives and nutmeg; mix well. Pour over cheese and bacon. Bake in preheated 450-degree oven for 10 minutes. Reduce oven temperature to 350 degrees. Bake for 15 minutes longer or until silver knife inserted about 1 inch from center comes out clean. Let stand for about 10 minutes before cutting.

Photograph for this recipe on this page.

HAM-BACON AND EGGS
SPECK EIER KUCHEN

1/4 lb. bacon, chopped
1/4 lb. smoked ham, chopped
Chopped onions to taste
4 eggs
1/4 c. milk or cream
Salt and pepper to taste

Fry bacon in skillet until crisp; remove from skillet. Fry ham in drippings until soft; remove ham. Fry onions until soft. Add bacon and ham to onions in skillet. Beat eggs; add milk, salt and pepper. Pour mixture into skillet. Cook over medium heat, stirring occasionally, until eggs are set. Serve on hot toast.

V. Irene Kaufman, V.P.
Preceptor Chap.
Spencer, Iowa

SUMMER SHADE SOUFFLE (FRANCE)

1 lb. hot bulk sausage
1 c. milk
3 tbsp. butter
1/4 c. flour
1/2 tsp. salt
1/4 tsp. pepper
1/8 tsp. paprika
1/8 tsp. soda
1/2 lb. grated sharp Cheddar cheese
5 eggs, separated

Crumble sausage into frying pan; brown. Drain off excess fat; set sausage aside. Scald milk in small saucepan. Melt butter in top of double boiler. Stir in flour;

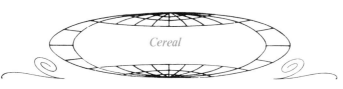

add hot milk, salt, pepper, paprika and soda. Cook, stirring, until thick. Add cheese; stir until melted. Remove from heat; cool for 15 minutes. Beat egg yolks until light. Beat whites until stiff. Add yolks to cheese mixture; fold into whites. Spread 1/2 of the sausage in casserole. Pour egg mixture over sausage. Sprinkle remaining sausage on top. Place casserole in pan of hot water. Bake at 300 degrees for 1 hour and 15 minutes. Do not open oven door until done. Serve immediately. Yield: 6-8 servings.

Barbara Lord
Alpha Theta No. 2437
Auburn, Alabama

SUNDAY EGGS (ITALY)

1 lb. fresh asparagus
1/2 med. onion, chopped
6 slices bacon, chopped
6 eggs
Salt and pepper to taste

Wash and chop fresh asparagus into 1-inch pieces. Brown onion and bacon together; add asparagus pieces. Cook, covered, over low heat for about 15 minutes. Beat eggs until fluffy; season with salt and pepper. Pour eggs over asparagus; cook until eggs are set. Yield: 4 servings.

Julie Imo, South County Coun. Treas.
Kappa Beta No. 7019
Saint Louis, Missouri

SEMOLINA CAKES WITH BUTTER AND CHEESE – GNOCCHI ALLA ROMANA

3 c. milk
1 1/2 tsp. salt
Pinch of ground nutmeg
Freshly ground pepper
3/4 c. semolina or farina
2 eggs, beaten lightly
1 c. grated Parmesan cheese
1/4 c. butter, melted

Combine milk, salt, ntumeg and several grindings of pepper in 3-quart saucepan; bring to a boil. Add semolina gradually, stirring constantly. Cook and stir until thick enough to support spoon standing in middle of semolina. Remove from heat. Combine eggs and 3/4 cup Parmesan cheese; stir into semolina. Mix well. Spoon onto large buttered baking sheet. Dip spatula in hot water; smooth and spread semolina into sheet about 1/4 inch thick. Refrigerate for at least 1 hour or until firm. Cut semolina into 1 1/2-inch circles; place in buttered 9-inch baking dish. Drizzle with melted butter and remaining cheese. Bake in preheated 400-degree oven for 15 minutes or until crisp and golden. Serve hot.

Jane Ann Hebert, Sec.
Alpha Phi No. 7325
Eau Claire, Wisconsin

PARTY ARMENIAN RICE

10 slices bacon, cut up
1 onion, chopped
2 tbsp. butter
2 c. long grain rice
1 pkg. slivered almonds
1 can sliced mushrooms
3 tbsp. soy sauce
3 cans consomme
3 cans beef bouillon

Fry bacon and onion together until crisp and brown. Add butter and rice; brown well. Add almonds, mushrooms and soy sauce; pour into large baking dish. Add consomme and bouillon; cover. Bake at 300 degrees for 3 hours or until done.

Kathy Sterling
Alpha Delta No. 3634
King Hill, Idaho

CALIFORNIA RANCH RICE

1 c. chopped onions
1/4 c. butter
4 c. cooked rice
2 c. sour cream
1 c. cream-style cottage cheese
Salt and pepper to taste
2 8-oz. cans whole unseeded chilies, cut into strips
2 c. grated Cheddar cheese

Saute onions in butter in large frying pan until limp. Add rice, sour cream, cottage cheese, salt and pepper; mix together. Spread 1/4 of the rice mixture in greased casserole. Add layer of 1/3 of the chilies and 1/2 cup cheese. Repeat, ending with layer of rice and reserving remaining 1/2 cup cheese. Bake at 375 degrees for 25 minutes. Sprinkle remaining 1/2 cup cheese over top; bake for 10 minutes longer. Yield: 8 servings.

Sandra Rose
Xi Alpha Tau X703
Woodland, California

CHINESE-FRIED RICE

2 c. diced cooked chicken
2 c. diced onions
1/2 c. diced green pepper
2 eggs, beaten
1/4 c. soy sauce
4 c. cooked rice
Salt and pepper to taste

Saute chicken, onions and green pepper until onions are soft and brown. Stir in eggs and soy sauce; mix well. Mix in cooked rice; cook over low heat for 10 minutes, stirring occasionally. Season to taste; add more soy sauce, if desired.

Connie Clanton, Corr. Sec.
Xi Iota Kappa No. 4649
Washington, Illinois

FRIED INSTANT RICE

6 slices bacon
3 eggs
2 beef bouillon cubes, dissolved
2 tbsp. soy sauce
2 lg. carrots, diced
1 lg. green pepper, diced
1 lg. onion, diced
Chopped mushrooms (opt.)
1/2 to 3/4 lb. ground beef
2 c. instant rice

Fry bacon in large skillet until crisp. Remove bacon; drain and crumble into small pieces. Set aside. Fry eggs in bacon drippings until firm. Remove eggs; dice and set aside. Pour bouillon into bacon grease. Add soy sauce and vegetables; cook until tender. Brown ground beef in small skillet. Cook rice according to package directions. Combine all ingredients; mix well.

Marilyn Miller
Xi Alpha Upsilon X738
Ironton, Ohio

JAPANESE-FRIED RICE

1 lb. cubed round steak
Soy sauce
2 eggs, slightly beaten
1/3 c. oil
1 clove of garlic, minced
3 lg. carrots, chopped
2 med. onions, chopped
3 c. cooked rice
Salt and pepper to taste
Parsley to taste

Marinate cubed steak in soy sauce. Fry eggs in hot oil until firm. Remove eggs from oil; set aside. Saute garlic in oil until browned. Add carrots and onions; saute until just tender. Add cubed steak; fry until well browned. Add rice; stir well. Season with salt and pepper; stir in parsley. Add soy sauce to taste. Chop eggs; stir into rice mixture. Heat thoroughly; serve immediately.

Nancy Gambrel
Eta Epsilon No. 6808
Oswego, Kansas

LEBANESE RICE – RUZZ

1/4 c. butter
2 curls vermicelli, broken
2 c. long grain rice
3 c. chicken broth
1 tsp. salt

Melt butter in large pan; add vermicelli. Stir until golden brown. Add rice; stir gently. Add chicken broth and salt; stir once. Cover; reduce heat to low. Cook for 20 minutes. Do not uncover or stir. Serve immediately.

Patricia Ann Williams
Xi Xi Nu X4096
Georgetown, Texas

MANDARIN RICE (CHINA)

2 or 3 eggs, beaten
3 tbsp. cooking oil
4 to 5 c. warm cooked rice
4 c. chopped green onions
1 c. cooked meat
1 c. cooked peas
2 tsp. salt
Soy sauce to taste

Scramble eggs to soft stage; remove from pan. Pour oil into same pan. Add rice; stir in onions, meat and peas. Cook quickly over high heat for 2 to 3 minutes. Add eggs, salt and soy sauce; mix well. Stir 1/4 to 1/3 cup water into rice, if cold and stuck together. A great way to use leftover meats.

Clara A. Newsom
Xi Omicron Beta X3391
Sutter Creek, California

EASY MEXICAN RICE

1 c. rice
2 tbsp. shortening
1/2 onion, minced
1/2 clove of garlic, minced
1 sm. can tomato paste
1/2 tsp. salt
1/4 tsp. sugar
1/4 tsp. pepper

Saute rice in shortening until golden. Add onion and garlic; saute until golden; Stir in tomato paste, 1 cup hot water, salt, sugar and pepper; bring to a boil. Reduce heat; cook, without stirring, until rice is tender and fluffy. Add water, if needed, to keep rice from sticking. One cup peas may be substituted for tomato paste and water, if desired.

Sandra R. Griffiths
Xi Zeta Rho X3110
Decatur, Illinois

FAVORITE MEXICAN RICE

1 c. long grain rice
2 tbsp. corn oil
1 sm. onion, minced
1/2 green pepper, chopped
2 tsp. salt
2 tsp. chili powder
1/4 tsp. ground cumin
1   1-lb. can tomatoes, sieved

Brown rice in hot oit; reduce heat. Add onion, green pepper, salt, chili powder, cumin and tomatoes; mix well. Add just enough water to cover. Simmer, covered, without stirring for about 30 minutes or until rice is tender. Remove cover; cook until all moisture is evaporated. Yield: 6-8 servings.

Betty Krieger, Serv. Chm.
Beta Upsilon No. 5500
Laplace, Louisiana

Cereal

POLYNESIAN RICE

1. c. rice
1/2 c. butter or margarine
1 tsp. oregano
Salt and pepper to taste
4 to 6 med. green onions, chopped
1 4-oz. can mushroom stems and pieces
3 or 4 chicken bouillon cubes

Brown rice in butter. Add 3 cups water, oregano, salt, pepper, onions and mushrooms; mix well. Add bouillon cubes; cook until almost dry. Bake in 350-degree oven for 30 to 45 minutes.

E. Dianne Bisig
Xi Zeta X202
Austin, Texas

PULAO (INDIA)

1 lg. onion, sliced
1 1/2 c. butter or margarine
2 c. rice
1 tbsp. salt
1 tsp. curry powder
1/2 tsp. ground cumin
1/8 tsp. cayenne pepper
1/8 tsp. ginger
1/8 tsp. pepper
1/8 tsp. turmeric
1 10-oz. package frozen peas, thawed

Saute onion in 1 cup butter in heavy saucepan until transparent. Add rice; saute for 5 minutes or until golden. Add 4 cups of water, salt, curry powder, cumin, cayenne pepper, ginger, pepper and turmeric. Mix well; cover tightly. Simmer for 25 minutes without stirring. Remove cover; place peas and remaining butter on top. Cover; cook slowly for 5 minutes longer or until peas are tender. Stir just to mix in peas and melted butter; serve immediately. Can be cooked ahead of time and reheated over hot water. Yield: 8 servings.

Rosalie Nelson
International Honorary Member
Redlands, California

SWEET RICE (PORTUGAL) ARROZ DOLCE

1/2 c. long grain rice
1 3/4 c. milk, heated
1/2 c. sugar
1 cinnamon stick
4 or 5 slices lemon peel
1/8 tsp. salt
3 eggs, beaten well
1 tbsp. butter or margarine
Ground cinnamon

Cook rice in 1 cup water until tender; let cool. Combine milk, sugar, cinnamon stick, lemon peel and salt in a saucepan. Bring to a boil. Add rice; mix well. Beat a small amount of the hot milk into eggs; beat egg mixture into hot mixture. Cook over low heat, stirring constantly, just until mixture thickens slightly. Do not boil. Add butter; stir until melted. Pour onto shallow platter or small plates; sprinkle cinnamon on top. Cool. Yield: 6 servings.

Geraldine V. Ford, Soc. Chm.
Zeta Nu No. 9060
Goldsboro, North Carolina

VENETIAN RICE WITH PEAS (ITALY) RISI E BISI

1/4 c. butter
4 strips bacon, chopped
1 sm. onion, minced
2 c. fresh or frozen peas
6 c. beef stock
2 c. rice
1 tsp. salt
1/2 tsp. pepper
2 tbsp. chopped parsley
3/4 c. Parmesan cheese

Melt butter in large pan. Add bacon pieces and onion; saute until bacon is crisp. Add peas and 3 cups of stock; simmer for 10 minutes. Add rice and remaining stock. Cook over medium heat for 20 to 25 minutes or until rice is tender, stirring frequently. Stir in salt, pepper, parsley and cheese; serve immediately.

Chelly Kenney
Alpha Rho No. 5302
Mountain Home A.F.B., Idaho

HOMEMADE FETTUCINI

2 c. sifted all-purpose flour
3 eggs
1/4 tsp. salt
Cornmeal
3/4 c. butter
6 tbsp. grated Parmesan cheese
1 8-oz. package cream cheese, softened
2 oz. Velveeta cheese

Place flour on pastry board; make well in center. Add eggs, salt and 1 tablespoon cold water; mix well with fingers. Knead, adding 1 tablespoon water as needed, until dough forms a ball and comes away clean from hands. Cover; let stand for 1 hour. Cut dough into 4 pieces; roll out paper thin. Place on towel to dry. Roll up dough; cut into 1/4-inch strips. Shake slices to unroll; place on waxed paper. Sprinkle a small amount of cornmeal over fettucini. Cook fettucini in boiling salted water for 10 minutes; drain well. Add half the butter; mix well. Add half the cheese; mix again. Place in warm bowl. Add remaining cheeses and remaining butter; mix well. Place bowl in hot oven for 2 minutes. Serve from bowl. Yield: 4 servings.

Mrs. Alyce D. Vanek
International Honorary Member
Laguna Hills, California

CHEESY FETTUCINI

1/4 c. butter, softened
1/4 c. heavy cream
1/2 c. grated Parmesan cheese
1 tbsp. salt
1   12-oz. package fettucini or egg noodles

Cream butter; stir in cream. Add cheese; mix well. Set aside. Boil 6 quarts water; add salt. Add fettucini; cook for 8 minutes. Drain. Stir in butter mixture.

Mrs. Marilyn Jensen
Xi Mu X958
Burnaby, British Columbia, Canada

LINGUINI WITH WHITE CLAM SAUCE (ITALY)

1/2 lb. linguini
1/4 c. olive oil
2 cloves of garlic, chopped
2 shallots, chopped
1/2 tsp. pepper
1 tsp. oregano
1 tsp. chopped parsley
1/2 c. dry white wine
1 can clams, drained
1/2 c. clam juice

Cook linguini according to package directions; drain. Do not rinse. Heat oil in skillet. Add garlic and shallots; cook until lightly browned. Add remaining ingredients; cook over low heat for 5 minutes, stirring constantly. Mix with linguini; serve at once. Yield: 4 servings.

Frances Kosenko
Alpha Tau No. 3131
Chelmsford, Massachusetts

MOSTACCIOLI ITALIANO

2 tbsp. olive oil
1 tbsp. butter
1/2 c. finely chopped onion
1/2 c. finely chopped celery
1 med. green pepper, finely chopped
1/2 clove of garlic, minced
1/4 c. chopped stuffed olives
1/4 c. chopped parsley
1   1-lb. jar spaghetti sauce with meat
1   8-oz. package mostaccioli
1/2 c. grated Cheddar cheese

Heat olive oil and butter in heavy saucepan. Saute onion, celery, green pepper and garlic for 10 minutes. Add olives, parsley and sauce; simmer for 10 minutes longer. Cook mostaccioli according to package directions; drain well. Toss with sauce in heated bowl. Sprinkle with cheese. Yield: 4 servings.

Mrs. Phyllis Brinegar, Pres.
Xi Epsilon Epsilon No. X4260
Evansville, Indiana

GERMAN NOODLES – SPAETZLE

2 c. flour
1 1/2 tsp. salt
2 eggs, beaten
1 c. milk

Sift flour and 1 teaspoon salt into bowl. Add eggs, mix well. Stir in milk gradually until batter is stiff but smooth. Fill kettle with water; add remaining salt. Bring to a boil. Place part of the batter in potato ricer; press batter into boiling water. Noodles will rice to top of water when done. Stir gently with fork; lift out with strainer. Repeat, using remaining batter.

Marvella Plapp
Preceptor Beta Iota XP1687
Leawood, Kansas

LEXINGTON BEST NOODLE PUDDING

1   8-oz. package med.-wide noodles
2   3-oz. packages cream cheese, softened
6 tablespoons butter or margarine, softened
3 lg. eggs
1/2 c. sugar
1 c. milk
1 c. apricot nectar
Topping

Cook noodles according to package directions; drain. Place hot noodles in large saucepan; add cream cheese and butter. Toss until both have melted. Turn into a buttered 2-quart oblong baking dish. Combine eggs, sugar, milk and apricot nectar in mixing bowl; beat just until combined. Pour over noodles; mix well. Sprinkle with Topping. Bake in preheated 350-degree oven for 45 minutes or until firm. Let stand for 5 to 10 minutes. Serve hot. Yield: 8 servings.

Topping

6 tbsp. butter or margarine
1 c. finely crushed corn flakes
1/2 c. sugar
1/2 tsp. cinnamon

Melt butter; stir in remaining ingredients.

Mary Dawn Cravens, Pres.
Gamma Psi No. 9189
Lexington, Kentucky

PINEAPPLE-CHEESE-NOODLE PUDDING

1   12-oz. package wide noodles
1   1-lb. can crushed pineapple, drained
1   8-oz. carton small curd cottage cheese
1 can evaporated milk
3/4 c. sugar
1 tsp. vanilla extract
Dash of salt
4 eggs, beaten
1/2 c. butter, melted
Cinnamon sugar

Boil noodles for 8 minutes; drain and set aside. Combine next 6 ingredients, mix well. Stir in eggs and butter. Add noodles. Pour into well-greased 13 x 9 x 2-inch baking pan; sprinkle with cinnamon sugar. Bake in 350-degree oven for 1 hour. Cut into squares. May serve warm or cold.

Mrs. Doris Josen, Corr. Sec.
Xi Kappa Zeta No. X4995
Sandusky, Ohio

RICH KUGEL (ISRAEL)

1/2 lb. medium noodles
1/2 c. melted butter
1/2 lb. cottage cheese
4 oz. cream cheese
1/3 pt. sour cream
1/2 c. sugar
1 1/2 tsp. vanilla extract
5 eggs, separated

Cook noodles according to package directions; drain. Add butter to noodles. Cream cottage cheese, cream cheese and sour cream with sugar; add to noodles. Stir in vanilla. Beat egg yolks; fold into noodles. Beat egg whites until very stiff; fold into noodle mixture. Pour into greased casserole. Bake at 350 degrees for 45 minutes. May add raisins or pineapple and sprinkle top with corn flakes before baking, if desired.

Virginia E. Rackiewicz, City Coun. Rep.
Preceptor Epsilon XP1320
Wilmington, Delaware

SPAGHETTI WITH CLAM SAUCE

2 cloves of garlic
1/2 c. chopped onion
1/2 c. olive oil
1 lg. can plum tomatoes
1 6 1/2-oz. can minced clams
Salt to taste
1 lb. spaghetti
Grated Romano cheese

Saute garlic and onion in oil until onion is transparent. Remove garlic. Puree tomatoes in blender. Add tomatoes and clams to onion; season with salt. Simmer for 40 minutes or until sauce is thick. Prepare spaghetti according to package directions. Pour clam sauce over spaghetti; sprinkle with cheese.

Carmela Smith
Xi Alpha Gamma No. X1426
Hampton, Virginia

SPAGHETTI ALLA CARBONARA (ITALY)

1/4 c. butter
2 eggs
2 egg yolks
1 c. freshly grated Parmesan cheese
1 lb. spaghetti
Salt
8 slices bacon, cut up
1 tsp. red pepper flakes (opt.)
1/2 c. cream
Pepper to taste

Cream butter until soft and fluffy; set aside. Beat eggs and egg yolks with whisk until well blended. Stir in 1/2 cup grated cheese; set aside. Add spaghetti and 1 teaspoon salt to 6 to 8 quarts water; cook until spaghetti is tender. Fry bacon over moderate heat until crisp; pour off half the bacon drippings. Stir red pepper and cream into bacon drippings; bring to a simmer. Keep warm. Drain spaghetti; place in bowl. Stir in butter, tossing spaghetti to coat well. Add cream mixture and egg mixture; toss to mix well. Season with salt and pepper. Sprinkle with remaining 1/2 cup cheese.

Evelyn M. Beckstrom
Psi Mu No. 5667
Chula Vista, California

SPAGHETTI ITALIANO

1/2 lb. ground beef
1 c. chopped onion
1 tsp. basil leaves, crushed
1 tsp. oregano leaves, crushed
1 lg. clove of garlic, minced
2 cans tomato soup
1 16-oz. can tomatoes, cut up

Brown ground beef in saucepan. Cook onion with seasonings until onion is tender; stir into browned beef. Add soup and tomatoes. Simmer for 30 minutes, stirring occasionally. Serve over spaghetti with Parmesan cheese. Yield: 4 cups sauce.

Photograph for this recipe on page 70.

SPAGHETTI AGLIO E OLIO (ITALY)

3 lg. cloves of garlic, minced
1/2 c. olive oil
2 tbsp. salt
1 lb. spaghetti
Freshly grated Parmesan cheese

Saute garlic in olive oil for 10 minutes; do not brown. Cover and keep hot. Add salt to 4 to 6 quarts rapidly boiling water. Add spaghetti gradually so that water continues to boil. Cook, uncovered, stirring occasionally, until tender. Drain in colander, reserving 1/4 cup spaghetti water. Stir reserved spaghetti water into garlic mixture. Pour over spaghetti; toss. Serve with Parmesan cheese.

Photograph for this recipe on page 110.

121

Vegetables

Vegetables are an exciting world of flavor, texture and color all to themselves, and cooks from England to Hawaii, from Mexico to Scandinavia have made imaginative use of all the delicious varieties. Probably more than any other food, vegetables reflect the cuisine of a country. Pork is as common to German cooking as it is to Hawaiian, but cauliflower, red cabbage, Brussels sprouts and baked onions are particularly German. Popular vegetables in the southern United States include back-eyed peas, okra and yellow squash, while favorite southern Italian vegetables might include tomatoes, eggplant, olives, pimento, spinach and escarole. Moreover, scallions, cucumbers, carrots, celery and beans may not seem an unusual group of vegetables until they are joined by bamboo shoots, lotus roots, and bean sprouts — then they are typically Japanese.

Vegetables are also superbly suited to countless methods of preparation and serving. Many can be served uncooked, to be cool, crisp and colorful; or, they can be pureed and used in delicious sauce. Vegetables can also be pickled, baked, steamed, dried, marinated and seasoned to achieve almost any texture and taste. All of this flavorful diversity is an undeniable expression of cooking creativity found in cooks all over the world.

Vegetables have earned their respect in every land because, regardless of how they are served, they bring a special sparkle to the table. Even more, vegetables have contributed significantly to balanced nutrition for thousands of years. You can present the personality of a new country to your family's meal every single day with these exciting vegetable recipes from Beta Sigma Phi. And for food that is nutritious, nothing is more lively and colorful than vegetables!

TORTA DI ASPARAGI (ITALY)

2 1/2 lb. fresh or 2 pkg. frozen asparagus
3 tbsp. butter
Salt, pepper and nutmeg to taste
1/2 c. Parmesan cheese
1 c. slivered ham
3 eggs, beaten

Cook asparagus until about half done; drain. Melt butter; add salt, pepper and nutmeg. Place asparagus in a buttered baking dish. Pour butter over top. Add cheese, reserving 3 tablespoons for top. Add ham; pour eggs over all. Top with reserved cheese. Bake at 350 degrees for 30 minutes. Yield: 4 servings.

Judith C. Stringer, Rec. Sec.
Xi Gamma Xi X3801
Port Orchard, Washington

ARTICHOKE HEARTS ELEGANTE (ITALY)

1 pkg. frozen artichoke hearts
1 tbsp. dried onion flakes
1 clove of garlic, crushed
1 tbsp. chopped parsley
1/2 c. bread crumbs
1 tsp. salt
1/2 tsp. pepper
1/4 c. olive oil
1/4 c. grated Parmesan cheese
1 avocado, chopped

Cook artichokes in boiling salted water for 5 minutes; drain well. Place in buttered casserole. Mix remaining ingredients and 2 tablespoons water. Sprinkle over artichokes. Bake at 400 degrees for 20 minutes.

Louise Lucidi
Xi Beta Beta X2120
Englewood, Colorado

STUFFED ARTICHOKES FELIPA

4 globe artichokes
1 c. dry bread crumbs
1/4 c. finely grated Romano cheese
1/2 tsp. salt
1/2 tsp. pepper
1 clove of garlic, chopped
1 tbsp. finely chopped parsley
1/4 c. olive oil

Cut off stalks and tips and all tough outer leaves of artichokes. Turn upside down; strike sharply on bread board until leaves open. Wash well with cold water; drain. Mix remaining ingredients except oil; fill each leaf with mixture. Place artichokes upright in 5-quart kettle. Pour olive oil over tops of artichokes. Fill kettle with enough hot water to cover artichokes halfway. Cover with lid; cook over medium-low heat for about 1 hour or until leaf pulls out with slight tug.

Phyllis Angela Niotta, Pres.
Omega Mu No. 5852
San Diego, California

CUBAN BLACK BEANS

1 lb. black beans
1 green pepper, cut in strips
2/3 c. olive oil
1 onion, chopped
4 cloves of garlic, mashed
1 green pepper, diced
4 tsp. salt
1/2 tsp. pepper
1/2 tsp. oregano
1 bay leaf
2 tsp. sugar
2 tsp. vinegar
2 tsp. wine

Combine beans, 10 cups water and green pepper strips in large kettle. Cook for 45 minutes. Combine oil, onion, garlic and diced green pepper in frying pan; brown. Remove 1 cup black beans from kettle; place in frypan, then stir into beans in kettle. Add salt, pepper, oregano, bay leaf and sugar. Cook for 1 hour. Add vinegar and wine. Reduce heat. Simmer for 1 hour and 30 minutes to 2 hours or to desired thickness. Serve over rice.

Mrs. Carol C. Odem
Xi Eta Sigma X4054
Tallahassee, Florida

VENEZUELAN-STYLE BLACK BEANS

2 lb. dried black beans
1 lg. onion, chopped
6 to 8 sm. sweet peppers, chopped
1/2 green bell pepper, chopped
4 or 5 cloves of garlic, chopped
1 tsp. cumin
1/2 c. cooking oil
1/4 c. sugar
1/2 tsp. salt

Soak beans in cold water to cover overnight. Change water; bring to a boil. Cook for about 3 hours or until tender, stirring frequently with wooden spoon. Fry onion, peppers, garlic and cumin in oil over low heat until tender; add to beans. Cook for 15 minutes. Add sugar; cook for 15 minutes. Add salt; cook for 5 minutes longer. Add more seasonings, if desired.

Joyce Palmer
Preceptor Alpha Sigma XP1293
Wellesley, Ontario, Canada

CHINESE GREEN BEANS

1 18-oz. package frozen green beans
1 can cream of celery soup
1/2 c. sliced celery
1 3-oz. can sliced mushrooms
1 8 1/2-oz. water chestnuts, drained and sliced
1 tbsp. soy sauce
3/4 c. chow mein noodles

Combine all ingredients except noodles; place in 2-quart casserole. Bake at 375 degrees for 45 minutes. Stir gently; top with noodles. Bake for 10 minutes longer. Yield: 6 servings.

Linda Panduren, Pres.
Rho No. 6575
Eielson AFB, Alaska

GARBANZO BEAN CASSEROLE

    2 1-lb. cans garbanzo beans
    1 c. chopped onion
    1 tsp. rosemary
    3 tbsp. minced parsley
    1 1-lb. can tomatoes, drained and chopped
    Salt and pepper to taste
    2 cloves of garlic
    1/2 c. olive oil

Combine beans with onion, rosemary, parsley and tomatoes; season with salt and pepper. Saute garlic in olive oil until lightly browned; discard garlic. Stir oil into bean mixture. Place in large casserole. Bake at 350 degrees for 1 hour. Yield: 8 servings.

Marie Johnson, Scrapbook Chm.
Xi Beta Xi X3083
Oklahoma City, Oklahoma

COWBOY BEANS

    2 c. pinto or red beans
    1/2 lb. ham or ham hock
    1 onion, thickly sliced
    2 cloves of garlic, minced
    1 bay leaf
    2 c. tomatoes
    1/2 c. chopped green pepper
    2 tsp. chili powder
    2 tbsp. brown sugar
    1/2 tsp. dry mustard
    1/4 tsp. oregano
    1/4 tsp. cumin
    Salt and pepper to taste

Soak beans for 2 hours in 6 cups boiling water. Cut ham in 1/2-inch cubes. Add to beans in soaking water; add onion, garlic and bay leaf. Bring to a boil; cover and cook on low heat for 1 hour and 30 minutes. Add remaining ingredients except salt and pepper. Simmer for 2 hours, stirring occasionally. Taste and add salt and pepper as needed. Yield: 8-10 servings.

Gertrude Hearty
Xi Alpha Eta X3207
Grantsville, Utah

GREEK BEANS

    1 1-lb. bag pinto beans
    1/2 No. 303 can tomatoes
    1 carrot, diced
    2 stalks celery, diced
    1 med. onion, sliced
    1 1/2 tsp. salt
    1 tsp. pepper

    1/4 tsp. garlic powder
    1/2 c. olive or salad oil
    1 tsp. minced parsley

Cover beans with water; simmer until half done. Add remaining ingredients; simmer until beans are tender but not soft. Yield: 6-8 servings.

Lois M. McAleer
Xi Alpha X168
Carson City, Nevada

POLYNESIAN BEETS

    1 16-oz. can sliced beets
    1 16-oz. can pineapple chunks
    1 or 2 tbsp. cornstarch
    1/3 c. sugar
    1 tbsp. vinegar
    Salt and pepper to taste
    2 tbsp. margarine

Drain beets and pineapple; reserve juices. Combine beet juice and pineapple juice in saucepan; cook over medium heat to boiling point. Mix cornstarch, sugar, vinegar, salt and pepper into a smooth paste; stir small amount of hot juice into paste. Cook, stirring constantly, until thickened. Add beets and pineapple; mix. Add margarine; simmer for 20 minutes. Serve hot or cold. Yield: 8-10 servings.

Mary E. Oakley, Corr. Sec.
Preceptor Nu XP437
Orlando, Florida

BROCCOLI-CHEESE CASSEROLE

    2 pkg. frozen chopped broccoli, thawed
    1 8-oz. jar Cheez Whiz
    1 can mushroom soup
    1 tbsp. melted butter
    1 c. Minute rice

Combine all ingredients in 9-inch casserole. Bake in 350-degree oven for 1 hour. May be prepared and refrigerated overnight before baking, if desired.

Eleanor DeVore, Pres.
Xi Beta X551
Cumberland, Maryland

CREAMY BROCCOLI CASSEROLE

    1 pkg. frozen chopped broccoli
    1 lb. Velveeta cheese, cubed
    1/4 c. margarine
    1/2 c. milk
    3 c. cooked Minute rice

Combine broccoli, cheese, margarine and milk in saucepan. Heat until cheese is melted; mix well. Stir in rice. Turn into casserole. Bake, uncovered, at 350 degrees for about 40 minutes.

Katherine L. Bell
Xi Gamma Theta X2998
Red Oak, Iowa

DELUXE BROCCOLI CASSEROLE

2 eggs, well beaten
1 can cream of mushroom soup
1 c. mayonnaise
1 c. grated Cheddar cheese
2 pkg. frozen chopped broccoli, thawed
Ritz cracker crumbs

Blend first 3 ingredients together; stir in cheese and broccoli. Pour into buttered 2-quart casserole. Top with crumbs. Bake at 350 degrees for 45 minutes. Yield: 8-10 servings.

Ruth Ann Emmerton, V.P.
Xi Delta Rho X4451
Saint Catharines, Ontario, Canada

SPECIAL BROCCOLI CASSEROLE

1   20-oz. bag frozen chopped broccoli
1/2 c. butter or margarine
1/2 lb. Velvetta cheese, cubed
1 stack Ritz crackers, crumbled

Cook broccoli for 5 minutes in salted water; drain. Melt 1/4 cup butter in pan; add broccoli and cheese. Cook until cheese melts, stirring constantly. Pour into well-greased 9 x 13-inch baking dish. Mix cracker crumbs with remaining 1/4 cup melted butter. Sprinkle over top. Bake at 350 degrees for 10 to 15 minutes or until bubbly.

Mrs. Mary E. Morris
Preceptor Beta Beta Chap.
Pomeroy, Ohio

BAYREUTH KRAUT (GERMANY)

1 head cabbage, shredded
1/2 c. shortening
1 tbsp. salt
1 tsp. pepper
1/2 c. red cooking wine (opt.)
3 tbsp. vinegar

Combine all ingredients; simmer for 3 hours, stirring occasionally. Cabbage should be soft and slightly brown.

Barbara Hunt
Xi Gamma Mu Chap.
Albany, Georgia

DUTCH-STYLE RED CABBAGE

1/2 c. chopped onion
2 tbsp. butter or margarine
3 c. shredded red cabbage
1 c. diced apples
3 whole cloves
1 1/4 tsp. salt
1/8 tsp. pepper
1 tsp. wine vinegar
1/4 c. stock

Saute onion in butter until limp and transparent; add remaining ingredients. Cover; cook for 10 minutes. Yield: 4 servings.

Geraldine S. Bryant, Pres.
Xi Gamma Gamma X3283
Central Point, Oregon

NORWEGIAN CABBAGE WITH SOUR CREAM

4 c. finely shredded cabbage
1 1/2 tsp. salt
1/2 tsp. pepper
2/3 c. (or more) sour cream
1 tbsp. dillweed

Combine cabbage and 1/4 cup water in casserole; cover. Cook in microwave over for 7 to 8 minutes or until crisp tender, stirring twice. Combine salt, pepper, sour cream and dillweed; mix into hot cabbage. Cook, covered for 1 minute longer.

Bonnie Bjerke
Preceptor Sigma XP584
Ottawa, Ontario, Canada

RED CABBAGE WITH APPLE

2   16-oz. jars sweet-sour red
      cabbage
1 med. tart red apple, cut in thin
      wedges and halved
1 med. onion, halved and sliced
1/4 c. raisins
1/2 tsp. caraway seed

Combine all ingredients in frypan or saucepan. Bring to a boil; cover. Reduce heat; cook slowly for 15 minutes or until apple is tender and raisins are plump. Drain, if desired. Yield: 6 servings.

Photograph for this recipe on page 69.

SOUR-SWEET CABBAGE (NORWAY)

1 green cabbage
1 tsp. salt
1/4 c. vinegar
1/4 c. sugar
2 tsp. caraway seed
2 tbsp. melted butter or bacon drippings

Cut cabbage in thin slices; place in saucepan with 2 cups water and salt. Cook until tender; add vinegar, sugar, caraway seed and butter. Simmer for at least 15 minutes longer.

Dr. Theodora E. Renneke
International Honorary Member
Minneapolis, Minnesota

TASTY RED CABBAGE

4 strips bacon, cut up
1 sm. red cabbage, shredded
1 med. onion, chopped
2 peeled tart apples, cored and quartered
Salt to taste
1 tbsp. sugar
1/4 tsp. ground cloves
Vinegar to taste

Fry bacon until crisp in large saucepan. Add cabbage, onion, apples, salt, sugar, cloves and 2/3 cup water. Bring to a boil; simmer for 1 hour, stirring occasionally and adding water, if needed. Add vinegar and additional sugar and salt to make desired sweet and sour taste.

Peggy Cohrs, Pres.
Xi Beta Phi X2064
Brooksville, Florida

CHINESE-STYLE CARROTS AND MUSHROOMS

12 spring carrots
2 yellow onions
3 tbsp. butter
1 1/2 c. sliced mushrooms
Juice of 1/2 lemon
3/4 tsp. salt
1/4 tsp. savory
1/4 tsp. ginger
1/8 tsp. mace
1/8 tsp. nutmeg
1/8 tsp. thyme
1/8 tsp. pepper
2 tbsp. minced parsley

Peel 12 tender young carrots; slice paper thin. Peel and thinly slice onions. Melt butter in a large skillet; add carrot, onions and mushrooms. Saute slowly until onions and mushrooms are tender. Add 1/2 cup water, lemon juice, salt and spices. Cover; simmer for about 25 minutes or until carrots are tender. Remove lid; simmer for several minutes longer. Stir in minced parsley just before serving. Yield: 6 servings.

Ruth Sterns
Preceptor Kappa XP1508
Tuscaloosa, Alabama

MARINATED CARROTS

2 lb. carrots, sliced
1 med. onion, diced
1/2 green pepper, diced
1 can tomato soup
1 c. sugar
3/4 c. salad oil
3/4 c. vinegar
1 tbsp. Worcestershire sauce
2 tsp. prepared mustard

Cook carrots until tender in small amount of boiling salted water; drain. Combine all remaining ingredients; add to carrots. Bring to a boil. Remove from heat; cool. Refrigerate overnight. Yield: 12 servings.

Barbara Moore, Corr. Sec.
Eta Chi No. 10332
Wendell, North Carolina

VICHY CARROTS (FRANCE) CAROTTES A LA VICHY

2 lb. carrots
3 tbsp. butter
4 tsp. sugar
1/2 tsp. salt

Scrub carrots well; do not scrape unless necessary. Cut into long narrow strips or slice very thin. Place in large saucepan with tightfitting cover. Add enough water to come 3/4 up height of carrots. Add butter, sugar and salt; cover. Cook over high heat without removing cover for 20 to 25 minutes or until water is evaporated and carrots are frying in butter. Sprinkle with parsley, if desired.

Jean L. McEnaney
Kappa Delta No. 9870
Farragut, Iowa

CAULIFLOWER-GREEN PEPPER AND BEEF (CHINA) YEH CHOY FA LUT TSIU NGAU YUK

3 tbsp. soy sauce
1 1/2 tsp. salt
2 tsp. sugar
3/4 c. sliced lean beef
1 tsp. fresh or dried ginger
3 tbsp. peanut oil
3 3/4 c. sliced cauliflower
1/4 c. sliced green pepper
1/2 tsp. cornstarch
1/8 c. sliced green onions with tops

Combine 1 tablespoon soy sauce, 1/2 teaspoon salt and 1 teaspoon sugar; add to beef. Let stand for 5 minutes. Soak ginger in 1 tablespoon water. Make sauce of remaining salt, sugar and soy sauce; add ginger juice. Heat 1/2 of the oil until very hot; add beef. Cook for 1 minute. Stir; remove beef from pan. Add remaining oil; heat. Add cauliflower and green pepper; stir and cook for 2 minutes. Add 1 cup water. Make a smooth paste of cornstarch and small amount of water; combine with ginger and soy sauce mixture. Stir into vegetables when vegetables begin to boil. Add onions; boil for 30 seconds, stirring constantly. Add beef; reheat. Serve very hot with steamed rice.

Sharon Anderson, City Coun. Pres.
Preceptor Beta Gamma XP1326
Bremerton, Washington

CAULIFLOWER-POTATO CURRY (PAKISTAN)

2 1/2 tbsp. shortening
1 med. onion, diced
1 med. tomato, cut into sm. wedges
1/4 tsp. salt
1/4 tsp. hot pepper sauce
1/4 tsp. turmeric
1/2 tsp. crushed cumin
1/2 tsp. crushed coriander
1   10-oz. package frozen cauliflower
1 lg. potato, peeled and quartered

Melt shortening in 2-quart saucepan; add onion, tomato, salt, hot pepper sauce, turmeric, cumin and coriander. Cook over very low heat until onion is tender. Add cauliflower and potato; mix well. Cover. Reduce heat to simmer. Do not add water. Cook until all moisture has been absorbed and vegetables are done. Serve hot with whole wheat bread puries or steamed rice.

Zelda Taylor, V.P.
Xi Alpha Chap.
Bozeman, Montana

DEEP-FRIED CAULIFLOWER (CZECHOSLOVAKIA) KVETAK

1 cauliflower
2 eggs
1/4 c. milk
Salt to taste
1/2 c. flour
2 c. bread crumbs

Separate cauliflower into flowerets. Beat eggs and milk together. Season cauliflower with salt; roll in flour. Dip in egg mixture; coat with bread crumbs. Heat oil to 400 degrees; fry cauliflower until golden brown. Remove from fryer; place is casserole. Bake at 350 degrees for about 10 minutes or until tender. Do not overcook.

Jarmila M. Schindeler
Mu No. 7729
Brooks, Alberta, Canada

CELERY TOULTA (ITALY)

1 lg. onion, finely chopped
1 clove of garlic, minced
2 tbsp. chopped parsley
3 tbsp. olive oil
5 eggs, slightly beaten
2 c. cooked chopped celery, drained well
1/4 c. bread crumbs
1/2 c. Parmesan cheese
Salt and pepper to taste
1/2 tsp. marjoram
1/2 tsp. basil
1/4 tsp. rosemary
Butter

Saute onion, garlic and parsley lightly in olive oil. Combine all ingredients except butter; mix well. Place in 8-inch square buttered casserole. Dot with butter; sprinkle with additional Parmesan cheese. Bake at 350 degrees for 25 minutes or just until set and lightly browned.

Lorraine Schau
Preceptor Alpha Lambda Chap.
San Rafael. California

CHINESE CELERY

1 tsp. salt
4 c. sliced celery
1 can cream of chicken soup
1   2-oz. can chopped pimento, drained
1   8-oz. can water chestnuts, drained and sliced
1/2 c. slivered almonds
1 c. coarse buttered bread crumbs

Add salt to 1/2 cup water; add celery. Boil for 5 minutes; drain. Add soup, pimento, water chestnuts and 1/2 of the almonds; mix well. Place in well-greased casserole. Top with crumbs and remaining almonds. Bake at 350 degrees for 20 to 30 minutes or until bread crumbs are brown.

Mary Jo Birley
Beta Sigma XP1494
Mount Carmel, Illinois

GRANDMA'S CREAMED CORN

2 cans creamed corn
1/2 to 3/4 c. milk
1/2 to 1 c. sugar
3 eggs, beaten
1 c. soda cracker crumbs
Butter

Mix corn, milk, sugar and eggs together. Add cracker crumbs for thickness. Turn into casserole; dot with butter. Bake in 350 to 375-degree oven until set.

Katie Spurgin, Parliamentarian
Gamma Theta No. 10427
Mackay, Idaho

COMPANY ITALIAN EGGPLANT PARMESAN

2   1-lb. eggplant
Salt
Flour
5 eggs, slightly beaten
Olive oil
3/4 c. (about) grated Parmesan cheese
4 c. spaghetti sauce with meat
1 lb. Cheddar cheese or mozzarella cheese, shredded

Slice unpeeled eggplant crosswise, about 1/4-inch thick. Sprinkle slices with salt; place in colander.

Weight down with plate to press out liquid for at least 2 hours. Dry with paper towels. Dip eggplant in flour, then in eggs. Fry in about 1/4-inch olive oil in large skillet in single layers until golden brown and tender. Drain on paper towels. Spread a small amount sauce over bottom of oblong baking dish; add layer of eggplant. Sprinkle with part of the Parmesan cheese and part of the Cheddar cheese. Repeat layers, ending with cheeses and sauce. Bake, covered, in preheated 350-degree oven for about 15 minutes. Uncover; bake for 10 minutes longer or until bubbly.

Georgia Schaefer, Publ.
Beta Nu No. 4292
Joseph, Oregon

BEEF-STUFFED EGGPLANT (ITALY)

3 sm. eggplant, cut in half
Salt
1/4 c. vegetable oil
1 1/4 lb. ground beef chuck
1 sm. onion, minced
1 c. drained canned tomatoes
Pepper to taste
1/2 c. fine dry bread crumbs
1 1/2 c. grated mozzarella cheese

Scoop out eggplant halves, leaving shell about 3/4-inch thick. Chop eggplant pulp removed from shells. Sprinkle with salt. Let stand for 30 minutes. Drain off excess liquid. Heat oil in a large skillet. Add ground chuck; saute until lightly browned. Add chopped eggplant and onion; continue cooking until onion is tender, stirring occasionally. Drain off excess fat and liquid. Stir in tomatoes. Season to taste with salt and pepper. Spoon mixture into eggplant shells. Sprinkle with bread crumbs and mozzarella cheese. Place in well-greased shallow casserole. Bake in preheated 350-degree oven for 20 to 25 minutes or until top is golden brown. Yield: 6-8 servings.

Photograph for this recipe on page 122.

STUFFED EGGPLANT ALL' ITALIANO

4 sm. or 2 med. eggplant
6 tbsp. olive oil
3 cloves of garlic, minced
1 med. onion, chopped
6 sprigs of parsley, minced
1 tbsp. capers
2 tbsp. coarsely chopped black olives
1/4 tsp. dried basil
1 1/2 c. fresh bread crumbs
1/8 to 1/4 tsp. dried chili peppers
1 tsp. salt
Juice of 1 lemon
3/4 c. grated Gruyere or Swiss cheese
8 to 12 thin slices tomato
Pepper to taste

Cut eggplant in half; scoop out pulp, leaving 1/2-inch shell. Chop pulp fine. Heat 2 tablespoons oil in skillet; add eggplant pulp. Cook, stirring for 1 minute. Combine garlic, onion and parsley; add to skillet mixture. Add capers, olives, basil, bread crumbs, chili peppers and salt; blend well. Add 3 tablespoons oil, lemon juice and 1/3 cup cheese. Stir again; fill eggplant shells. Cover shells with slightly overlapping tomato slices. Sprinkle with additional salt and pepper. Top with remaining cheese; drizzle remaining oil over top. Place on baking sheet. Bake in preheated 350-degree oven for 30 minutes or until hot and bubbling.

Teresa Lynn Crofoot
Kappa Delta No. 9501
Emporia, Kansas

SHRIMP-STUFFED EGGPLANT

3 sm. eggplant
2 bell peppers, chopped
1 c. chopped onion
1 tsp. salt
1/8 tsp. cayenne pepper
2 tsp. garlic salt
1/2 tsp. pepper
1/2 c. butter
1 lb. fresh shrimp, peeled and deveined
2 c. cooked rice
Bread crumbs

Cut eggplant in half; spoon out pulp, leaving shell. Combine pulp, bell peppers, onion and seasonings in saucepan with 1/2 cup water. Cook until tender. Melt butter in skillet; add shrimp. Cook until tender. Add rice and eggplant mixture; cook for 5 minutes or until water has evaporated. Spoon into eggplant shells; sprinkle with bread crumbs. Place in baking dish; add 1/2 cup water to baking dish. Bake at 350 degrees for 45 minutes.

Vlasta Bell
Xi Alpha Zeta X3025
Rayne, Louisiana

GREEN PEPPERS STUFFED WITH EGGPLANT (BRAZIL)

1/4 c. oil
1 lg. eggplant, peeled and cut into 1/2-in. cubes
1 1/3 c. tomato sauce
1/2 c. grated Parmesan cheese
1 clove of garlic, crushed
2 lg. green peppers, seeded and
    halved lengthwise

Heat oil in frying pan; fry eggplant until soft. Add tomato sauce, half the cheese and garlic. Cook green peppers in boiling salted water for 5 minutes. Drain well. Fill green pepper halves with eggplant mixture; sprinkle tops with remaining cheese. Bake in preheated 350-degree oven for 20 minutes. Yield: 4 servings.

Annelle Mizell
Xi Epsilon Gamma X2317
Petersburg, Illinois

ITALIAN GREEN PEPPERS

1/2 c. sliced onion
2 cloves of garlic, minced
2 tbsp. olive oil
1   1-lb. can stewed tomatoes or 3 to
    4 med. tomatoes, chopped
2 tsp. sugar
1 1/2 tsp. salt
1/4 tsp. pepper
1/4 tsp. oregano
1/4 tsp. basil
5 lg. green peppers, cut in 1-in. strips

Saute onion and garlic in oil in large skillet until golden. Add tomatoes and seasonings; blend well. Simmer, uncovered, for about 20 minutes or until slightly thickened. Parboil green pepper strips, uncovered, for about 15 minutes. Drain well; combine with tomato mixture in skillet. Cook, uncovered, for about 15 minutes or until peppers are tender.

Jeanne Urban, Pres.
Xi Epsilon Omicron X4943
Wichita, Kansas

MUSHROOM DELIGHT

1 lb. fresh mushrooms
2 tbsp. flour
1 tsp. salt
1/2 tsp. pepper
3 tbsp. margarine, melted
1/3 c. shredded Cheddar cheese
1   8-oz. carton sour cream
2 tsp. minced parsley

Clean mushrooms and remove stems. Combine flour, salt and pepper in plastic bag. Add mushrooms; shake to coat well. Saute mushrooms in margarine for 10 minutes. Add cheese and sour cream; stir until cheese is melted. Do not boil. Sprinkle with parsley. Serve over buttered toast, if desired. Yield: 4-6 servings.

Jeanne Poll, Pres.
Laureate Mu PL291
Holland, Michigan

BRAISED ENDIVE AND
MUSHROOMS (FRANCE)

1/2 c. butter or margarine
6 heads endive, trimmed and cut into
    halves
1 lb. fresh mushrooms
1/2 c. white wine
1/2 c. Ocean Spray cranberry-orange
    relish

Melt butter in a large skillet. Add endive and mushrooms; saute until lightly browned. Add wine; cover. Simmer for about 20 minutes or until tender. Stir in cranberry-orange relish. Heat to serving temperature. Yield: 6 servings.

Photograph for this recipe on page 122.

STUFFED MUSHROOMS
CHAMPIGNONS FARCIS

16 fresh mushrooms
6 tbsp. butter
1 tbsp. olive oil
3 tbsp. finely minced shallots
3 tbsp. finely minced onion
3 tbsp. fine white bread crumbs
3 tbsp. cream
1/4 c. grated Swiss cheese
Salt and pepper to taste
1/4 c. minced parsley
1/2 tsp. tarragon
1/4 c. grated Parmesan cheese

Wash mushrooms; remove stems. Pat caps dry. Melt butter in heavy saucepan. Dip mushroom caps in butter; place in shallow baking pan, hollow side up. Chop mushroom stems; squeeze in towel to extract juice. Add oil to butter; saute shallots, onion and mushroom stems until limp. Remove from heat. Add remaining ingredients except Parmesan cheese; mix well. Fill mushroom caps with stuffing; sprinkle with Parmesan cheese. Bake in 375-degree oven for 15 to 20 minutes.

Mrs. Pat Torrington, Treas.
Xi Gamma Omega No. 3603
Storm Lake, Iowa

FRESH ONION TARTLETS
(FRANCE)

1 1/2 c. finely chopped onions
1/4 tsp. Italian seasoning
1/4 c. butter or margarine
1/3 c. bleu cheese
12   3-in. unbaked pastry shells
3 lg. eggs, lightly beaten

1 c. light cream
1/2 tsp. salt
1/8 tsp. pepper

Saute onions and Italian seasoning in butter until onions are limp. Stir in cheese until melted. Spoon about 1 tablespoon onion mixture into each pastry shell. Combine eggs, cream, salt and pepper. Spoon over onions. Bake in preheated 425-degree oven for 15 minutes. Reduce oven temperature to 350 degrees. Bake for 20 minutes longer or until custard is set. Yield: 12 tarts.

Photograph for this recipe on opposite page.

SAUTEED ONIONS

1 med. onion, sliced
1/2 green pepper, chopped
1/4 c. chopped mushrooms
Butter or margarine
1/2 fresh ripe tomato, peeled and mashed
1/2 tsp. salt
1/8 tsp. pepper
2 tsp. grated Danish cheese

Saute onion, green pepper and mushrooms in butter until brown. Add tomato; heat through. Stir in salt and pepper. Add cheese, 1 spoonful at a time, stirring well after each addition.
This recipe is from Papasan's Steak House in Nagoya, Japan. Yield: 1 serving.

Rosanna Fahl
Xi Gamma Xi Chap.
Oroville, California

TARTE AUX OIGNONS (FRANCE)

3 or 4 lg. onions, chopped
2 tbsp. butter
2 c. Bechamel sauce
2 eggs, beaten
3/4 c. cream
1/2 tsp. salt
1/4 tsp. pepper
1/4 tsp. dry mustard
1 9-in. unbaked pastry shell
Paprika (opt.)

Saute onions lightly in butter until soft. Combine onions and Bechamel sauce. Beat eggs with cream; pour into sauce mixture. Add seasonings; pour into pie shell. Sprinkle lightly with paprika. Bake at 450 degrees for 30 minutes or until filling is set and crust is browned.

Patricia Elliott, Pres.
Xi Gamma X1449
Burton, New Brunswick, Canada

IMPERIAL GREEN PEAS
(JAPAN)

1 10-oz. package frozen green peas
and celery

1 tbsp. butter
1/2 tsp. salt
1 chicken bouillon cube
1 tbsp. cornstarch
1 5-oz. can water chestnuts, drained
and thinly sliced

Add peas, celery, butter and salt to 1/2 cup boiling water in saucepan; cover. Cook over low heat for about 2 to 3 minutes or until peas and celery are tender but still crisp. Remove from heat. Add bouillon cube; stir until dissolved. Blend 1/4 cup cold water and cornstarch. Add cornstarch mixture, 1 cup boiling water and water chestnuts to peas and celery. Cook just until thickened, stirring gently. Yield: 4 servings.

Photograph for this recipe above.

PEAS ORIENTAL

1 lb. mushrooms, sliced thick
Butter
3 pkg. frozen peas
2 sm. cans water chestnuts, drained and sliced
2 sm. cans bean sprouts, drained and rinsed
2 cans cream of mushroom soup
2 cans French-fried onion rings

Saute mushrooms in butter. Cook peas just until separated. Combine mushrooms, peas and remaining ingredients except onion rings in casserole. Bake for 30 minutes in 350-degree oven. Crumble onion rings over top; bake for 5 or 10 minutes longer. Canned buttered sliced mushrooms may be substituted for fresh mushrooms; do not saute.

Letty Ayres
Laureate Iota Chap.
Independence, Missouri

POTATO APPLES (SWITZERLAND) FUNGGI

2 apples, pared and quartered
3 tbsp. sugar
3 tbsp. butter
1 onion, sliced
6 potatoes, peeled and cubed
1 1/2 tsp. salt
2 tbsp. cider

Combine apples, sugar and 3 cups water in saucepan. Bring to a boil; cook for 3 minutes. Melt butter in large saucepan. Add onion; saute for 10 minutes, stirring frequently. Add potatoes, salt, cider and apple mixture with liquid. Cover; cook for 30 minutes or until very soft. Mix well. Serve hot in individual dishes with meats.

Mavourneen Rustell, Off. Staff
Beta Sigma Phi International
Kansas City, Missouri

UKRAINIAN POTATO BABKA

3 lg. potatoes, peeled and halved
1 c. cream-style cottage cheese
2 tbsp. butter
2 eggs, separated
1/2 tsp. salt
1/8 tsp. white pepper

Cook potatoes in boiling salted water for about 20 minutes or until tender. Drain well. Mash hot potatoes with cottage cheese and butter in mixing bowl. Add

egg yolks, salt and pepper; beat until fluffy. Beat egg whites until stiff peaks form; fold into potato mixture. Spoon into greased 1-quart casserole or souffle dish. Bake at 375 degrees for 25 to 30 minutes or until puffed and golden. Serve immediately. Yield: 6 servings.

Jenna Glenn, Treas.
Eta Lambda No. 6451
Knoxville, Iowa

POTATOES FROM THE BASQUE COUNTRY (FRANCE)

2 1/4 c. chicken broth
1/4 c. celery leaves
1/4 c. white wine
2 1/2 c. Idaho instant potato flakes
Salt and pepper to taste
1 clove of garlic, crushed
1 green pepper, chopped
1 onion, chopped
1 tomato, chopped
12 stuffed green olives, sliced
1/4 c. butter or margarine

Combine broth, celery leaves and wine; bring to a boil. Whisk lightly into potato flakes. Season with salt and pepper; keep warm. Saute garlic, vegetables and olives in butter. Make a nest in center of potatoes; pour in vegetables. Yield: 5 servings.

Photograph for this recipe below.

MASHED POTATOES WITH HORSERADISH SAUCE (GERMANY)

8 to 10 potatoes
Salt to taste
2 tbsp. butter
Freshly ground pepper to taste
1 c. sour cream
2 tbsp. horseradish
Minced parsley
Melted butter

Cook potatoes in boiling salted water until tender; drain well. Sprinkle with salt. Mash potatoes, adding butter and pepper. Add sour cream, horseradish and a small amount of parsley. Whip potatoes. Pour melted butter over top; serve immediately.

Sandra Bell, Pres.
Zeta Gamma No. 2720
Shelby, Ohio

SPINACH-CHEESE PIE (GREECE)
SPANAKOPETA

1/4 c. chopped onion
1/4 c. butter
2 pkg. frozen chopped spinach, cooked
    and drained
2 eggs
1   16-oz. carton dry cottage cheese
1/4 lb. feta cheese, crumbled
Salt to taste
1/8 tsp. pepper
Melted butter
1 lb. phyllo or strudel leaves

Saute onion in 1/4 cup butter. Add spinach; mix well. Beat eggs in large bowl. Stir in cottage cheese, feta cheese, salt, pepper and spinach mixture, using a wooden spoon; mix well. Brush 8 x 12 x 2-inch baking pan lightly with melted butter. Place 8 phyllo leaves in baking dish, 1 at a time, brushing each leaf with melted butter. Keep unused leaves covered with damp paper towels. Spread spinach mixture over phyllo. Cover with remaining phyllo leaves, brushing each leaf with melted butter. Bake in preheated 350-degree oven until golden brown. Yield: 8-10 servings.

Geraldine B. Goumas, Pres.
Xi Gamma Zeta No. 3720
Upper Nyack, New York

SPINACH-RICE AND CHEESE CASSEROLE

1 pkg. frozen chopped spinach
1 c. rice, cooked
Grated cheese
Bacon

Cook spinach according to package directions; drain well. Place spinach in square baking pan; spread rice over spinach. Sprinkle with enough cheese to cover rice generously. Cover cheese with bacon slices. Bake

in 350-degree oven until cheese is melted. Broil for 1 minute or until bacon is crisp.

Patty Harris, Corr. Sec.
Alpha Eta No. 4574
Las Vegas, Nevada

SPINACH SOUFFLE

1 pkg. frozen chopped spinach
4 eggs, separated
1/4 c. Parmesan cheese

Cook spinach according to package directions; drain well. Beat egg whites until firm peaks form. Combine beaten egg yolks and cheese; mix well. Fold egg whites into egg yolk mixture; fold in spinach. Place in well-buttered casserole. Bake at 350 degrees for 30 minutes or until done.

Barbara Baird, Treas.
Xi Xi Chap.
Lakemont, Pennsylvania

MEXICAN SQUASH CASSEROLE

12 med. yellow summer squash, sliced
1 sm. onion, sliced
2 cans cream of chicken soup
2 cans green roasted chilies
Salt and pepper to taste
1 pkg. corn tortillas
2   1/2 c. grated American cheese
Paprika

Steam squash and onion together in saucepan until limp. Do not overcook squash. Drain well. Pour into large mixing bowl. Add soup and chilies; season with salt and pepper. Mix well. Cover bottom of large oblong baking dish with tortillas. Spread half the squash mixture over tortillas; sprinkle with part of the grated cheese. Repeat layers, ending with a generous layer of grated cheese. Sprinkle paprika over cheese; cover. Bake at 350 degrees for 30 minutes or until cheese is bubbly. Remove from oven; let stand for 15 minutes before serving. Yield: 6 servings.

Maria Herrera, Treas.
Xi Alpha Delta X666
Austin, Texas

MEXICAN-STYLE ITALIAN SQUASH

2 tbsp. margarine
1 med. onion, chopped
2 lb. zucchini, sliced
1 can chopped green chilies
12 oz. Montery Jack cheese, shredded

Saute first 3 ingredients until golden. Add chilies and cheese; cook over low heat until squash is tender and cheese is melted. Can be prepared and baked as a casserole.

Kay Lowery, Pres.
Psi No. 2619
Roswell, New Mexico

ZUCCHINI PARMESAN (ITALY)

8 to 10 sm. zucchini
3 tbsp. olive oil
2/3 c. coarsely chopped onions
1/4 lb. mushrooms, sliced
2/3 c. grated Parmesan cheese
2 6-oz. cans tomato paste
1 tsp. salt
1/2 tsp. MSG
1/2 tsp. garlic salt or 1 clove
of garlic, minced
1/8 tsp. pepper

Trim off ends of zucchini; cut crosswise into 1/8-inch slices. Heat olive oil in saucepan; add zucchini, onions, and mushrooms. Cover; cook over low heat for 10 to 15 minutes or until tender, stirring occasionally. Remove from heat; mix in about 1/2 of the grated cheese. Combine remaining ingredients; pour over zucchini mixture. Blend lightly; place in casserole. Sprinkle with remaining cheese. Bake at 350 degrees for 20 to 30 minutes or until done. Yield: 8 servings.

Linda A. Koenig, Ext. Off.
Xi Epsilon Chi X2744
Granite City, Illinois

ZUCCHINI PIE

3 c. coarsely grated unpeeled zucchini
Salt to taste
1 4-oz. can whole green chilies
3/4 c. sliced green onions with tops
1 1/2 tbsp. butter or margarine
1 tbsp. flour
1 thick 9-in. pie crust
1 c. grated Cheddar cheese
1/2 c. shredded Montery Jack cheese
3 eggs
1 1/2 c. evaporated milk
Freshly ground pepper to taste

Place zucchini on sheet of foil; sprinkle with salt. Let stand for 30 minutes. Squeeze out moisture. Cut chilies into 1/2-inch pieces. Cook green onions slowly in melted butter for about 1 minute. Stir in zucchini; cook until zucchini is glazed. Blend in flour until smooth. Spread in pastry shell; sprinkle with chilies and half the cheeses. Beat eggs with milk; season lightly with salt and pepper. Pour into pastry shell; sprinkle with remaining cheeses. Bake at 400 degrees for 15 minutes. Reduce temperature to 350 degrees; bake for 20 to 25 minutes longer or until custard is set. Cool for 15 minutes before serving.

Beverly Woodford
Beta Iota No. 8903
Custer, South Dakota

DANISH SWEET POTATOES

1/2 c. margarine
1 c. (packed) brown sugar
2 cans syrup-packed sweet potatoes
1/2 tsp. salt
1/4 c. cornstarch

Melt margarine over low heat in saucepan; add brown sugar. Simmer, stirring, for about 5 minutes or until sugar is dissolved. Add syrup from 1 can of sweet potatoes; bring to a boil. Drain remaining can of sweet potatoes; reserve syrup. Arrange sweet potatoes in casserole. Combine reserved syrup with salt and cornstarch; add to mixture in saucepan. Boil for 1 minute; pour over sweet potatoes. Bake at 350 degrees for 1 hour.

Linda Ramberg Schmidt
Xi Xi No. 2525
Tioga, North Dakota

SOUTHERN SWEET POTATO SOUFFLE

3 c. cooked mashed sweet potatoes
1 c. sugar
1/2 tsp. salt
2 eggs
1/2 c. milk
1 tsp. vanilla extract
Melted margarine
1 c. (packed) brown sugar
1/3 c. flour
1 c. chopped nuts
1 c. coconut

Combine first 6 ingredients; stir in a scant 3 tablespoons melted margarine. Pour into baking dish. Combine brown sugar, flour and nuts; blend in 1/4 cup melted margarine. Add coconut; spread over potato mixture. Bake in 350-degree oven for 30 minutes.

Marcene P. Powell, Rec. Sec.
Eta Omicron No. 10246
Washington, Georgia

SWEET POTATO-CRANBERRY CASSEROLE (SOUTH AMERICA)

1 c. dried apricots
6 med. sweet potatoes, cooked, peeled
and sliced
6 bananas, cut into 1-inch slices
1 c. Ocean Spray whole berry
cranberry sauce
1/4 c. melted butter or margarine
1/2 c. flaked coconut

Cook apricots in 2 cups hot water until tender. Drain and reserve liquid. Arrange alternate layers of potatoes, apricots, bananas and cranberry sauce in a 1 1/2-quart casserole, ending with potatoes. Mix reserved apricot liquid with butter. Pour over casserole. Bake in preheated 375-degree oven for 35 minutes. Sprinkle top of casserole with coconut; bake for 10 minutes longer or until coconut is lightly browned. Garnish with additional cranberry sauce. Yield: 6-8 servings.

Photograph for this recipe on page 122.

SWEET POTATOES PANAMANIAN

6 sweet potatoes, cooked
1/4 c. butter
1 c. chicken broth
Garlic salt to taste

Peel potatoes; mash. Add butter, broth and garlic salt. Mix well. Add more broth and butter if potatoes seem dry. Place in greased casserole. Bake at 350 degrees until heated through.

Armine S. Atkinson, W. and M. Chm.
Preceptor Phi XP1361
Mesa, Arizona

SWISS CHARD ITALIANO

2 lb. washed Swiss chard
1/2 lb. bacon, diced
1 lg. onion, diced
1 lg. can tomatoes, diced
1 sm. can tomato juice

Cook Swiss chard in boiling water until tender. Drain; set aside. Cook bacon and onion in Dutch oven until done. Add tomatoes and juice; simmer over low heat for 30 minutes. Add Swiss chard; simmer for 15 minutes. Yield: 6 servings.

Lila Warrell, Pres.
Xi Gamma Pi X2584
Muncie, Indiana

THREE-VEGETABLE CASSEROLE

1 10-oz. package frozen baby lima beans
1 10-oz. package frozen cauliflower
1 10-oz. package frozen chopped broccoli
1 10-oz. can cream of mushroom soup
1 sm. jar Cheez Whiz
2 tbsp. milk
1 can French-fried onions

Precook lima beans for several minutes; drain. Pour boiling water over cauliflower and broccoli; drain well. Arrange vegetables in layers in buttered casserole. Combine soup, Cheez Whiz and milk in saucepan; heat until well blended. Pour over vegetables. Bake at 350 degrees for 30 minutes. Arrange onions over top. Bake for 10 minutes longer.

Dianne Wiltgen, Ext. Off.
Xi Delta Omega X4355
Calmar, Iowa

TOMATO FLIP (ENGLAND)

2 tbsp. margarine or butter
1 sm. onion, chopped
1 29-oz. can tomatoes
6 oz. sharp Cheddar cheese, grated

Melt margarine in skillet over medium heat; saute onion for 5 minutes. Add tomatoes; mash lightly. Simmer for 20 minutes. Add cheese; simmer for 20 min-

utes longer, stirring until cheese is melted. Serve over toast or as vegetable dish.

Virginia Gail Gaskell, Ritual of Jewels
Gamma Delta No. 4080
Walla Walla, Washington

TOMATOES ROMANO (ITALY)

1 c. herb-seasoned stuffing mix
1/4 c. shredded sharp Cheddar cheese
Pepper to taste
1/4 c. margarine, melted
4 underripe or green tomatoes, halved
Grated fresh Romano cheese

Combine stuffing mix, Cheddar cheese and pepper; add margarine. Toss to combine. Line shallow baking pan with foil. Place tomatoes in baking pan. Spoon about 2 tablespoons crumb mixture on each tomato half. Sprinkle Romano cheese on top. Bake in preheated 400-degree oven for about 15 minutes or until tomatoes are tender.

Sharlene Mattioda, City Coun. Pres.
Xi Zeta X600
Hot Springs, Arkansas

FINNISH TURNIP LOAF

6 c. diced turnips
1 tsp. sugar
Pinch of pepper
Pinch of nutmeg
1/2 c. cream
2 eggs, slightly beaten
1/4 c. soft bread crumbs
1 tbsp. melted butter

Cook turnips in boiling salted water for 20 minutes or until tender. Drain and mash. Add next 5 ingredients; blend thoroughly. Turn into buttered 6-cup casserole. Toss bread crumbs and butter together; sprinkle over casserole. Bake in 375-degree oven for 1 hour. Serve hot. Yield: 6 to 8 servings.

Dr. Leona F. Paterson
International Honorary Member
Calgary, Alberta, Canada

MERSEYSIDE MASH (ENGLAND)

6 sm. turnips
10 carrots
1/2 c. butter
Salt and pepper to taste

Peel and slice turnips and carrots; boil in salted water until tender. Drain; mash with butter. Season with salt and pepper. Serve piping hot. Yield: 6 servings.

Valerie J. Cox
Xi Theta Rho X2566
Austin, Texas

Breads

All around the world, bread is considered the staff of life. Arabic street vendors call "Allah is Merciful" as they sell their flat, round loaves to passersby. The Jewish *challah* loaf is traditionally baked for the Sabbath. It commemorates the 12 loaves offered for the 12 Tribes at The Temple in Jerusalem before the Dispersion. Christians also have an imaginative array of holiday breads, each with its own traditional spices and shape. Often, a trinket is hidden in the bread — the Twelfth Night loaf in Mexico holds a figure of the Christ Child. In Sweden, the Yule season opens on December 13 with a young girl of the house serving *Lussekatter* buns to her family in honor of St. Lucia. English maidens recognize their patron saint on November 25 with customary loaves called *St. Catharine's Wigs.*

Leavened bread did not become common to man's diet until after the Middle Ages. Once it did, however, the amazing imagination of the world's cooks created an almost endless array of favorite breads. We can now enjoy dark breads from northern Europe, corn bread from America, pastries from Scandinavia, Austria and France, strudel from Germany, scones from Canada and the British Isles, as well as gingerbread, banana bread, oatmeal bread, pancakes, waffles and biscuits.

With the availability of so many commercially prepared breads and baked goods, baking is no longer the crucial household chore that it was only a few generations ago. However, Beta Sigma Phi sisters recommend it as a form of family togetherness, and a creative and rewarding experience that fills the house with an indescribably wonderful aroma. There is something that everyone in the family can do to produce a loaf of bread, cinnamon rolls, corn muffins, or brown bread if they wish. Moreover, the results are so mouthwatering that the whole family may never eat anything but homemade breads again!

COLORADO BISCUITS

3 c. flour
4 1/2 tsp. baking powder
2 1/2 tbsp. sugar
3/4 tsp. cream of tartar
3/4 tsp. salt
3/4 c. shortening
1 egg
1 c. milk

Sift flour, baking powder, sugar, cream of tartar and salt together. Cut in shortening until mixture resembles cornmeal. Beat egg and milk together slightly. Add to dry ingredients; beat vigorously for several seconds. Turn out on a floured board; knead and shape into ball. Let rest for several minutes. Roll out 1/2 inch thick; cut into desired shapes. Place on baking sheet. Bake in preheated 450-degree oven for 12 minutes or until done. Yield: 20 biscuits.

Janice Venrick, Soc. Com. Chm.
Eta Psi No. 9487
Akron, Colorado

EASTER BISCUITS (ENGLAND)

3 c. all-purpose flour
1 tsp. baking powder
1 tsp. mixed spices
1 tsp. cinnamon
3/4 c. margarine or butter
3/4 c. sugar
1/2 c. (or more) currants
2 eggs, beaten

Sift flour, baking powder, mixed spices and cinnamon into a bowl; add margarine. Cut into small pieces; rub in with fingertips until mixture resembles fine bread crumbs. Stir in sugar and currants. Add eggs; mix to form stiff dough. Roll out on a lightly floured board to 1/4-inch thickness. Cut in rounds with a 3 1/2-inch fluted cutter. Place on greased baking sheets. Bake in preheated 350-degree oven for 15 to 20 minutes or until lightly browned. Cool on wire rack.

Joan G. Routt, Soc. Chm.
Preceptor Alpha Sigma XP760
San Angelo, Texas

MULESHOE BISCUITS

1 pkg. dry yeast
2 c. buttermilk
5 c. flour
3 tsp. baking powder
1 tsp. soda
1/2 tsp. salt
1/4 c. sugar
1 c. shortening
Melted butter

Combine yeast with 2 tablespoons warm water. Add to buttermilk; set aside. Sift dry ingredients together; cut in shortening. Add buttermilk mixture; mix well. Knead dough on floured board; divide into 3 parts. Roll out 1/2 inch thick; cut with biscuit cutter. Dip in melted butter; fold in half. Place on baking sheet. Let rise for 15 to 20 minutes. Bake at 400 degrees for 15 minutes. Dough can be frozen or kept in refrigerator for 3 to 4 days.

Frances Walker, Ext. Off.
Xi Sigma Beta No. 4798
White Deer, Texas

CHAPATI (INDIA)

2 c. whole wheat flour
2 c. all-purpose flour
1 tsp. salt
3 tbsp. melted butter

Sift flours and salt together. Mix in butter with fork. Add just enough water to make a soft dough; knead for 5 to 8 minutes. Cover with plastic wrap; let stand for 1 hour. Knead dough again; form into 10 small balls. Roll out into paper thin circles. Cook on lightly greased hot griddle until brown, turning frequently. Lightly grease griddle after each baking. Serve hot brushed with butter.

Edythe Shelton, Soc. Chm.
Preceptor Mu Chap.
Salina, Kansas

CHEESE PUFFS (FRANCE)
LES PETITES GOUGERES

1/4 c. margarine
1/2 tsp. salt
Dash of white pepper
1 c. unsifted flour
4 eggs
1 c. shredded Swiss cheese

Heat 1 cup water, margarine, salt and pepper in saucepan until water is boiling and margarine has melted. Add flour all at once; beat vigorously until mixture leaves the side of pan. Remove from heat. Add eggs, one at a time, beating well after each addition. Continue beating until mixture is smooth. Stir in cheese until well blended. Drop mixture by tablespoonfuls onto lightly greased baking sheet. Bake at 375 degrees for about 45 minutes or until done. Yield: 12 puffs.

Phyllis Gray
Xi Alpha Omicron X1528
Orlando, Florida

MUSHROOM CORN MUFFINS

1 4-oz. can mushroom stems and pieces
Milk
1 egg, beaten
3 tbsp. chopped almonds
1 12-oz. package corn muffin mix

Drain mushrooms; add enough milk to mushroom liquid to measure 2/3 cup. Add egg to liquid. Chop mushrooms into small pieces. Add mushrooms, almonds and liquid to muffin mix; mix well. Spoon bat-

ter into well-greased muffin pan, filling cups half full. Bake according to package directions for 20 minutes. Yield: 18 muffins.

Helen E. Reigel, Pres.
Laureate Epsilon PL192
Harrisburg, Pennsylvania

COOL-RISE SESAME BRAID

    5 1/2 to 6 1/2 c. all-purpose flour
    2 pkg. Fleischmann's yeast
    1 3/4 c. warm milk
    2 tbsp. sugar
    1 tbsp. salt
    3 tbsp. Fleischmann's margarine
    Peanut oil
    1 egg white, beaten
    2 tbsp. sesame seed

Pour flour onto waxed paper. Pour 1/2 cup warm water into large warm bowl. Sprinkle in yeast; stir until dissolved. Add warm milk, sugar, salt and margarine. Add 2 cups flour. Beat with rotary beater for about 1 minute or until smooth. Add 1 cup flour. Beat vigorously with a wooden spoon for about 150 strokes or until smooth. Add enough additional flour to make a soft dough. Turn out onto lightly floured board. Knead for about 8 to 10 minutes or until smooth and elastic. Cover with plastic wrap, then towel. Let rest for 20 minutes. Divide dough in half. Roll each half on a lightly floured board into 9 x 12-inch rectangle. Cut each rectangle lengthwise into 3 equal strips. Braid 3 strips together; seal ends tightly. Place in greased 8 x 4 x 2 5/8-inch bread pan. Repeat with remaining 3 strips. Brush with peanut oil. Cover pans loosely with waxed paper brushed with oil. Top with plastic wrap. Refrigerate for 2 to 24 hours. Remove from refrig-

erator. Uncover dough carefully. Let stand, uncovered, for 20 minutes at room temperature. Puncture any bubbles which may have formed with a greased toothpick or metal skewer. Brush with beaten egg white. Sprinkle with sesame seed just before baking. Bake in a 400-degree oven for 30 to 40 minutes or until done.

Photograph for this recipe on this page.

PAN DE ELOTE

    1 1-lb. can cream-style corn
    1 c. Bisquick
    1/2 c. milk
    1 egg, beaten
    2 tbsp. melted butter
    1 4-oz. can diced green chilies
    1/2 lb. Jack cheese, grated

Combine corn, Bisquick, milk, egg, butter and green chilies. Turn 1/2 of the batter into well-greased 2-quart Pyrex baking dish. Cover with grated cheese. Spread remaining batter over cheese. Bake at 400 degrees for about 35 to 40 minutes or until browned.

JoAnn Miller, Newport Harbor Area Coun. Pres.
Preceptor Eta Rho XP1650
Huntington Beach, California

ZIPPY MEXICAN CORN BREAD

    1 egg
    1 c. milk
    1 1/2 c. self-rising cornmeal
    1/2 c. self-rising flour
    1/4 c. minced bell pepper
    1/2 tsp. chili powder
    1 tbsp. oil

Beat egg until pale yellow; blend in milk. Stir in cornmeal slowly. Blend in flour until smooth. Add bell pepper and chili powder. Preheat pan with oil. Add corn bread batter. Bake in preheated 450-degree oven until done. Yield: 6-8 servings.

Patricia C. Clark, Pres.
Xi Epsilon X662
Tuscaloosa, Alabama

ENGLISH SHORTBREAD

    2 c. flour
    1/2 c. sugar
    1 tbsp. cornstarch
    Pinch of salt
    1 c. butter
    Powdered sugar

Combine first 4 ingredients; cut in butter. Knead until smooth; shape into ball. Cut in half. Spread with fingers into 2 8-inch pans. Bake at 275 degrees for about 1 hour or until lightly browned. Cut while hot; sprinkle with powdered sugar.

Francey L. Morris
Pi Omega No. 8577
Rittman, Ohio

FRIED CHEESE CAKES (RUSSIA)
SYRNIKI

> 1 lb. very dry pot cheese
> 1/2 tsp. salt
> 2 eggs, lightly beaten
> 1/2 c. all-purpose flour
> Butter

Force cheese through food mill or sieve. Beat in salt, eggs and flour until thoroughly mixed and very smooth. Chill for 2 hours. Shape a small amount of dough at a time with floured hands into flat round 2-inch cakes, keeping remaining dough chilled. Fry over medium heat in hot butter for 10 minutes; reduce temperature. Cook for 10 to 15 minutes longer, turning once during frying to brown on both sides. Serve with sour cream and minced dill.

Judith L. Mitchell
Xi Alpha Gamma X3284
Anniston, Alabama

FRIED MATZAH (ISRAEL)

> 2 eggs
> Dash of salt
> Egg-type matzah
> 1 to 2 tbsp. butter

Measure eggs; add half as much water. Add salt; beat well. Run sheet of matzah under hot water to soften. Melt butter in frying pan over medium heat. Break matzah; dip pieces in egg mixture. Fry in butter just until golden, turning once. Serve hot.

Kathryn I. Gundersen
San Gabriel Valley Coun. Treas.
Xi Epsilon Phi X3281
Monrovia, California

ITALIAN BREADSTICKS
GRISSINI

> 1 pkg. dry yeast
> 1 tsp. salt
> 1/2 c. soft shortening
> 1 tbsp. sugar
> 2 c. flour
> 1 egg yolk
> Sesame seed or coarse salt

Dissolve yeast in 2/3 cup warm water. Combine salt, shortening, sugar and 1/2 of the flour. Knead in remaining flour on cloth for 5 minutes or until smooth. Cover; let rise for about 1 hour or until doubled in bulk. Divide dough in half; cut each half into 24 pieces. Roll each piece into pencil shapes, 6 to 10 inches long. Place 1 inch apart on greased baking sheet. Brush with egg yolk; sprinkle with sesame seed. Bake in preheated 400-degree oven for 20 to 25 minutes.

Margaret Greb, Treas.
Xi Alpha Eta X3444
Waukesha, Wisconsin

BEER BREAD

> 3 c. self-rising flour
> 3 tbsp. (heaping) sugar
> 1 12-oz. can beer at room temperature
> Melted butter

Combine flour and sugar; add beer gradually, stirring well for 1 minute. Pour into greased loaf pan. Bake at 350 degrees for 20 minutes. Brush well with melted butter. Bake for 20 to 25 minutes longer or until bread tests done.

Shirley Futch
Eta Theta No. 5712
Plant City, Florida
Janet Kroh, Pres.
Xi Gamma Phi X4805
Woodbridge, Virginia

BUTTERMILK BREAD (ENGLAND)

> 3 c. flour
> 2 tsp. baking powder
> 1 tsp. soda
> 1 tsp. salt
> 2/3 c. sugar
> 1 3/4 c. buttermilk
> 2 eggs, lightly beaten
> 2 tbsp. melted butter or margarine
> 1 1/2 c. floured raisins

Sift dry ingredients together; add buttermilk, eggs, butter and raisins. Mix well. Spoon into greased and lightly floured loaf pan. Bake at 350 degrees for 55 minutes.

Clara Norris
Preceptor Laureate Alpha PL111
Roseburg, Oregon

CAPE BRETON BANNOCK

> 1 1/2 c. bran
> 1 c. whole wheat flour
> 1 c. all-purpose flour
> 1 1/2 tsp. salt
> 1 tsp. soda
> 1 tsp. baking powder
> 2 tbsp. brown sugar
> 1/2 c. wheat germ
> 1/2 c. coconut
> 1 c. sunflower seed
> 1/4 c. oil
> 1 1/2 c. buttermilk
> 1/2 c. chopped candied orange peel (opt.)

Combine first 10 ingredients. Combine oil, buttermilk and orange peel in blender container; blend just enough to mix. Stir liquid into dry ingredients to make a moist dough. Form a large ball; place on buttered baking sheet. Press out to 1 or 1 1/2 inches thick and an oval shape. Cut a cross on top for good luck. Bake at 400 degrees for about 25 minutes or until

browned. Cool on rack; cut in slices 1/2 inch thick. Serve spread with butter.

Edna Staebler
International Honorary Member
Waterloo, Ontario, Canada

BLACK BREAD (RUSSIA)

4 c. unsifted rye flour
3 c. unsifted all-purpose flour
1 tsp. sugar
2 tsp. salt
2 c. whole bran cereal
2 tbsp. caraway seed, crushed
2 tsp. instant coffee
2 tsp. onion powder
1/2 tsp. fennel seed, crushed
2 pkg. Fleischmann's yeast
1/4 c. vinegar
1/4 c. dark molasses
1 sq. unsweetened chocolate
1/4 c. Fleischmann's margarine
1 tsp. cornstarch

Combine flours. Combine 2 1/3 cups flour mixture with next 8 ingredients in a large bowl; mix well. Combine 2 1/2 cups water, vinegar, molasses, chocolate and margarine in saucepan. Heat over low heat until liquids are warm. Margarine and chocolate do not need to melt. Add to dry ingredients gradually. Beat for 2 minutes at medium speed of electric mixer, scraping bowl occasionally. Add 1/2 cup flour mixture, or enough flour mixture to make a thick batter. Beat at high speed for 2 minutes, scraping bowl occasionally. Stir in enough additional flour mixture to make a soft dough. Turn out onto lightly floured board. Cover dough with bowl; let rest for 15 minutes. Knead for about 10 to 15 minutes or until smooth and elastic; dough may be sticky. Place in greased bowl, turning to grease top. Cover; let rise in warm place for about 1 hour or until doubled in bulk. Punch dough down; turn out onto lightly floured board. Divide dough in half. Shape each half into a ball, about 5 inches in diameter. Place each ball in center of greased 8-inch round cake pan. Cover; let rise in warm place, for about 1 hour or until doubled in bulk. Bake in 350-degree oven for about 45 to 50 minutes or until done. Combine cornstarch and 1/2 cup cold water. Cook over medium heat, stirring constantly, until mixture boils; continue to cook, stirring constantly, for 1 minute. Brush cornstarch mixture over tops of loaves as soon as bread is baked. Return bread to oven; bake for 2 to 3 minutes longer or until glaze is set. Remove from pans; cool on wire racks.

Photograph for this recipe on page 136.

IRISH SODA BREAD

3 c. sifted all-purpose flour
1/3 c. sugar
2 1/2 tsp. soda
1 1/2 tsp. salt

2 tbsp. butter
1 3/4 c. old-fashioned rolled oats
1/2 c. chopped candied green cherries
2 tsp. caraway seed (opt.)
2 c. raisins
1 3/4 c. buttermilk
1 egg

Blend flour, sugar, soda and salt in bowl. Cut in butter until blended. Mix in oats, cherries, caraway seed and raisins. Combine buttermilk and egg; add gradually to flour mixture, stirring until blended. Turn batter into greased 9 ro 10-inch round cake pan. Cut a deep cross in top. Bake at 375 degrees for 45 to 50 minutes. Serve warm.

Marlys Meagher
Alpha Omega No. 1800
Pueblo, Colorado

COUNTY CORK SODA BREAD (IRELAND)

4 c. sifted flour
3 tsp. baking powder
1 tsp. salt
1/2 tsp. soda
1 c. California seedless raisins
1 tbsp. caraway seed
1 3/4 c. buttermilk
1/4 c. cooking oil

Resift flour with baking powder, salt and soda. Add remaining ingredients; mix just enough to moisten. Shape dough into 2 mounds on greased baking sheet. Cut deep cross in top of each loaf with sharp knife. Bake in 350-degree oven for 50 minutes.

Photograph for this recipe below.

SESAME BREAD

1 pkg. dry yeast
1/4 c. sugar
1 tsp. salt
1 c. margarine
2 eggs. beaten
3 1/2 c. flour
1/3 c. sesame seed

Dissolve yeast in 1 1/4 cups warm water; mix well. Add sugar, salt, 1/2 cup melted margarine and eggs. Work in flour. Cover; let rise in warm place for 1 hour. Stir down. Pour batter in greased 9 x 12-inch baking pan. Combine remaining 1/2 cup margarine and sesame seed; heat until melted. Spread over batter. Let rise until doubled in bulk. Bake in 400-degree oven for 25 minutes. Cut in squares to serve.

Merlyn Stanton, Treas.
Alpha Eta Zeta No. 7967
Canadian, Texas

POCKET BREAD (ISRAEL) PETA

1 pkg. dry yeast
1/2 tsp. salt
3 1/2 c. flour
1/4 c. poppy or caraway seed

Blend yeast and 1 1/4 cup warm water; let stand for 5 minutes. Stir in salt. Mix in flour gradually to form a stiff dough. Turn dough on floured board; knead for 5 minutes or until smooth, adding flour as needed to prevent sticking. Cut into 8 equal pieces; cover dough with cloth. Let rise until doubled in bulk. Turn out on floured board; roll into 5-inch circles. Dampen top with water; sprinkle with poppy seed. Place 1 inch apart on greased baking sheets. Cover with cloth; let rise in a warm place for about 45 minutes or until almost doubled in bulk. Bake at 450 degrees for 8 to 10 minutes. Yield: 8 servings.

Shirley Fay Smith, Pres.
Preceptor Beta Omega XP749
San Diego, California

POORIS

1 c. unsifted flour
1/2 c. whole wheat flour
1 tsp. salt
1 qt. (about) corn oil

Stir flours and salt together. Stir in 1/2 cup cold water and 1 tablespoon corn oil. Mixture will be crumbly. Work with hands until smooth dough forms. Divide into 8 balls. Roll each ball very thin on lightly floured board or cloth. Cut 5-inch circle from each. Pour corn oil into deep fryer or skillet, filling no more than 1/3 full. Heat over medium heat to 375 degrees. Place dough circles carefully in hot oil and fry for about 45 seconds to 1 minute on each side, turning once, until well puffed and slightly browned. Drain on paper towels. Yield: 8 servings.

Photograph for this recipe on page 2.

QUICK SPINACH BREAD (ITALY)

Frozen bread dough to make 2 loaves
3   10-oz. packages frozen chopped spinach
1 to 1/2 lb. Italian sausage
Garlic to taste
Minced onion to taste
Oregano to taste
Grated Parmesan cheese

Thaw frozen dough according to package directions. Thaw spinach; do not cook. Peel skin from sausages; fry until done, stirring to break up. Add spinach, garlic, onion and oregano. Add a generous amount of Parmesan cheese. Let cool. Roll 1 piece dough out to large square; spread 1/2 of the sausage mixture on one side of square. Roll up; place on cookie sheet in horseshoe shape. Repeat with remaining dough and sausage mixture. Bake at 350 degrees for 30 minutes or until golden brown.

Mrs. Angela Galen. Pres.
Alpha Eta No. 9465
Bloomington, Indiana

BUTTERFLY ROLLS (CZECHOSLOVAKIA)

1/3 c. sugar
1/3 c. vegetable shortening, melted
1 pkg. dry yeast
2 eggs, beaten
1 tsp. salt
2 1/2 c. flour
Melted margarine

Add sugar to shortening. Dissolve yeast in 1 cup warm water. Add sugar mixture to eggs; mix well. Add yeast mixture. Combine salt and flour; add to egg mixture. Let rise until doubled in bulk. Divide into 3 balls. Roll each ball into a circle; cut in 12 wedges. Roll toward point, starting from rounded edge of each wedge. Place on greased baking sheet. Brush with margarine. Let rise until doubled in bulk. Bake at 400 degrees for 10 minutes or until golden brown.

Marcia V. Haworth
Exemplar Preceptor Iota XP274
Sugar Creek, Missouri

CRESCENT ROLLS

Sugar
1 tbsp. warm milk
1 pkg. yeast
3 eggs
4 c. unsifted flour
1 c. hot milk
1/4 c. melted butter
1 tsp. salt

Dissolve 1 tablespoon sugar in warm milk; add yeast and dissolve thoroughly. Beat eggs; add 1/3 cup sugar and yeast mixture. Add flour alternately with hot milk. Add melted butter and salt. Cover; refrigerate overnight. Remove dough from refrigerator 4 hours

Breads

before using. Roll out half the dough into a 1/4-inch thick circle. Brush with additional melted butter. Cut into 16 wedges. Roll up, starting at large end; place, point side down, on baking sheet. Repeat with remaining dough. Bake at 450 degrees for 7 to 8 minutes or until browned.

Brenda Bruton, V.P.
Phi Epsilon Beta P1662
Pampa, Texas

CRUNCH ROLLS

1 pkg. dry yeast
1 c. milk, scalded
1/2 c. shortening
1/4 c. sugar
1 1/4 tsp. salt
1 1/4 c. rolled oats
2 eggs
2 1/2 c. sifted flour

Soften yeast in 1/4 cup warm water. Pour milk over shortening, sugar and 1 teaspoon salt; cool to lukewarm. Stir in 1 cup oats. Add 1 egg, 1 egg yolk and softened yeast. Stir in flour; beat well. Cover; let rise in warm place for about 1 hour or until doubled in bulk. Punch down. Fill greased muffin cups about 1/2 full. Cover; let rise in warm place for about 30 minutes or until about doubled in bulk. Combine remaining oats and remaining salt for topping. Brush roll tops lightly with egg white; sprinkle with topping. Bake at 375 degrees for 15 to 20 minutes or until golden brown. Yield: 18 rolls.

Loree Girod
Xi Alpha Pi X1822
Tacoma, Washington

FILLED ROLLS (RUSSIA)
PIROSIIKI

Biscuit mix
1/2 c. sour cream
1 c. finely chopped cooked carrots
2 hard-boiled eggs, finely chopped
1 tbsp. finely chopped ripe olives
1 tbsp. finely chopped parsley
1/2 tsp. salt
1/4 tsp. pepper

Prepare 1 recipe biscuit dough according to package directions. Roll dough out until about 1/4 inch thick. Cut with round cutter. Brush each piece with sour cream. Combine carrots, eggs, olives, parsley, salt and pepper. Place heaping teaspoon of mixture on each pastry round. Fold pastry over; pinch edges together. Prick pastry with fork. Place on baking sheet. Bake in 375-degree oven for 25 minutes or until lightly browned. Yield: About 24.

Micki Blasczyk, Corr. Sec., City Coun. Rep.
Xi Alpha Iota X3511
Rochester, Minnesota

WHOLE WHEAT HOT ROLLS

2 tbsp. dry yeast
1 tsp. sugar
1/4 c. honey
1 3/4 c. scalded milk
1/2 c. oil
2 tsp. salt
2 well-beaten eggs
5 1/2 to 6 c. whole wheat flour
1/4 tsp. ginger

Dissolve yeast and sugar in 1/2 cup warm water. Add honey to milk; cool. Add oil, salt, eggs and yeast mixture. Sift flour and ginger into yeast mixture; mix well. Cover; let rise until doubled in bulk. Punch down; let rise again. Spoon into greased muffin tins; let rise until light. Bake at 375 degrees for 15 minutes.

Regina Merrill
Laureate Alpha PL189
Salt Lake City, Utah

BRITISH WHOLE WHEAT SCONES

3 1/3 c. whole wheat flour
1/2 tsp. soda
1/4 c. butter
1 1/2 tbsp. honey
1/2 c. raisins
2 eggs
1 c. milk
1 tbsp. lemon juice

Combine flour and soda; cut butter into flour mixture. Add honey and raisins. Beat eggs; add milk and lemon juice. Add egg mixture to flour mixture; mix well. Add more milk if dough is too dry to roll. Roll dough 3/4 inch thick. Cut into 2-inch circles. Place on lightly greased baking sheet. Bake at 425 degrees for 20 minutes. Yield: 25 scones.

Barbara Potter, Pres.
Chi No. 4720
Loring AFB, Maine

OATMEAL SCONES (SCOTLAND)

3 c. rolled oats
3 c. all-purpose flour
2 c. shortening
1 tbsp. salt
1 c. (packed) brown sugar

Combine oats and flour; cut in shortening. Blend in salt and brown sugar. Stir in 1/4 cup cold water. Roll about 1/4 inch thick on highly floured board. Cut in squares. Place 1 inch apart on ungreased cookie sheet. Bake in preheated 400-degree oven for 20 minutes or until golden brown. Yield: 3-4 dozen scones.

V. Gail Lokey, V.P.
Xi Alpha Nu X2959
Old Hickory, Tennessee

HONEY SCONES (SCOTLAND)

2 c. flour
1/4 c. sugar
1 tbsp. baking powder
1/2 tsp. salt
6 tbsp. butter or margarine
1/4 c. milk
2 tbsp. honey
1 egg

Stir flour, sugar, baking powder and salt together; cut in butter until fine crumbs form. Blend in milk, honey and egg with fork; stir in flour all at once. Turn out on floured board; knead until dough holds together. Pat dough into 9-inch circle; cut into 8 wedges. Place on greased cookie sheet. Bake in preheated 400-degree oven for 10 minutes or until browned. Brush tops with melted butter; serve with warm honey. Yield: 8 servings.

Faith E. Edmonson
Kappa Rho No. 7397
Harrisonville, Missouri

IRISH SCONES

2 c. sifted flour
2 tsp. baking powder
1/2 tsp. soda
1/4 c. sugar
1/3 c. shortening or 1/2 c. margarine
1/2 c. raisins
1 egg, beaten
2/3 c. sour milk

Sift dry ingredients together; cut in shortening. Add raisins; mix well. Combine egg and sour milk; reserve about 2 tablespoons egg mixture. Add remaining egg mixture to raisin mixture; turn into 8 or 9-inch layer pan. Brush top of scones with reserved egg mixture. Bake in preheated 400-degree oven for 20 minutes or until done.

Lorretta Weller
Theta Alpha No. 9446
Wasaga Beach, Ontario, Canada

SWEDISH LIMPA BREAD

2 c. beer
1/4 c. (packed) brown sugar
2 tbsp. molasses
1 1/2 tbsp. shortening
1/2 tsp. cumin seed
1 tsp. fennel seed
1 pkg. dry yeast
1 tsp. grated orange rind
3 c. all-purpose flour
1 tsp. salt
2 c. rye flour

Combine first 6 ingredients in pan; bring to a boil. Reduce heat; simmer for 3 minutes. Cool to lukewarm. Add yeast; stir to dissolve. Stir in orange rind and all-purpose flour. Cover; let rise for 30 minutes. Add salt and enough rye flour to make stiff dough. Let rise until doubled in bulk. Knead for 10 minutes. Pat into rectangle; roll as for jelly roll. Place on greased cookie sheet; let rise for 20 minutes. Prick top with toothpick. Bake at 350 degrees for 40 to 50 minutes.

Doris Rascher
Xi Theta Beta Chap.
Yucaipa, California

AEBLESKIVERS (DENMARK)

2 c. buttermilk
2 tbsp. sugar
1/4 c. melted butter
2 eggs, separated
2 c. flour
2 tsp. baking powder
1/2 tsp. salt
1/2 tsp. soda

Combine first 3 ingredients; add lightly beaten egg yolks. Combine dry ingredients; add to buttermilk mixture. Beat until smooth. Fold in beaten egg whites. Fill well-greased cups of Danish Aebleskiver pan 3/4 full. Bake on top of stove until golden brown. Turn in cup with fork or knitting needle to brown other side. A piece of apple, raisins or a nut may be placed in middle of each skiver just before turning. May be rolled in sugar after baking and served with syrup, honey or jam.

Shirley J. Lehmann, Rec. Sec.
Theta Gamma No. 9857
Golden, Colorado

CHUCHEL (SWITZERLAND)

3 egg, beaten
1 c. milk
1 c. flour
1/2 tsp. salt
1 tsp. baking powder
2 tbsp. sugar
1 tbsp. butter

Combine eggs and milk. Beat in sifted dry ingredients. Melt butter in frypan. Pour half the batter at a time into pan and brown. Turn and brown other side. Cut into small pieces. Serve with applesauce, syrup or honey and cheese. Yield: 3 servings.

Sheri Duerst, Pres.
Preceptor Theta Delta XP1720
San Marcos, California

APPLE CREAM COFFEE CAKE

1/2 c. chopped walnuts
2 tsp. cinnamon
1 1/2 c. sugar
1/2 c. butter or margarine, softened
2 eggs
1 tsp. vanilla extract

2 c. sifted flour
1 tsp. baking powder
1/2 tsp. salt
1 tsp. soda
1 cup sour cream
1 apple, sliced

Combine walnuts, cinnamon and 1/2 cup sugar; set aside. Cream butter at high speed of electric mixer. Add 1 cup sugar gradually; beat until light and fluffy. Add eggs, 1 at a time, beating well after each addition. Add vanilla; beat until blended. Sift flour with baking powder, salt and soda; add to batter alternately with sour cream at low speed. Spread half the batter in greased 9-inch tube pan; top with apple slices and half the walnut mixture. Add remaining batter; top with remaining walnut mixture. Bake in 375-degree oven for 40 minutes or until done. Cool for 30 minutes; remove from pan.

Angie Overholt, City Coun. Past Pres.
Laureate Kappa XP636
Hamilton, Ontario, Canada

PECAN-FILLED POTECA (YUGOSLAVIA)

3 to 4 c. unsifted flour
1/4 c. sugar
1 tsp. salt
1 pkg. Fleischmann's yeast
Milk
1/2 c. Fleischmann's margarine
2 eggs
1 c. (firmly packed) brown sugar
1 tsp. orange extract
2 c. finely chopped pecans
Confectioners' sugar frosting

Combine 1 cup flour, sugar, salt and dry yeast in a large bowl; mix well. Combine 1/2 cup milk, 1/2 cup water and margarine in a saucepan. Heat over low heat until liquids are warm. Margarine does not need to melt. Add to dry ingredients gradually; beat for 2 minutes at medium speed of electric mixer, scraping bowl occasionally. Add 1 egg and 1/2 cup flour or enough flour to make a thick batter. Beat at high speed for 2 minutes, scraping bowl occasionally. Stir in enough additional flour to make a soft dough. Turn out onto lightly floured board; knead for about 8 to 10 minutes or until smooth and elastic. Place in greased bowl, turning to grease top. Cover; let rise in warm place for about 1 hour and 30 minutes or until doubled in bulk. Punch dough down; turn out onto lightly floured board. Roll dough out to a 20 x 15-inch rectangle. Combine 1/4 cup margarine, brown sugar and remaining egg; stir in 2 tablespoons milk and orange extract. Blend in pecans. Spread filling over dough. Roll up as for jelly roll, starting at wide side of dough. Seal edges. Pull dough gently to make a 25-inch roll. Form into a snail shape on a large greased baking sheet. Cover; let rise in warm place for about 1 hour or until doubled in bulk. Bake in a 325-degree oven for 40 to 45 minutes or until done. Remove from baking sheet; cool on wire rack. Frost with confectioners' sugar frosting.

Photograph for this recipe on this page.

COTTAGE CHEESE CAKE (ESTONIA) KOHUPIIMA KOOK

1 pkg. dry yeast
1/2 c. milk
1/2 c. butter or margarine
1/2 tsp. salt
Sugar
Flour
4 eggs
1/2 tsp. lemon peel or orange peel
2 lb. dry cottage cheese
1 c. sour cream
1 tsp. caraway seed or 2 tsp. vanilla extract
1/2 c. raisins

Dissolve yeast in 1/4 cup lukewarm water. Bring milk and butter to a boil. Add salt and 2 tablespoons sugar; let cool. Beat 1 cup flour, 1 egg and yeast into milk mixture. Beat in 1 3/4 cups flour and lemon peel gradually. Knead for several minutes; place in greased bowl. Cover; let rise for 1 hour to 1 hour and 30 minutes or until doubled in bulk. Punch down; press dough over bottom and sides of greased 9 x 13-inch pan. Let rise for 30 minutes. Place cottage cheese, 2 egg yolks, 3/4 cup sugar, sour cream, 1 tablespoon flour and caraway seed in blender container; blend until smooth. Beat 2 egg whites until stiff. Fold egg whites and raisins into cottage cheese mixture; pour into dough crust. Beat remaining egg with 1 teaspoon sugar; brush over cottage cheese mixture. Bake at 350 degrees for 30 to 35 minutes or until done.

Lillian Tamm White, Treas.
Xi Iota Upsilon X4683
Ashland, Ohio

HOLIDAY POTECA

1 cake yeast
3/4 c. warm milk
1/4 c. sugar
1 tsp. salt
1 egg
1/4 c. butter or shortening
3 1/2 to 3 3/4 c. flour, sifted
Walnut Filling
Raisins (opt.)
Cinnamon to taste (opt.)

Dissolve yeast in 1/4 cup warm water. Add milk, sugar, salt, egg and butter; blend thoroughly. Add flour gradually to make a soft dough; knead until smooth and elastic. Place in greased bowl; cover with damp cloth. Let rise for about 2 hours or until doubled in bulk. Place dough on large floured cloth. Roll and pull dough carefully in circle until 1/4 inch to paper thin. Spread filling on dough until completely covered to edge. Sprinkle on raisins and cinnamon. Roll as for jelly roll, lifting cloth to keep dough from breaking. Pinch to seal edges. Place in greased 13 x 9 x 2-inch pan or on cookie sheet in S-shape; cover with waxed paper. Let rise for about 1 hour or until doubled in bulk. Bake at 325 degrees for 40 to 45 minutes or until done. Cool before slicing.

Walnut Filling

1/4 c. warm milk
2 c. ground walnuts
1/4 c. soft butter
1/2 c. (packed) brown sugar
1 or 2 eggs
1/4 c. honey

Combine all ingredients; mix well.

Hazel Minerich, Pres.
Preceptor Alpha Omega XP1258
Sedro-Woolley, Washington

JEWISH COFFEE CAKE

Sugar
2 tsp. cinnamon
1 c. chopped nuts
1 c. butter
2 eggs
2 c. flour
1 tsp. soda
2 c. sour cream
1 tsp. vanilla extract

Combine 1/4 cup sugar, cinnamon and nuts; set aside. Cream butter, eggs and 1 1/4 cups sugar together. Add flour, soda and sour cream; mix in vanilla. Batter will be stiff. Spread half the batter into greased and floured ring pan; sprinkle 1/2 of the nut mixture over top. Spread remaining batter over nuts; sprinkle with remaining nut mixture. Bake in 350-degree oven for 45 to 55 minutes or until done.

Gloria Dyer, Treas.
Pi Tau No. 4725
Fremont, California

BOHEMIAN APPLE STRUDEL

1 sm. egg
2 1/2 c. flour
Melted butter
Sugar
Dash of salt
2 c. bread crumbs
2 c. raisins
1/4 c. cinnamon
2 tbsp. currants
5 lb. apples, peeled and shredded

Mix egg with 3/4 cup lukewarm water. Stir in flour, 1/2 cup butter, 2 tablespoons sugar and salt; mix well. Shape dough in 2 balls; let stand for about 10 minutes. Combine remaining ingredients with 4 cups sugar; mix well for filling. Roll out 1 ball of dough very thin; brush with butter. Spread half the filling over dough. Roll out remaining dough. Place over filling; brush with butter. Spread remaining filling over dough. Roll up as for jelly roll; place on baking sheet. Bake at 350 degrees for about 45 minutes or until done, brushing with melted butter about 3 times.

Anna Baker
Preceptor Eta XP887
Whitefish, Montana

KUCHEN

1 c. milk, scalded
1 pkg. dry yeast
1/2 c. sugar
3 eggs, beaten
1/2 c. shortening
1 tsp. salt
Raisins
Dash of cinnamon
Dash of nutmeg
Flour
Cream Filling
Fresh fruit

Cool milk to lukewarm. Dissolve yeast in 1 cup lukewarm water. Add milk, sugar, eggs, shortening, salt, raisins and spices; mix well. Add enough flour to make a soft dough. Place in greased bowl; cover. Let rise until doubled in bulk. Punch down; let rise again. Roll out as for pie dough; place in pie pan. Fill with Cream Filling; top with fruit. Sprinkle with additional cinnamon. Bake at 375 degrees until filling sets. Yield: 5-6 servings.

Cream Filling

1 c. cream or sour cream
3/4 c. sugar
2 eggs, well beaten
1/4 tsp. salt

Combine all ingredients; mix well.

Vi Tracer
Preceptor Alpha XP126
Missoula, Montana

OSLO CAKE

1/2 c. butter or margarine
Dash of salt
1 c. flour
1 tsp. almond extract
4 eggs

Bring butter and 1 cup water to a boil in saucepan; remove from heat. Add salt, flour and almond extract; mix well. Add eggs, one at a time, beating well after each addition. Spread on cookie sheet. Bake at 425 degrees for 30 minutes or until done. Spread with frosting of powdered sugar, milk, butter and almond extract, if desired.

Nancy E. Maki, Ext. Off.
Xi Alpha Nu X3829
Pierce, Idaho

FROSTED PINEAPPLE SQUARES

Sugar
3 tbsp. cornstarch
1/4 tsp. salt
5 egg yolks
1 1-lb. 14-oz. can pineapple chunks
3 3/4 to 4 1/4 cups unsifted flour
1 pkg. Fleishmann's yeast
1/2 c. milk
1 c. Fleischmann's margarine
Confectioners' sugar frosting

Mix 1/2 cup sugar, cornstarch and salt together in saucepan. Stir in 1 slightly beaten egg yolk and undrained pineapple chunks. Cook over medium heat, stirring constantly, until mixture comes to a boil. Set aside to cool. Combine 1 1/3 cups flour, 1 teaspoon sugar and dry yeast in a large bowl; mix well. Combine milk, 1/2 cup water and margarine in a saucepan. Heat over low heat until liquids are warm. Margarine does not need to melt. Add to dry ingredients gradually. Beat for 2 minutes at medium speed of electric mixer, scraping bowl occasionally. Add 4 egg yolks and 1/2 cup flour or enough flour to make a thick batter. Beat at high speed for 2 minutes, scraping bowl occasionally. Stir in enough additional flour to make a soft moist dough. Divide dough in half. Roll out 1/2 of the dough on floured board to fit bottom of ungreased 15 x 10 x 1-inch jelly roll pan. Spread with cooled pineapple filling. Roll remaining dough large enough to cover filling. Seal edges together. Snip surface of dough with scissors to let steam escape. Cover; let rise in warm place for about 1 hour or until doubled in bulk. Bake in 375-degree oven for about 35 to 40 minutes or until done. Let cake cool in pan. Frost while warm with confectioners' sugar frosting. Cut into squares to serve.

Photograph for this recipe on page 136.

DANISH KRINGLE

2 c. flour
Butter

3 eggs
3/4 tsp. almond extract
1/2 tsp. vanilla extract
3/4 c. powdered sugar
2 tbsp. cream

Combine 1 cup flour, 1/2 cup butter and 1 tablespoon water as for pie crust. Roll out on floured board, making two 4 x 14 1/4-inch strips. Pat in cookie sheet. Place 1 cup boiling water and 1/2 cup butter in saucepan; bring to a boil. Remove from heat; add remaining 1 cup flour, stirring until smooth. Add eggs, 1 at a time, beating well after each addition. Stir in 1/4 teaspoon almond extract and vanilla extract. Spread on top of each strip. Bake at 350 degrees for 1 hour. Combine powdered sugar, cream, 1 tablespoon butter and remaining 1/2 teaspoon almond extract; mix well. Spread over each strip while warm.

Eleanor Rensvold
Preceptor Alpha XP125
Fargo, North Dakota

GERMAN CRULLERS — RULL KUCHEN

3 c. flour
2 tsp. baking powder
1 tsp. soda
1 tsp. salt
2 eggs, beaten
1 c. milk
1 c. sour cream
Oil for frying

Mix first 7 ingredients together to make a soft dough. Roll out thin; cut into 2 x 5-inch strips. Cut slit in center of each strip; pull one end of dough through slit. Fry in deep hot oil until golden brown.

Betty Berlage, Pres.
Preceptor Alpha Beta XP638
Colorado Springs, Colorado

MEXICAN CRULLERS — CHURROS

1/2 c. butter
1 c. all-purpose flour
Dash of salt
3 or 4 eggs
Confectioners' sugar

Pour 1 cup water in saucepan; bring to a boil. Add butter; stir until melted. Add flour and salt; stir over heat until mixture forms a ball. Cool slightly. Beat in eggs, 1 at a time, beating well after each addition. Place in pastry bag with a star tube. Squeeze out dough in spirals into 370-degree deep fat; fry until brown. Drain; sprinkle with confectioners' sugar.

Mrs. Pat Kipfer, Treas.
Iota Kappa No. 10409
Hemlock, New York

FRIED CRULLERS (MIDDLE EAST) GOZLEME

1/8 tsp. salt
1/2 c. butter
2/3 c. sifted flour
3 eggs
1/2 c. raisins
2 tbsp. chopped candied fruit
1 tbsp. rose water
Vegetable oil for deep frying
Confectioners' sugar

Combine 1/2 cup water, salt and butter in saucepan. Cook until butter melts. Add flour all at once, beating vigorously with wooden spoon until mixture forms ball and leaves side of pan. Remove from heat. Add eggs, 1 at a time, beating well after each addition. Beat in raisins, fruit and rose water. Heat the oil to 370 degrees. Drop dough into oil by teaspoonfuls; fry until brown. Do not crowd so crullers can turn themselves. Drain; sprinkle with confectioners' sugar. Yield: About 24 crullers.

Charlotte Nesseth, Sec.
Preceptor Delta XP477
Tomah, Wisconsin

LITHUANIAN CRULLERS GRUZDAI

6 egg yolks
1 whole egg
5 tbsp. sugar
1/4 tsp. salt
3 tbsp. melted butter
1/4 c. milk
3 c. flour
1 tsp. vanilla extract or rum flavoring
Oil for frying
Powdered sugar

Beat egg yolks and egg together. Add sugar, salt, butter and milk; mix well. Add flour and vanilla; finish mixing in flour by hand. Knead dough until smooth; divide into 2 or 3 portions. Roll out each portion as thin as possible. Cut into strips about 1 1/2 inches wide; cut diagonally into 3 inch lengths. Make a small slit in center of each piece using knife. Fold one end through slit and pull out with a slight stretch. Fry in hot oil until lightly browned. Drain on paper towels. Let cool. Dust with powdered sugar. One tablespoon brandy may be substituted for vanilla extract. Yield: 6-8 dozen.

Mary J. Kazak, W. and M. Chm.
Xi Zeta Lambda X2961
Aurora, Illinois

HUNGARIAN DOUGHNUTS

1 cake yeast, crumbled
1 tbsp. sugar
3 c. lukewarm milk
4 egg yolks
2 tbsp. butter
1 tsp. salt
6 c. flour
Powdered sugar

Add yeast and sugar to lukewarm milk. Stir until yeast is dissolved. Mix egg yolks with butter; add yeast mixture. Add salt and enough flour to make a soft dough; beat well with wooden spoon. Let stand for 1 hour. Roll dough about 1 inch thick on floured board. Cut with doughnut cutter or glass dipped in flour. Place on floured board or cloth; cover. Let rise in warm place for 1 hour. Fry in hot deep fat until golden brown. Sprinkle generously with powdered sugar.

Theresa E. Kish, V.P.
Xi Sigma No. 3188
Norwalk, Connecticut

LOVE CAKES (POLAND) CHRUSCIKI

12 egg yolks
1 c. whipping cream
1/2 tsp. salt
1 tsp. vanilla extract
Flour
Powdered sugar

Combine egg yolks, cream, salt and vanilla with enough flour to make a soft dough; knead for 1 hour. Cut dough in sections; roll out very thin. Cut into 3 x 1 1/2-inch strips. Make a 1/2-inch slit in middle of each strip; pull one end through slit. Fry in hot deep fat until golden brown. Sprinkle with powdered sugar.

Joyce M. Rehm
Xi Iota Kappa X4514
Maumee, Ohio

POLISH CHRUST

6 egg yolks
6 tbsp. sugar
1 c. cream
2 tbsp. rum
2 c. (about) flour
Confectioners' sugar

Cream egg yolks and sugar until pale and thick. Combine cream and rum; blend into egg mixture. Add enough flour to make stiff dough. Divide dough into 4 parts; roll out each piece very thin on a floured board, keeping remaining dough covered to prevent drying. Cut into strips, about 1 inch wide and 5 inches long. Fry in deep hot fat until golden brown; drain on paper towels. Sprinkle with confectioners' sugar.

Suzanne Porter
Psi Iota Chap.
Amarillo, Texas

ROSEMARIE'S DOUGHNUTS (ITALY) ZEPPOLE

1 lb. ricotta cheese
6 or 7 eggs
1 tsp. vanilla extract
3 tbsp. sugar
2 1/2 c. flour
Oil for frying
Powdered sugar

Combine first 5 ingredients; mix thoroughly. Drop by rounded teaspoonfuls into hot oil in frying pan. Zeppole will flip over as one side browns. Remove and drain on paper towel when browned on both sides. Sprinkle with powdered sugar; place in bowl when cool.

Rosemarie Bardenheier, Hist.
Xi Xi Rho X3343
Anaheim, California

SWEET POTATO DOUGHNUTS (GUAM) BONELDS CAMUTE

1 1/2 c. flour
3 tbsp. baking powder
1 c. sugar
1 c. coconut milk
4 c. mashed sweet potatoes

Sift flour and baking powder together. Add flour mixture, sugar and coconut milk to sweet potatoes; mix well. Shape dough into balls the size of a lemon. Fry in deep hot fat until golden brown. Drain on paper towels. May be rolled in powdered sugar, if desired.

Evelyne M. Chaffey, V.P.
Xi Delta Eta X3120
Erie, Pennsylvania

FINNISH BRAIDS

1 1/2 tsp. dry yeast
1 c. warm milk
4 eggs
1/3 c. butter, melted
1 c. sugar
8 to 10 cardamom seed, crushed
4 1/2 c. flour

Combine 1/2 cup lukewarm water and yeast; stir until dissolved. Add milk. Combine with 3 well-beaten eggs, butter, sugar and cardamom seed. Add flour; knead until smooth. Let rise until doubled in bulk. Punch down; let rise again. Divide dough in half. Divide each half into 3 pieces. Shape into 1-inch rolls. Braid together; tuck ends under. Place braids on baking sheet. Beat remaining egg with fork; brush on braids. Sprinkle with additional sugar. Bake at 350 degrees for 40 minutes.

Andrea Paw, Publ. Chm.
Xi Beta Epsilon X4172
Chilliwack, British Columbia, Canada

FINNISH BREAD

4 c. flour
2 c. butter
1 1/4 c. sugar
1/2 c. finely chopped walnuts
1 egg white, beaten until foamy

Combine flour, butter and 1 cup sugar. Mix well. Roll with hands into long thin rolls. Combine walnuts and 1/4 cup sugar. Dip rolls in egg white; dredge with walnut mixture. Place on buttered cookie sheet. Bake in 400-degree oven for 8 to 12 minutes or until done.

Irma Chancellor
Alpha Zeta XP1350
Nevada, Iowa

FLASKPANNKAKA (SWEDEN)

1/2 lb. bacon, chopped
5 eggs, beaten
3 c. milk
1 1/2 c. flour
1 tbsp. sugar
1 tsp. salt

Fry bacon until crisp; pour into 10 x 13 x 2-inch pan. Cool. Combine remaining ingredients; mix well. Pour over bacon and drippings. Bake at 400 degrees for 25 minutes. Cut into squares; serve with syrup or preserves.
This recipe won the Fort Worth Star Telegram Recipe Contest in 1972.

Kathleen M. Lynass, Ushering Chm.
Xi Xi Rho X4116
Fort Worth, Texas

KOLACHE CRESCENTS

1 8-oz. package cream cheese, softened
1 lb. butter, softened
1 2-lb. box cake flour
1 lb. walnuts, finely ground
1 1/2 c. sugar
1 c. melted butter
1 or 2 eggs, separated
Powdered sugar

Blend cream cheese and softened butter together until smooth. Add flour; mix well. Shape into balls, about 1 inch in diameter. Refrigerate overnight. Combine walnuts and sugar; add melted butter, a small amount at a time. Fold in small amount of egg white at a time to make of spreadable consistency. Roll balls in powdered sugar; place small amount filling on dough. Roll up in shape of crescent. Place on baking sheet; brush with beaten egg yolks. Bake at 350 degrees for 15 minutes.

Victoria Quigley
Zeta Nu No. 2840
Quincy, Illinois

HUNGARIAN BUTTERHORNS

4 c. flour
1/2 tsp. salt
1 cake yeast
1 1/2 c. butter
3 eggs, separated
1/2 c. sour cream
2 tsp. vanilla extract
1 c. sugar
1 c. finely chopped nuts
1 lb. confectioners' sugar

Sift flour and salt into mixing bowl. Crumble yeast into flour; cut in butter. Add beaten egg yolks, sour cream and 1 teaspoon vanilla; mix well. Shape into 8 equal balls; wrap. Chill for at least 1 hour or overnight. Beat egg whites until soft peaks form. Add sugar gradually; beat until stiff peaks form. Add nuts and remaining teaspoon vanilla. Sprinkle table with confectioners' sugar. Roll out 1 ball of dough at a time into 9-inch circle; cut into 8 wedges. Place 1 teaspoon filling onto each wedge; roll to center. Place on baking sheets. Bake in 400-degree oven for 15 to 18 minutes. Let cool; sift confectioners' sugar over butterhorns. Yield: 64 butterhorns.

Jan Simmermann, Soc. Chm.
Xi Beta X163
Saint Louis, Missouri

KOLACHE SQUARES (POLAND)

1 8-oz. package cream cheese,
   softened
2 c. flour
1 c. margarine, softened
1 can Solo filling

Combine cream cheese, flour and margarine; mix with wooden spoon. Chill dough. Roll out 1/4 inch thick; cut into squares or rounds. Place 1 teaspoon filling in center of each square. Place on ungreased cookie sheet. Bake at 375 degrees for 15 minutes or until golden brown.

Mary K. Simms, Pres.
Preceptor Beta XP149
Waukegan, Illinois

ALOHA BREAD

2 c. sifted flour
1 tsp. soda
1/2 tsp. salt
2 tsp. baking powder
1/2 c. butter
1 c. sugar
2 eggs, beaten
1 c. mashed bananas
1 c. undrained crushed pineapple
2 c. chopped nuts
Juice of 1 orange

Sift dry ingredients together. Cream butter and sugar together; add eggs. Blend well. Combine all ingredients; mix until well combined. Turn into greased and floured loaf pan. Bake at 350 degrees for 1 hour to 1 hour and 10 minutes.

Judith O'Neil, Rec. Sec.
Nu No. 5860
Keene, New Hampshire

AUSTRALIAN ALMOND BREAD

3 egg whites
1/2 c. sugar
1 c. all-purpose flour
4 oz. sliced unblanched almonds

Beat egg whites until soft peaks form. Beat in sugar slowly until stiff peaks form. Fold in flour and almonds. Place in greased loaf pan. Bake in 350-degree oven for 30 to 40 minutes or until done. Let cool in pan. Remove; wrap in foil. Let stand for 3 days. Slice very thin; place on cookie sheet. Bake in 350-degree oven until crisp and golden brown.

Jean Fullmer
Lambda No. 3307
Newcastle, Wyoming

EASTER BREAD (FINLAND)

5 1/4 to 6 1/4 c. unsifted flour
3/4 c. sugar
1/2 tsp. salt
1 tsp. ground cardamom
1 tbsp. grated orange peel
1 tsp. grated lemon peel
2 pkg. Fleischmann's yeast
3/4 c. milk
1/2 c. Fleischmann's margarine
2 eggs
1/2 c. chopped blanched almonds
1/2 c. golden raisins
Confectioners' sugar frosting

Combine 1 1/2 cups flour with next 6 ingredients in a large bowl; mix well. Combine milk, 1/2 cup water and margarine in a saucepan. Heat over low heat until liquids are warm. Margarine does not need to melt. Add to dry ingredients gradually; beat for 2 minutes at medium speed of electric mixer, scraping bowl occasionally. Add eggs and 1 cup flour, or enough flour to make a thick batter. Beat at high speed for 2 minutes, scraping bowl occasionally. Stir in enough additional flour to make a soft dough. Turn out onto lightly floured board; knead for about 8 to 10 minutes or until smooth and elastic. Place in greased bowl, turning to grease top. Cover; let rise in warm place for about 1 hour or until doubled in bulk. Punch dough down; turn out onto lightly floured board. Knead in almonds and raisins. Divide in half; shape into 2 smooth balls. Place in 2 greased 8-inch round cake pans. Cover; let rise in warm place for about 1 hour or until doubled in bulk. Bake in 375-degree oven for 35 to 40 minutes or until done. Remove from pans and place on wire racks to cool. Frost with confectioners' sugar frosting.

Photograph for this recipe on opposite page.

GERMAN CHRISTMAS STOLLEN

2 c. milk
1 c. sugar
2 tsp. salt
2 c. shortening
2 cakes yeast
4 eggs, beaten
1/2 tsp. almond extract
8 c. flour
1 c. mixed chopped cherries and citron
1 c. mixed candied fruit
1 c. raisins
2 tbsp. grated lemon rind
2 tbsp. grated orange rind
1 c. chopped almonds

Scald milk; stir in sugar, salt and shortening. Cool to lukewarm. Dissolve yeast in 1/4 cup lukewarm water; stir into milk mixture. Add eggs, almond extract and 4 cups flour; mix well. Add remaining flour and remaining ingredients; knead until dough is smooth. Place in bowl; cover. Let rise until doubled in bulk. Divide in 3 or 4 pieces; roll out each piece lightly to 3/4-inch thickness. Fold over as for an omelet; place on greased cookie sheet. May place dough in loaf pans, if desired. Let rise for 2 or 3 hours or until doubled in bulk. Bake at 375 degrees for 30 to 40 minutes or until done.

Patricia L. Benda, Treas.
Xi Alpha Gamma X4008
Ledyard, Connecticut

HONEY BREAD (ETHIOPIA)
YEMARINA YEWOTET DABO

1 pkg. dry yeast
1 egg

1/2 c. honey
1/2 tsp. cinnamon
1/4 tsp. cloves
1 1/2 tsp. salt
1 c. lukewarm milk
6 tbsp. melted butter
4 to 4 1/2 c. flour

Sprinkle yeast over 1/4 cup lukewarm water in small bowl; let stand for 2 to 3 minutes. Stir to dissolve. Combine egg, honey, cinnamon, cloves and salt in large bowl; mix well. Add yeast mixture, milk and 4 tablespoons butter. Stir in flour, 1/2 cup at a time. Work in additional flour to make a stiff dough. Turn out on floured surface. Knead dough for 5 minutes. Shape into ball; place in lightly buttered bowl. Cover; let rise for 1 hour or until doubled in bulk. Butter 3-quart casserole with remaining 2 tablespoons butter. Punch down dough; knead for 1 to 2 minutes. Shape into ball; place in casserole. Cover; let rise for 1 hour. Bake at 300 degrees for 50 to 60 minutes. Turn out of pan onto rack; let cool. Serve with butter and honey.

Dolores Davis, Corr. Sec.
Xi Beta Delta X3727
Memphis, Tennessee

PEAR BREAD (SWITZERLAND)
BIERABROT

1 lb. dried pears
1 lb. prunes
1 lb. dried apples
1 lb. raisins
1 lb. pitted dates
Wine or grape juice
2 or 3 cakes yeast
Flour
1 tbsp. salt
1 3/4 c. sugar
1 tsp. nutmeg
1 tsp. cinnamon
1 tsp. cloves
2 tbsp. aniseed
1/4 lb. citron (opt.)
1 c. chopped nuts
1/4 c. molasses

Combine first 5 ingredients in bowl; cover with wine. Let stand overnight. Pour into large saucepan; boil until fruit is very tender. Drain and reserve juice. Dissolve yeast in 1 cup lukewarm water. Add enough water to reserved juice to measure 4 cups liquid. Stir into yeast mixture; mix in 5 cups flour. Let stand for 1 hour or until light. Add salt and enough flour to make a stiff dough. Turn out on floured surface; knead until smooth and elastic. Place in greased bowl; cover. Let rise in warm place until doubled in bulk. Place in large pan; add remaining ingredients. Work with hands until well mixed. Shape into loaves; place in greased loaf pans. Cover; let rise until doubled in bulk. Bake in 300-degree oven for about 2 hours or until done.

Marjorie Hefty, Pres.
Xi Alpha Gamma X2547
Tucson, Arizona

NORWEGIAN CHRISTMAS BREAD
JULE KAGE

1 c. lukewarm milk
1/2 c. sugar
1/2 tsp. salt
1 tsp. powdered cardamom
1 cake yeast
1 sm. egg
2 tbsp. soft shortening
3 1/4 to 3 1/2 c. flour
1/4 c. chopped citron
1/2 c. white or dark raisins

Combine milk, sugar, salt and cardamom. Crumble in yeast; stir until dissolved. Add egg and shortening; mix well. Add remaining ingredients to make a stiff dough; turn out on floured board. Knead until smooth and elastic. Place in greased bowl. Cover; let rise for about 2 hours or until doubled in bulk. Knead again; shape into loaves. Place in greased loaf pans; cover. Let rise for 30 to 45 minutes or until doubled in bulk. Bake in 350-degree oven for 45 to 60 minutes or until brown.

Maculate Palumbo, Pres.
Xi Delta Phi X3537
Kane, Pennsylvania

HAWAIIAN BREAD

1 No. 2 1/2 can crushed pineapple
1 10-oz. package moist coconut
4 eggs
1 1/2 c. sugar
4 c. flour
2 tsp. salt
2 tsp. soda

Combine pineapple and coconut in mixing bowl. Beat eggs until light; add sugar. Add to pineapple mixture; mix well. Sift flour; measure. Sift again with salt and soda; add to pineapple mixture. Mix until well blended. Pour into 3 greased 5 x 9-inch loaf pans. Bake at 325 degrees for 1 hour. Remove from oven; turn out on wire racks. Serve warm or cold.

Bobbye Ruth Robins, W. and M. Com.
Xi Epsilon Chi X1689
Lynwood, California

PORTUGUESE SWEET BREAD

5 lb. flour
Sugar
1 tsp. salt
2 tbsp. butter
1/4 c. shortening
2 1/2 yeast cakes
16 eggs, slightly beaten
1/2 can evaporated milk
1/2 tbsp. vanilla extract

Sift flour, 5 cups sugar and salt together. Cut in butter and shortening. Combine yeast, 1/2 cup lukewarm water and 2 1/2 teaspoons sugar; do not stir. Let stand until bubbly. Add 15 eggs, milk, vanilla and 3 cups

lukewarm water to yeast; mix well. Work into flour mixture. Knead dough until smooth and elastic. Place in greased bowl; turn to grease top. Let rise until doubled in bulk. Turn out dough on floured surface; shape into 5 loaves. Place in greased loaf pans. Let rise until even with top of pans. Brush top of loaves with remaining beaten egg. Bake at 350 degrees for 1 hour or until done.

Betty W. Hodgen, W. and M. Chm.
Preceptor Alpha Kappa XP966
Saint Petersburg, Florida

SPECIAL CHRISTMAS BREAD
SCHUITZ BROT

Flour
2 tbsp. sugar
2 pkg. dry yeast
1 pkg. mincemeat
1 1/2 c. prune juice
2 c. cooked pitted prunes
1 c. raisins, soaked
1 c. whole nuts
2 tsp. salt
1 c. (packed) brown sugar
1 c. shortening

Combine 3 cups flour, sugar, yeast and 1 cup warm water to make a sponge. Cover; let stand in warm place for 1 hour. Cook mincemeat according to package directions, using prune juice instead of water. Add prunes, raisins, nuts, salt, brown sugar and shortening; mix well. Place 6 cups flour in large bowl. Add sponge and prune mixture; mix until flour is quite moist. Sprinkle 1 cup flour on bread board; knead dough until all flour is worked in. Place in greased bowl; cover. Let rise in warm place for about 1 hour and 30 minutes or until doubled in bulk. Punch down; let rise again. Divide dough into 3 loaves; place in greased loaf pans. Grease tops of loaves; let rise until doubled in bulk. Bake in 300-degree oven for 1 hour. Reduce heat to 250 degrees; bake for 30 minutes longer. May be frosted. Let age for 3 days before serving.

Janell Martin, W. and M. Chm.
Xi Alpha Pi X4041
Heyburn, Idaho

SWEDISH CHRISTMAS BREAD

3/4 c. milk, scalded
6 tbsp. butter
3/4 c. sugar
2 1/4 tsp. salt
3 pkg. dry yeast
3 eggs, beaten
7 1/2 c. sifted flour
1 tsp. ground cardamom
Cinnamon sugar

Combine milk, butter, sugar and salt; stir until butter is melted. Cool to lukewarm. Dissolve yeast in 3/4 cup

lukewarm water in large bowl. Add milk mixture, eggs and about half the flour; beat until smooth. Reserve 1/4 cup flour; add remaining flour and cardamom. Knead in reserved flour until smooth and elastic. Place in greased bowl; turn to grease top. Cover; let rise in warm place for about 1 hour and 30 minutes or until doubled in bulk. Punch down; divide in half. Shape each half into a loaf; place in greased pans. Cover; let rise until doubled in bulk. Brush tops with additional milk; sprinkle with cinnamon sugar. Bake in 375-degree oven for 45 minutes or until done.

Barbara J. Ross, V.P.
Xi Alpha Tau X2559
Ardmore, Oklahoma

TEA LOAF

      1 c. strong tea
      1/2 c. raisins or dates
      1 1/4 c. flour
      1/2 c. sugar
      1 tsp. nutmeg
      1 tsp. cinnamon
      1/4 tsp. cloves
      1 tsp. soda
      1/2 tsp. salt
      1/4 c. shortening

Add tea to raisins; set aside. Sift dry ingredients together into mixing bowl. Cut in shortening until mixture resembles cornmeal. Add tea mixture; stir just until moistened. Pour into greased small loaf pan. Bake in preheated 350-degree oven for 45 to 50 minutes or until done.

Mrs. D. Haennel
Epsilon Beta No. 6421
Kitchener, Ontario, Canada

ZUCCHINI BREAD

      3 eggs
      1 c. oil
      2 c. sugar
      2 c. grated zucchini
      2 tsp. vanilla extract
      3 c. flour
      1 tsp. soda
      1/2 tsp. baking powder
      1 tsp. salt
      1 tsp. cinnamon
      1/2 c. chopped walnuts

Beat eggs. Add oil, sugar, zucchini and vanilla; mix well. Sift dry ingredients together. Add to zucchini mixture; beat well by hand. Mix in walnuts. Place in 2 greased loaf pans. Bake at 325 degrees for 1 hour or until done.

Karole Johnson
Gamma Tau No. 6631
El Dorado, Arkansas

UKRAINIAN EASTER BREAD

      2 pkg. yeast
      1 1/2 c. sugar
      3 c. hot milk
      10 c. (about) flour
      6 eggs
      2 egg yolks
      Grated rind of 1 orange
      3 tsp. vanilla extract
      1/2 c. butter, softened
      1 tsp. cinnamon
      1/2 c. cooking oil

Dissolve yeast in 1/2 cup lukewarm water; let stand for 10 minutes. Dissolve sugar in milk; let cool. Place 8 cups flour in bowl; stir in yeast and milk mixture. Beat eggs and egg yolks; add to dough. Work in orange rind, vanilla, butter and cinnamon, using hands. Knead in remaining 2 cups flour, a small amount at a time, to make a stiff dough. Knead for about 10 minutes. Add oil; knead for 5 minutes or until all oil is absorbed. Place in greased bowl; let rise for 2 hours or until doubled in bulk. Punch down; let rise again. Place dough in greased loaf pans; let rise. Dough may be brushed with beaten egg before baking, if desired. Bake in 350-degree oven for 40 to 45 minutes or until done.

Eldeen I. Chupa
Alpha Iota No. 8432
Tisdale, Saskatchewan, Canada

FRENCH TOAST (MEXICO)
TORREJAS DE COCO

      4 c. sugar
      1 coconut, shredded
      1 sliced loaf egg bread
      3 eggs
      1 tbsp. flour
      1 c. shortening
      1 cinnamon stick
      3 tbsp. raisins
      1/4 c. chopped blanched almonds

Dissolve 1 cup sugar in 1/2 cup water in saucepan over medium heat. Bring to a boil; boil for 3 minutes. Add coconut; cook for about 15 minutes or until moisture is absorbed and coconut is dry. Remove from heat; cool slightly. Spread part of the coconut mixture between 2 slices bread. Repeat, using all bread. Beat eggs with flour; dip both sides of sandwiches in egg mixture. Fry in shortening in skillet for about 1 minute on each side. Drain on absorbent paper. Combine remaining 3 cups sugar, cinnamon stick and 1 cup water in large skillet; bring to a boil. Boil for 5 minutes or until syrupy. Add browned sandwiches; simmer for several minutes, turning once. Place on serving dish; garnish with raisins and almonds. Strain syrup over all. Yield: 12 servings.

Billie Mercer, 1st V.P.
Alpha Upsilon No. 9284
Polson, Montana

APPLE MUFFINS

2 c. sifted flour
3/4 tsp. salt
4 tsp. baking powder
1/4 c. sugar
3/4 tsp. cinnamon
1/4 tsp. nutmeg
1 egg, beaten
1 c. milk
1/3 c. melted shortening
3/4 c. chopped apples
Cinnamon sugar

Combine first 6 ingredients; stir in egg, milk and shortening. Add apples; pour into muffin tins. Sprinkle with cinnamon sugar. Bake at 375 degrees for 25 minutes. Yield: 12 servings.

Becky Rampy, Corr. Sec.
Xi Tau Theta X5058
Palestine, Texas

ENGLISH TEA MUFFINS

2 c. flour
1/4 c. sugar
1 tbsp. baking powder
1/2 tsp. salt
1 egg, beaten
1 c. milk
1/4 c. cooking oil
Orange marmalade
Sour cream

Sift flour, sugar, baking powder and salt together. Combine egg, milk and oil; add to dry ingredients. Mix well. Fill greased muffin cups 2/3 full. Bake at 425 degrees for 20 to 25 minutes. Split muffins; toast. Top with marmalade and sour cream. Broil until bubbly. Yield: 1 dozen.

Suella Coram, Corr. Sec.
Xi Alpha Phi X754
Delaware, Ohio

BAKED PANCAKE (FINLAND) KROPSU

3 eggs
2 c. milk
1 c. flour
1/2 tsp. salt
1/4 c. butter

Place eggs in bowl; beat well. Stir in milk and flour alternately; mix in salt. Melt butter in 9 x 13-inch pan in 400-degree oven. Pour melted butter into egg mixture; stir just to mix. Pour egg mixture into sizzling hot pan. Bake for 40 minutes. Cut into pieces; serve with sausage, ligonberry sauce or syrup.

Cheryl Lowery, Pres.
Xi Kappa No. 1068
Menomonie, Wisconsin

FRENCH BREAKFAST PUFFS

1/3 c. shortening or butter
1 c. sugar
1 egg
1 1/2 c. flour
1 1/2 tsp. baking powder
1/2 tsp. salt
1/4 tsp. nutmeg
1/2 c. milk
1/2 c. melted butter
1 tsp. cinnamon

Combine shortening, 1/2 cup sugar and egg; mix until well blended. Combine flour, baking powder, salt and nutmeg; blend into egg mixture alternately with milk. Fill greased muffin tins 2/3 full. Bake at 350 degrees for 20 to 25 minutes or until golden brown. Combine butter, remaining 1/2 cup sugar and cinnamon. Roll hot puffs in butter mixture. Serve warm.

Karen Copley
Preceptor Beta Eta XP1316
Eureka, Illinois
Marjorie Swinford, Corr. Sec.
Laureate Theta PL325
Portland, Oregon

COMPANY POTATO LEFSE (NORWAY)

1/2 c. (heaping) butter
1/2 c. whipping cream
1 tbsp. salt
8 c. mashed Russet potatoes
4 c. (scant) flour

Add butter, cream and salt to hot mashed potatoes. Cool. Mix in flour. Roll out balls of dough on lightly floured board until paper thin. Bake rounds on hot griddle, turning to lightly brown both sides.

Violet A. Perkins, Corr. Sec.
Xi Rho Beta X3922
Tustin, California

COTTAGE CHEESE PANCAKES (YUGOSLAVIA) POLACHINKE

3/4 c. flour
4 eggs
1 tsp. salt
1 1/2 c. milk
1 carton creamed cottage cheese
1/4 c. sugar
1/2 c. sour cream

Combine flour, 3 eggs, salt and 1 cup milk; mix well to make thin batter. Pour through strainer into pitcher. Pour a small amount of the batter into greased 8 or 10-inch skillet to make a thin pancake. Fry until light brown; turn and brown lightly on other side. Combine cottage cheese, remaining egg and sugar for filling; mix well. Place 2 to 3 spoonfuls filling on each pancake; spread evenly. Roll as for jelly roll; place, side by side, in buttered oblong pan. Combine remaining 1/2 cup

milk with sour cream; pour over filled pancakes. Bake at 350 degrees for 45 minutes or until milk is almost absorbed.

Mrs. Joseph Jasper, 2nd V.P.
Xi Epsilon Kappa X2195
Middletown, Ohio

EASY NORWEGIAN LEFSE

3 c. hot mashed potatoes
1/2 c. butter
1 tbsp. sugar
1 tsp. salt
1 1/2 c. flour, sifted

Combine mashed potatoes and butter; stir until butter is melted. Let cool. Add remaining ingredients; mix well. Shape into balls; chill thoroughly. Roll out on lightly floured surface until very thin. Bake on preheated griddle or heavy frypan, turning once to brown both sides. Lefse will blister and brown in spots. Serve with butter and sprinkle with cinnamon sugar, if desired.

Donna Blume, Treas.
Preceptor Alpha Gamma XP1600
Bloomfield, New Mexico

FINNISH BREAKFAST PANCAKE

2 c. milk
1 c. cream
3 eggs, beaten
3 tsp. sugar
1 c. flour
1 tsp. (scant) salt
1/2 c. butter

Combine milk, cream and eggs; add sugar, flour and salt. Mix well to make a smooth batter. Melt butter in large jelly roll pan; pour in batter. Bake at 400 to 425 degrees for 20 minutes or until edges are lightly browned and puffy. Cut in squares; serve topped with cinnamon sugar, jam, jelly, syrup or fruit. Yield: 4-8 servings.

Donna J. Hamilton, Corr. Sec.
Zeta Xi No. 8022
Auburn, Washington

GERMAN PANCAKE

1/4 c. margarine
3 eggs, well beaten
1 tbsp. sugar
Nutmeg or cinnamon to taste
1/2 c. flour
1/2 c. milk
1/4 tsp. grated lemon peel (opt.)

Melt margarine in 10-inch pan on low heat. Place eggs in mixing bowl; beat in sugar and nutmeg. Add flour, a small amount at a time, beating well after each addition. Pour 1/2 of the melted margarine into batter; beat well. Add milk, a small amount at a time, beating

constantly. Pour into butter in pan. Bake in preheated 400-degree oven for 15 to 20 minutes. Serve with preserves or fresh or frozen fruit. May be baked in muffin tins, if desired.

Carol Bray, Co-Chm.
Theta Alpha No. 9446
Wasaga Beach, Ontario, Canada

POLISH PANCAKES— POLLACHENKY

1 egg
1 tsp. vanilla extract
1/2 tsp. baking powder
3/4 tsp. salt
1 tbsp. sugar
2 c. flour
2 c. milk

Beat egg. Add vanilla, baking powder, salt and sugar; stir well. Add flour and milk; stir until smooth. Batter will be very thin. Pour into frying pan; spread out thin, covering pan. Brown on both sides. Repeat, using all batter. Spread with butter and jam or pancake syrup; roll up and serve.

Elaine Stanko
Preceptor Alpha XP200
Baltimore, Maryland

SWEDISH PANCAKES

1 c. flour
1/2 tsp. salt
5 tbsp. sugar
2 c. milk
3 eggs, well beaten

Sift flour, salt and sugar together; blend in milk and eggs. Pour about 1/4 cup batter in well-greased griddle, tilting to spread batter thin. Brown on both sides. Repeat until all batter is used.

Mary Johnson
Preceptor Chi No. 1092
Davenport, Iowa

SOPAIPILLAS

4 c. all-purpose flour
1 1/4 tsp. salt
3 tsp. baking powder
3 tbsp. sugar
2 tbsp. shortening
1 1/4 c. milk

Sift dry ingredients together; cut in shortening. Blend in milk. Knead until smooth. Let rest for 30 minutes to 1 hour. Roll out on floured surface. Cut into diamond shapes. Fry in deep fat at 370 to 380 degrees, turning frequently until all sides are brown.

Elsie Bingenheimer, Sec.
Preceptor Beta XP141
Bismarck, North Dakota

Desserts

In most countries, sweets are synonymous with special occasions. Some desserts, such as Austrian *Linzer Torte* and the French *Peche Melba* were named in honor of a particular person or place. Many other classic desserts developed anonymously around seasons, saints and holidays. Jews celebrate *Purim* with *Hamentaschen,* prune-filled, three-cornered buns that represent the donkey-like ears of Haman, the treacherous Persian official exposed by Queen Esther. German *springerle* developed along with pagan celebrations of *Julfest* (the Winter Solstice), and are now a regular part of their Yule season. Cheesecake, a favorite of the Greeks, is often linked to Socrates' ill-tempered wife Xanthippe. She is said to have thrown his favorite on the floor and stomped it rather than let her philosophical husband enjoy it.

Nothing can compare with a sample selection of the world's great desserts. A list of some favorites might include an elegant French Mousse, German Apple Strudel, honey and nut cakes from the Middle East, Scandinavian cookies and pastries, Viennese Tortes, American Strawberry Shortcake, an ambrosia of fruits from the Pacific Islands, and a fancy English Trifle. Cooks of every nation love to prepare desserts because the results are always an excellent way to display creative cooking talents — desserts are colorful and artistic, and always taste magnificent. Moreover, desserts are an enjoyable way to include eggs, cheese, milk, cream, fruits, gelatin and other wholesome foods in the menu plan without complaints from finicky eaters.

Homemade desserts, both plain and fancy from all over the world, make regular appearances on Beta Sigma Phi tables because there is no better way to make mealtime special. Also, desserts do not have to be expensive or too sugar-and-calorie laden for most families if the ingredients are carefully chosen. Remember, no matter how delicious and satisfying a meal is, there is always room for a homemade dessert!

IRISH COFFEE

1 1/2 oz. Irish whiskey
1 or 2 tsp. sugar
Strong, hot black coffee
Whipped cream

Pour Irish whiskey and sugar into prewarmed stemmed glasses or mugs. Fill to within 1 inch of top with hot coffee. Stir to dissolve sugar. Float whipped cream to brim. Do not stir. True flavor is obtained by drinking through the cream.

Judi Shannon, Pres.
Xi Beta Beta X2120
Parker, Colorado

EGGNOG DELUXE

12 eggs, separated
1 3/4 c. sugar
1 tsp. vanilla extract
3/4 c. light rum
1/2 tsp. nutmeg
1 1/2 pints Brandy
1 qt. milk
1 1/2 qt. unwhipped cream
6 tbsp. sugar

Beat egg yolks until fluffy. Add 1 3/4 cups sugar, vanilla, rum, nutmeg and Brandy, stirring well. Store in refrigerator overnight, stirring occasionally. Beat egg whites until soft peaks form. Add 6 tablespoons sugar, one tablespoon at a time, beating until stiff peaks form. Add milk and whipping cream to first mixture. Fold in egg whites. Serve with additional nutmeg sprinkled on top. Yield: 40 servings.

Alexina L. Strozier, Pres.
Xi Lambda X1620
Hampton, South Carolina

CAFE DIABLE (FRANCE)

3 sm. sugar cubes
1/4 c. butter or margarine
1 c. whole coffee beans
Grated rind and juice of 1 orange
Chopped peel of 1 apple
1 2-in. piece of cinnamon stick
12 cloves
6 tbsp. Cognac
6 tbsp. Kirsch
6 tbsp. Curacao
1 1/4 c. freshly made coffee

Place sugar cubes and butter in chafing dish or diable pan over direct flame. Melt butter but do not brown. Add coffee beans, orange rind, apple peel, cinnamon stick and cloves. Pour in Cognac, Kirsch and Curacao; heat, stirring constantly. Apply lighted match; flame Cognac mixture. Stir in coffee and orange juice after flame dies; let heat to steaming. Pour through strainer into demitasse cups. Yield: 4-6 servings.

Photograph for this recipe above.

AFTERDINNER DRINK

3 1/2 c. sugar
2 oz. instant coffee
4 c. vodka
1 2-in. vanilla bean

Bring 2 cups water to a boil. Stir in sugar and instant coffee. Add vodka and vanilla bean. Store in dark place for 1 month. Serve over ice or ice cream. Yield: 1 1/2 gallons.

Dixie D. Carlton
Xi Delta Delta Chap.
Jay, Florida

IPPOLITO HOLIDAY EGGNOG

2 eggs, well beaten
1 15-oz. can sweetened
   condensed milk
1 tsp. vanilla extract
1/4 tsp. salt
1 qt. milk
1 c. heavy cream, whipped
Nutmeg
Rum (opt.)

Combine eggs, condensed milk, vanilla and salt until thoroughly blended. Gradually beat in milk. Fold in whipped cream. Sprinkle with nutmeg. Lace with rum, if desired.

Marie Ippolito
Xi Beta Lambda Chap.
Rockaway, New Jersey

GOLDEN PINEAPPLE PUNCH

8 46-oz. cans pineapple juice
7 46-oz. cans apricot nectar

2 lg. cans frozen orange juice
8 qt. pineapple sherbet
8 qt. club soda

Mix pineapple juice, apricot nectar, frozen orange juice, and 1 quart water well. Add sherbet. Whip lightly. Add club soda to serve. Garnish with slices of pineapple and maraschino cherries. Yield: 200 servings.

Clara Christine Farmer
Xi Gamma Gamma X2337
Richmond, Indiana

O'MEARA TAVERN PUNCH

1/2 gal. light rum
1/2 gal. Cognac
1 qt. dark rum
1/2 fifth apricot Brandy
48 oz. Rose's lime juice
4 c. sugar

Combine all ingredients with 6 quarts water. Stir until well blended. Chill. Garnish with lemon, lime and orange slices. Serve over ice. Yield: 40-48 servings.

Jackie M. Ericson
Preceptor Alpha Xi XP504
Santa Barbara, California

RUSSIAN TEA

1 c. unflavored tea
1 1/4 c. Tang
1 c. sugar
1   3-oz. package lemonade mix
1/4 tsp. cinnamon
1/4 tsp. ground cloves

Mix ingredients together with 1 quart water. Store in tightly covered jar. Serve 3 or 4 heaping teaspoonfuls to 1 cup hot water or to taste.

Bettye Flynn
Preceptor Alpha Sigma XP546
Hayward, California

SPICED WINE (GERMANY)
GLUHWEIN

2 bottles red wine
1/2 bottle water
1 c. sugar
2 sticks cinnamon
6 to 8 whole cloves
Thin lemon slices

Combine all ingredients except lemon slices in a saucepan. Bring to a rapid boil. Turn to low heat. Simmer for 1 or 2 hours. The longer it simmers the spicer it will be. Pour into punch bowl. Add lemon slices. Yield: 15 to 20 cups.

Beverly A. Mackey
Delta Delta Phi Chap.
San Bernardino, California

WASSAIL

1 gal. cider
2/3 46-oz. can pineapple juice
2/3 of 6-oz. frozen orange juice
Juice of 2 lemons
Cloves to taste
3/4 box cinnamon sticks

Combine all ingredients in a saucepan. Simmer for 30 minutes. Pour into punch bowl. Garnish with sliced oranges.

Meri Rees
Xi Iota Omicron X4802
Crystal Lake, Illinois

PINK AND YELLOW
COCONUT APPLES (MEXICO)

1 1/2 c. sugar
1/2 c. milk
1/4 tsp. cream of tartar
1   7-oz. package finely grated
   coconut
Red food coloring
Yellow food coloring
Powdered sugar
Raisins

Combine sugar, milk and cream of tartar in medium saucepan. Cook over high heat, stirring until sugar is dissolved and mixture comes to a boil. Boil to 225 degrees on candy thermometer. Remove from heat. Stir in coconut. Divide in half into 2 small bowls. Tint half pink and half yellow. Cool to room temperature, about 2 hours. Shape mixture into 1 1/2-inch balls. Roll in powdered sugar. Press raisin on top of each ball. Let stand for 2 days. Yield: 1 1/2 dozen.

Frances C. Lorenz, Corr. Sec.
Preceptor Zeta XP261
Pottsville, Pennsylvania

ITALIAN CREAM PUFFS

1/2 c. Crisco
Dash of salt
1 c. flour
3 eggs
15-oz. Ricotta cheese
1 c. sugar
1 1/2 tbsp. vanilla extract
1 lg. bar hard chocolate

Combine 1 cup water, Crisco and salt in saucepan. Bring to a full boil. Pour immediately into mixing bowl. Add flour; mix at medium speed. Add eggs, one at a time, mixing well after each addition. Drop by teaspoon onto ungreased cookie sheet. Bake at 350 degrees for 50 minutes. Cool for 1 hour and 30 minutes. Mix Ricotta, sugar and vanilla. Shove hard chocolate into filling. Fill cream puffs with filling. Serve at once.

Georgiana Shorman, V.P.
Xi Zeta Psi X3767
Baynton Beach, Florida

FRENCH ALMOND CREPES

1/3 c. flour
1 tbsp. sugar
Dash of salt
1 egg
1 egg yolk
3/4 c. milk
Melted butter
Almond Cream Filling
Grated unsweetened chocolate
Confectioners' sugar

Place first 6 ingredients and 1 tablespoon melted butter in mixing bowl. Beat until smooth. Refrigerate several hours or until thick. Heat heavy 6-inch skillet; grease lightly. Pour in 2 tablespoons batter. Lift skillet from heat; tilt from side to side until batter covers bottom evenly. Return to heat. Cook until underside of crepe is lightly browned, about 1 1/2 minutes. Invert skillet over paper towels to remove. Repeat. Spread about 2 tablespoons Almond Cream Filling on unbrowned side of each crepe. Roll up. Place folded side down in buttered 13 x 9 x 2-inch baking dish. Brush crepes with additional melted butter. Bake at 350 degrees for 20 to 25 minutes. Sprinkle with grated unsweetened chocolate. Sift confectioners' sugar over all. Serve warm with whipped cream.

Almond Cream Filling

1 c. sugar
1/4 c. flour
1 c. milk
2 eggs
2 egg yolks
3 tbsp. butter
2 tsp. vanilla extract
1/2 tsp. almond extract
1/2 c. ground toasted blanched almonds

Mix sugar and flour together in saucepan. Add milk. Cook, stirring until thick. Cook, stirring for 1 or 2 minutes longer. Beat eggs and egg yolks slightly; stir a small amount of hot mixture into eggs; return to hot mixture. Bring just to a boil, stirring constantly; remove from heat. Stir in butter and flavorings. Add ground almonds; mix until well blended. Cool to room temperature.

Sandra Bell, Pres.
Zeta Gamma No. 2720
Shelby, Ohio

ALMOND CAKE FROM ALBUFEIRA (PORTUGAL)

1 1/2 c. sugar
1/2 tsp. almond extract
1 c. all-purpose flour, sifted
1/2 tsp. baking powder
1/2 tsp. soda
1/4 tsp. salt
1 egg
1/2 c. buttermilk
1/2 tsp. vanilla extract

1/3 c. melted butter, cooled
2/3 c. sliced almonds

Combine 3/4 cup sugar and 6 tablespoons water in 1-quart saucepan. Boil until mixture reaches 220 degrees on candy thermometer. Remove from heat. Stir in almond extract. Set syrup aside. Sift flour, 3/4 cup sugar, baking powder, soda and salt into bowl. Beat egg, buttermilk and vanilla together in separate bowl until smooth. Stir in butter. Add flour mixture. Mix with spoon until nearly smooth. Turn into a buttered 9-inch springform pan. Bake in preheated 350-degree oven until cake tests done, about 35 minutes. Remove from oven. Cover top with almonds. Pour hot almond syrup evenly over hot cake letting syrup soak into cake. Broil in oven about 6 inches from source of heat until almonds are lightly toasted. Cool on rack. Loosen sides from pan using knife. Cool completely before releasing springform. Yield: 8-10 servings.

Julia Ann Powers, Pres.
Xi Beta Rho X4086
Corton, West Virginia

APPLE-DATE DREAM (GERMANY)

2 c. sifted all-purpose flour
1 c. sugar
1 1/2 tsp. soda
1 tsp. salt
1 tsp. ground cinnamon
1/2 tsp. ground allspice
2 eggs, slightly beaten
1   21-oz. can apple pie filling
1/2 c. cooking oil
1 tsp. vanilla extract
1 c. chopped dates
1/4 c. chopped walnuts

Sift flour, sugar, soda, salt, cinnamon and allspice together. Combine eggs, pie filling, oil and vanilla. Stir into flour mixture; mix well. Stir in dates and walnuts. Pour into greased and floured 13 1/2 x 8 3/4 x 1 3/4-inch baking dish. Bake in 350-degree oven for 40 to 45 minutes. Cool. Cut into squares. Serve with a dollop of whipped cream or vanilla ice cream, if desired. Yield: 12 servings.

R. Virginia Herriman, Pres.
Preceptor Gamma XP198
McLean, Virginia

APPLE KUCHEN

1/2 c. butter or margarine, softened
1 pkg. yellow cake mix
1/2 c. flaked coconut
1   20-oz. can sliced pie apples,
    well drained or 2 1/2 c. sliced
    pared baking apples
1/2 c. sugar
1 tsp. cinnamon
1 c. sour cream
2 egg yolks or 1 egg

Cut butter into dry cake mix until crumbly. Mix in coconut. Pat mixture lightly into ungreased oblong

pan, building up sides slightly. Bake in preheated 350-degree oven for 10 minutes. Arrange apple slices on warm crust. Mix sugar and cinnamon. Sprinkle on apples. Blend sour cream and egg yolks; drizzle over apples. Bake for 25 minutes or until edges are light brown. Serve warm. Yield: 12-15 servings.

Mrs. Lowber Gugino Hendricks
Xi Pi X1492
Little Rock, Arkansas

FRESH APPLE CAKE

    2 c. unsifted flour
    2 c. sugar
    2 tsp. soda
    1 tsp. each nutmeg and cinnamon
    1/2 tsp. salt
    4 c. diced raw apples
    1/2 c. chopped walnuts
    1/2 c. soft butter
    2 eggs, beaten
    1 c. (packed) dark brown sugar
    1/4 c. butter
    1/4 c. milk

Sift first 5 ingredients together. Add apples, walnuts, butter and eggs. Beat until well combined; mixture will be thick. Pour into greased and floured 13 x 9 x 2-inch pan. Bake at 325 degrees for 1 hour or until cake tests done. Cool slightly in pan on wire rack. Combine remaining ingredients in a saucepan. Bring to a boil. Boil for 1 minute. Pour glaze over hot cake.

Becky Suder
Preceptor Alpha Epsilon XP648
Cincinnati, Ohio

MOTHER'S APPLE CAKE
(DENMARK) MORS AEBLEKAGE

    1 1/2 c. Zwieback crumbs
    2 tbsp. sugar
    1/4 c. butter
    6 to 8 almond macaroons
    1/4 c. cooking Sherry
    3 1/2 c. thick applesauce

Brown crumbs with sugar and butter over low heat. Place macaroons in bottom of glass bowl. Pour Sherry over to soften. Add layer of applesauce, then layer of crumbs. Alternate layers until ingredients are used. Top with whipped cream. Garnish with dots of currant jelly. Cake is better made the day before serving.

Barbara Boien Erickson
Preceptor Beta Pi XP1484
Edwardsville, Illinois

SWEDISH APPLE CAKE
APPLEKAKA

    1/4 c. butter
    3/4 c. sugar

    1 egg
    1/2 c. milk
    1 c. flour, sifted
    2 tsp. baking powder
    1/4 tsp. salt
    1 tsp. vanilla extract
    Apple slices
    Nutmeg

Cream butter and sugar. Add egg and milk; mix well. Sift flour, baking powder and salt together, stir gradually into creamed mixture. Add vanilla. Beat for 2 minutes at medium speed. Pour batter into greased 8-inch round and floured pan. Place thin apple slices in design around pan, pushing slices down into batter. Sprinkle with nutmeg and additional sugar. Bake in 375-degree oven for 30 minutes or until cake tests done. Serve with whipped cream if desired.

Eleanor A. Adams, Treas.
Xi Phi X3033
Bowie, Maryland

BABY ORANGE BABAS

    1 pkg. yellow cake mix
    3/4 c. sugar
    3/4 c. orange juice
    3 tbsp. orange rind

Prepare cake mix according to package directions. Place well-greased paper hot drink cups on a cookie sheet. Spoon in batter, filling cups 1/2 full. Bake at 375 degrees for 25 minutes or until cake tests done. Combine sugar, 3/4 cup water, orange juice and orange rind. Cook mixture for 5 minutes. Cool cakes for 2 minutes. Turn out onto a serving plate. Drizzle with hot orange syrup, soaking cakes well. Chill. Serve cold with whipped cream. Yield: 9-10 servings.

Caroline Howard, Pres.
Xi Alpha X253
Little Rock, Arkansas

BUTTER MOCHI (JAPAN)

    1/4 lb. butter
    1 lb. mochiko
    3 c. milk
    1 tsp. vanilla extract
    2 tsp. baking powder
    2 1/2 c. sugar
    5 eggs
    1 c. flaked coconut (opt.)

Melt butter; set aside to cool. Mix next 6 ingredients together until well blended. Add butter. Add coconut flakes; mix well. Pour into greased 9 x 13-inch pan. Bake at 350 degrees for 1 hour. Mochi will rise unevenly during baking but will settle during cooling. Excess butter will be absorbed during cooling. Mochiko is sweet rice flour.

Susan Wong, Pres.
Rho No. 6133
Honolulu, Hawaii

BRIDWELL CHOCOLATE CAKE

3 c. flour
2 c. sugar
1/2 c. cocoa
1 tsp. soda
1 tsp. salt
2 c. water
3/4 c. oil
2 tbsp. vinegar
1 tbsp. vanilla extract

Combine all ingredients in large mixing bowl; blend well for about 3 minutes. Pour into greased and floured 13 x 9-inch pan. Bake at 350 degrees for 25 to 35 minutes or until cake tests done. Do not overbake.

Debbie Bridwell, Corr. Sec.
Gamma Zeta No. 3248
Frontenac, Kansas

COCOA SPICE CAKE (ARABIA)

2 c. flour
1/2 tsp. salt
1/2 tsp. cardamon
2 tbsp. cocoa
1/2 tsp. nutmeg
1 1/4 c. sugar
1 tsp. soda
2 tsp. baking powder
1 tsp. cinnamon
1 tsp. cloves
2 eggs
1 c. milk
2/3 c. shortening
3/4 c. orange juice

Mix together first 10 ingredients. Add next 4 ingredients. Mix well by hand, incorporating as much air as possible. Pour into 2 greased and floured cake pans. Bake at 350 degrees for 30 to 35 minutes or until cake tests done. Cool on wire racks.

Cocoa Frosting

2/3 pkg. powdered sugar
1/3 c. shortening
2 tbsp. cocoa
1/3 c. strong coffee

Combine all ingredients until of spreading consistency. Frost Cake. Top with nuts or coconut.

Jo Beth Gaddey
Beta Nu Chap.
Carmi, Illinois

FUDGE CUPCAKES

4 sq. semisweet chocolate, melted
  and cooled
2 sticks margarine
1 3/4 c. sugar
1 c. flour
4 eggs, beaten

1 tsp. vanilla extract
1 c. chopped pecans

Combine all ingredients. Mix by hand until smooth. Fill paper-lined cupcake pans 2/3 full. Bake at 325 degrees for 35 minutes. Needs no frosting.

Pat Heitschmidt, Office Staff
Beta Sigma Phi
Kansas City, Missouri

OLD-FASHIONED COCOA CAKE

3/4 c. margarine
2 c. sugar
2 c. flour
1/2 c. cocoa
2 tsp. soda
1/2 tsp. salt
2 eggs
1 tsp. vanilla extract

Cream margarine and sugar together. Add 1 1/2 cups boiling water; mix well. Sift flour, cocoa, soda and salt together. Add to water mixture; beat well. Add eggs and vanilla; mix well. Pour into 2 greased and floured 8-inch layer pans. Bake at 350 degrees for 25 to 30 minutes or until cake tests done. Frost cooled cake with favorite icing. This recipe is over 100 years old.

Melba Robb, W. and M. Chm.
Beta Zeta XP685
Susanville, California

GRANDMOTHER'S CHOCOLATE FUDGE CAKE (GERMANY)

3 sq. unsweetened chocolate
2 1/2 c. sifted cake flour
2 tsp. soda
1/2 tsp. salt
1/2 c. butter or margarine
2 1/4 c. (firmly packed) brown sugar
3 eggs
1 1/2 tsp. vanilla extract
1 c. sour cream

Melt chocolate in small bowl over hot water; cool. Sift flour, soda and salt on waxed paper. Beat butter, brown sugar and eggs about 5 minutes. Beat in vanilla and cooled melted chocolate. Stir in dry ingredients alternately with sour cream until batter is smooth. Stir in 1 cup boiling water. Batter will be thin. Pour at once into 2 greased 9-inch round pans. Bake at 350 degrees for 35 minutes.

Grandmother's German Fudge Frosting

3 sq. unsweetened chocolate
1/2 c. butter, softened
1/2 c. milk
2 tsp. vanilla extract
1 lb. powdered sugar
1 c. chopped nuts (opt.)

Melt chocolate and butter over low heat. Add milk, vanilla and powdered sugar. Beat until smooth. Add chopped nuts; mix well. Frost cake.

Marjorie K. E. Lessman, Pres.
Xi Alpha Kappa X2494
Dalton, Nebraska

SICILIAN CREAM CAKE
(ITALY)

    1 11-oz. frozen pound cake, thawed
    1 1/2 c. ricotta cheese
    1/4 c. sugar
    1/4 c. Creme de Cacao
    1/4 c. mini-chocolate pieces
    1/4 c. mixed candied fruit
    1 c. ready-to-spread chocolate
        frosting
    Confetti decorettes

Cut cake horizontally into 3 layers. Combine cheese, sugar and 3 tablespoons Creme de Cacao in mixing bowl. Beat with electric mixer until smooth. Fold in chocolate pieces and candied fruit. Spread bottom cake layer with 1/2 of the ricotta mixture. Place second layer on top. Spread remaining ricotta over second layer. Place third layer on top. Combine frosting with remaining Creme de Cacao. Spread on top and sides of cake. Sprinkle with decorettes. Chill for 30 minutes. Yield: 6 servings.

Donna Ayres, Pres.
Omega Psi No. 5909
Fremont, California

SWEET AND SOUR KRAUT CAKE
(GERMANY)

    1/2 c. butter
    1 1/2 c. sugar
    3 eggs
    1 tsp. vanilla extract
    2 c. sifted all-purpose flour
    1 tsp. baking powder
    1 tsp. soda
    1/4 tsp. salt
    1/2 c. cocoa
    1 8-oz. can sauerkraut, drained,
        rinsed and finely snipped

Cream butter and sugar until light in large mixing bowl. Beat in eggs, one at a time, beating well after each addition. Add vanilla. Sift flour, baking powder, soda, salt and cocoa together. Add to creamed mixture alternately with 1 cup water, beating well after each addition. Stir in sauerkraut. Turn into greased and floured 13 x 9 x 2-inch baking pan. Bake in 350-degree oven for 35 to 40 minutes or until cake tests done.

Sour Cream Chocolate Frosting

    1 6-oz. package semisweet chocolate chips
    4 tbsp. butter
    1/2 c. sour cream
    1 tsp. vanilla extract
    1 1-lb. box confectioners' sugar

Melt chocolate chips and butter over low heat. Remove from heat. Blend in sour cream, vanilla and salt. Add sifted confectioners' sugar; mix until smooth and of spreading consistency. Spread over cooled cake.

Carol Moerlien, Pres.
Nu Zeta No. 6426
Granite City, Illinois

WALNUT-HONEY CAKE
(GREECE) KARIDOPITA

    6 eggs, separated
    1/2 tsp. salt
    1/2 tsp. cream of tartar
    1 1/2 c. sugar
    1 c. sifted all-purpose flour
    2 tsp. baking powder
    1/2 tsp. cinnamon
    1/4 tsp. cloves
    3 c. ground walnuts
    1/2 c. honey
    2 tsp. lemon juice

Beat egg whites with salt and cream of tartar until stiff. Beat in 1 cup sugar gradually. Beat egg yolks with same beater until light colored; fold into egg white mixture. Sift flour, baking powder and spices together; fold into batter gradually. Fold in walnuts. Turn into ungreased 10-inch tube pan. Bake at 375 degrees for about 35 minutes or until cake tests done. Invert over neck of bottle; let hang until cold. Turn out onto serving plate. Combine remaining 1/2 cup sugar, honey and 1/2 cup water in saucepan. Simmer for 5 minutes. Remove from heat; stir in lemon juice. Spoon warm honey syrup gradually over cake, allowing syrup to absorb before adding more. Decorate cake with walnut halves.

Photograph for this recipe below.

CREOLE PECAN CAKE

3/4 c. butter or margarine
2 c. sugar
3 egg yolks
3 c. cake flour
1/4 tsp. salt
2 tsp. baking powder
3/4 c. milk
1 tsp. vanilla extract
6 egg whites, stiffly beaten
1 tsp. cinnamon
1/2 tsp. cloves
1 1/4 c. pecans, chopped

Cream butter. Add sugar gradually; cream together well. Beat in egg yolks. Sift flour 3 times, adding salt and baking powder the third time. Add to creamed mixture alternately with milk and vanilla. Fold in stiffly beaten egg whites. Divide batter into 2 parts. Add cinnamon and cloves to one part. Add chopped pecans to second part. Grease and flour four 8-inch cake pans. Pour pecan batter in 2 pans. Pour spice batter in 2 pans. Bake at 375 degrees for 25 to 30 minutes. Cool for 10 minutes. Remove from pans; cool on rack.

Brown Sugar Frosting

4 c. (packed) brown sugar
2 egg whites
1 tsp. vanilla extract
Pecans, finely chopped

Mix brown sugar and 1/2 cup water together. Bring to a boil. Boil to soft-ball stage. Beat egg whites until stiff peaks form. Add sugar mixture to egg whites slowly, beating until stiff. Add vanilla; mix well. Frost cake. Sprinkle top and sides with finely chopped pecans.

Sandy Howell, V.P.
Gamma Gamma No. 7398
Kelso, Washington

DANISH LAYER CAKE

1/4 c. butter
1 c. sugar
4 eggs
1 c. sifted flour
1 tsp. baking powder
1 tsp. vanilla extract
Custard filling
Raspberry jam
1/2 pt. whipped cream, sweetened

Cream butter and sugar well. Add eggs, one at a time, beating well after each addition. Add flour and baking powder gradually; mix well. Add vanilla. Pour into 4 greased 8-inch cake pans. Bake at 375 degrees for about 10 minutes. Remove from pans immediately. Spread custard between 2 bottom layers, raspberry jam between second and third layers and custard between third and fourth layers. Frost with sweetened whipped cream.

Grace Rose
Preceptor Laureate Beta PL149
Racine, Wisconsin

DOUBLE TOFFEE DELIGHT

1 1/2 c. (firmly packed) brown sugar
1 c. chopped nuts
1 tbsp. cinnamon
2 c. all-purpose flour
1 c. sugar
2 tsp. baking powder
1 tsp. salt
1 pkg. dry vanilla instant pudding mix
1 pkg. dry butterscotch instant
    pudding mix
1 c. water
3/4 c. cooking oil
1 tsp. vanilla extract
4 eggs

Combine brown sugar, nuts and cinnamon; set aside. Combine remaining ingredients in a large mixer bowl. Beat for 2 minutes at medium speed, scraping bowl occasionally. Pour 1/2 of the batter into greased 13 x 9-inch baking pan; sprinkle with 1/2 of the brown sugar mixture. Pour remaining batter over brown sugar mixture; sprinkle with remaining brown sugar mixture. Bake at 350 degrees for 40 to 45 minutes until cake tests done.

Alicia D. Rodriguez, Rec. Sec.
Tau Pi No. 5208
Brawley, California

ENGLISH FRUITCAKE

1/2 tsp. allspice
1/2 tsp. ground cloves
1/2 tsp. cinnamon
1/2 tsp. nutmeg
1/2 tsp. baking powder
1/2 tsp. salt
2 1/2 c. flour
16 oz. diced glazed fruit
1 1/4 lb. seedless raisins
3/4 lb. currants
1/2 lb. diced mixed peel
2 oz. shelled slivered almonds
1 c. butter
1 c. sugar
5 eggs
10 oz. Sherry or Brandy

Sift together allspice, cloves, cinnamon, nutmeg, baking powder, salt and flour. Mix glazed fruit, raisins, currants, mixed peel and almonds in separate bowl. Add sifted flour mixture; mix well. Grease and line with waxed paper a 9 x 5 x 3-inch loaf pan. Lightly grease waxed paper. Cream butter; add sugar gradually. Add eggs; beat until light and fluffy. Add flour mixture and Sherry, beating until just mixed. Pour into prepared pan. Bake in preheated 275-degree oven for 3 hours and 30 minutes. Place a pan of water in oven for approximately half the baking time. This will keep cake moist. Cool cake in pan. Remove paper. Wrap cake in cheesecloth, then foil. Store in tightly-covered container. Brush with Sherry or Brandy occa-

sionally. Store for 30 days or more before serving. Yield: 6 lbs.

Doreen Prodger, V.P.
Preceptor Rho XP569
Saint Catharines, Ontario, Canada

ITALIAN FRUITCAKE

3/4 c. flour
1/4 tsp. baking powder
1/4 tsp. soda
1/4 tsp. salt
3/4 c. (packed) brown sugar
2 c. dates
1 1/2 c. dry apricots
3 c. walnuts
3 eggs, beaten
1 tsp. vanilla extract

Mix first 5 ingredients together in a large bowl. Stir in fruit and walnuts, completely covering with flour. Add eggs; mix well. Add vanilla; mix well. Pour into well-greased and floured loaf pan. Bake at 325 degrees for 1 hour and 30 minutes until cake tests done. Cool. Slice thin to serve. Leave fruits and nuts whole for a prettier cake.

Tina Marie Parker, Treas.
Xi Zeta Iota X2851
North Olmsted, Ohio

SWEET LUCY'S

1/2 c. butter
1 1/2 c. (packed) brown sugar
4 eggs
3/4 c. whiskey
3 tbsp. milk
3 c. flour
3 tsp. soda
1 tsp. cloves
1 tsp. cinnamon
1 tsp. nutmeg
1 1/2 lb. candied cherries, cut up
1 1/2 lb. candied pineapples, cut up
2 lbs. white raisins
6 c. chopped nuts

Cream butter and brown sugar. Add eggs, one at a time, beating well after each addition. Add whiskey and milk. Sift dry ingredients together. Mix fruit and nuts with 1/4 cup flour mixture. Add dry ingredients to sugar mixture. Add fruits and nuts. Pour into small paper-lined muffin cups. Bake for 25 to 30 minutes at 250 degrees.

Lucille Riedel, Pres.
Preceptor Laureate Eta TL278
Schertz, Texas

FILLED JAPANESE FRUITCAKE

1 c. butter
4 c. sugar
6 eggs, separated
Flour
4 tsp. baking powder
2 tsp. cinnamon
1 tsp. cloves
1 tsp. nutmeg
1 c. milk
1 c. coconut
1 c. chopped pecans
1 box seedless raisins
2 lemons, peeled
2 oranges, peeled

Cream butter and 2 cups sugar until light and fluffy. Beat egg yolks; add to creamed mixture. Sift 3 cups flour with next 4 ingredients. Add alternately with milk to sugar mixture. Dredge 1/2 cup coconut, pecans and raisins in flour. Stir into beaten mixture. Fold in stiffly beaten egg whites. Pour into 4 greased layer pans. Bake at 350 degrees for 30 minutes. Cool on wire racks. Combine 1 1/2 cups water, 2 cups sugar and 4 tablespoons flour in a saucepan. Cut lemons and oranges into small bits; add to saucepan. Cook over medium heat until mixture is thick, like honey, stirring constantly. Add 1/2 cup coconut. Cook for 2 minutes longer. Cool. Spread between layers and on top and sides of cake.

Mrs. Patsy M. Lynch, Rec. Sec.
Gamma Sigma No. 7277
Tuscaloosa, Alabama

LAYERED JAPANESE FRUITCAKE

1 c. margarine
4 c. sugar
4 eggs
3 c. flour
2 tsp. baking powder
1 c. milk
1 c. chopped nuts
1 tsp. each cloves, cinnamon and
    allspice
Juice of 2 lemons
1 c. coconut
1 c. hot water
1 med. can crushed pineapple
4 tbsp. (heaping) flour

Cream margarine and 2 cups sugar. Add eggs, one at a time, beating well after each addition. Sift flour and baking powder together. Add alternately with milk to creamed mixture. Divide batter in half. Pour into 2 greased 9-inch layer pans. Bake in preheated 350-degree oven for 30 to 40 minutes or until cake tests done. Combine remaining ingredients in saucepan. Cook until thickened. Split each layer, making 4 layers. Spread icing between layers and on top and side of cake.

Helen J. Jobe, Pres.
Xi Gamma Alpha X2450
Mexico, Missouri

RUM CREAM CAKE (ITALY)
ZUPPA INGLESE

4 eggs
2/3 c. sugar
1/2 tsp. salt
2/3 c. sifted flour
1/2 c. cornstarch
1/2 c. dark rum
1 recipe Custard Filling
1 c. heavy cream, whipped
1 tbsp. chopped candied fruit

Beat eggs until fluffy in large mixing bowl with electric mixer at medium high speed. Add sugar and salt gradually, beating for about 12 minutes or until mixture is doubled in bulk and mounds slightly when dropped from spoon. Sift flour and cornstarch over egg mixture. Fold in gently until well mixed. Pour into 2 greased and lightly floured 9-inch round cake pans. Bake in 350-degree oven for about 25 minutes or until cake tests done. Cool for 10 minutes. Remove from pans; cool completely on wire rack. Split each layer in half. Sprinkle cake layers with rum. Place bottom layer on serving plate. Spread with 1/3 of the Custard Filling. Repeat with remaining cake and Custard Filling, ending with cake layer. Frost with whipped cream. Garnish with candied fruit. Yield: 12 servings.

Custard Filling

1/2 c. sugar
1/4 c. cornstarch
1/8 tsp. salt
2 c. milk
3 egg yolks, slightly beaten
1 1/2 tsp. vanilla extract

Stir sugar, cornstarch and salt together in medium saucepan. Stir in milk gradually. Bring to a boil, stirring constantly, over medium heat. Boil for 1 minute. Stir about 1/2 cup hot mixture into egg yolks; stir into remaining hot mixture in saucepan. Cook over low heat, stirring constantly, for 2 minutes. Stir in vanilla. Chill. Yield: 2 3/4 cups.

Photograph for this recipe on page 1.

GLAZED PRUNE CAKE

2 c. flour
1 tsp. soda
1/4 tsp. salt
1 tbsp. cinnamon
1 tbsp. allspice
1 1/2 c. sugar
1 c. corn oil
3 eggs
1 c. buttermilk
1 tsp. vanilla
1 c. chopped nuts
1 1/2 c. coarsely cut prunes, cooked,
    drained and pitted
Butterscotch Glaze

Sift first 5 ingredients together. Beat next 2 ingredients together in a large mixing bowl. Add eggs, one at a time, beating well after each addition. Add dry ingredients alternately with buttermilk. Add vanilla; mix well. Stir in nuts and prunes; mix well. Pour into greased, floured and waxed paper-lined tube pan. Bake at 350 degrees for about 1 hour. Pour Butterscotch Glaze over hot cake. Let stand in pan a few minutes. Remove cake from pan while still warm.

Butterscotch Glaze

1 c. sugar
1/2 c. buttermilk
1/4 c. margarine
1/4 c. light corn syrup
1/2 tsp. soda
1/2 tsp. vanilla extract

Combine all ingredients in large saucepan. Bring to a boil. Boil for 10 minutes. Pour over hot cake.

Elise Jane Clapp, Hawaii Conv. Co-Chm.
Xi Theta Chap.
Pearl City, Hawaii

GREEK HONEY CAKE

1 c. butter or margarine
3 c. sugar
6 eggs, separated
2 c. flour
2 tbsp. baking powder
1 tsp. cinnamon
1 c. milk
1 c. chopped nuts
1/2 c. honey
1 tsp. lemon juice

Cream butter and 2 cups sugar together. Add egg yolks, one at a time, beating well after each addition. Sift flour, baking powder and cinnamon together. Add to creamed mixture alternately with milk, beating well after each addition. Fold in stiffly beaten egg whites, a small amount at a time. Add nuts; mix well. Pour into greased 13 x 9-inch pan. Bake at 350 degrees for 40 to 45 minutes. Combine 1 cup sugar, 2 cups water, honey and lemon juice in saucepan. Cook to desired thickness, stirring constantly. Cool syrup slightly. Pour over warm cake. Cut into squares while warm.

Mary Monezis, Honorary Mem.
Xi Iota Delta X4351
Weirton, West Virginia

GREEK NUT CAKE
KARIDOPETA

1 c. butter
2 1/4 c. sugar
5 eggs
2 1/2 c. all-purpose flour
2 tsp. baking powder
1 tsp. cinnamon
1 c. chopped walnuts

Cream butter and 1 1/2 cups sugar until light and fluffy. Add eggs, one at a time, beating well after each addition. Beat until thick and light lemon colored. Sift flour, baking powder and cinnamon into a bowl. Add dry ingredients to creamed mixture gradually, stirring well. Stir in walnuts. Pour mixture into greased 12 x 8-inch pan. Smooth top with knife. Bake in preheated 350-degree oven for 30 to 35 minutes until golden. Combine 1 1/2 cups water and 3/4 cup sugar in saucepan. Bring to a boil over high heat. Boil for 10 minutes. Cool. Pour syrup over hot cake. Serve cut into diamonds or squares. Serve hot or cold.

Beverly Richardson, Treas.
Xi Alpha Tau X4132
Twin Falls, Idaho

GREEK ORANGE CAKE – RAVANI

    1 stick margarine
    3 2/3 c. sugar
    4 eggs, separated
    1 c. flour
    2 tsp. baking powder
    1 c. cream of wheat
    1/2 c. milk
    Grated rind of 1 orange
    2 tsp. vanilla extract

Cream butter and 2/3 cup sugar until light and fluffy. Add egg yolks, one at a time, beating well after each addition. Sift flour and baking powder together. Add cream of wheat and milk to creamed mixture; mix well. Stir in flour mixture; beat well. Add orange rind and vanilla; beat well. Fold in stiffly beaten egg whites, a small amount at a time. Pour into a greased 13 x 9-inch baking pan. Bake at 350 degrees for 45 minutes. Cool cake. Combine 3 cups sugar and 3 cups water in a saucepan. Bring to a boil. Boil for 15 minutes, stirring constantly. Pour hot syrup over cool cake. Cut into diamond shapes.

Lorraine Alkousakis, Ext. Off.
Chi Sigma Chap.
Davis, California

HUMMINGBIRD CAKE

    3 c. flour
    2 c. sugar
    1 tsp. soda
    Dash of salt
    1 tsp. cinnamon
    1 1/2 c. vegetable oil
    3 eggs
    1 can crushed pineapple including
        juice
    2 c. chopped bananas
    1 c. chopped pecans
    1 8-oz. package cream cheese
    1 stick butter
    1 tsp. vanilla extract
    1 box powdered sugar

Sift flour, sugar, soda, salt and cinnamon together. Stir in next 5 ingredients in order listed. Do not beat. Pour into 13 x 9-inch pan or 10-inch tube pan. Bake in preheated 350-degree oven for 1 hour and 10 minutes. Mix cream cheese, softened butter and vanilla; beat until smooth. Add powdered sugar gradually, beating until smooth. Frost cake.

Pat Bird
Gamma Delta No. 5016
Blue Creek, West Virginia

HOT MILK SPONGE CAKE
(NEW ZEALAND)

    3 eggs
    1 c. sugar
    1 c. flour
    1 tsp. baking powder
    Pinch of salt
    1 tbsp. hot milk
    Raspberry jam
    1 c. whipping cream, whipped and
        sweetened
    Confectioners' sugar

Beat eggs and sugar together for 15 minutes until light and fluffy. Sift flour, baking powder and salt together. Fold into egg mixture. Add hot milk. Pour into well-greased and waxed paper-lined 8-inch round cake pan. Place in oven immediately. Bake at 350 degrees for 15 minutes. Turn on rack to cool. Split layer in half. Spread raspberry jam on bottom half; top with whipped cream. Place top layer in place. Sprinkle with confectioners' sugar.

Bobbie Herbert, Exec. Coord. Com. Chm.
Xi Beta Omicron No. 2787
Armonk, New York

HUNGARIAN CAKE

    1 c. quick-cooking oats
    1 c. sugar
    1 1/2 c. (packed) brown sugar
    1/2 c. Crisco
    2 eggs
    1 1/2 c. flour
    1 tsp. cinnamon
    1 tsp. soda
    1/2 tsp. salt
    1 1/2 tsp. vanilla extract
    1 c. chopped pecans
    1/2 c. evaporated milk
    1/2 c. flaked coconut

Pour 1 1/4 cups boiling water over oats. Set aside to cool. Add sugar, 1 cup brown sugar, Crisco, eggs and flour. Beat on medium speed for 2 minutes. Stir in by hand cinnamon, soda, salt, 1/2 teaspoon vanilla and 1/2 cup pecans. Mix thoroughly. Pour into a greased 9 x 13-inch pan. Bake at 350 degrees for 30 minutes. Combine 1/2 cup brown sugar, 1/2 cup pecans, milk, coconut and 1 teaspoon vanilla; mix well. Pour over cake. Place under broiler until golden brown. Cool cake.

Betty Branch, Serv. Chm.
Preceptor Beta Rho XP1537
Temple Terrace, Florida

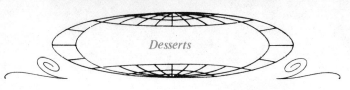

ITALIAN CREAM CAKE

1 stick butter
1/2 c. shortening
2 c. sugar
5 eggs, separated
2 c. flour
1 tsp. soda
1 tsp. salt
1 c. buttermilk
1 sm. can coconut
1 tsp. vanilla extract
1 c. chopped pecans

Cream butter and shortening. Add sugar; beat until smooth. Add egg yolks; beat well. Sift flour, soda and salt together. Add to creamed mixture alternately with buttermilk. Add coconut, vanilla and pecans. Fold in stiffly beaten egg whites. Pour into 3 greased and floured pans. Bake at 350 degrees for 25 minutes. Cool.

Frosting

1   8-oz. package cream cheese, softened
1/2 stick butter
1 box powdered sugar
1 tsp. vanilla extract
1 c. chopped pecans

Beat cream cheese and butter until smooth. Add sugar; beat well. Add vanilla; mix well. Spread on cooled cake. Sprinkle with pecans.

Muriel Nelsen
Preceptor Eta Phi No. 1696
Salinas, California
Sandra Johnson, City Coun. Pres.
Delta Chi No. 4730
Chickasha, Oklahoma

PINA COLADA PUDDING CAKE

1 pkg. white cake mix
2 sm. packages coconut cream instant
   pudding mix
4 eggs
1/4 c. oil
2/3 c. Bacardi rum
1   8-oz. can crushed pineapple and
   juice
1   9-oz. carton Cool Whip
1 c. coconut

Combine cake mix, 1 package pudding mix, eggs, 1/2 cup water, oil and 1/3 cup rum; mix well. Beat for 4 minutes at medium speed of electric mixer. Pour into 3 greased and floured cake pans. Bake at 350 degrees for 20 to 25 minutes. Do not underbake. Cool in pans for 15 minutes. Remove from pans; cool on racks. Combine pineapple, remaining pudding mix and rum. Beat until well blended. Fold in Cool Whip. Frost cake. Sprinkle with coconut. Chill.

Barbara Thornton
Epsilon Mu No. 7839
Mansfield, Louisiana

RAISIN GINGERBREAD (NEWFOUNDLAND)

1 c. raisins
1/2 c. shortening
1/3 c. sugar
6 tbsp. dark molasses
2 eggs, beaten
2 1/2 c. flour
1/2 tsp. salt
2 tsp. ginger
2 tsp. cinnamon
1 tsp. soda
3/4 c. buttermilk

Rinse raisins in hot water. Drain and dry on a towel. Cream shortening and sugar; stir in molasses. Add beaten eggs; beat well. Sift flour with salt and spices. Dissolve soda in buttermilk. Add alternately with sifted flour to egg mixture, beating well after each addition. Stir in raisins. Pour into greased 8 x 12-inch baking pan. Bake at 350 degrees for 40 minutes. Serve hot with butter.

Sylvia L. Roop, Corr. Sec.
Zeta No. 6657
Grand Falls, Newfoundland, Canada

REFRIED BEAN CAKE (MEXICO)

2 c. Bisquick
2 eggs
3/4 c. milk
1/3 c. margarine or oil
Sugar
1 1/2 c. refried beans
1 tsp. cinnamon
1/2 tsp. cloves
1/2 c. raisins
3/4 c. chopped walnuts
1 c. (packed) brown sugar
1 1/2 to 2 c. powdered sugar
Chopped nuts or coconut

Mix Bisquick, eggs, milk and margarine together. Add 1 1/2 cups sugar and refried beans. Beat for 3 minutes or until beans are well blended. Stir in spices, raisins and walnuts. Pour into well-greased and floured pan. Bake at 350 degrees for 40 minutes. Brown 1/3 cup sugar in skillet. Add 1/4 cup water and brown sugar; stir well. Cool. Beat in enough powdered sugar to spreading consistency. Add chopped nuts or coconut, if desired. Spead frosting over cake.

Almeda Swaney, Treas.
Xi Xi Beta X3186
Long Beach, California

RICOTTA CAKE (ITALY)

1 pkg. yellow cake mix
3 lb. ricotta
8 eggs
1 c. sugar
2 tbsp. vanilla extract

Pinch of salt
Cinnamon

Prepare cake mix according to package directions. Pour into greased 13 x 9 x 2-inch pan. Combine ricotta, eggs, sugar, vanilla and salt. Beat until thoroughly mixed. Pour over cake batter. Bake at 350 degrees for 30 minutes. Sprinkle with mixture of cinnamon and additional sugar. Bake for 1 hour longer.

Carolyn Zaza
Beta Nu No. 6437
Waterbury, Connecticut

SPICY YOGURT CAKE (GREECE)
TOURTA ME YIAOURTI

1/2 c. butter or margarine
1 c. sugar
3 eggs
2 c. sifted flour
1 tsp. salt
2 tsp. baking powder
1 c. yogurt
1 tsp. soda
1 tsp. vanilla extract
3/4 c. raisins
1 tsp. cinnamon
1/2 tsp. nutmeg
1/2 tsp. cloves
1/2 c. chopped walnuts

Cream butter and sugar. Add eggs; beat well. Sift flour, salt and baking powder together. Add gradually to batter, beating on medium speed. Combine yogurt and soda; add to batter a few tablespoons at a time. Add vanilla. Mix raisins, spices and walnuts together. Pour half the batter into a buttered 9-inch pan. Sprinkle half the raisin mixture over batter. Pour on remaining batter; top with remaining raisin mixture. Bake at 350 degrees for 40 to 45 minutes. Greeks prefer this recipe made as cupcakes.

Glenda Rice, Pres.
Xi Beta Omicron Chap.
Wakita, Oklahoma

ZUCCHINI CAKE

3 eggs
2 c. sugar
1 c. oil
2 c. grated zucchini
2 c. flour
1 tsp. baking powder
2 tsp. soda
1 tsp. salt
3 tsp. cinnamon
1/4 tsp. cloves
1/2 tsp. ginger
3/4 c. raisins
1 1/2 c. chopped nuts

Combine eggs, sugar and oil; beat until smooth. Add grated zucchini; stir until combined. Sift flour, baking powder, soda, salt, cinnamon, cloves and ginger together. Add raisins and nuts to dry ingredients. Stir into zucchini mixture. Pour into greased and floured 9 x 13-inch baking pan. Bake at 325 degrees about 1 hour and 20 minutes or until cake tests done. Apples, carrots, cucumbers or any type of squash, or a combination may be substituted for zucchini.

Kitty Lint, Corr. Sec.
Preceptor Gamma Zeta XP787
San Diego, California

GERMAN CHEESECAKE
KASEKUCHEN

1/3 c. margarine
Sugar
4 eggs
Flour
1 8-oz. package cream cheese,
  softened
1 tsp. vanilla extract
2 tbsp. milk

Cream margarine and 1/3 cup sugar until light and fluffy. Blend in 1 egg. Add 1 1/4 cups flour; mix well. Spread dough on bottom and 1 1/2 inches high around sides of 9-inch springform pan. Bake for 5 minutes in preheated 450-degree oven. Combine softened cream cheese, 3/4 cup sugar, 2 tablespoons flour and vanilla, mixing at medium speed in electric mixer until blended. Blend in 3 eggs, one at a time, beating well after each addition. Stir in milk; mix well. Pour into pastry-lined pan. Bake at 450 degrees for 10 minutes. Reduce temperature to 250 degrees; continue baking for 25 to 30 minutes. Cool. Remove from springform pan. Chill for several hours.

Irmi Harrell
Theta Nu No. 8477
Mustang, Oklahoma

LYNN'S CHEESECAKE

16 graham crackers, crushed
2/3 c. melted butter
1 8-oz. package cream cheese,
  softened
Sugar
2 eggs, beaten
1/2 pt. sour cream
1/2 tsp. vanilla extract
1 can cherry or blueberry filling

Combine cracker crumbs and melted butter in a 9-inch pie pan. Pat over bottom and sides of pan evenly. Beat cream cheese, 1 1/3 cups sugar and eggs together, mixing well. Pour into lined pie pan. Bake at 350 degrees for 22 minutes. Blend sour cream, 1/4 cup sugar and vanilla. Pour over cream cheese layer. Bake at 350 degrees for 8 minutes longer. Cool. Top with cherry pie filling.

Lynn Elaine Rardin
Eta Kappa Chap.
Reston, Virginia

PEACHES AND CREAM CHEESECAKE

1 lg. can peaches
1 1/2 c. flour
2 tsp. baking powder
1 c. milk
6 tbsp. margarine
2 eggs
1/2 tsp. salt
2 sm. packages vanilla pudding mix
6 tbsp. peach juice
2 8-oz. packages cream cheese, softened
Sugar
1 tsp. cinnamon

Drain peaches, reserving juice. Combine next 7 ingredients in mixing bowl. Beat for 2 minutes. Pour into greased 9 x 13-inch pan. Arrange peaches over batter. Combine next 2 ingredients and 1 cup sugar in small bowl. Beat for 2 minutes. Spoon over top of peaches to within 1 inch of edge of batter. Combine 2 tablespoons sugar and cinnamon. Sprinkle over cream cheese filling. Bake at 350 degrees for 30 to 35 minutes. Filling will be soft. Chill immediately.

Alice Martin
Wakeman Chap.
Wakeman, Ohio

MOLDED RAISIN BLANC MANGE

1/2 c. sugar
5 tbsp. cornstarch
1/4 tsp. salt
4 c. milk
1 1/2 tsp. vanilla extract
1/2 c. golden raisins

Stir sugar, cornstarch and salt together in 2-quart saucepan. Stir in milk gradually until smooth. Bring to a boil, stirring constantly, over medium heat; boil for 1 minute. Remove from heat. Stir in vanilla and raisins. Pour into 4-cup mold. Chill for 4 hours or until set. Unmold on serving plate.

Photograph for this recipe on page 2.

BRANDY-CHOCOLATE CREAM (GERMANY) SCHOKOLADENCREME

1/2 lb. sweet cooking chocolate
4 eggs, separated
1/2 c. Brandy or whiskey
Whipped cream
Nuts

Melt chocolate in double boiler. Add egg yolks, one at a time, beating well after each addition. Add Brandy, stirring well. Cool. Beat egg whites until stiff. Fold into chocolate mixture. Pour into serving glasses. Garnish with whipped cream and nuts. Chill in refrigerator.

This fine recipe was given to me by my mother-in-law in Germany. It was her own prize-winning recipe. Yield: 6 servings.

Christel Conradi, Pres.
Preceptor Beta Rho XP1537
Tampa, Florida

CHOCOLATE-CRUSTED BAVARIAN

1 1/2 c. chocolate wafer crumbs
1/3 c. melted butter
1 tbsp. unflavored gelatin
1 c. milk
3 eggs, separated
1/2 c. sugar
1/4 tsp. salt
1 tsp. vanilla extract
3/4 c. whipping cream
13 8-oz. bars milk chocolate

Mix chocolate crumbs and butter thoroughly. Press a thin layer over sides and bottom of a lightly buttered 8-inch square cake pan. Chill. Soften gelatin in 1 cup cold water. Scald milk in top of double boiler. Beat egg yolks slightly. Add sugar and salt. Stir a small amount of scalded milk into egg yolks. Stir egg yolks into scalded milk, stirring constantly. Return to double boiler. Cook until mixture coats a metal spoon. Remove from heat. Add gelatin; stir until dissolved. Strain into bowl. Add vanilla. Fold in stiffly beaten egg whites. Chill until partially congealed. Pour cream into chilled bowl; beat until stiff. Fold into slightly congealed mixture. Pour into crumb-lined pan. Grate chocolate directly over the custard mixture, distributing evenly. Chill for several hours or overnight. Cut into squares to serve. Dip pan in hot water for a second to remove squares from pan easily. Yield: 8 servings.

Kathleen Bromley, Pres.
Alpha Chap.
Toronto, Ontario, Canada

CHOCOLATE MOUSSE

4 sq. semisweet chocolate
4 eggs, separated
1/2 c. powdered sugar
Dash of salt

Combine chocolate and 1/4 cup water in top of double boiler. Melt chocolate over hot, not boiling, water, stirring occasionally. Remove from heat; set aside to cool. Beat egg yolks in large bowl. Beat in sugar gradually. Continue to beat until mixture is pale yellow. Beat egg whites in second large bowl at medium speed until foamy. Add salt; beat until stiff peaks form. Stir about 1 cup egg whites into chocolate mixture, then fold remaining egg whites into chocolate mixture. Pour mousse into serving dishes. Refrigerate for several hours or overnight.

Candy Gergen
Theta Delta No. 9912
Burlington, Colorado

DANISH DESSERT

1/2 pt. heavy cream
Sugar
1 1-lb. can applesauce
1/3 lb. graham crackers, crushed

Whip cream and sweeten to taste. Layer applesauce, graham crackers and whipped cream in shallow serving bowl. Refrigerate until well chilled before serving.

Mary Lou Brannon, Pres.
Preceptor Alpha Kappa XP1555
Dubuque, Iowa

EGGNOG BAVARIAN WITH MELBA SAUCE

3 env. unflavored gelatin
1/2 c. milk
1 qt. eggnog
2 egg whites
1/8 tsp. salt
2 tbsp. sugar
1/4 to 1/3 c. rum
3/4 c. whipping cream, whipped
1 c. finely chopped walnuts
1 10-oz. package frozen raspberries
1/2 c. currant jelly
3 tbsp. cornstarch

Stir gelatin into milk to soften. Add 1 cup eggnog. Heat gently until gelatin melts. Stir in remaining eggnog. Cool until mixture thickens. Beat egg whites with salt until stiff, adding sugar gradually; fold in rum. Fold egg whites, cream and walnuts into gelatin. Pour into 2-quart mold. Chill until firm. Place frozen raspberries into saucepan. Heat until raspberries are thawed and soft. Press through a sieve to remove seeds; return strained raspberries to pan. Add currant jelly. Mix cornstarch with 1 tablespoon water; add to raspberries. Cook until clear and thickened, stirring frequently. Chill. Serve over Eggnog Bavarian.

Linda E. Edwards, Sec -Treas.
Delta Beta No. 4108
Pryor, Oklahoma

IRISH COFFEE PUDDING (IRELAND)

6 eggs, separated
3/4 c. sugar
2 1/2 tbsp. unflavored gelatin
1 c. strong black coffee
1/4 c. Irish Whiskey or Irish Mist
2 1/4 c. heavy cream, whipped
1/2 c. crushed walnuts

Beat egg yolks with sugar until lemon colored. Dissolve gelatin in hot coffee. Add small amount hot coffee mixture to egg yolks; mix well. Add egg yolks to coffee mixture; mix well. Place egg mixture in top of double boiler over hot water. Do not boil. Beat mixture until it begins to thicken. Add whiskey and continue beating until thick and creamy. Remove from heat. Chill for 1 hour and 30 minutes. Fold in 1 1/4 cups whipped cream. Beat egg whites until foamy. Fold into cream mixture. Pour into angel food cake pan. Chill until set. Serve with 1 cup whipped cream sprinkled with walnuts.

Una C. Teelin
Alpha Delta No. 1050
Baraboo, Wisconsin

MYSTERY POPPY SEED DESSERT

1/2 c. all-purpose flour
1/2 c. finely crushed saltine crackers
1/2 c. finely crushed graham crackers
1/2 c. chopped black walnuts
1/2 c. butter or margarine, melted
1 1/2 c. sugar
1/4 c. poppy seed
3 tbsp. cornstarch
1 env. unflavored gelatin
2 c. milk
4 eggs, separated
1 tsp. vanilla extract
1/2 tsp. cream of tartar

Combine flour, cracker crumbs and walnuts. Stir in butter. Press mixture into 9 x 9 x 2-inch baking dish. Bake in 375-degree oven for 10 minutes. Cool. Combine 1 cup sugar, poppy seed, cornstarch and gelatin in medium saucepan. Stir in milk. Cook and stir until thickened and bubbly. Beat egg yolks. Add a small amount of hot mixture to egg yolks, stirring constantly. Return all to saucepan. Cook and stir for 2 minutes. Add vanilla. Cover and cool until partially set. Beat egg whites and cream of tartar until soft peaks form. Add remaining sugar gradually, beating until stiff peaks form. Fold into cooled poppy seed mixture. Turn into prepared crust; cover. Chill overnight. Serve with whipped cream and additional chopped nuts, if desired.

Virginia Woolf
Xi Alpha Alpha X4700
Amory, Mississippi

PRUNE PUDDING

1 lb. prunes
1 c. sugar
3 tsp. unflavored gelatin
3 egg whites

Soak prunes overnight in enough water to cover. Remove pits. Place in saucepan with small amount of water. Cook slowly for 1 hour. Add sugar; let cool. Put through colander until smooth. Soften gelatin in 1/3 cup water. Beat egg whites until stiff. Fold into prune mixture. Mix gelatin into prune mixture. Pour into mold. Chill until firm.

Clarise M. Merrill
Preceptor Phi Chap.
Apache Junction, Arizona

RUM SOUFFLE (DENMARK)

4 egg yolks
1 c. sugar
1/4 c. rum
1 env. unflavored gelatin
1/2 pt. heavy cream
3 egg whites

Beat egg yolks and 1/2 cup sugar until light lemon colored. Add rum. Dissolve gelatin in 1/4 cup water over boiling water. Stir into egg yolk mixture. Beat cream until stiff. Beat egg whites until stiff; add remaining sugar gradually. Fold whipped cream into the egg yolk mixture. Fold in stiffly beaten egg whites. Pour into a serving dish. Chill for 4 to 6 hours. Garnish with additional whipped cream and shaved unsweetened chocolate.

Judy Sherman
Delta Eta Chap.
North Delta, British Columbia, Canada

SNOW PUDDING (NORWAY)

1 tbsp. unflavored gelatin
2/3 c. sugar
3 unbeaten egg whites
1/4 tsp. salt
1 tsp. vanilla extract
16 graham crackers, crushed
Rum Sauce

Place gelatin in 4 tablespoons cold water; soak 5 minutes. Add 1 cup boiling water and stir. Add sugar; stir until dissolved. Cool slightly. Add egg whites, salt and vanilla. Let set until partially congealed. Beat until light and fluffy. Turn into 9 x 9-inch pan. Chill until firm. Cut into 1-inch squares. Roll in graham cracker crumbs. Pile lightly in sherbet glasses. Serve with Rum Sauce.

Rum Sauce

2 egg yolks
1/3 c. sugar
1/3 c. melted butter
2 tbsp. rum
1/3 c. heavy cream, whipped

Beat egg yolks until light and thick. Add sugar gradually, beating after each addition. Add butter and rum. Fold in whipped cream. Chill. Yield: 8 servings.

Julie Volz, Sec.
Alpha Zeta No. 1173
Bedford, Indiana

TALI'S FRENCH DELIGHT

1 c. all-purpose flour
1 stick margarine, softened
1/2 c. chopped walnuts
1 8-oz. package cream cheese, softened
1 c. confectioners' sugar
1 16-oz. carton Cool Whip

1 4 1/2-oz. box instant chocolate pudding mix
1 4 1/2-oz. box instant vanilla pudding mix
3 c. milk
1/2 lg. Hershey bar with almonds, grated (opt.)

Mix flour, margarine and walnuts in 13 x 9 1/2-inch baking pan. Press into place with fingers. Bake in 350-degree oven for 20 minutes. Let cool. Cream together cream cheese, confectioners' sugar and 1 cup Cool Whip. Spread mixture over cooled crust. Prepare pudding mixes according to package directions, using 3 cups milk. Spread over cream cheese mixture. Combine grated chocolate with remaining Cool Whip. Spread over pudding mixture. Chill for several hours.

Tali Lee Holton
Sigma Gamma No. 10033
Orange Park, Florida

ZUPPA INGLESE (ITALY)

2 pkg. vanilla pudding mix
Cinnamon stick
1 lb. cake, thinly sliced
1 jigger each grenadine, whiskey and rum
Whipped cream
Maraschino cherries

Prepare pudding mix according to package directions, adding cinnamon stick. Place layer of pound cake in 8-inch square pan. Sprinkle with grenadine, whiskey and rum. Spoon pudding over all. Continue to layer ingredients until all are used, ending with pudding layer. Top with whipped cream. Decorate with cherries. Chill for several hours.

Gloria M. Ridolfi
Preceptor Beta XP346
Anchorage, Alaska

GRANDPA'S PUDDING
(FRANCE) BLANC MANGE

8 anisette sponge cookies
6 tbsp. sugar
6 tbsp. cornstarch
1/4 tsp. salt
4 c. milk
1 1/2 tsp. vanilla extract
4 oz. milk or semisweet chocolate,
    chopped or grated
Cinnamon sugar

Break each sponge cookie into 4 pieces; place in 2 1/2-quart bowl. Combine sugar, cornstarch and salt in top of double boiler, over boiling water. Add milk. Cook over medium heat, stirring constantly. As soon as pudding begins to thicken, remove from heat. Stir in vanilla. Pour 1/2 of the pudding into bowl over cookies. Sprinkle 1/2 of the chocolate on top of pudding. Pour in remaining pudding. Sprinkle with remaining chocolate. Cover with cinnamon sugar. Cool to room temperature, uncovered.

Barbara Catuosco
Xi Alpha Delta No. 4865
West Islip, New York

BURNT STRAWBERRY CREAM (ENGLAND)

3 c. cooked rice
3 c. milk
1/3 c. sugar
1/4 tsp. salt
2   3-oz. packages cream cheese,
    softened
1 1/2 tsp. vanilla extract
1 c. cream, whipped
1   16-oz. package frozen sweetened
    strawberries, drained
1/3 c. (packed) brown sugar

Combine rice, milk, sugar and salt in saucepan. Cook over medium heat until thick and creamy, about 30 minutes, stirring frequently. Remove from heat. Add cream cheese and vanilla. Stir until cheese is dissolved. Chill. Fold in whipped cream. Chill thoroughly. Slice strawberries in half over bottom of a 7 1/2 x 12 x 2-inch baking dish. Spoon pudding over strawberries. Sprinkle with brown sugar. Place under broiler for 1 to 2 minutes or until sugar melts. Serve immediately. Sliced, fresh strawberries sprinkled with sugar may be used.

Margaret E. Taylor, Pres.
Preceptor Alpha Kappa XP778
Fort Collins, Colorado

CARAMEL FLAN (COSTA RICA)

1 3/4 c. sugar
3 egg whites
8 egg yolks
2   13-oz. cans evaporated milk
2 tsp. vanilla extract
6 tbsp. Brandy or rum (opt.)

Pour 1 cup sugar in greased flan or baking pan. Place in oven until sugar melts and turns golden. Tip pan to coat sides. Let cool. Beat egg whites and egg yolks together. Add milk, remaining sugar and vanilla. Beat until sugar is dissolved. Pour into flan pan. Place pan in larger pan containing 1 inch hot water. Bake in preheated 350-degree oven for 1 hour or until firm. Chill before serving. Heat Brandy; pour over flan. Ignite. Serve flaming. Yield: 8-10 servings.

Elaine J. Williams, Ext. Off.
Preceptor Tau XP397
Yakima, Washington

RICE CUSTARD
ROZ EB HALEEB

1 qt. milk
1/4 c. rice
3 tbsp. cornstarch
3/4 c. sugar
3/4 tsp. orange blossom water

Heat milk over medium heat until crust forms, about 10 minutes. Add rice. Stir slowly until milk boils. Cook on low heat for 20 minutes. Mix cornstarch with small amount of water to make paste. Add to milk-rice mixture; mix well. Add sugar. Stir until custard begins to thicken. Add orange blossom water; remove from heat. Cool. Pour into custard cups. Yield: 6 servings.

Carreme Curry
Xi Alpha Gamma X4904
Hattiesburg, Mississippi

ZABAGLIONE (ITALY)

2 c. cold milk
3 c. cold light cream
2 pkg. vanilla instant pudding mix
2 egg whites
1/4 c. sugar
1/3 c. Sherry

Pour milk and cream into mixing bowl. Add pudding mix. Beat slowly with egg beater just until well mixed, about 1 minute. Do not overbeat. Mixture will be thin. Let stand about 5 minutes to set. Beat egg whites until stiff but not dry. Beat in sugar gradually, sprinkling a small amount at a time over the surface of egg white. Continue beating until very smooth and glossy. Fold egg whie mixture into pudding. Chill. Pour Sherry over the top just before serving. Do not stir. Serve in sherbet glasses. Yield: 8 servings.

Glenna Page, V.P.
Xi Omicron Eta X3470
Mission Viejo, California

SCANDINAVIAN APPLE PUDDING

Sugar
1/4 tsp. salt
1 No. 2 can unsweetened applesauce
3 c. bread cubes
1/2 c. melted margarine
1/2 tsp. cinnamon
1/2 tsp. nutmeg
2 tbsp. butter

Add 1/3 cup sugar and salt to applesauce. Brown bread cubes in melted margarine in skillet, tossing lightly with fork. Stir in applesauce. Pour into 8-inch square baking dish. Sprinkle with mixture of 2 tablespoons sugar, cinnamon and nutmeg. Dot with butter. Bake at 375 degrees for 1 hour. Yield: 6 servings.

Shirley Ann Snyder
Xi Theta Chi X4361
Robinson, Illinois

BAKED INDIAN PUDDING

3 tbsp. cornmeal
3 c. scalded milk
1/3 c. molasses
1/2 c. sugar
1 tbsp. melted butter
1/2 tsp. cinnamon
1/2 tsp. ginger
1/2 tsp. salt
1 egg, beaten

Add cornmeal to milk gradually, stirring constantly until slightly thickened. Add molasses. Add sugar, butter, spices and salt to beaten egg. Add small amount of egg mixture to hot milk mixture. Stir egg mixture into hot mixture; mix well. Pour into greased pudding dishes. Bake in 300-degree oven for 2 hours.

Linda Greene
Eta Chi No. 10489
Snellville, Georgia

CHEESE PUDDING (SWEDEN)
OSTPUDDING

2/3 c. flour
1 pt. milk
1/2 tsp. almond extract
4 eggs, well beaten
3 c. creamed cottage cheese
1 c. sugar

Fold first 3 ingredients into eggs, cottage cheese and sugar. Pour into a greased baking dish. Place in pan of hot water to bake. Bake at 400 degrees for 1 hour until brown. Serve with fresh lingonberries.

Mrs. Cheri Bowden
Gamma Gamma No. 6387
Grand Island, Nebraska

INDIAN BREAD PUDDING

1 1/2 c. sugar
1 tbsp. vanilla extract
1 1/2 tsp. ground allspice or cinnamon
10 slices white toast
2 c. shredded Cheddar cheese
1 1/2 c. seedless raisins

Melt sugar in a heavy skillet over low heat. Stir constantly with a wooden spoon until sugar is melted and syrup is golden brown. Remove from heat. Stir in 3 cups water slowly. Add vanilla. Add allspice and return to heat. Cook, stirring, until all sugar is dissolved. Arrange half the toast slices in bottom of greased 9 x 9-inch pan, breaking pieces to fit around corners. Sprinkle toast with 1/2 of the cheese and 1/2 of the raisins. Repeat layers. Pour sugar syrup over layers. Bake in preheated 375-degree oven until cheese is melted and syrup is bubbly, about 10 minutes. Yield: 8 servings.

Florence M. Sanchez, Corr. Sec.
Delta No. 485
Santa Fe, New Mexico

EVE'S PUDDING

3 lg. cooking apples, peeled and cored
2 tbsp. sugar
Juice of 1/2 lemon
3 oz. butter, softened
Grated rind of 1/2 lemon
3 oz. caster sugar
1 egg
5 oz. self-rising flour
Pinch of salt
2 or 3 tbsp. milk

Cut apples into thick slices. Combine apples, sugar, lemon juice and 1 tablespoon water in a saucepan. Cook until apples are tender. Place in bottom of a pie plate. Combine butter and lemon rind in a mixing bowl. Add caster sugar; mix until light and fluffy. Beat in egg. Sift flour and salt together. Fold into egg mixture. Stir in enough milk to make pouring consistency. Spread over apples. Bake at 375 degrees for 40 minutes. Serve hot with cream.

Margaret R. Johnson, V.P.
Preceptor Delta XP193
Fruitport, Michigan

ORANGE PUDDING

Sugar
2 tbsp. flour
2 eggs, separated
1 c. milk
2 oranges, peeled and sectioned

Combine 1 cup sugar and flour. Beat egg yolks slightly. Stir in milk; blend well. Add gradually to sugar-flour mixture. Cook over medium heat until thickened. Cool in saucepan. Beat egg whites until stiff; add to cooled pudding. Sprinkle oranges with 2 tablespoons sugar. Stir oranges into cooled pudding; mix well. Garnish with small pieces of additional orange.

Kathie Connor
Xi Delta Delta X4221
Saint Thomas, Ontario, Canada

MONMOUTH PUDDING (WALES)

Grated rind of 1 lemon
1 oz. sugar
1 oz. butter
3/4 pt. milk
6 oz. bread crumbs
3 egg yolks
4 or 5 tbsp. strawberry jam, heated

Add grated lemon rind, sugar and butter to milk. Bring to a boil. Pour mixture over bread crumbs. Allow to cool for 15 minutes. Stir egg yolks into cooled mixture. Pour half the mixture into greased baking dish. Spread with melted jam. Add remaining mixture. Cover with remaining jam. Bake at 325 degrees for 40 to 45 minutes.

Roberta Wakefield
Preceptor Zeta Eta XP1292
Long Beach, California

FILBERT PRALINE CREAM

4 eggs, separated
Sugar
1/3 c. all-purpose flour
2 1/2 c. milk
Dash of salt
1/2 c. Filbert Praline Powder
1 tsp. vanilla extract
1 tsp. rum flavoring

Beat egg yolks and 1/3 cup sugar until thick and lemon colored. Stir in flour. Heat milk just to boiling point; pour into egg yolk mixture gradually, beating constantly. Bring to a boil over medium heat. Boil gently for 2 minutes, beating constantly with wire whip. Add salt to egg whites; beat until foamy. Add 1 tablespoon sugar; beat until soft peaks form. Fold egg whites into hot egg yolk mixture; fold in 1/4 cup Filbert Praline Powder and flavorings. Turn into serving dish. Chill for 2 to 3 hours. Sprinkle with remaining 1/4 cup Filbert Praline Powder just before serving. Yield: 6-8 servings.

Filbert Praline Powder

3/4 c. sugar
1 tsp. light corn syrup or 1/8 tsp.
   cream of tartar
3/4 c. filberts

Combine sugar, 1/4 cup water and corn syrup in small saucepan. Cook over medium heat, stirring constantly, until sugar is dissolved and mixture boils. Stir in filberts. Cook over high heat, without stirring, until mixture is the color of molasses. Pour onto oiled cookie sheet; let cool. Break into small pieces. Process in electric blender until powdered. Store praline powder in covered container in refrigerator. Use as topping for puddings, pies, cakes, ice cream and fruit. Yield: 2-2 1/2 cups.

Photograph for this recipe above.

ENGLISH PLUM PUDDING

1/4 tsp. soda
1 c. molasses
2 c. flour
1/4 tsp. each allspice, cloves,
   cinnamon and salt
1 c. currants
1 c. raisins
1 c. chopped dates
1 c. glazed fruit
1 c. diced beef suet
1 c. walnuts
1 c. milk
1 egg, beaten
1 c. Brandy (opt.)
1/2 c. butter
2 c. confectioners' sugar, sifted
1 tsp. Bourbon

Stir soda into molasses. Sift flour and spices together. Stir in fruits, suet and walnuts; mix well. Add molasses mixture, milk and egg; mix well. Add Brandy. Pour into greased mold, filling 2/3 full. Cover tightly. Place on rack in covered container with small amount of boiling water. Steam for 3 hours. Cream butter and sugar. Add Bourbon; mix well. Serve sauce over hot pudding.

Beatrice E. Faircloth, Pres.
Preceptor Theta Theta XP1759
Stockton, California

TRADITIONAL ENGLISH STEAMED PUDDING

1 c. chopped dates
2 tbsp. shortening
1 c. (packed) brown sugar
1 egg, well beaten
1/2 c. chopped nuts
1 tsp. grated lemon rind
1 1/2 c. sifted flour
1 tsp. salt
1 tsp. soda
1/2 c. butter or margarine
1 1/2 c. sifted confectioners' sugar
2 tsp. vanilla extract
Sugar cubes
Lemon or orange extract

Pour 1 cup boiling water over dates and shortening. Stir brown sugar into egg. Blend in date mixture, nuts and lemon rind. Sift flour, salt and soda together. Add to date mixture. Pour into well-greased 1-quart mold. Steam tightly covered for 2 hours. Cream butter until soft. Blend in confectioners' sugar and vanilla gradually; mix well. Pour over unmolded pudding. Soak sugar cubes in lemon extract. Arrange around pudding. Touch a lighted match to one sugar cube; the pudding will be encircled with bright flames. Serve immediately.

Kathy Kasiorek, V.P.
Zeta Rho No. 8397
McKeesport, Pennsylvania

RICE PORRIDGE (NORWAY)
RISENGROT

3 pt. milk
1/2 c. (heaping) rice
1 tsp. salt

Bring milk to a boil. Add rice; stir well. Reduce heat; cover. Simmer gently for 1 hour, stirring occasionally. Add salt 5 minutes before porridge is done. Serve with pat of butter on each serving, sprinkled with sugar and powdered cinnamon. It is customary to serve Raspberry Cordial with this dish.

Thelma M. Krell
Beta No. 9031
Spokane, Washington

RUSK PUDDING

1 box Holland rusk, crushed
1 c. sugar
Melted butter
2 c. milk
1 tbsp. cornstarch
4 egg yolks
1 tsp. vanilla extract
1 egg white

Combine crushed rusk, 1/2 cup sugar and enough melted butter to moisten; mix well. Spread 3/4 of the crumb mixture on bottom of 12 x 8-inch pan. Mix milk, 1/2 cup sugar, cornstarch, egg yolks and vanilla. Cook until thickened. Beat egg white until stiff. Layer custard and egg white in crumb-lined pan. Top with remaining crumb mixture. Bake at 350 degrees until egg white slightly browns. Cool. Serve with whipped cream.

Leslie Jannereth
Xi Gamma Chi X3437
Kentwood, Michigan

STEAMED CRANBERRY PUDDING
(GERMANY)

2 c. cranberries
Flour
1/2 tsp. salt
2 tsp. soda
1/4 c. dark corn syrup
1 c. sugar
1/2 c. cream
1/2 c. butter
1 tsp. vanilla extract

Cut cranberries in half; sprinkle lightly with flour. Add 1 1/2 cups flour and salt. Stir soda into 1/2 cup water until foamy; add to cranberry mixture. Add corn syrup. Place in 2-quart mold; steam tightly covered for 1 hour and 30 minutes. Combine sugar and cream. Cook for 5 minutes. Add butter and vanilla; mix well. Serve hot over steamed pudding.

Connie Cynkar
Alpha Sigma No. 8391
Great Falls, Montana

STEAMED JAM SPONGE
(ENGLAND)

1/2 c. butter or margarine
2/3 c. sugar
2 eggs
1 c. flour
1/2 tsp. baking powder
1/4 tsp. salt
1 tsp. grated lemon rind
Milk
2 tbsp. jam or marmalade

Cream butter and sugar until light and fluffy. Add eggs, one at a time, beating well after each addition. Sift flour, baking powder and salt together; add lemon rind. Fold into creamed mixture. Add enough milk to make soft batter. Spread jam in bottom of a greased mold. Pour batter on top of jam; cover. Steam over boiling water for 2 hours.

Pauline Lockwood, Rec. Sec.
Xi Gamma Tau X4416
Owego, New York

APPLE FRITTERS

3 eggs
1/4 c. milk
2 c. chopped peeled apples
1 1/2 c. biscuit mix
2 tbsp. raisins
1 tbsp. sugar
3/4 tsp. cinnamon
1/4 tsp. nutmeg
Oil
Confectioners' sugar or
cinnamon-sugar mixture

Beat eggs and milk just until foamy. Stir in chopped apples and biscuit mix. Add raisins, sugar and spices; mix well. Heat 2 to 3 inches oil in frypan to 360 degrees. Drop batter by rounded tablespoonfuls into hot oil. Fry until golden brown on both sides, about 2 1/2 minutes. Drain on paper towels. Roll in confectioners' sugar. Serve warm.

Barbara King, Pres.
Xi Alpha Lambda X1827
Norfolk, Virginia

APPLE-MINT CRISP (SPAIN)
PASTEL DE MANZANA

4 med. tart apples, peeled
1 tbsp. softened butter
1 c. sugar
1 c. all-purpose flour
1/2 tsp. baking powder
1 egg
1 tbsp. dried mint leaves
1 tbsp. ground cinnamon
1 c. heavy cream, whipped (opt.)

Cut apples lengthwise into 1/4-inch slices. Coat bottom and sides of 8 x 8 x 2-inch baking dish with

butter. Set aside. Combine sugar, flour and baking powder. Sift into mixing bowl. Make a well in center. Drop in egg. Mix together with 2 knives until well mixed. Stir mint leaves and cinnamon into large mixing bowl. Add apples; toss until slices are coated evenly. Arrange slices in baking dish; sprinkle flour mixture over all, spreading into a smooth layer. Bake in preheated 350-degree oven for 45 minutes or until top is crusty. Remove from oven. Cover with foil; set aside to cool. Serve at room temperature with whipped cream.

Audrey B. Carr, Treas.
Preceptor Mu XP1464
Bountiful, Utah

DUTCH APPLE PIE

2 c. flour
1/2 c. oatmeal
1 c. (packed) brown sugar
3/4 c. melted butter
1 1/4 tsp. salt
2 to 4 c. diced apples
1 c. water
1 c. sugar
1 tsp. (or more) vanilla extract
3 tbsp. cornstarch

Mix first 4 ingredients and 1 teaspoon salt together until crumbly. Reserve 1 cup mixture for topping. Spread remaining mixture evenly in 8 x 8-inch deep dish. Cover crumb mixture with apples. Bring remaining ingredients to a boil. Boil until mixture is thick. Pour syrup over apples. Top with reserved crumb mixture. Bake at 350 degrees for 55 minutes or until crust is brown. Serve warm with ice cream. Yield: 6-10 servings.

Mrs. Roy McBride, Corr. Sec.
Xi Eta Eta X2219
McKinney, Texas

APRICOT DUMPLINGS (AUSTRIA)
APRIKOSEN KNODEL

2 lb. potatoes
2 1/2 c. flour
3/4 c. plus 2 tbsp. sugar
2 tbsp. cream of wheat, uncooked
2 tbsp. oil
2 egg yolks, beaten
2 tsp. salt
2 1/2 lb. fresh apricots or
    plums
Sugar cubes, cut in halves
1 stick margarine, melted
2 c. fine bread crumbs, toasted

Boil potatoes in skin. Peel warm potatoes and mash. Add flour, 2 tablespoons sugar, cream of wheat, oil, egg yolks and 1 teaspoon salt. Knead into a ball. Shape into a roll. Remove pits from apricots without cutting all the way through; replace with sugar cube. Cover each fruit piece with a portion of the dough; shape into a ball. Bring 3 cups water and 1 teaspoon salt to a boil. Drop dumplings into boiling water. Simmer gently for 10 to 15 minutes. Remove dumplings with slotted spoon. Roll in melted margarine then in toasted bread crumbs. Arrange in baking dish; sprinkle with 3/4 cup sugar. Serve with additional hot melted margarine and sugar.

Eva E. Hodges
Gamma Delta No. 4443
Mount Airy, North Carolina

AVOCADO FRUIT CUP (BRAZIL)
PUREE DE ABACATE

1 lg. ripe avocado
1 tsp. (or more) sugar
2 tsp. lime or lemon juice
2 tbsp. Creme de Cacao

Cut avocado in half. Scoop out pulp; press through coarse sieve. Add sugar and lime juice. Whip mixture with fork. Pile into 2 sherbet glasses. Chill for several hours. Spoon Creme de Cacao over each serving. Yield: 2 servings.

Rebecca Traum, Pres.
Xi Beta Eta No. 2291
Arvada, Colorado

FRIED BANANAS
(PHILIPPINE ISLANDS)

6 bananas, cut 3 in. long
Lumpia wrappers or thawed
    won ton wrappers
Oil
1 tsp. cinnamon
1/2 c. sugar

Wrap bananas in lumpia wrappers. Fry in hot oil until golden brown. Roll in mixture of cinnamon and sugar. Serve hot. Yield: 6 servings.

Virginia Ann Thomas
Xi Gamma Beta No. 3958
Annandale, Virginia

HAWAIIAN BANANA CRISP

5 med. bananas
1/4 tsp. salt
1/2 c. vanilla wafer crumbs
1/4 c. butter or margarine
1/3 c. (packed) brown sugar
1/4 tsp. cinnamon

Slice bananas crosswise into 1/2-inch slices. Arrange in buttered casserole. Sprinkle lightly with salt. Combine wafer crumbs with butter using pastry blender. Add sugar and cinnamon; blend. Sprinkle evenly over bananas. Bake at 350 degrees for 18 to 20 minutes or until top is browned. Serve with whipped cream or ice cream.

Velma F. Larison, Soc. Com. Chm.
Preceptor Eta XP902
Midwest City, Oklahoma

DUNFILLAN BRAMBLE DESSERT

1/4 c. butter
1 c. flour
3/4 c. sugar
1 egg
2 tbsp. milk
1/4 tsp. baking powder
1 tsp. grated lemon rind
1 lb. fresh brambles or 1 No. 303 can
    blackberries

Cut butter into flour until crumbly. Mix in 1/4 cup sugar. Beat egg with milk and baking powder. Make a well in center of flour; pour in egg mixture. Blend thoroughly. Mix in lemon rind. Stew the brambles with 1/2 cup sugar and water to cover until tender. Place brambles and juice in deep 10-inch pie pan. Spoon batter over evenly. Bake at 350 degrees for 20 minutes. Yield: 4-6 servings.

Lillian M. Watkins, Pres.
Preceptor Epsilon Tau XP1229
Pasadena, California

CHERRY DELIGHT

1 2/3 c. graham cracker crumbs
1/4 c. sugar
1/3 c. melted butter
1 can cherry pie filling
1 c. whipping cream, whipped
3 c. miniature marshmallows

Blend crumbs, sugar and butter. Reserve 1/3 cup for topping. Press the remainder into a 9-inch square pan. Pour the cherry pie filling over crumb mixture. Fold marshmallows into whipped cream. Spread over filling. Sprinkle reserved crumbs over top. Refrigerate overnight.

Nancy LePoidevin
Zeta Pi No. 8068
Saint Catharines, Ontario, Canada

DREAMY CHERRY DESSERT

6 egg whites
Pinch of cream of tartar
2 c. sugar
2 c. crushed soda crackers
2 c. chopped walnuts
1 pkg. Dream Whip
2 cans cherry pie filling

Beat egg whites and cream of tartar until stiff peaks form. Add sugar; beat well. Fold in crushed crackers and walnuts. Place in 9 x 13-inch pan. Bake at 350 degrees for 25 minutes. Remove from oven. Cool completely. Prepare Dream Whip according to package directions. Smooth over cooled crust. Top with cherry pie filling. Yield: 15-20 servings.

Constance Liebherr
Alpha Iota No. 4988
Minden, Nevada

POACHED STUFFED PEARS (GERMANY)

4 ripe pears, peeled
Lemon juice
4 dried figs
1 c. Blue Nun wine
1 to 2 tbsp. sugar (opt.)
1 1-in. piece of cinnamon stick
1/4 tsp. vanilla extract

Brush pears with lemon juice. Scoop out cores from bottom, using spoon or melon scoop. Press figs into cavities. Combine wine, sugar and cinnamon stick in Dutch oven or large saucepan; heat, stirring constantly. Add pears; cover. Simmer for 10 minutes. Remove pears to serving dish; remove cinnamon stick. Add vanilla to wine; pour over pears. Serve warm. Yield: 4 servings.

Photograph for this recipe above.

MELON DOLMA (TURKEY) KAVUN DOLMASI

1 med. honeydew or casaba melon
2 c. seeded cubed grapes, cherries,
    strawberries, peaches, pears, plums
    and apricots
3 tbsp. sugar
1 lime
2 tbsp. rum, sweet vermouth or Cointreau
Fresh mint leaves

Slice through top of melon. Reserve top for cover. Remove seeds. Scoop out pulp into balls; place in bowl. Scrape melon so inside is smooth; dry inside. Mix fruit with melon balls. Add sugar, juice of 1/2 lime and

rum; mix well. Fill melon with fruit mixture. Cut remaining half lime into thin slices. Place on top of fruit. Decorate with mint leaves. Replace reserved top; wrap melon in foil. Refrigerate for 4 to 5 hours. Remove foil and cover to serve. Place on a bed of ice. Serve with cookies. Yield: 6 servings.

Jean R. Flynn, Soc. Chm.
Xi Alpha Chi X2636
Springfield, Virginia

PINEAPPLE WITH CUSTARD SAUCE
PINA CON NATILLAS

1 lg. or 2 med. fresh ripe pineapples
1/2 c. sugar
2 to 3 tbsp. rum or 1 tsp. rum flavoring
1/4 c. butter
1 pt. half and half
1/4 tsp. salt
1 egg plus 2 egg yolks
1 tsp. cornstarch
1 tsp. vanilla extract

Cut thick slice from top of pineapple. Scoop out pulp; cut into bite-sized chunks. Mix with 1/4 cup sugar and rum. Return to shell. Dot with butter; replace cut slice. Wrap in foil. Bake at 350 degrees for 20 minutes. Scald half and half in top of double boiler. Add salt. Beat 1/4 cup sugar with eggs; add to scalded half and half. Add cornstarch and vanilla; mix well. Cook, stirring constantly until mixture is smooth and thickened. Chill. Serve over warm pineapple. Yield: 8-10 servings.

Loretta Tucker, City Coun. Pres.
Preceptor Laureate Upsilon PL298
Woodland, California
Jeanette A. Arnold
Norfolk No. 8004
Norfolk, Nebraska

CHOCOLATE STRAWBERRIES

1 6-oz. package semisweet chocolate
    pieces
1 pt. fresh strawberries, washed and
    drained

Melt chocolate over hot but not boiling water; remove from heat. Dip strawberries in chocolate to coat, holding by stem ends; place on waxed paper. Let stand at room temperature until chocolate is set. Place over hot water if chocolate becomes too thick; heat until of dipping consistency.

Photograph for this recipe on this page.

SNOWCAP STRAWBERRIES

1 egg white
3/4 c. sugar
1 1/2 tsp. light corn syrup
1/4 tsp. salt

1/2 tsp. vanilla extract
2 pt. fresh strawberries, washed and
    drained

Combine egg white, sugar, 1/4 cup water, corn syrup and salt in top of double boiler; blend with electric mixer. Place over rapidly boiling water. Beat at high speed until mixture forms peaks when beater is raised. Remove from heat; add vanilla. Beat until thick and of a spreading consistency. Remove from heat. Dip strawberries into vanilla mixture to coat, holding by stem end. Place on waxed paper; let stand at room temperature until coating is set.

Photograph for this recipe above.

BAKED IN STRAWBERRY
SHORTCAKE

1 1/2 c. sifted flour
3/4 c. sugar
2 tsp. baking powder
1/2 tsp. salt
1/2 c. milk
1 egg
2 tbsp. melted butter
2 1/2 c. sliced strawberries
1/4 c. butter

Sift 1 cup flour, 1/2 cup sugar, baking powder and salt together. Add milk, egg and melted butter. Beat for 2 minutes. Turn into greased 8 x 8-inch pan. Top with sliced strawberries. Mix 1/2 cup flour, 1/4 cup sugar and butter to coarse crumbs. Sprinkle over strawberries. Bake at 375 degrees for 35 to 40 minutes.

Mary Jane McLeod
Tau No. 10088
Baden, Germany

SCALLOPED PINEAPPLE

2 c. sugar
1 stick margarine, softened
3 eggs, beaten
1 c. milk
2 cans pineapple tidbits, drained
4 c. bread cubes

Combine sugar, margarine, eggs and milk. Add pineapple. Fold in bread cubes. Place in ungreased casserole. Bake at 325 degrees for 35 to 40 minutes. Yield: 6 servings.

Dorothy Wainwright
Xi Beta Omicron X3506
Portsmouth, Virginia

PUMPKIN-CARDAMOM DESSERT (INDIA) KUDDO HALWA

2 c. uncooked oats
1/2 c. butter, melted
1/2 c. (packed) brown sugar
1/2 c. hot water
1 1/4 tsp. cardamom
1 tsp. cinnamon
1/2 tsp. salt
1 c. cooked pumpkin
1/8 tps. cloves
Nutmeg
1 qt. coffee ice cream
Whipped cream

Combine oats, butter, brown sugar, water and 1/2 teaspoon each cardamom, cinnamon and salt into mixing bowl; mix well. Press on bottom and side of large baking pan. Bake at 325 degrees for 30 minutes. Cool. Fold pumpkin, 3/4 teaspoon cardamom, cloves, 1/2 teaspoon cinnamon and 1/8 teaspoon nutmeg into ice cream. Spread over crust; cover. Freeze at least 4 hours. Remove 10 to 15 minutes before serving. Cut into squares. Top with whipped cream. Sprinkle with additional nutmeg. Yield: 12 servings.

Zoe C. Walter, Past Pres.
Xi Gamma Beta X2113
Lake Worth, Florida

ANN'S FOUR-FRUIT SHERBET

1 c. mashed bananas
2/3 c. sugar
1/2 tsp. grated orange rind
1/3 c. orange juice
1 tbsp. lemon juice
1 c. cranberry juice
6 drops of red food coloring
1 egg white, stiffly beaten

Combine bananas, sugar, orange rind, orange juice and lemon juice. Beat until mixutre is smooth. Stir in cranberry juice and food coloring. Turn into 4-cup refrigerator tray. Freeze until firm. Break mixture into chunks in chilled mixing bowl. Beat with chilled beater until smooth. Fold in beaten egg white; mix well. Return to freezer. Let stand at room temperature for a few minutes before serving. Spoon into sherbet glasses. Yield: 6 servings.

Alma Yardley
Preceptor Delta XP365
Lincoln, Nebraska

FRUIT ICE (BELGIUM) SORBET DES ILES

Juice of 3 or 4 oranges
Juice of 4 or 5 lemons
4 or 5 ripe bananas, mashed
1 c. sugar
1 egg white

Mix fruit juices, bananas and sugar. Pour into 9 x 9-inch pan. Cover with Saran Wrap. Freeze for 1 hour. Beat egg white until stiff. Pour fruit mixture into chilled bowl. Fold egg white into fruit mixture. Return to 9 x 9-inch pan. Freeze for 2 hours or until firm. Cut into small squares. Serve in sherbet dishes.

Charlotte G. Nier, V.P.
Xi Beta Xi XI628
Huntingdon, Pennsylvania

PINEAPPLE-COCONUT SHERBET (INDONESIA)

1 sm. ripe pineapple
Sugar
1 env. unflavored gelatin
1/4 c. water
1 1/2 c. cream of coconut
2 egg whites
1 tbsp. rum

Pare, halve and core pineapple. Chop pulp very fine or put through food grinder, using a fine blade. Measure out 2 cups. Combine with 1/2 cup sugar in a large bowl; mix well. Let stand 30 minutes. Soften gelatin in water in small pan. Place over very low heat until gelatin dissolves and mixture is clear. Stir gelatin into pineapple mixture. Blend in cream of coconut. Pour into 9-inch square pan. Freeze until firm, about 3 hours. Break frozen mixture into chunks in large chilled bowl. Beat with electric mixer until smooth, about 5 minutes. Beat egg whites until foamy. Beat in 3 tablespoons sugar, 1 tablespoon at a time, until forms soft peaks. Fold meringue into pineapple-coconut mixture. Stir in rum. Spoon sherbet into chilled 6-cup mold or bowl. Cover with foil or plastic wrap. Freeze about 6 hours or overnight. Unmold to serve. Yield: 1 1/2 quarts.

Carol Gesalman
Beat Pi Chap.
Johnstown, Pennsylvania

FRUIT KUCHEN

1 1/4 c. flour
1 tsp. baking powder

1/2 tsp. salt
1 1/4 c. sugar
1/4 c. shortening
1/4 c. milk
1 egg
1 qt. raspberries, cherries, strawberries,
    quartered apples or sliced peaches
1/4 c. butter

Sift 1 cup flour, baking powder, salt and 1/4 cup sugar together. Cut in shortening with a pastry blender. Beat together milk and egg. Add to flour mixture. Spread in a greased 8 x 12-inch cake pan. Cover with raspberries. Combine 1 cup sugar, butter, 1/4 cup flour; mix well. Sprinkle over top of raspberries. Bake at 350 degrees for 50 minutes.

Betty Ellen Tatlock
Xi Epsilon X4947
Seymour, Indiana

STRAWBERRY PIZZA

1/4 c. powdered sugar
1 stick butter, melted
1 c. flour
1 can sweetened condensed milk
1 pkg. cream cheese
1/3 c. lemon juice
1 tsp. vanilla extract
2 pt. frozen strawberries
4 tbsp. cornstarch

Combine powdered sugar, butter and flour; mix well. Press into a pizza pan. Bake at 350 degrees for 8 to 10 minutes. Let cool. Cream condensed milk and cream cheese until smooth. Stir in lemon juice and vanilla. Spread over crust. Combine strawberries and cornstarch in saucepan. Cook, stirring constantly, over medium heat until thick. Cool. Spread over filling. Refrigerate overnight.

Renee Mathews, Pres.
Alpha Theta Delta No. 8365
Canyon, Texas

ORANGE CRUNCH

1 stick butter
1 c. flour
1/4 c. sugar
1/2 c. chopped pecans
1 qt. orange sherbet

Combine first 4 ingredients. Pat onto cookie sheet. Bake at 350 degrees for 15 minutes. Crumble into bowl. Reserve 1/2 cup for topping. Pat remainder into serving bowl. Spread sherbet over crumbs. Top with reserved topping. Freeze for several hours.

Nancy L. Clower
Alpha Sigma No. 2809
Elkins, West Virginia

MEXICAN CREAM CAKE

1 angel food cake
1 pt. chocolate ice cream

1 pt. vanilla ice cream
1 pt. whipping cream
2 tbsp. Kahlua
4 to 6 tbsp. sugar
1/2 c. toasted slivered almonds

Slice 1/2 inch thick layer from top of cake; set aside. Hollow out cake leaving 1/2 inch thick sides. Alternate layers of chocolate and vanilla ice cream, filling cake shell to top. Replace top slice; press gently to secure to ice cream. Whip cream until stiff, adding Kahlua and sugar. Frost cake with flavored whipped cream; sprinkle with almonds. Place cake, uncovered, in freezer until cream is firm. Will keep for several weeks in freezer.

Evelyn Chandler, Ext Off.
Xi Gamma Tau No. 1438
Nacogdoches, Texas

STRAWBERRY-CHEESE DELIGHT

2 c. coconut
2 tbsp. sugar
1 tbsp. flour
2 tbsp. margarine, melted
1   10-oz. jar strawberry preserves
1   8-oz. package cream cheese, softened
3/4 c. confectioners' sugar
1/2 c. chopped pecans
1 tbsp. milk
1 tsp. almond extract
1 c. heavy cream

Combine coconut, sugar and flour. Blend in margarine. Press mixture onto bottom of 9-inch springform pan or 8-inch square pan. Bake at 350 degrees for 5 minutes. Chill. Spread half the preserves over crust. Combine cream cheese, 1/2 cup confectioners' sugar, pecans, milk and almond extract; mix until well blended. Spread cream cheese mixture over preserves. Combine cream and 1/4 cup confectioners' sugar. Whip until stiff. Spread over cream cheese mixture. Garnish with remaining preserves. Freeze until firm.

Mrs. Nancy Thorbecke, V.P.
Xi Epsilon Epsilon X4260
Evansville, Indiana

PAVLOVA (NEW ZEALAND)

4 egg whites
1 c. caster sugar
2 tbsp. cornstarch
1 tsp. vinegar
1 tsp. vanilla extract

Beat egg whites until stiff. Add sugar, a small amount at a time. Add cornstarch, vinegar and vanilla; stir well. Grease a cookie sheet. Cover with paper dampened with cold water. Pour batter onto paper. Shape as desired. Bake at 250 degrees for 1 hour and 15 minutes. Serve with fruit and whipped cream.

Beverley Hanrahan, Serv. Com. Mem.
Xi Omicron X568
Lewiston, New York

DUTCH APPLE PIE

1 unbaked pie shell
Apple slices
1/2 c. (packed) brown sugar
2 tbsp. butter
2 tbsp. flour
1/2 tsp. salt
1/2 tsp. (or more) cinnamon
3/4 c. water
1 tbsp. lemon juice
1 tsp. vanilla extract

Fill pie shell with apple slices to rim. Combine remaining ingredients in a saucepan. Cook until thick. Cool. Pour over apples. Bake in preheated 400-degree oven for 25 minutes or until apples are tender.

Mimi Temple
Lambda No. 3623
Minnedosa, Manitoba, Canada

SWEDISH APPLE PIE

1 egg
1/4 tsp. vanilla extract
3/4 c. sugar
1/2 c. flour
1 tsp. baking powder
1/4 tsp. salt
1/2 tsp. ground cinnamon
1 1/2 c. chopped tart apples
1/2 c. chopped black walnuts

Beat egg in medium mixing bowl. Add vanilla. Combine sugar, 1/4 cup flour, baking powder, salt and cinnamon. Add to beaten egg. Dredge apples and walnuts in remaining flour. Stir into egg mixture. Pour in well-greased 8-inch pie pan. Bake at 350 degrees for 30 to 40 minutes or until top is browned and firm. Serve warm topped with vanilla ice cream.

Mary S. Dorning
Beta Rho No. 3461
Paris, Tennessee

FROZEN CHOCOLATE PIE

Confectioners' sugar
1/2 c. butter, softened
6 squares semisweet chocolate, melted
    and cooled
1 tsp. vanilla extract
4 eggs
1 baked 9-inch pie shell
1 c. chilled whipping cream

Blend 1 cup confectioners' sugar and butter on low speed in small mixer bowl until fluffy. Blend in chocolate and vanilla. Beat in eggs on high speed, one at a time, beating thoroughly after each addition. Pour into baked pie shell. Cover with plastic wrap. Freeze for several hours or until firm. Remove from freezer 15 minutes before serving; remove plastic wrap. Beat cream and 2 tablespoons confectioners' sugar in

chilled bowl until stiff. Pile onto pie. Top with chocolate curls.

Carolyn Sue McClelland, Pres.
Xi Mu X4252
Lewes, Delaware

MUD PIE FROM HAWAII

1 1/2 c. chocolate cookie crumbs
1/3 c. melted butter
1 1/2 qt. Kona coffee ice cream
1   9-oz. jar hot fudge sauce
3/4 c. cream, whipped
1/4 c. almonds or macadamia nuts

Mix chocolate cookie crumbs with melted butter. Press into 9-inch pie pan. Bake at 375 degrees for 8 minutes. Cool. Freeze. Spread softened ice cream in crust. Freeze for 1 hour. Spread fudge sauce over ice cream. Freeze for 30 minutes. Mound whipped cream on pie. Sprinkle with almonds. Freeze for 3 hours. If coffee ice cream is unavailable use 1 1/2 quarts vanilla ice cream flavored with 1 1/2 teaspoons instant coffee. Yield: 10-12 servings.

Mrs. Warren H. Brown
International Honorary Member
McCall, Idaho

COTTAGE CHEESE PIE
TVAROHOVY PAJ

1 baked pie shell
2 c. dry cottage cheese
Butter
3/4 c. raisins
2 eggs, beaten
1 c. milk
1/2 c. sugar
1 tsp. lemon extract

Fill pie shell with cottage cheese. Dot with butter. Sprinkle raisins over cheese. Combine eggs, milk, sugar and lemon extract; mix well. Pour over cottage cheese. Bake at 275 degrees about 30 minutes or until custard is set.

Marian Ring
Xi Sigma Chap.
Sheridan, Wyoming

DUTCH PEACH PIE
(HOLLAND)

1 egg
3/4 c. sugar
1 tbsp. (heaping) shortening
1/2 c. milk
2 c. flour
3 tsp. baking powder
Sliced peaches
Custard Topping

Combine first 6 ingredients until smooth. Pat into 9-inch pie pan. Top with sliced peaches. Bake at 350 degrees for 45 minutes. Serve with warm Custard Topping.

Custard Topping

1 egg
3/4 c. sugar
1 pt. milk
2 tbsp. cornstarch
Pinch of salt
1 tbsp. vanilla extract

Combine all ingredients in a saucepan. Cook until thick, stirring constantly.

Patricia L. Long, Advisor
Sigma No. 2148
Hagerstown, Maryland

APRICOT TART (FRANCE)
FLAN AUX ABRICOTS

1   30-oz. can apricot halves
1 pkg. vanilla pudding and pie
   filling mix
1 c. heavy cream
1 egg, beaten
4 tbsp. Grand Marnier or apricot
   Brandy
1 baked 10-in. tart shell or pie
   shell, cooled
4 maraschino cherry halves
2 tbsp. sugar
1 tbsp. cornstarch

Drain apricots, reserving 1 1/4 cups syrup; chill apricots. Combine pudding mix, cream, egg and 1/2 cup reserved syrup in medium saucepan. Bring to a boil over medium heat, stirring constantly. Remove from heat; cool slightly. Stir in 3 tablespoons Grand

Marnier; beat custard mixture until smooth. Spoon into tart shell. Chill for at least 1 hour. Slice all but 4 of the apricots into quarters at least 45 minutes before serving time. Arrange 4 whole apricot halves evenly around edge of pie filling. Form an apricot flower in center of each pie quarter, using a cherry half as center and 1/4 of the apricot slices as petals. Blend sugar and cornstarch in small saucepan; stir in remaining 3/4 cup apricot syrup. Boil syrup mixture for 1 minute, stirring constantly. Remove from heat. Stir in remaining 1 tablespoon Grand Marnier. Spoon warm glaze over top of tart. Chill until serving time. Yield: 6-8 servings.

Photograph for this recipe on this page.

CANADIAN PRIZE
BUTTER TARTS

1 recipe pie pastry
1/3 c. butter
1 c. (packed) brown sugar, sifted
2 tbsp. cream
1/2 c. currants
1 egg, beaten
1 tsp. vanilla extract

Line tassie pans with pastry. Cream butter. Add brown sugar; beat well. Fold in remaining ingredients, mixing well. Place 1 spoonful mixture in pastry-lined tassie pans. Bake at 450 degrees for 8 minutes. Reduce temperature to 350 degrees and continue baking until browned.

Beverly Teerink, Pres.
Rho No. 2306
Coeur D'Alene, Idaho

SCANDINAVIAN PRUNE
TARTS

1 1/2 lb. prunes
1/2 c. sugar
1 tsp. vanilla extract
5 c. flour
1/2 c. lard
1 lb. butter, at room temperature

Cook prunes in 2 1/2 cups water until soft. Add sugar and vanilla. Beat to a paste. Cool. Sift flour; cut in lard. Add enough water to make dough similar to pie crust. Roll out to 1/4-inch thickness on well-floured board. Spread butter on half the dough. Turn down other half and pat with hands until butter is mixed in. Roll to 1/4-inch thickness. Repeat process 5 or 6 times until butter is used up. Roll as for jelly roll. Place in refrigerator overnight. Roll out to 1/4-inch thickness; cut into 4-inch squares. Place spoonful of prune filling in center. Cut corners and turn up in pinwheel-fashion. Pinch center edges together. Place on cookie sheet. Bake at 400 degrees for 20 minutes or until light golden brown. Yield: 60 tarts.

Delores Pitcher, Pres.
Preceptor Alpha Nu XP1222
Sterling Heights, Michigan

BLACK FOREST CHERRY TORTE (GERMANY) SCHWARZWALDER KIRSCHTORTE

3 1/2 c. whipping cream
3 eggs, well beaten
1 tsp. almond extract
2 c. flour
1 3/4 c. sugar
2 tsp. baking powder
1/2 tsp. salt
2   2-lb. cans Bing cherries
4 tbsp. cornstarch
2 tbsp. Brandy extract
1/2 c. confectioners' sugar
1/3 bar sweet cooking chocolate, grated

Whip 1 1/2 cups cream until stiff. Fold in eggs and almond extract. Sift flour, 1 1/2 cups sugar, baking powder and salt together. Fold gently into egg mixture. Spread in 2 greased and floured 8 or 9-inch cake pans. Bake in preheated 350-degree oven for 30 to 35 minutes or until cake tests done. Cool. Drain cherries, reserving juice. Mix cornstarch and 1/4 cup sugar in saucepan. Add water to juice to measure 2 cups; stir into cornstarch mixture. Cook over medium heat until thick and clear. Cool to lukewarm. Add extract. Dip 36 cherries into thickened juice; set aside for garnish. Add remaining cherries to juice. Whip 2 cups cream; add confectioners' sugar slowly. Whip until stiff. Invert one cake layer onto cake plate. With decorating tube or spoon form a thin ring of whipped cream around outer edge of cake layer. Fill center with cherry filling. Top with second cake layer. Cover sides and top with whipped cream. Press grated chocolate into sides of cake. Garnish with reserved 36 cherries.

Erika Marguerite MacLean, Publ. Chm.
Xi Gamma X1117
Portsmouth, New Hampshire

APRICOT DOBOSCH TORTE (AUSTRIA)

6 eggs, separated
Sugar
1 c. flour

Beat egg whites in large bowl until foamy; add 1/3 cup sugar gradually, beating until stiff peaks form. Beat egg yolks with 1/2 cup sugar until thick and pale yellow; fold into egg whites. Fold in flour gradually. Grease and flour bottoms of six 9-inch layer cake pans; divide batter equally and spread thinly in each pan. Bake in 350-degree oven for 15 minutes or until golden. Remove layers from pan using sharp knife; cool on racks.

Chocolate Butter Cream And Fillings

3/4 c. sugar
3 eggs
2 egg yolks
2 oz. semisweet chocolate, melted
1 tsp. instant coffee powder
1 tsp. vanilla extract

1 c. sweet butter, softened
1   17-oz. can apricot halves, drained
1/4 c. apricot preserves
1/2 c. chopped toasted filberts

Beat sugar, eggs, egg yolks, chocolate, coffee powder and vanilla together in top of double boiler; cook over simmering water for 10 to 15 minutes or until thickened, stirring frequently. Cool completely. Beat butter until fluffy; beat into chocolate mixture gradually. Set aside. Quarter 3 apricot halves for top. Chop remaining apricots; mix with preserves. Spread 3 cake layers with Chocolate Butter Cream, using 1/3 cup cream for each. Spread 2 cake layers with apricot mixture. Stack together on serving plate, beginning and ending with Chocolate Butter Cream layers. Invert remaining cake layer onto top. Spread remaining Chocolate Butter Cream over side of cake; press in filberts. Spread additional preserves on top. Garnish with reserved apricot slices and chocolate curls. Chill for 3 hours before serving.

Photograph for this recipe on page 104.

BAVARIAN TORTE

1/2 c. butter or margarine, softened
Sugar
3/4 tsp. vanilla extract
3/4 c. flour
2/3 c. finely chopped pecans
1   8-oz. package cream cheese, softened
1 egg
1/2 tsp. cinnamon
1   29-oz. can sliced cling peaches, drained

Beat butter at medium speed in large bowl. Add 1/2 cup sugar and 1/4 teaspoon vanilla. Add flour gradually; continue beating until well mixed. Stir in pecans. Press mixture into bottom and 1 inch up side of 10-inch springform pan with lightly floured hands. Beat cream cheese and 1/4 cup sugar on medium speed until smooth. Beat in egg and 1/2 teaspoon vanilla until well blended. Pour into lined pan. Combine 1 teaspoon sugar and cinnamon. Add peaches; toss gently. Arrange pinwheel-fashion on top of cream cheese mixture. Bake in preheated 450-degree oven for 10 minutes. Reduce temperature to 400 degrees; bake 25 minutes longer. Cool for 20 minutes. Remove sides of pan. Serve.

Carole J. Krupski, Soc. Chm.
Rho Tau Chap.
Naperville, Illinois

SCHWARZWALDER KIRSCHTORTE MIT KIRSCHWASSER (GERMANY)

1   10-in. chocolate sponge cake
2 pt. whipping cream
2 oz. sugar
Kirschwasser
1 can cherry pie filling

Chocolate shavings
Confectioners' sugar

Slice cake into 2 layers. Beat whipping cream with sugar and 1/2 cup Kirschwasser until stiff. Pipe 3 rings of whipped cream, using a plain 1/2-inch tube, on bottom cake layer, leaving space between each to fill with cherry pie filling. Place cherry pie filling in each ring of whipped cream. Place second layer on top. Sprinkle with Kirschwasser. Spread whipped cream on top and sides of torte. Sprinkle completely with fine chocolate shavings. Dust with confectioners' sugar. Decorate with whipped cream rosettes and red cherries. Keep refrigerated.

Ella A. Blackburn, Treas.
Xi Zeta Theta X2030
Abilene, Texas

FILBERT CREME TORTE (GERMANY)

10 eggs, separated
1 1/2 c. sugar
3 tbsp. cake flour
2 c. ground toasted filberts
1/2 c. peach preserves
1/2 tsp. grated lemon peel
1 tbsp. lemon juice
1 pt. heavy cream
1/2 c. (firmly packed) dark brown
    sugar
Whole filberts

Beat egg yolks until thick in large mixing bowl. Add sugar gradually, beating until mixture is light and fluffy. Fold in flour and filberts. Beat egg whites until stiff but not dry. Mix 1/3 of the egg whites into egg yolk mixture; fold in remaining egg whites gently. Pour batter into 3 waxed paper-lined, greased and floured 9-inch cake pans. Bake in 350-degree oven for 35 to 40 minutes or until cakes test done. Cool slightly before removing from pans. Remove from pans; cool thoroughly. Combine preserves, lemon peel and lemon juice; mix well. Whip cream with brown sugar until stiff. Place 1 torte layer on serving platter. Spread with 1/2 of the preserves mixture and 2 tablespoons whipped cream. Top with second layer; repeat process. Place third layer on top. Frost top and side with remaining cream. Slice whole filberts, using sharp knife. Spread in shallow pan. Bake in 400-degree oven for 10 minutes. Garnish torte with toasted sliced filberts.

Photograph for this recipe on this page.

PECAN TORTE (GERMANY)

5 eggs, separated
3 eggs
1 c. sugar
5 pkg. vanilla sugar
1 c. ground pecans
2 tsp. rum
1 pt. whipping cream, whipped

Mix egg yolks and next 3 ingredients until fluffy. Add pecans and rum gradually. Fold in stiffly beaten egg whites. Pour into springform cake pan. Bake at 350 degrees for 45 minutes. Cool overnight. Cut in half horizontally. Fill and cover with whipped cream. Vanilla sugar may be bought in gourmet food stores.

Mrs Gerda P. Kibbe
Alpha Upsilon No. 8446
Oxford, Mississippi

GENOA TORTE (ITALY)
TORTA DI GENOVA

6 eggs
1 c. sugar
1 tsp. grated lemon rind
1 tsp. grated orange rind
1 1/3 c. cake flour, sifted
Apricot Frosting

Beat eggs until light and fluffy. Add sugar gradually, beating well. Add lemon and orange rinds; continue beating until thick and lemon colored. Fold in sifted flour, 2 tablespoons at a time. Pour mixture into 9 x 13-inch cake pan. Bake in 350-degree oven for 25 to 30 minutes or until cake tests done. Frost with Apricot Frosting.

Apricot Frosting

1 c. sifted confectioners' sugar
4 tbsp. apricot jam
2 tbsp. Brandy

Combine all ingredients; blend well. Add a small amount more of confectioners' sugar for right consistency to spread, if necessary.

Flora Marcotte
Xi Eta Nu X2237
Bryan, Texas

BAKLAVA

3 c. ground walnuts
1/4 c. confectioners' sugar
1/4 tsp. cinnamon
1 lb. phyllo
1 c. margarine, melted
1 1/2 c. sugar
1 c. light corn syrup
2 tbsp. lemon juice
1 cinnamon stick

Mix walnuts, confectioners' sugar and cinnamon together in a bowl. Cut away dry ends from phyllo, working quickly to keep phyllo moist. Cover unused portions with damp towel during preparation of recipe. Brush bottom and sides of 13 x 9 x 2-inch baking pan with margarine. Arrange 1 sheet phyllo in bottom of pan, overlapping sides. Brush lightly with margarine. Fold in ends. Brush with margarine. Trim remaining sheets of phyllo even with short sides of pan. Place a layer of 6 sheets in pan, brushing each sheet with margarine. Fold sides over, brushing with margarine again before adding next sheet. Brush lightly. Do not soak pastry. Sprinkle about 3/4 cup walnut mixture over pastry. Add about 4 more sheets phyllo on top. Sprinkle top with 3/4 cup walnut mixture. Continue layering phyllo, brushing with margarine and sprinkling with walnut mixture until all phyllo and walnut mixture are used, ending with 5 sheets of phyllo. Fold sides of last sheet under. Brush with margarine. Make 3 lengthwise cuts halfway to bottom of pan. Slash each row diagonally on the surface, making cuts about 2 inches apart, to form diamond pattern. Bake in 350-degree oven for 1 hour and 15 minutes. Cover if top gets too brown. Mix sugar, 1 cup water, corn syrup, lemon juice and 1 cinnamon stick together in 3-quart saucepan. Bring to a boil, stirring constantly. Boil for 15 minutes. Remove cinnamon stick. Pour syrup slowly over baked Baklava as soon as removed from oven. Let stand for at least 24 hours. Does not require refrigeration.

Photograph for this recipe on page 1.

HAWAIIAN HONEYMOONS

1 c. butter
1/2 c. sugar
2 c. flour
1 c. flaked coconut
1 tsp. vanilla or almond extract
1 c. chopped pecans
1 c. honey
1 c. crushed pineapple, drained
Pecan halves

Cream butter and sugar until fluffy. Add flour, coconut, vanilla and pecans, blending well. Roll into marble-sized balls. Place on ungreased cookie sheet. Bake for 15 to 20 minutes in 350-degree oven. Cool. Combine honey and crushed pineapple. Bring to a boil. Boil for 10 minutes or until honey turns dark brown and pineapple is orange color. Sauce will be thick. Cool. Glaze cooled cookies. Top with pecan half.

Ruth Carpenter, Regional Coun. Pres.
Preceptor Gamma XP238
Billings, Montana

ALMOND COOKIES (IRAQ)
LAWZ KHUBZ

1/4 c. shortening
4 eggs
1 1/2 c. sugar
1 tsp. grated lemon rind
1 1/2 c. ground almonds
2 1/2 c. sifted all-purpose flour
1/2 tsp. salt

Cream shortening. Stir in unbeaten eggs, sugar, lemon rind and almonds. Beat for 15 minutes. Sift flour with salt. Stir in flour gradually. Mix to a stiff dough. Shape into walnut-sized balls. Place on waxed paper-lined cookie sheet about 2 inches apart. Bake in 350-degree oven for 5 to 10 minutes or until cookies are golden brown. Cool on wire rack. Yield: 5 dozen.

DeLette E. Wittenwyler, Pres.
Xi Delta Rho X2801
Princeton, Florida

MEXICAN WEDDING CAKES

1 c. butter
1/2 c. powdered sugar
2 c. flour
1 c. pecans

Cream butter and powdered sugar. Add flour gradually. Add pecans. Chill for 15 minutes. Roll into small balls. Place on ungreased cookie sheet. Bake at 375 degrees for 10 minutes. Sprinkle with additional powdered sugar while still warm. Yield: 3 dozen.

Robbie McGee, Pres.
Alpha No. 7250
Springfield, Missouri

NORWEGIAN JELLY BARS

2 eggs, separated
1/2 c. butter
1/2 c. powdered sugar
1 c. flour
Red currant jelly
1/2 c. sugar
1/2 c. chopped pecans

Combine egg yolk with next 3 ingredients; mix well. Pack into ungreased 8-inch square pan. Bake for 10 minutes in 350-degree oven. Remove from oven. Spread with jelly. Beat egg whites and sugar into stiff meringue. Fold in chopped pecans. Spread evenly over jelly. Bake for 25 minutes at 350 degrees. Cool. Cut into squares to serve.

Clara S. Wilbanks, Treas.
Alpha Theta Zeta No. 8409
Houston, Texas

CAN SIZE CHART

8 oz. can or jar ....1 c.	1 lb. 13 oz. can or jar
10 1/2 oz. can (picnic can) ....1 1/4 c.	or No. 2 1/2 can or jar ....3 1/2 c.
12 oz. can (vacuum) ....1 1/2 c.	1 qt. 14 fl. oz. or 3 lb. 3 oz.
14-16 oz. or No. 300 can ....1 1/4 c.	or 46 oz. can ....5 3/4 c.
16-17 oz. can or jar	6 1/2 to 7 1/2 lb.
or No. 303 can or jar ....2 c.	or No. 10 can .... 12-13 c.
1 lb. 4 oz. or 1 pt. 2 fl. oz.	
or No. 2 can or jar ....2 1/2 c.	

EQUIVALENT CHART

3 tsp. .... 1 tbsp.		2 pt. ....1 qt.	
2 tbsp. ....1/8 c.		1 qt. ....4 c.	
4 tbsp. ....1/4 c.		5/8 c. ....1/2 c. + 2 tbsp.	
8 tbsp. ....1/2 c.		7/8 c. ....3/4 c. + 2 tbsp.	
16 tbsp. ....1 c.		1 jigger ....1 1/2 fl. oz.(3 tbsp.)	
5 tbsp. + 1 tsp. ....1/3 c.		2 c. fat ....1 lb.	
12 tbsp. ....3/4 c.		1 lb. butter .... 2 c. or 4 sticks	
4 oz. ....1/2 c.		2 c. sugar ....1 lb.	
8 oz. ....1 c.		2 2/3 c. powdered sugar ....1 lb.	
16 oz. ....1 lb.		2 2/3 c. brown sugar ....1 lb.	
1 oz. .... 2 tbsp. fat or liquid		4 c. sifted flour ....1 lb.	
2 c. ....1 pt.		4 1/2 c. cake flour ....1 lb.	

3 1/2 c. unsifted whole wheat flour ....1 lb.
8 to 10 egg whites ....1 c.
12 to 14 egg yolks ....1 c.
1 c. unwhipped cream ....2 c. whipped
1 lb. shredded American cheese ....4 c.
1/4 lb. crumbled blue cheese ....1 c.
1 chopped med. onion ....1/2 c. pieces
1 lemon .... 3 tbsp. juice
1 lemon .... 1 tsp. grated peel
1 orange ....1/3 c. juice
1 orange .... about 2 tsp. grated peel
1 lb. unshelled walnuts .... 1 1/2 to 1 3/4 c. shelled
1 lb. unshelled almonds ....3/4 to 1 c. shelled
4 oz. (1 to 1 1/4 c.) uncooked macaroni .... 2 1/4 c. cooked
7 oz. spaghetti ....4 c. cooked
4 oz. (1 1/2 to 2 c.) uncooked noodles ....2 c. cooked
28 saltine crackers ....1 c. crumbs
4 slices bread ....1 c. crumbs
14 square graham crackers ....1 c. crumbs
22 vanilla wafers ....1 c. crumbs

SUBSTITUTIONS FOR A MISSING INGREDIENT

1 square *chocolate* (1 ounce) = 3 or 4 tablespoons cocoa plus 1/2 tablespoon fat.

1 tablespoon *cornstarch* (for thickening) = 2 tablespoons flour.

1 cup sifted *all-purpose flour* = 1 cup plus 2 tablespoons sifted cake flour.

1 cup sifted *cake flour* = 1 cup minus 2 tablespoons sifted all-purpose flour.

1 teaspoon *baking powder* = 1/4 teaspoon baking soda plus 1/2 teaspoon cream of tartar.

1 cup *sour milk* — 1 cup sweet milk into which 1 tablespoon vinegar or lemon juice has been stirred; or
1 cup buttermilk (let stand for 5 minutes).

SUBSTITUTIONS FOR A MISSING INGREDIENT

1 cup *sweet milk* = 1 cup sour milk or buttermilk plus 1/2 teaspoon baking soda.

1 cup *canned tomatoes* = about 1 1/3 cups cut-up fresh tomatoes, simmered 10 minutes.

3/4 cup *cracker crumbs* = 1 cup bread crumbs.

1 cup *cream, sour, heavy* = 1/3 cup butter and 2/3 cups milk in any sour milk recipe.

1 cup *cream, sour, thin* = 3 tablespoons butter and 3/4 cup milk in sour milk recipe.

1 cup *molasses* = 1 cup honey.

1 teaspoon *dried herbs* = 1 tablespoon fresh herbs.

1 *whole egg* = 2 egg yolks for custards.

1/2 cup *evaporated milk* and 1/2 cup *water* or 1 cup *reconstituted nonfat dry milk* and 1 tablespoon *butter* = 1 cup whole milk.

1 package *active dry yeast* = 1 cake compressed yeast.

1 tablespoon *instant minced onion, rehydrated* = 1 cake compressed yeast.

1 tablespoon *instant minced onion, rehydrated* = 1 small fresh onion.

1 tablespoon *prepared mustard* = 1 teaspoon dry mustard.

1/8 teaspoon *garlic powder* = 1 small pressed clove of garlic

METRIC CONVERSION CHARTS FOR THE KITCHEN

VOLUME

1 tsp.	4.9 cc	2 c.	473.4 cc
1 tbsp.	14.7 cc	1 fl. oz.	29.5 cc
1/3 c.	28.9 cc	4 oz.	118.3 cc
1/8 c.	29.5 cc	8 oz.	236.7 cc
1/4 c.	59.1 cc	1 pt.	473.4 cc
1/2 c.	118.3 cc	1 qt.	.946 liters
3/4 c.	177.5 cc	1 gal.	3.7 liters
1 c.	236.7 cc		

CONVERSION FACTORS:

Liters	X	1.056	=	Liquid Quarts
Quarts	X	0.946	=	Liters
Liters	X	0.264	=	Gallons
Gallons	X	3.785	=	Liters
Fluid Ounces	X	29.563	=	Cubic Centimeters
Cubic Centimeters	X	0.034	=	Fluid Ounces
Cups	X	236.575	=	Cubic Centimeters
Tablespoons	X	14.797	=	Cubic Centimeters
Teaspoons	X	4.932	=	Cubic Centimeters
Bushels	X	0.352	=	Hectoliters
Hectoliters	X	2.837	=	Bushels
Ounces (Avoir.)	X	28.349	=	Grams
Grams	X	0.035	=	Ounces
Pounds	X	0.454	=	Kilograms
Kilograms	X	2.205	=	Pounds

WEIGHT

1 dry oz.	28.3 Grams
1 lb.	454 Kilograms

(NEAREST CONVENIENT EQUIVALENTS)

CUPS SPOONS	QUARTS OUNCES	METRIC EQUIVALENTS
1 teaspoon	1/6 ounce	5 milliliters 5 grams
2 teaspoons	1/3 ounce	10 milliliters 10 grams
1 tablespoon	1/2 ounce	15 milliliters 15 grams
3 1/3 tablespoons	1 3/4 ounces	50 milliliters
1/4 cup (4 tablespoons)	2 ounces	60 milliliters
1/3 cup (5 1/3 tablespoons)	2 2/3 ounces	79 milliliters
1/3 cup plus 1 tablespoon	3 1/2 ounces	100 milliliters
1/2 cup (8 tablespoons)	4 ounces	118 milliliters
1 cup (16 tablespoons)	8 ounces	1/4 liter 236 milliliters
2 cups	1 pint 16 ounces	1/2 liter less 1 1/2 tablespoons 473 milliliters
2 cups plus 2 1/2 tablespoons	17 ounces	1/2 liter
4 cups	1 quart 32 ounces	946 milliliters
4 1/3 cups	1 quart, 2 ounces	1 liter 1000 milliliters

CONVERSION FORMULAS:

To convert Centigrade to Fahrenheit: multiply by 9, divide by 5, add 32.

To convert Fahrenheit to Centigrade: subtract 32, multiply by 5, divide by 9.

(MOST CONVENIENT APPROXIMATION)

POUNDS AND OUNCES	METRIC	POUNDS AND OUNCES	METRIC
1/6 ounce	5 grams	1/4 pound (4 ounces)	114 grams
1/3 ounce	10 grams	4 1/8 ounces	125 grams
1/2 ounce	15 grams	1/2 pound (8 ounces)	227 grams
1 ounce	30 grams (28.35)	3/4 pound (12 ounces)	250 grams
		1 pound (16 ounces)	454 grams
1 3/4 ounces	50 grams	1.1 pounds	500 grams
2 2/3 ounces	75 grams	2.2 pounds	1 kilogram 1000 grams
3 1/2 ounces	100 grams		

Index

190

Index

Index

Index

Index

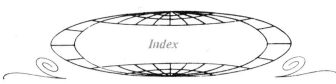

Index

Index

Index

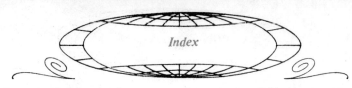

Index

COLOR PHOTOGRAPH RECIPES

PHOTOGRAPHY CREDITS

Best Foods, a Division of CPC International Inc.; National Live Stock and Meat Board; National Kraut Packer's Association; Spanish Green Olive Commission; California Apricot Advisory Board; Campbell's Soup Company; The J. M. Smucker Company; PET, Inc.; California Avocado Advisory Board; Ruth Lundgren Company; The Olive Administrative Committee; National Association of Frozen Foods Packers; Seven Seas; Diamond Walnut Kitchen; United Fresh Fruit and Vegetable Association; Fleischmann's Margarine; McIlhenny Company; National Macaroni Institute; Pineapple Growers Association; American Lamb Council; International Shrimp Council; Ruffino Orvieto Secco Wine Company; California Strawberry Advisory Board; Peter Pan Peanut Butter; The Quaker Oats Company; Ocean Spray Cranberry, Inc.; General Foods Kitchens; Idaho Potato Commission; Fleischmann's Yeast; California Raisin Advisory Board; Sterno Company; Filbert-Hazelnut Institute; Schieffelin and Company; Turkish American Filbert Institute.

FAVORITE RECIPES® OF BETA SIGMA PHI INTERNATIONAL
COOKBOOKS

Add to Your Cookbook Collection Select from These ALL-TIME Favorites

BOOK TITLE	ITEM NUMBER
Recipes From The World Of Beta Sigma Phi (1978) 200 Pages	01341
Dieting To Stay Healthy (1977) 200 Pages	00949
Meats (1968) 384 Pages	70076
Desserts (1968) 384 Pages	70068
Holiday (1971) 288 Pages	70041
Fondue & Buffet (1972) 192 Pages	70033
Bicentennial Heritage Recipes (1976) 200 Pages	70262
Party Book (1973) 192 Pages	70378
Gourmet (1973) 200 Pages	70025
Money-Saving Casseroles (1974) 200 Pages	70009
Save and "Win" (1975) 200 Pages	70017

FOR ORDERING INFORMATION

Write to:
Favorite Recipes Press
P. O. Box 77
Nashville, Tennessee 37202

BOOKS OFFERED DURING 1978 SUBJECT TO AVAILABILITY.